365 Days of Family Devotions

5-Minute Prayers, Bible Lessons, and Activities to Help Kids, Teens, and Parents Grow Closer to God and to Each Other

Welcome Aboard, Check Out This Limited-Time Free Bonus!

Ahoy, reader! Welcome to the Ahoy Publications family, and thanks for snagging a copy of this book! Since you've chosen to join us on this journey, we'd like to offer you something special.

Check out the link below for a FREE e-book filled with delightful facts about American History.

But that's not all - you'll also have access to our exclusive email list with even more free e-books and insider knowledge. Well, what are ye waiting for? Click the link below to join and set sail toward exciting adventures in American History.

Access your bonus here

https://ahoypublications.com/

Or, Scan the QR code!

Table of Contents

Introduction

A family Bible study book is a wonderful way to grow together in faith. Parents can introduce their children to Bible themes and messages that can stay with them a lifetime, with fun activities making every day's devotional even more memorable.

This guide has been lovingly curated to share heartfelt messages that will inspire readers to look further, deeper, and grow their faith together, every day. To fit into the rhythm of your busy family life, the full experience, including the reading, family questions, prayer, and activity, is designed to take approximately five minutes. This brief but intentional time ensures that even on your busiest days, you can stay connected to God's Word and to one another.

To make the most of your daily time together, we recommend gathering basic craft supplies, such as a dedicated scrapbook, markers, glue, and colored paper, so they are ready for each day's activity.

Please remember that the prayers and scrapbook activities provided are intended as helpful guidelines rather than rigid rules. If your family feels led to pray longer, or if a particular activity sparks a more creative or elaborate idea, we encourage you to expand upon them. These are simply seeds meant to plant the truth in your hearts; feel free to let them grow in whatever way best suits your family's unique personality.

Enjoy the next 365 days and make the memories last: journal comments from each family member that you can revisit, create a Bible study scrapbook, and save photos of all the fun activities you do together.

Your faith-inspired journey as a family starts now.

JANUARY

January 1
God's Word Is Our Rock

"The LORD is my rock, my fortress and my deliverer; my God is my rock, in whom I take refuge, my shield and the horn of my salvation, my stronghold." - Psalm 18:2

When was the last time you as a family built something together, like a gate to keep stray dogs out of your yard, only for it to break down? What did you do differently to make it work and stay firm? Did you check your foundation to ensure you were building on solid ground?

Faith is pretty much like that, with God being our solid foundation that we can find refuge in. When we put our trust in God in every part of our lives, from school to work to studies, we make the best declaration, namely that we are rooted in faith.

Being believers does not imply that we will not go through any hardships at any point. Life happens, but how we handle it can speak volumes. We could still have a bad day, get angry at someone, get stuck in traffic, or get sick, but as long as we have faith, we will get through it all.

Think for a moment how you would normally react when you are angry at someone. Would you lash out and say mean things? Or, would you guard your words and pray for a calm mind? Battling difficulties is part of our daily lives, but we have a choice of what we choose to be our foundation. And choosing God's Word is always a step in the best direction. So, how do we ensure that we steer the course? We focus on our daily Bible studies, take to heart the lessons that we have learned and apply them in our daily lives. Together as a family, we can encourage one another to stay true to our faith, and when we stumble, we can help one another get back up.

Let us build this year on the belief that we will keep with us faith and live in the presence of God's eternal love and grace. We will be challenged, but with faith, it is all surmountable.

With that said, let's get into some food for thought:

1. Think about a time our family faced a challenge. How did we deal with it? Were we scared, angry or did we need extra help?
2. What is the first building block we can put in place today as the first part of our faith foundation?
3. Are there any storms that our family is facing at the moment? How will we make sure that we put our trust in God?

📖 PRAYER

Heavenly Father, You really are our rock, our safe place, the steady ground underneath our feet. Guide us, Father, help us to stay strong, and when it feels like we cannot go on, help us push through life's challenges.

Thank you, Almighty Father.

Amen.

👪 FAMILY ACTIVITY

Head out to your garden or to the beach if you prefer. Gather rocks or stones, and build a foundation together as a family. Stack your rocks or stones, then write your family members' names in the ground or sand next to it. Now, consider the foundation you built your structure on. Is it solid? Will it last? Take a picture and save it in your journal or in your online photo library. Make notes about what you learned from this activity.

January 2
Created in God's Image

"So God created mankind in His own image, in the image of God He created them; male and female He created them." – Genesis 1:27

Do you ever find it difficult to believe how unique you are? Perhaps you look in the mirror and see someone who, in your eyes, is just average. You might feel that there is nothing special or worth discussing.

Today's verse, from the first book of the Bible, flips the script on these feelings. It makes us aware just how important we are to God and that we were created with purpose. Of course, being created in God's image doesn't mean that we are exactly like God, but rather that we are created to reflect His character. This can be seen in traits such as showing love towards family, friends, and neighbors, showing compassion for those in need, and following a course of life that is just.

So, what does this uniqueness mean for Christians? First, we should focus on showing respect to one another. Not just our family circle, but also others. Something as simple as a thank you at a convenience store, or helping elderly neighbors carry their groceries to their homes, are just some examples of how we can bring the spirit of our divine creation to life. Remember, you can start with small gestures to get into this way of living as God's beautifully created children. You'll see soon enough how these actions will add up to create a bigger part of a whole.

Are you ready to put this love for others into action? Here are some ideas: Identify someone in your community who needs a little extra help every day. Can it be someone who needs a lift to the grocery store, as they do not have a car?

Reach out to them and find out how you can help them. Reflect on those qualities that you most admire in each of your family members. What makes your parents and siblings unique? Brainstorm together with your family how you can foster respect and a sense of community.

✐ PRAYER

God, thank you so much for creating us in Your image. Thank you for a beautiful affirmation in the Bible that we are created with divine purpose. Guide us from today to reflect this wonderful testament in everything that we do. Please make us aware of anyone who might need our assistance and help us to always be available for those who need us, even if it is someone with whom we might not be best friends with. Also, Lord, help us to be kind to our family members and to appreciate everything that makes them so special to us. Amen.

♟ FAMILY ACTIVITY

Get some art supplies together to make a big poster. Colorful markers, pens, glitter, glue, tape, string, and some pictures of family members too. Sit together around the dinner table and make a list of the unique qualities you would like to highlight in each family member. Perhaps Dad is the one who always gets things fixed in the house, and Mom always makes sure that you are on time for school. Glue a picture of each family member onto your poster and add these qualities. Put the poster up where everyone can see it every day, such as on the side of the fridge or in the living room.

January 3
God's Love Never Fails

"The steadfast love of the Lord never ceases; His mercies never come to an end; they are new every morning; great is Your faithfulness." – Lamentations 3:22–23

Have you ever loved something so much that it almost felt like your heart would burst? It could have been a treasured soft toy when you were younger, or a family pet that added warmth and laughter to your home.

Nothing could change the love that you felt, it was always there, always part of you. God's love is described as steadfast, always there, never wavering, never going away. It is there, 24/7 and it will never change.

Sometimes, it might feel like we do not deserve this love. We might make mistakes, or we could have done something to hurt someone else which made us feel terrible and worried how God might have felt about us now. In times like these, it is important that you remember: God loves us completely.

Even if we feel broken and incomplete or even fallible, He loves us. So, when you feel you have strayed from the path that God put before you, seek out His Love. Confess in prayer if you feel you have done something wrong, and ask for his guidance to stay on a path of faith.

It might be tough admitting when you've made a mistake, but remember this: Admitting and asking for forgiveness will make you feel so much better.

Here's some questions you as a family can work through today:

1. What has been one situation when you have doubted whether you deserved God's love or not? Why did it make you feel this way?
2. What is one way that you and your family can constantly remind yourself of God's unwavering love?
3. What is one thing you can start doing today to become an example of this love too?

✎ PRAYER

Dear God, your love is a shining light on our path. As a family, we praise you for a wonderful example of how love should be: unwavering, steadfast and rooted in faith. If we ever lose sight of your divine love for us, help us remember that you hold us close 24/7 every day, and that you lovingly watch over us.

Thank you for filling our lives with a wonderful love that never ends. Help us to show unconditional love too. Guide our words and thoughts to be examples of the love you have for us.

Amen.

♣ FAMILY ACTIVITY

Get pink card board and twine. Cut out hearts, write the name of each family member on a heart, then use a paper punch to put holes at the top. Thread the twine through the holes, then hang up your mobile in a special spot at home, like over the top of a book case. Keep some extra pink carton for when you would like to add more names to your project.

January 4
Jesus Is the Way

"Jesus answered, "I am the way and the truth and the life. No one comes to the Father except through Me." – John 14:6

For today's lesson, let's imagine you are planning a family trip. Think about what you would be packing in, like board games, toys, mobile devices, snacks, or even tents and outdoor equipment if you are going out in nature.

The most important thing is of course your map or a reliable GPS on your phone. The latter can help you stay on course, take the right roads and get to wherever you need to go without getting lost. You listen to the voice you hear from your phone and know you will get to be where you need to be. In our spiritual lives, we have the best guide: It's God, of course! His Scripture, His lessons and the way He inspires us to do good all serve as markers on our road map to life. In the Bible,

He gives us clear inspiration of how to live faith-inspired lives. See it as our Spiritual GPS, unlocked with words that are divinely inspired. Whenever you feel lost, look to God and his teachings. Trust in Him to show you the path when you have become lost. It might feel hard sometimes, but stay strong in faith and prayer. The journey will become so much easier when you put your trust in God and his divinely inspired words.

Let's think together as a family about how life's roadmaps have impacted our lives:

1. Was there ever a time that you drove to a holiday destination but you became completely lost? What did you do to get back on route? Did you relook your map or ask directions?

2. What is sometimes the habit you struggle with the most? Is it consistently praying, being kind to others or accepting other people as they are? How can you get back on route?

3. What was the most important lesson you learned today about God's guidance in your life?

PRAYER

God, thank you for reminding us today that you provide Spiritual guidance for us every day.

Thank you for Your Word and how it can help us navigate life and its challenges.

Give us open hearts today to always accept the guidance you give us. Should we struggle with challenges this week, help us to hear Your voice and follow.

Help us to be brave when we feeling anything but bravery, and help us to follow the right path. Thank you for loving us so much.

Amen.

FAMILY ACTIVITY

Bring today's lesson to life by creating a big map. Use a large piece of cardboard of paper to draw out a route, then add post its, or little flags with toothpicks and small triangles if you have these materials available. Decide how you will mark each "destination", such as going to Daily Sunday Service, going to Bible study, helping out someone in need. You can have as many destinations as you like, there is no limit.

January 5

God Knows Me

"You have searched me, Lord, and You know me. You know when I sit and when I rise; You perceive my thoughts from afar." – Psalm 139:1–2

It can be easy to feel lonely when the world feels so much bigger than us. We might feel like no one understands us, that we are not worth much or do not have value.

No matter how busy or noisy the circumstances around us get, we can often feel alone. Here's the good news: Even when we have days like this, the Bible reminds us that God knows us, even our most private thoughts and what we wish for.

It feels almost unreal, doesn't it? Having Someone who knows us better than anyone, Who loves us so much and to top it all, Someone who created us with a special purpose in life. And best of all? We can take comfort in the fact that we do not pretend to be anyone else but ourselves.

God sees us as we are and He knows everything about us. We can honestly come to Him in prayer and speak to Him about our worries and concerns, just like we would speak to a parent or trusted partner. This week, let's make it a priority to accept that we are seen and loved, and anything but lonely.

Here are some food for thought:

1. How can we as a family remind one another that we are loved by an ever-present Heavenly Father?

2. What is the most important thing to remember when we feel lonely?

3. Was there ever a time that a family member felt emotionally drained and unworthy? How did we go about to raise them up and remind them of their value.

PRAYER

Loving God, You know each of us the best. Thank you for accepting us just the way we are.

Thank you for reminding us through your Word that we are never alone, that we have a place in the world and that we are your children.

Should we start feeling doubt about whether we are important in the world, help us remember that each of us has a place.

Strengthen us as a family and help us to support each other too. Help us celebrate each one and love one another always.

Amen.

FAMILY ACTIVITY

On small pieces of paper, write down a few simple things each family member likes (e.g., "loves pizza," "likes to draw," "favorite color is blue"). Put them in a bowl and have everyone take turns drawing a piece of paper and guessing who it is describing. This is a fun way to celebrate how well you know and love each other, which is just a small reflection of how God knows and loves you.

January 6
Trust in the Lord

"Trust in the Lord with all your heart and lean not on your own understanding; in all your ways submit to Him, and He will make your paths straight." –
Proverbs 3:5–6

Have you ever been in a situation where it felt like the future was scary and unknown? Perhaps you as a family were moving to a new city, or you started a new school that you didn't know. This type of uncertainty can make you feel worried and unsure, which is something no one really wants to feel, right?

There is one thing that can change the way you feel about uncertainty: Trust.

Today's Scripture gives a good example of how trust in God works: Simply trust with your whole heart!

Life can sometimes feel like you are trying to put together a puzzle without the picture on the box. We can't see the final outcome, and it's tempting to just guess where the pieces go.

This verse tells us to trust God with the whole picture, even when we can't see how all the pieces fit together. "Leaning on our own understanding" means trying to figure everything out by ourselves.

God's plan is so much bigger and better than anything we could imagine. When we choose to trust Him and follow His lead, He promises to guide us on the right path.

Remember this week, when you feel like you do not know or understand the path that you are on, that your Heavenly Father is walking with You and guiding you. Put your trust in Him, and pray for strength to stay strong in this trust.

Let's go through some questions as part of our Bible study today:

1. Can you think of a time when you battled to put your trust in someone? Why were you unsure and what changed your mind?
2. What are some things we can do as a family to show God we trust Him?
3. What does it mean for God to "make our paths straight"?
4. How can we make it easier as a family to trust one another?

PRAYER

Lord, we learned about trust today, something that can be hard sometimes, especially when we are uncertain about the future and the path before us.

Thank you, Heavenly Father, that we can put our trust in You. You know how all the pieces of life fit together, and You will guide us forward.

Help us this week to put our trust in your Heavenly wisdom and to put our faith in you. Guide our steps and make our paths straight.

Amen.

FAMILY ACTIVITY

Find a blindfold and a small, simple obstacle course in a room (use pillows or blankets as obstacles). Take turns with a blindfold on and have a family member guide you through the course using only their voice. Take pictures for your family scrapbook and add them to your daily Bible study moments. Write next to each picture what you learned about this activity and what you needed to do to trust someone to guide you when you couldn't see. Then, write down what this means for you as a Christian and how you can make a daily effort to trust God with every aspect of your life.

January 7
God Is with Us

"Have I not commanded you? Be strong and courageous. Do not be afraid; do not be discouraged, for the Lord your God will be with you wherever you go." – Joshua 1:9

When was the last time you needed to be courageous? Like fearless, even when your knees felt like jelly and you had no idea if you would succeed?

Or were you in a situation that called for you to be strong in faith and resilience?

Joshua was in such a situation, and his was a massive task that could make many people feel unsure.

He had to lead his people, the Israelites, into a new land. Think about it for a moment. In Biblical times, there were no GPS devices, no social media, nothing.

Joshua was probably nervous, but God gave him a promise: "I will be with you wherever you go." This same promise still counts for us today.

When you're afraid of a new school year, a test, or a difficult conversation, God is right there with you. When you're feeling lonely or discouraged, He is there too. Knowing that God is with us gives us the courage to face anything. We don't have to be brave on our own; we can be strong because He is with us.

And when times of doubt do cross your path, remember Joshua's story. Sometimes, we have no idea of what is in store for us in new situations. Our Heavenly Father reminds us through His Word in times like these we are surrounded by His Love.

That's quite a promise, right?

Let's have a look at some questions for today's family Bible study:

1. When was a time during the past month where you had to pray for courage? Was it for something big, like an exam, or something small like driving to a new location for the first time? What did it feel like when you got the courage you needed?

2. Have you as a family ever experienced a situation, such as moving to a new house or even a new country, where you needed extra courage? How often did you pray?

3. Consider the example of Joshua that we spoke about today. What did it mean for you to revisit this story and be reminded of the lessons learned in this Scripture?

📖 PRAYER

Dear God, today's lesson about courage has been an important lesson that we needed to hear.

It is not always easy to be brave, especially when we are scared or unsure, but we know that You are always with us.

Help us to remember this week that You are always with us, and that when we are alone, we can reach out in prayer.

Strengthen our hearts

Amen.

♟ FAMILY ACTIVITY

Create a "God is with Us" box. Decorate a small box and fill it with encouraging verses or small items that remind you of God's presence, like a rock (our rock), a small cross, or a picture of your family. Keep it in a central place in your home and encourage family members to look at it when they need a reminder of God's love and presence. At the end of the week, go through the box and pick out your favorite verses. Paste them into your family scrapbook and make notes about why you picked out these items.

January 8

His Word Lights Our Path

"Your word is a lamp for my feet, a light on my path." – Psalm 119:105 (NIV)

Have you ever come home at night in total darkness? Did you immediately reach for your mobile phone to put on the torch function? Or did you have a torch with you in your car that you could use?

And did finding the path to your front door feel like it took forever?

In life, we might find ourselves trying to navigate forward in the "dark". We might be facing unexpected situations, just got bad news or are simply feeling like the world is just too much.

It happens. Life can be tough, and we might not always feel like we have a guiding light in front of us.

Then you turn on a flashlight. The light doesn't show you the full path in front of you, but it shows you how the next step looks.

This is exactly how God's Word works. It's a flashlight for our lives. It gives us the wisdom and guidance we need for the next decision. Although we do not instantly get all the answers, we are put on a path where we can make wise choices.

So, how do we find this light when it feels like we are surrounded by "darkness"? We pray. We read our Bible. And we seek out God's Wisdom.

This is an ongoing journey. We might stumble along the way as we learn to find the right path, knowing that God is our light and lamp helps us to better handle life's challenges.

Here are some questions for your family Bible study about today's lesson:

1. Can you think about a time that felt dark and scary in your life? Was it uncertainty about a new job or new school? How did you manage to overcome fear?
2. Which Bible verse is your favorite to remember when times are tough and uncertain?
3. Are you facing a challenge today in your daily or spiritual life? Are you unsure what to pray for?
4. Who is a hero from Biblical times that you feel succeeded in seeing the lamp at his or her feet?

📖 PRAYER

Heavenly Father, we often face times when it feels like there is just darkness. No light, no sight, just uncertainty.

Thank you for giving us light to see the path ahead of us. We praise you for guiding us forward, even when we do not know all the steps waiting for us.

We ask today to open our hearts to accept the light you provide for us, through Your Word and through our prayers.

Help is as a family to support one another to seek out this light.

Bless our words, bless our hearts and bless the love of support we share as a family.

Amen.

♟ FAMILY ACTIVITY

For today's family activity, you will be creating a lantern out of paper. Cut out large strips of paper to create the shape, then glue or use tape to put the pieces together. Put the lamp on the dinner table or in your living room, and make it part of your daily Bible study. Take a picture of your lamp and paste the printout into your Bible study scrapbook. Write down what this lamp has meant for you as a reminder of God's guidance and love for your family.

January 9
We Are God's Children

"Yet to all who did receive Him, to those who believed in His name, He gave the right to become children of God." – John 1:12

Think for a moment what it means to you to be someone's child. A son or daughter, someone who belongs to a specific family.

This belonging can provide an anchor in life that helps you feel secure in the world. Sure of where you fit into life's puzzle.

Being a child of God means we have a very special connection. We are treasured, cared for and created for a wonderful purpose.

Today's verse tells us that when we choose to believe in Jesus, we are welcomed into God's family. This is a big deal! It means we have a Heavenly Father who loves us perfectly, cares for our needs, and is always there for us. It means we are brothers and sisters in Christ, part of a huge family all over the world. We have a new identity: we belong to God.

What does belonging look like?

Think about how you are a parent, or your own parents, and what it means to belong in their family inner circle.

Your children, or you as a child, always have a place at the table. You are loved. You are cared for. You never have to doubt whether you have a place in the world. It has already been prepared for you by your Heavenly Father.

Let's sit together and go through today's Bible study questions:

1. What does it mean to you to be a child of God? What does it mean for you as a Christian to know this truth?
2. As a parent, what connection do you see between your relationship with your children and how there are similarities in the connection between you and your Heavenly Father?
3. As a family, how can we show others that we are part of God's family but also see our neighbors and friends as part of this family too?
4. What are the core parts of a family that keeps us united? And how can we use this knowledge to strengthen our bond as a family united in Christ?
5. Think of a family in Biblical times that embraced being God's children. What can we learn from them?

✍ PRAYER

Heavenly Father, thank You for making us Your children.

We are so grateful to be part of Your family.

Help us to live in a way that shows others what it's like to be loved by You.

Amen.

⛪ FAMILY ACTIVITY

Choose an evening that you as a family can have a "Family Celebration Event". Keep your camera close to take pictures that you can add to your family Bible study scrapbook. Choose something that you and your family will enjoy the most, such as a board game challenge evening or a Bible quiz night. Use this opportunity to talk to one another about what it means to be part of both an earthly family and God's family.

January 10
God Listens to Our Prayers

"This is the confidence we have in approaching God: that if we ask anything according to His will, He hears us." – 1 John 5:14

Have you ever asked for something with high hopes that your wish would come true? Perhaps you wanted a puppy for your birthday, or you wanted a shiny new bike for Christmas.

In life, we often might yearn for things, tangible and spiritual. Our wishes might be about more than "things" that can be bought.

Today's Bible verse reminds us that even when we feel like our prayers are hitting a brick wall, we are heard by our Heavenly Father. From where we are praying does not matter. We could be praying from a car, from our living room or even the garden.

The important thing is to never forget that God hears us.

Does this mean that we will get anything we ask for when we pray? Ready today's scripture again, it says "according to His will."

In other words, when we pray for things that we know are good and right, things that align with what He wants for our lives.

We might not get an answer immediately, or get the answer that we expected. We can be sure though that He's listening and will answer in a way that is best for us.

Let's reflect on this lesson with a couple of questions:

1. Have you ever asked for something and you didn't receive it? How did this make you feel, and in hindsight, did you understand why it was better that you didn't receive it?
2. Now, let's turn the first questions around. When was a time that you asked or prayed for something and you did receive it? Why do you think you did receive what you asked for?
3. How can we as a family become more resilient in prayer and open our hearts to God's Will?
4. How will we make a better effort this week to seek out God's Will first before our own needs?

PRAYER

Heavenly Father, it is wonderful to know that You hear our prayers without fail.

Thank you for the Bible that tells us that our words never fall on deaf ears.

Help us this week to seek out Your will, to open our hearts and to be open to receiving blessings that are aligned with Your will

Give us faith to trust whatever outcome our prayers will have, and give us peace as we wait for Your answers.

Amen.

FAMILY ACTIVITY

Use a page of your Bible study scrapbook to create a prayer journal for the week. Draw a column for each family member, jot down your requests and write underneath these words why you chose those requests. Discuss as a family what the best way would be to celebrate when God answers our requests. And, if you like, add on the page when there was a time in the past when a big prayer was answered, and what you learned from this.

The Lord Is My Shepherd

"The Lord is my shepherd, I lack nothing. He makes me lie down in green pastures, He leads me beside quiet waters, He refreshes my soul." – Psalm 23:1–3

Have you ever visited a farm where you saw how a shepherd guided sheep into the fields? Or how they gathered the sheep back to take them back to their shed?

Being a shepherd is a job that goes beyond herding. It means taking care of something, or someone, other than yourself. It is about looking after their needs, their requirements and helping them when they go astray.

In this psalm, we are reminded that God is our Heavenly Shepherd. He protects us, ensures our needs are met, and when we stray on our path, he helps us to get back on track.

God also helps us when we face danger, and He brings us back to peace too.

That is not where our Heavenly guidance ends. When we feel overwhelmed or tired, we can trust that God will heal our hearts and minds. And when we feel we are missing something, we can remember that in Him, we lack nothing. He gives us rest for our souls.

It can be so easy to always feel like it is up to us to find direction in life. To sort out our own problems and worries. What we need to remind ourselves of is that God will refresh us and heal our hearts.

He ensures that we will have exactly what we need, and help us to find the path that will get us there.

Let's discuss further what we have learned today:

1. What does "being a shepherd" mean to you? What would a shepherd typically do or be expected to do as part of their role?
2. Think of a time when you felt utterly lost? How did praying to God help you see reason?
3. What are some ways God acts as a "shepherd" for our family?
4. What does it mean that God "refreshes our soul"?

📖 PRAYER

Heavenly Father, we praise you as our savior and as our divine Shepherd

Every day, we are in awe of how you take care of our every need and bring us back to peace.

Please refresh our souls and help us to follow Your guidance.

Help us to never be stubborn, and to trust in your Heavenly Will for our lives.

Amen.

♣ FAMILY ACTIVITY

Use a blank page in your Bible study scrapbook to draw a path from the bottom left to the top corner. This path symbolizes how God as your shepherd guides you on the right paths every day. Make notes on this "map" of typical stumbling blocks you might face, such as uncertainty, sadness or fear. Write a solution underneath each about how you would pray to overcome these challenges, even when things are hard.

January 12
Made New in Christ

"Therefore, if anyone is in Christ, the new creation has come: The old has gone, the new is here!" – 2 Corinthians 5:17

Have you ever messed up and wished that you could have a redo to right things? Perhaps you hurt a friend's feelings or made such a big mistake that you felt there was no turning back from it.

We might feel like our hearts and lives are tarnished forever, and that there is no coming back from the mistakes we've made.

Here's the good news that we are reminded of in today's Bible study. When we accept Jesus into our lives, He doesn't just make us better; He makes us completely new. He takes away the shame and guilt of our past mistakes and gives us a fresh start.

So, what do we need to do to remind ourselves that we are made anew?

The first is to pray to God to help us clear our thoughts and not stay stuck in the memories of our mistakes. We need to trust Him in guiding us to be better, live better and believe that we can become better in every part of our lives.

The old things are gone, and a brand-new beginning is here, right now. A new beginning created by God just for you as a family.

Support one another this week and serve as constant reminders for your family members that God's grace has washed you clean of sin.

Let's go through some food for thought for this week's Bible study:

1. What does it mean for you as a family that "the old is gone"? Was there anything in the past that you felt held you back in your spiritual lives, and how has God's grace helped you to embrace the "new" that is promised in this Bible verse?
2. What are some things about being a "new creation" that you are excited about?
3. How can we forgive each other and give each other a "new start" when we make mistakes?
4. What are some old habits or ways of thinking we can leave behind and replace with new, good habits?

✎ PRAYER

God, knowing that we are made anew is incredible.

Thank You for making us new in Christ. We are so grateful for the fresh start and the new life You have given us.

Help us to leave our old mistakes behind and to live as the new creations You have made us to be.

Amen.

♟ FAMILY ACTIVITY

Give everyone a blank piece of paper. On one side, have them write or draw something they want to leave behind from the past, such as a bad habit, a worry, or a mistake. Then, on the other side, write or draw a new good thing they want to start. Tear up the "old" side and keep the "new" side as a reminder of their fresh start. Paste these papers into your family Bible study scrapbook as part of your 365 days of renewed worship.

January 13
God's Plan Is Good

"'For I know the plans I have for you,' declares the Lord, 'plans to prosper you and not to harm you, plans to give you hope and a future.'" – Jeremiah 29:11

In yesterday's Bible study lesson, we spoke about being made anew. Today, we are continuing a lesson that is linked to this: Being open to following new paths that your Heavenly Father has put before you.

Think back for a moment to a time when you had to take a detour. Perhaps your school bus was late and you had to walk or home, or your car wouldn't start and you needed to commute to with in another way.

Life can throw us some curveballs when we least expect them, but how we handle situations when things do not go our way speaks volumes.

It is human to wonder why something is happening to you, to even get angry, but it is important to remember that even if life is not following the path you want it to take, that you trust God's plan.

He knows better than anyone what the best way forward is, and trusting this wisdom will keep you resilient.

So, when life isn't going your way, remind yourself to trust that so many wonderful things are still to come on your path. It will take a little time, but it will be worth it when God's plan for you is revealed, blessing by blessing.

This doesn't mean everything will be easy immediately. Things will not instantly change. What it does mean though is that even in tough times, we can trust that God is working behind the scenes for our good. His plans lead to a future filled with hope.

Let's think about this hope a bit further and go through the following Bible study questions as a family:

1. When was the last time when you had to make a detour in life? What was the outcome and how did your faith in your Heavenly Father guide you to get the best possible outcome?

2. How can we trust in God's plan when things are difficult? How can we remind ourselves in our prayers and through our Bible studies that better things are coming?

3. What is the best way to share this promise of hope with someone who is struggling? And how can we set an example of how God's presence in our lives helps us to persevere?

4. Think about an important character in the Bible who relied on trusting God. How were they victorious, even when times were tough and things looked bleak?

5. What is the best way to hold onto hope when the plans we had for ourselves are not working out?

✒ PRAYER

Lord, thank you for reminding us today that you have wonderful things in store for us.

Thank You for the good plans You have for our lives. Help us to trust in Your promises, even when we don't understand the path we are on. Fill our hearts with hope for the future You have for us.

Amen.

♟ FAMILY ACTIVITY

Have a "What's Next?" game. Take a simple story and have each family member add a new sentence to build the next part of the story. Talk about how God's plan unfolds one step at a time, and we can trust Him with each part of our story. Then, create a page in your family scrapbook with the title "What's Next?". Use finger paint to make handprints on the page, and write down the words "thousands of blessings" on this page, as a reminder that these blessings are part of your journey.

January 14
Obeying God

"Walk in obedience to all that the Lord your God has commanded you, so that you may live and prosper and prolong your days in the land that you will possess." –
Deuteronomy 5:33

Before we start today's Bible lesson, let's reflect on one of the first examples of obedience in the Bible in the story of the Garden of Eden. What were the consequences of Adam and Eve's actions when they were not obedient to God?

Obeying God is part of our Christian calling. We do not simply exist to live only for ourselves. That would have been the easy route to follow, but we know from our scripture and Bible studies that obeying our Heavenly Father is a command asked from the beginning of time.

This might sound like you will be tied down to rules for your whole life. Just remember: these commands are there for our own good. They are rooted in the love our Heavenly Father has for us and all the good He wants us to experience in our lives.

He knows what is best for us, and today's verse says that walking in obedience leads to life and prosperity.

Now, remember that prosperity doesn't mean instant riches or cool things. It is so much more: Incredible spiritual gifts and so many blessings for your family.

Take these truths with you this year:

1. Following God's way leads to a life that is full, joyful, and secure.
2. Obedience is an act of trust, showing God that we believe His way is the best way.

Here are some questions to work through with your family today:

1. When was a time you didn't obey rules at school or work? What were the consequences, and what did you learn from this experience? What do you wish you did differently?
2. How can we help each other as a family to obey God?
3. Why do you think God's commands are for our good?
4. If you think about the Ten Commandments, which command do you feel resonates the most in your life?
5. What does it mean to you to live a life that is secure and full of joy, thanks to God's abundant blessings?

PRAYER

Dear God, thank you for teaching us that obedience leads to a blessed spiritual life.

Thank you for teaching us that obedience is a beautiful command that enriches our lives.

Help us to be obedient to all You have commanded us. We know Your ways are best for us. Give us the strength to follow You so that we may live a full life.

And inspire us as a family to follow a path that is shaped by Your will.

Amen.

FAMILY ACTIVITY

Open a new page of your family Bible study scrapbook. Draw a big cross in the center and make the heading in the page: God, our Heavenly Father and Leader. Write down what makes our God an awesome God, and Talk about how God is our ultimate leader, and which verses in the Bible reminds us of how He makes us feel safe and secure.

January 15

God Gives Peace

"Do not be anxious about anything, but in every situation, by prayer and petition,
with thanksgiving, present your requests to God. And the peace of God, which
transcends all understanding, will guard your hearts and your minds in Christ Jesus."
– Philippians 4:6–7

Have you ever been so worried about something in your life that it almost felt like you couldn't breathe? Perhaps it was a financial situation, or a test you had to write the next day or even a big project that kept you awake all night.

Worry can be scary. It can make you feel like there is no hope, causing your heart to race and clouding your thoughts with terrible ideas.

In today's Bible lesson, we learn an important lesson: God is always in control, in every situation.

Paul's words in Philippians are true and encouraging. God has given us a tool to help manage and overcome anxiety and stress.

Can you guess what this could be?

It's prayer, of course!

Think about it. What is our first response when we are worried and unsure? For many of us, it can be locking that stress and anxiety into the back of your mind, trying to manage it on your own ... but we do not have to.

When we start praying, we stop trying to hide our worries. We speak with our Heavenly Father, asking for guidance, for support, for solutions. And sometimes, even sharing our stress can be a starting point to help us on a path of healing.

Even more importantly: when we bring our worries to our Heavenly Father, we do not carry them along anymore.

Our worries will not disappear immediately, but we will get courage to push through our challenges. We will remember once more how God has helped us in the past, and that He is faithful

As a family, you can live this beautiful truth together by being open and honest about your fears, and praying together for salvation.

So, when next you are feeling anxious, remember God's peace for your life. He loves you and cares about you.

Let's wrap up today's Bible study with some reflection questions:

1. Think about the past year. What are some things that made you feel anxious or worried?
2. What should we remember when we are feeling anxiety and stress?
3. What have you learned today about prayer when you are worried about something in your life?

PRAYER

Heavenly Father, thank you for today's lesson about how we can manage worries.

It can be tough sometimes to see a silver lining when we are battling with our emotions, but thank you for giving us the peace we need.

Keep our hearts open this year to accept the grace we receive from you, and that we can heal from worry.

Amen.

▲ FAMILY ACTIVITY

Get your scrapbook ready to document today's family activity. Each family member must write down a worry on a piece of paper. Use an envelope and paste it, with the pieces of paper, into your book. Next to it, write Given to God. Then, write down one thing that each family member is thankful for this week underneath the envelope. Pray together, and revisit the scrapbook page and record how God answered your prayers or gave you peace during the waiting.

January 16
God Is Our Might Warrior

"The Lord your God is with you, the Mighty Warrior who saves. He will take great delight in you; in his love he will no longer rebuke you, but will rejoice over you with singing." - Zephaniah 3:17

Have you ever had a best friend or family member that might make you feel completely safe? Someone who will help you when you are in a difficult situation and do so without only love in their heart?

It's a wonderful feeling, right? That knowledge that you are protected by someone who is overjoyed when you are happy and feel safe.

Even better is to know that we already have such a wonderful presence in our lives: Our Heavenly Father.

Our Bible lesson for today reminds us that we never walk alone in this world. God is with us every day, giving us strength and courage when we need it in life.

We might often feel like we need to rely on ourselves to have perseverance in life, but through His Word God reminds us to put our trust in Him.

So, what does this mean for a family? We need to hold on to this truth, even when we are facing challenges or hardships in life.

Some situations might seem scary, such as financial worries, battling with school work or even illness. The important thing is to remember that in those moments, God is present in our lives. He will never forget us, his children, or leave us.

Knowing this truth changes how we live. True, it doesn't mean we will never get scared, but we will know how to move beyond fear as we stay anchored in faith and prayer.

Let's remember to not stay stuck in that mindset of wanting to solve everything on our own. Let's put our trust in God first, and live our lives fearless.

Here are some questions to inspire us even more for today's Bible study:

1. What has today's lesson taught you about trusting God when you are scared?
2. What does it mean for you as a family to have a constant warrior by your side?
3. How can we remind ourselves to trust the protection of God when we are facing difficult times?

✐ PRAYER

Heavenly Father, we often find ourselves fearing the worst in our lives. There are so many things that we can get scared about, which makes it hard sometimes to realize that we are not alone.

Help us, Father, to learn how to trust in Your divine presence. Teach us how to rise about fear and draw on the courage that we receive from You.

Keep our family close to You and help us to encourage one another with this truth.

Amen.

♟ FAMILY ACTIVITY

Open another blank page in your family scrapbook. Draw a picture of a big shield. Let each family member choose a word that they feel best describes God as our Heavenly Warrior. Use bright bold colors for the design, and keep the book open on the page this week as a reminder of what we learned today.

January 17
God Gives Strength

"The Lord is my strength and my shield; in him my heart trusts, and I am helped; my heart exults, and with my song I give thanks to him." – Psalm 28:7

Close your eyes for a moment. Think about what the word strength means to you as a family. Picture it in your mind. Do you immediately think of someone with big muscles, someone who never gets scared or someone that can push any obstacle out of the way?

Or, do you think first of your Heavenly Father?

We've already revealed a big truth just now in today's Bible study. God is our strength, even when we are feeling tired, depleted or that our troubles are just too heavy to bear.

It can be hard to sometimes believe in strength when we feel hopeless or weak. The way forward is to shake off any fear we might harbor in our hearts and focus on the love and support of our Heavenly Father.

One of our Bible heroes is an exceptional example of this. David, small in stature but big in courage thanks to God, faced a giant. A huge man that instilled fear in those that saw him.

David could have easily hid in the shadows, but spurred on by courage he received from God, he used the simplest of tools to defeat Goliath. He trusted God for strength and protection, and he received exactly that.

God's strength goes beyond our human perception. It can help us push through when we are at our most vulnerable, and help us endure when we feel overwhelmed.

Families can rely on God's strength in daily life. When a child feels nervous about a test, they can pray for courage. When parents feel overwhelmed by responsibilities, they can ask God for strength to keep going. His strength never runs out.

This is our shield against any challenge. Let's proudly carry it in our hearts, and when we despair, let us remember that God is near and always protects us.

Here are some extra questions to think about today:

1. How does the story of David inspire you as a family? Was there ever a time that you felt anxious and worried, but overcame your feelings through your faith in Christ?

2. Is there something specific that you need strength for at this moment, like a test or work struggle? How will you pray about this to Your Heavenly Father?

3. What are some ways that we can depend on strength from God in our daily lives?

4. How can we support one another as a family when we feel weak and scared? How can we encourage each other through God's Word and in prayer?

✎ PRAYER

Dear God, we are in awe once more today as we are reminded of the wonderful strength you give us every day.

You are our strength and shield. You give us courage when we are afraid and help us to endure when things get tough.

Forgive us for those times when we struggled to stay rooted in faith when we were tired.

Help us to trust You each day. Fill our family with Your Spirit so that we can live with joy and thanksgiving.

Amen

♟ FAMILY ACTIVITY

Create a page in your Bible study scrapbook with the heading "God is my strength". Let each family member write on a piece of paper something that they received strength for in the past week. Paste these words onto the page and decorate them with hearts and stars. Leave some space on the page where you can add more pieces of paper if you like.

January 18
God Is Our Rock

"For who is God, but the Lord? And who is a rock, except our God?" –
2 Samuel 22:32

When was the last time you and your family went on a hike in nature? Did you do some climbing over big rocks or followed a hiking trail? And how did the ground beneath your feet feel?

Rocks are known to be strong. They are not easy to move and they make us feel safe.

We need to feel the "rock" in our lives to be clear in our thoughts and certain about our destination in life.

Today's Bible lesson reminds us that God is our rock: the foundation of our faith Who keeps us steady even when the world around us feels unsteady.

God's care, wisdom and support goes beyond material things, beyond any earthly belongings. He gives us a strong spiritual home to live in, and keeps us on firm footing, no matter which storm we are facing.

So, how can families rely on God as their rock? It starts with trusting His Word, obeying His commands, and relying on His promises. When challenges come, the family that stands on His truth will not be shaken.

God is our place of refuge when life feels uncertain. When we believe without fail, and put our trust in Him, we will experience a firm foundation of faith that gives sense to our world.

Let's go through some family questions as part of today's Bible study:

1.   What does it mean for God to be our rock?
2.   What are some "shaky" foundations people often trust instead of God?
3.   How can our family make sure we are building our lives on God's Word?

📖 PRAYER

Heavenly Father, Your are our rock and our refuge

Thank you for providing firm ground for our feet even when we feel uncertain about taking those first steps.

Guide our hearts to be open to receiving Your blessings this week.

And help us to trust even when times are hard.

Amen.

♟ FAMILY ACTIVITY

Go to the beach or a park and collect rocks of various shapes and sizes. Clean them up at home, then let each family member paint a rock with a powerful message that "God is our rock". Place these rocks in your living room window sills, or put them outside in the garden in your flower bed. Take a picture and add it to your Bible study scrapbook.

January 19
God Is Our Helper

"My help comes from the Lord, the Maker of heaven and earth." – Psalm 121:2

When was the last time you asked for help, and what was it for? Did you ask your parents for help with your homework, or did you ask a colleague to help with a project you were working on?

Everyone needs help, and families need help with daily challenges.

Today's lesson reminds us that our ultimate help comes from the Lord, the Maker of heaven and earth.

One of the most powerful questions and affirmations in the Bible is: "I lift up my eyes to the hills. From where does my help come?" The answer is immediate: "My help comes from the Lord." This means God, Who created everything, helps His children without fail in so many ways.

He gives wisdom when we need direction, peace when we feel anxious, and strength when we are tired. He sends people into our lives to encourage us, support us, and remind us of His truth.

Families can practice asking for God's help together. Instead of worrying, stop and pray. When decisions need to be made, ask God for wisdom. When someone feels discouraged, remind them that the Lord is our helper.

Let's go over today's Bible study questions:

1. What does Psalm 121 teach us about where our help comes from?
2. Why is it important to look to God for help instead of only to people or things?
3. What are some ways God has helped you in the past?
4. How can our family turn to God for help this week?

PRAYER

Heavenly Father, thank You for being our helper. Thank You that we can trust You in every situation. Forgive us when we try to do everything on our own. Teach us to call on You for help each day. Help our family to remember that You are faithful and powerful. In Jesus' name, amen.

FAMILY ACTIVITY

Create a "Help List" on a piece of paper. Each family member writes one area where they need God's help this week. Pray over the list daily. At the end of the week, write notes about how God answered or gave peace. Place the list in your Bible study scrapbook under the title "God Our Helper."

God Is Love

"Anyone who does not love does not know God, because God is love." – 1 John 4:8

Love is one of the most powerful emotions in the world. It can lift our spirits, make us feel cherished and ready to take on any challenge that we might face in the world.

Think about the love your parents have for you. They would do anything for you and love you just the way you are. In the same way, your children cherish and adore you as parents, also loving you unconditionally.

And even more importantly, think about how much God loves you as His children.

Love is one of the most powerful truths about God. Scripture says He is love. Everything He does flows from His perfect love.

In other words, He sets the example of how love can change the world around us. There are so many examples in the Bible that show His love. He created the world out of love. He cared for Israel out of love. He sent prophets and leaders to guide His people out of love. Most importantly, He sent Jesus to die for us out of love. John 3:16 says, "For God so loved the world, that he gave his only Son, that whoever believes in him should not perish but have eternal life."

God's love is not like human love that changes or fades. His love is constant, faithful, and unconditional. Even when we sin, He offers forgiveness. Even when we wander, He calls us back.

This is a powerful truth that we need to stay anchored in, every day.

Families are called to reflect God's love in daily life. This means being patient, forgiving, and kind. It means putting others before ourselves. When families live in love, they show the world what God's love looks like in action.

Let's go through today's Bible study questions:

1. What does it mean that God is love?

2. How has God shown His love in your life?

3. Why is it important for families to love one another?

4. What are some practical ways we can show God's love this week?

PRAYER

Heavenly Father, thank You for being love itself. Thank You for sending Jesus as the greatest example of love. Forgive us when we fail to love others well. Fill our family with Your love so that we can be patient, kind, and forgiving. Help us to reflect Your love in our home and in our community. In Jesus' name, amen.

FAMILY ACTIVITY

On a poster board, write "Our Family of Love" at the top. Each family member writes ways they can show love at home, school, or work. Decorate the poster and place it in your home. At the end of the week, write a reflection about what happened and add it to your Bible study scrapbook.

January 21
God Is Patient

"The Lord is merciful and gracious, slow to anger and abounding in steadfast love."
– Psalm 103:8

What does it mean to be patient? Does it mean you never lose your temper, watch your words and think carefully when you speak? Or perhaps that you remain calm when you need to make important choices?

The Bible certainly teaches us a lot about patience. Think, for instance, about Abraham (Abram) and Sarah (Sarai) who waited for years for Isaac. They needed to be patient to receive one of the greatest gifts of their lives from God.

And of course, there is the greatest example of patience: God Himself.

God's patience is one of His most comforting qualities. He does not lose His temper quickly or give up on His children. Instead, He shows mercy, grace, and steadfast love.

Throughout the Bible, God's patience is clear. He gave Israel chance after chance to repent when they turned away. He was patient with His disciples and taught them like a loving father would.

God's patience also means He allows us room to grow in our faith. Second Peter 3:9 says, "The Lord is not slow to fulfill his promise as some count slowness, but is patient toward you, not wishing that any should perish, but that all should reach repentance." His patience is a gift that gives us the chance to turn back to Him.

This sets a wonderful example for families. We need to be patient with one another, even when we sometimes feel frustrated or want things to move at a faster pace. Being patient allows us to follow God's example of love.

Let's now go through today's Bible study questions:

1. What can we do this week to be more patient with one another as a family?
2. Are there other examples in the Bible about patience that we can further study this week?
3. What did we learn about God's patience this week?
4. Have you ever struggled being patient in the past, and how did you learn to be more patient?

✎ PRAYER

Heavenly Father, thank you for setting the perfect example of patience for us.

Thank you for being patient with us, and allowing us to grow in faith.

Teach us this week to be patient with our family and with others.

Give us open hearts to love one another and to accept that others do not think or act like we would do.

Teach us to love as You love. In Jesus' name, amen.

♟ FAMILY ACTIVITY

Create a "Patience Challenge." Each family member writes one area where they need more patience (for example, waiting, speaking kindly, or finishing chores). At the end of the week, talk about progress and thank God for His help. Add your notes to your Bible study scrapbook under the title "God Is Patient".

January 22
God Forgives

"If we confess our sins, he is faithful and just to forgive us our sins and to cleanse us from all unrighteousness." – 1 John 1:9

Making mistakes often happens in our lives. And worse of all: These mistakes can make us feel like we will never be forgiven or that we can never right the wrongs that we caused.

Perhaps you accidentally kicked a ball that smashed through your wife's window. Or maybe you broke someone at work's cup when you took it out of a cabinet.

Here's what you need to remember about making mistakes: When you are honest and confess to someone if you made a mistake that impacted them, you are taking the first steps towards forgiveness.

It is certainly the same when we confess our sins to our Heavenly Father.

We might be broken human beings, but that doesn't mean we cannot be forgiven. God offers forgiveness through Jesus, and He will make us anew when we confess.

Confession doesn't mean we completely forget our sins and wrongdoings. What it does mean is that our guilt can be wiped away and our relationship with our Heavenly Father can be restored.

Making mistakes can sometimes make us feel like we want to hide and just forget what we did. The Bible guides us to realize that when we confess our sins, a huge load can be removed from our shoulders.

So, let's support one another this week with the powerful affirmation that forgiveness is possible when we confess, no matter how "big" or "small" we feel our sins are.

Let's go through today's Bible study questions:

1. Has there ever been a time when you wronged someone close to you? How did it make you feel?
2. What does it mean for you that God forgives us when we confess our sins?
3. How can families practice forgiveness every day?
4. How can we set the example of forgiveness when someone wronged us?

PRAYER

Heavenly Father, thank you for today's affirmation that when we confess our sins, we can receive forgiveness.

It can be hard sometimes to truly believe that we can be forgiven when we've messed up big time.

Teach us to have open hearts and to be ready to receive forgiveness when we confess our sins.

Help us to also be humble when we need to confess to family or friends when we did something wrong.

Amen.

FAMILY ACTIVITY

Make a "Forgiveness Cross." On slips of paper, write down sins or mistakes you want to confess. Place the slips in an envelope and tape it to a paper cross. Write 1 John 1:9 at the top. Place the cross in your Bible study scrapbook as a reminder that God forgives completely.

January 23
God Is Good

"Oh, taste and see that the Lord is good! Blessed is the man who takes refuge in him!"
– Psalm 34:8

Today's lesson unpacks an important truth: what it means to be good.

Close your eyes for a moment, and picture a person who you think embodies pure goodness. Is it your mother or granny, or perhaps a friend who is always willing to listen?

These people without a doubt reflect the divine goodness of our Heavenly Father, the best possible example of what being good truly embodies.

God's goodness can be seen in so many examples in the Bible. He provided manna in the desert, gave Hannah a son after many years of waiting and protected Moses when his mother put him in a basket to keep him safe from Egyptians. And when Jesus was born, he would show kindness as an adult by healing others and showing compassion, even for those that society saw as sinners.

At the heart of God's goodness is that it can be seen in both big miracles and even everyday blessings such as having food at home and a warm bed to sleep in at night.

James 1:17 says, "Every good gift and every perfect gift is from above, coming down from the Father of lights."

So, how can you as a family become more aware of seeing this goodness?

Start by acknowledging every day that you are grateful for every blessing that you receive, even when life feels hard sometimes.

Romans 8:28 reminds us that "for those who love God all things work together for good." Even in trials, God is working for the good of His children.

Look beyond the trials this week. Be more aware of the goodness in your life. Show gratitude, and embrace goodness as a family in how you treat each other as well as friends and neighbors.

Let's reflect on today's lesson with a couple of questions:

1. Think of a time that you experienced. God's goodness in your life. What happened, and how did it make you feel to experience this goodness?
2. How can families remind one another of this goodness in their daily lives?
3. And how can we bring goodness to the world around us? What can we do to help others who are struggling?

🕮 PRAYER

Heavenly Father, thank you for the blessing of goodness in our lives.

Thank you for kindness and love, and that we have everything we need.

Forgive us when we forget to give thanks or doubt Your goodness. Teach our family to notice Your blessings each day and to trust that You are always working for our good.

Amen.

⛪ FAMILY ACTIVITY

Create a "Goodness Journal" page in your family Bible study scrapbook. Each family member must write down one way they saw God's goodness each day for a week. At the end of the week, read them aloud together.

January 24
God Guides Our Steps

"The steps of a man are established by the Lord, when he delights in his way." –
Psalm 37:23

Every step we take in our lives, whether we are talking about physical steps to move forward or the actions that we choose to move forward, impacts our future.

Every day we make choices. Some are big, like where to work or where to go to school, while others can seem small, such as which ice cream to buy on a Saturday afternoon.

Families are reminded in Psalm 37 that when we delight in God and walk in His ways, He guides our steps.

God's guidance is steady and trustworthy. Proverbs 3:5-6 says, "Trust in the Lord with all your heart, and do not lean on your own understanding. In all your ways acknowledge him, and he will make straight your paths." When we try to figure everything out on our own, we stumble. When we seek God first, He shows us the way forward.

God guides His people through his Word, and we see so many examples of this goodness in the Bible. God led Israel with a cloud and fire in the desert. He guided Ruth to Boaz, who became part of God's plan for the Messiah. He guided the wise men to Bethlehem with a star.

Today, He continues to guide his children, and families can trust in His divine grace when they need to make important decisions.

Knowing that we have this incredible guidance gives us courage and confidence in our daily lives. We know that we are cared for and loved.

Let's dig a little deeper into today's lesson with some discussion questions:

1. Have you ever felt uncertain about a decision you needed to make? How did prayer help you get clarity?
2. What does it mean for you as a family that God guides your steps, every day?
3. How can you as a family become more aware of God's guidance in everyday life?

📖 PRAYER

Heavenly Father, thank You for guiding our steps.

We praise you for being a shining beacon of hope on our path, even when we feel uncertain about what lies ahead for us.

Help us to never lose sight of

Amen.

⛪ FAMILY ACTIVITY

Draw footprints on a page in your Bible study scrapbook. In each footprint, write one way God has guided your family in the past. Write "God Guides Our Steps" on top of the page. Take some time to go through each footprint, and thank God for helping us during these specific times.

January 25
God Listens to Prayer

"I call on you, my God, for you will answer me; turn your ear to me and hear my prayer." – Psalm 17:6

Prayer is more than speaking words into the air. It is talking with the living God who hears every word and cares about every concern. David knew this truth well when he wrote, "I call on you, my God, for you will answer me."

God listens when His children pray. Sometimes He answers quickly, other times He teaches us patience. Sometimes His answer is "yes," other times "no," or "wait." Every answer is given in wisdom and love. First John 5:14 says, "This is the confidence we have in approaching God: that if we ask anything according to his will, he hears us."

Families should remember that prayer is not limited to church or mealtimes. God invites us to pray in every situation: before school, in the middle of a busy day, or when facing worry at night.

Prayer also draws families closer together. When we share requests and pray together, we carry one another's burdens. We remind each other that God is faithful and that we are never alone.

Here are some questions to discuss during today's Bible study session:

1. Why is it important to believe that God listens when we pray?
2. How has God answered prayers in your life or in our family?
3. What can we learn when God's answer is different from what we expected?
4. How can we make prayer a bigger part of our family life?

PRAYER

Heavenly Father, thank You for listening to our prayers.

Thank You that You never ignore us or grow tired of hearing from us.

Forgive us when we forget to come to You first.

Teach our family to pray with faith and patience, trusting that You always answer in love.

In Jesus' name, amen.

FAMILY ACTIVITY

Make a "Prayer Jar". Write requests on slips of paper and place them inside. At the end of the month, read through the slips and write how God answered each one. Place both the requests and the answers in your Bible study scrapbook under the title "God Listens to Prayer". Use two envelopes that you stick onto a page to keep the strips of paper neat and tidy.

January 26
God Gives Wisdom

"If any of you lacks wisdom, you should ask God, who gives generously to all without finding fault, and it will be given to you." – James 1:5

What does wisdom mean to you? Is it always saying and doing the right things? Perhaps knowing so much about life that you feel you cannot go wrong?

Today's lesson reminds us that God is wisdom, and he provides wisdom to those who ask for it in prayer.

We need to also remember that wisdom is more than knowledge. Knowledge is knowing facts; wisdom is knowing how to use them in a way that honors God. James tells us that when we lack wisdom, we should ask God. He does not hold back or criticize; He gives generously.

Wisdom begins with reverence for God. Proverbs 9:10 says, "The fear of the Lord is the beginning of wisdom." True wisdom comes from respecting God's authority and living according to His Word. Without it, even smart decisions can lead to trouble.

And the great news is, we have the best source to get examples of wisdom: our Bibles.

God's Word is a key source of wisdom. The more we read and obey Scripture, the wiser we become. God also provides wisdom through prayer and through the counsel of faithful believers.

Here are some questions to go through in today's Bible study:

1. What is the difference between wisdom and knowledge?
2. How does James 1:5 encourage us when we feel unsure about decisions?
3. What are some areas in our family where we need God's wisdom right now?
4. How can we practice seeking wisdom each day?

✎ PRAYER

Lord, thank You for promising to give wisdom when we ask.

Thank You for guiding us with patience and love. Forgive us when we rely only on ourselves.

Fill our family with wisdom from Your Word and Your Spirit. Help us to make choices that honor You.

⛪ FAMILY ACTIVITY

Create a "Wisdom Tree" on a page in your Bible study scrapbook. Write James 1:5 at the top. On each branch, write an area where your family needs wisdom. As God answers, add leaves with notes about His guidance.

January 27
God Gives Comfort

*"Praise be to the God and Father of our Lord Jesus Christ, the Father of compassion
and the God of all comfort." – 2 Corinthians 1:3*

In today's lesson, we reflect on comfort in times of sorrow. Those times when we were at our lowest low and how we were able to move forward, thanks to the comfort that our Heavenly Father provides.

It can feel super hard to get through difficult times. Kids might have fights with their best friends, parents might face financial difficulties and stress.

When life brings moments of sorrow, we can feel disappointed, lonely and scared. This is why, in such moments, we need to seek God's comfort.

In those moments of despair, God reveals Himself as the "God of all comfort". His compassion reaches into our pain and brings peace that the world cannot give.

Paul reminds us that God not only comforts us but also equips us to comfort others. Second Corinthians 1:4 says, "He comforts us in all our troubles, so that we can comfort those in any trouble with the comfort we ourselves receive from God." When families experience God's comfort, they can then encourage others who are hurting.

God comforts through His Word, which reminds us of His promises. He comforts through His Spirit, who brings peace to the heart. He also comforts through people: friends, church family, and even parents and children comforting one another at home.

Comfort does not mean problems vanish. It means we are not crushed by them. God's presence carries us through pain and gives us hope.

So, the next time someone in your family feels overwhelmed by sorrow, provide comfort and remind them of how God can ease our sorrows and hurt.

Let's reflect further on today's Bible study with the following questions:

1. What does it mean that God is the "God of all comfort"?
2. How has God comforted you during hard times?
3. Why is it important for families to comfort one another?
4. How can we bring God's comfort to someone else this week?

✎ PRAYER

Compassionate Father, thank You for being the God of all comfort.

Thank You for holding us in times of sorrow. Forgive us when we forget to turn to You. Teach our family to seek comfort in Your Word and to share that comfort with others.

In Jesus' name, amen.

♟ FAMILY ACTIVITY

Each family member draws or writes one way God has comforted them. Collect the drawings and place them together on one scrapbook page with the title "The God of All Comfort".

January 28
God Gives Hope

"May the God of hope fill you with all joy and peace as you trust in him, so that you may overflow with hope by the power of the Holy Spirit." – Romans 15:13

Think about a time that you felt filled with hope and courage. Was it a test that you were sure you were going to do well in, or a promotion that you were sure you were going to get?

Today's Bible lesson reminds us that hope is the confident expectation of God's goodness. It is rooted in God's promises and His faithfulness. Paul calls Him "the God of hope."

Hope and trust goes hand in hand. We do not simply blindly hope, we trust our Heavenly Father to help us persevere and receive blessings according to His will.

This is an important message for families to remember. Children need hope when the future feels scary. Parents need hope when challenges press in. God promises joy and peace when we trust Him, filling us with hope through the Holy Spirit.

The Bible shows how God gives hope. Abraham hoped for a son and trusted God's promise. Hannah hoped in God through prayer, and He answered. The prophets spoke of the Messiah, and their hope was fulfilled in Jesus. Today, our hope rests in the risen Christ, who gives eternal life.

Hope changes how we live each day. It helps us endure trials, encourages us to keep praying, and gives us strength to encourage others.

And if we foster an awareness of hope, we can encourage our families to trust in God, to hope and know that He will answer according to His will.

This deliverance might not be instant, but we can be assured that it will come.

So, let's remind each other this week that God gives hope. God encourages, and He loves us so much.

Here are some questions to work through as part of today's Bible study:

1. What does Romans 15:13 teach us about God as the source of hope?
2. How is biblical hope different from wishful thinking?
3. What promises from Scripture give you hope today?
4. How can our family encourage one another to stay hopeful?

PRAYER

God of hope, thank You for filling us with joy and peace.

Thank You for giving us hope in Jesus Christ. Forgive us when we lose sight of Your promises.

Fill our family with hope that overflows to others. Teach us to trust You in every situation.

Amen.

FAMILY ACTIVITY

Make an A4-size "Hope Board". On this poster, write Romans 15:13. Each family member adds Bible verses, drawings, or notes that give them hope. Place the board in your scrapbook at the end of the week.

January 29
God Is Faithful

"Jesus Christ is the same yesterday and today and forever." – Hebrews 13:8

What does being faithful mean to you and your family? Is it staying true to your values and faith? Or does it mean that you have an active prayer and Bible study habit that you follow every day?

Today's Bible lesson reminds us that God's faithfulness means He always keeps His promises. He never changes, never fails, and never abandons His children.

His love and mercy are new every morning, a reminder that He can be trusted in every season.

Throughout the Bible, God proved His faithfulness. He kept His promises to Noah, Abraham, Israel, and David.

And the greatest promise fulfilled was the coming of Jesus, our Savior.

Families can rest in this truth. Life is uncertain, but God is steady. People may fail us, but God remains faithful.

Even when we are unfaithful, He remains true to His Word. Second Timothy 2:13 says, "If we are faithless, he remains faithful—for he cannot deny himself."

Trusting God's faithfulness helps families face trials with peace. It reminds us that God's promises stand firm, no matter how circumstances change.

So, make it your family goal this week to trust God anew in the days and weeks to come.

Believe in the blessings that your Heavenly Father has in store for you, and embrace them wholeheartedly.

Here are some questions to inspire today's Bible study lesson:

1. What does it mean that God is faithful?
2. How has God shown faithfulness in the Bible?
3. How has He shown faithfulness in your life?
4. Why is it important for families to remember God's faithfulness?

PRAYER

Faithful God, thank You for keeping every promise.

Thank You that Your mercies are new every morning. Forgive us when we doubt Your Word.

Teach our family to remember Your faithfulness and to live with trust.

In Jesus' name, amen.

FAMILY ACTIVITY

Start a "Faithfulness Timeline" in your scrapbook. Write down moments when God showed His faithfulness to your family. Add to it over time as new examples happen.

God Is Strong

"Be strong in the Lord and in the strength of his might." – Ephesians 6:10

What does it mean to be strong?

Strength in this world often looks like power, control, or independence. When we hear the word "strong", we might also think of resilient athletes and those who do endurance sports, making it look easy to move forward.

Then there are those people who display a strength in character. It could be our parents who seem unshakeable in their faith and beliefs, or a grandma and grandad who persevered during tough times in their lives.

Today's Bible lesson reminds us that God is our true source of strength. So often, we might feel like we have to dig out strength on our own, but the truth is, all we need to do is pray and trust in our Heavenly Father to give us exactly what we need.

Paul told the Ephesians to "be strong in the Lord," not in themselves. The same message applies to us and our families today.

We also need to remember God's strength is unshakable. He created the heavens and the earth. He parted the Red Sea. He raised Jesus from the dead. That same strength is available to His children through the Holy Spirit.

Families need God's strength to face challenges. It can be hard when times are tough, but together, we can stay strong in our faith and persevere.

Here are some family questions to discuss for the next couple of minutes:

1. How does God's strength look different from human strength?
2. What part of God's armor encourages you the most?
3. How can our family rely on God's strength each day?

✐ PRAYER

Lord, thank You for being our strength.

Thank You for giving us courage through the Holy Spirit. Forgive us when we try to depend on ourselves. Clothe our family in Your armor and help us to stand firm in faith.

Amen.

♟ FAMILY ACTIVITY

Draw a picture of God's armor in your Bible study scrapbook with the heading "Be Strong in the Lord". Label each piece with its name from Ephesians 6. Discuss how each piece protects believers.

January 31
God Is Our Refuge

"God is our refuge and strength, a very present help in trouble." – Psalm 46:1

Quick question: What makes your home feel like a safe space? Is it knowing Mom and Dad are near? Is it the security your home has or the area it is based in? Or is it something simpler, like your bedroom that feels like a castle of comfort?

Do you seek out these safe spaces when you feel you need to hide from the world or need refuge when something bad happens?

Today's Bible lesson reminds us that God is our refuge and our strength. These gifts are always present when trouble comes, and in times when we feel safe too.

It might feel unreal at times, knowing we have this kind of safe space that we can take shelter in. Yet, it is a trust that we can rest in when life feels overwhelming.

Another important lesson from today's Bible study is to remember that God's refuge is not about escaping every problem in our lives. It is about His presence giving peace in the middle of them. The psalm continues, "Therefore we will not fear though the earth gives way." Even if everything shakes, God remains steady.

There are many stories of the Bible that show how God provided refuge for his children. Noah found safety in the ark. Israel found refuge when God parted the Red Sea. Daniel found protection in the lion's den.

So, when you feel scared or even alone this week, keep today's Bible study close to your heart. As a family, encourage one another to pray for strength in times of trouble.

Trust God in everything, from this month to the months ahead.

As we wrap up our month of January Bible lessons, let's reflect on the following questions for a couple of minutes:

1. What does Psalm 46:1 teach us about God as our refuge?
2. How does His presence change the way we face trouble?
3. What are some ways God has been a refuge for your family?
4. How can we remind each other to run to God for safety?

PRAYER

Lord, thank You for being our refuge and strength.

Thank You for being present in times of trouble. Forgive us when we forget to run to You. Keep our family close to You and give us peace in Your presence.

In Jesus' name, amen.

FAMILY ACTIVITY

Build a small "Refuge Fort" from blankets and pillows. Sit inside together and read Psalm 46. Write down your family's prayer for God's refuge and add it to your Bible study scrapbook under the title "God Is Our Refuge".

FEBRUARY

February 1
Finding Hope

"Do not gloat over me, my enemy! Though I have fallen, I will rise. Though I sit in darkness, the Lord will be my light." - Micah 7:8

Life is full of ups and downs. The book of Micah paints a picture of a nation in deep spiritual darkness. The people had fallen far from God's ways, and as a result, they were facing judgment and hardship.

The prophet Micah speaks a message of unshakeable hope. He personifies Israel's faith, declaring that even in their lowest moment they would not be defeated.

This is a beautiful lesson for families today: our failures are not our final destination. Just as the sun rises after the darkest night, God promises to be our light, guiding us out of our struggles and into His presence.

The "enemy" in this verse can be many things: a person who wishes us harm, our own self-doubt, or even the spiritual forces of darkness.

The message is clear: we are not to let them have the final word. Our circumstances might seem overwhelming, and we might feel like we've fallen, but our hope is not in our own strength. It's in the character of God. He is a God who lifts the fallen and illuminates the darkness. This verse reminds us that even when we are at our weakest, we can find strength in His promise to be our light. It is a promise of restoration, a promise that our story isn't over when we fall. It is a promise that with God, a new chapter of victory is always possible.

Let's reflect for a couple of minutes on this lesson with today's Bible study questions:

1. Think about a time you felt like you had "fallen" or were in a dark place. How did you rely on God to be your light during that time?
2. What does it mean to you that God is a God of restoration?
3. How can you apply the message of Micah 7:8 to a current challenge you or your family is facing?

PRAYER

Heavenly Father, thank you for being our light in the darkness. We confess that there are times we feel like we have fallen, and the enemy of our souls tries to gloat over our mistakes. Lord, help us to remember that our story is not over. In Jesus' name, Amen.

FAMILY ACTIVITY

Draw a picture in your family Bible study scrapbook of a flashlight.

Let each family member write one sentence of a time that God shined a light on something that they were concerned or worried about.

Discuss as a family what it meant to get clarity on these situations and how it helped you to grow closer to God.

February 2
God Gives Rest

"Come to me, all who labor and are heavy laden, and I will give you rest." –
Matthew 11:28

Have you ever been so emotionally or spiritually tired that it feels like you will never be able to recharge?

Everyone feels weary at times. Children may feel tired after studying hard for tests and being worried that they will not do well. Parents may feel overwhelmed with work, bills, and the pressures of daily life.

Here's what you as a family need to know: You are not alone.

Jesus invites the weary to come to Him, promising rest for their souls.

This rest is not only physical. It is deeper than a good night's sleep. It is the peace of knowing sins are forgiven, the relief of knowing God carries our burdens, and the security of knowing He controls tomorrow. True rest is found only in Jesus.

From the beginning, God designed rest for His people. After creating the world, He rested on the seventh day. He gave Israel the Sabbath to remind them that rest is part of worship. Rest is not laziness. It is trust. When we rest in God, we declare that He is in control and we are not.

Jesus showed this kind of rest when He slept in the boat during a storm (Mark 4:38). Even though his disciples panicked, He remained calm and trusted His Father.

This is a wonderful example for families. Even in the worst of storms, God is with us. He provides rest, even if our schedules and work lives get busy.

So, let's inspire one another this week to not let being busy get in the way of our daily Bible studies and prayers.

Make it a priority to set out time every time for spiritual connection.

Let's reflect on the lessons we learned today for a couple of minutes:

1. What have you learned today about why it is important to rest?
2. How will you and your family make it easier to stick to your Bible study schedule? Chat for a minute about what works best, such as after dinner or the morning after breakfast.
3. What does spiritual rest mean to you? What does it feel like and why is it important?

🕮 PRAYER

Heavenly Father, thank You for providing rest and refuge.

Thank you for listening to our prayers when we need to speak about worries and concerns.

Help us to always know that there is no need to carry our sorrows on our own, and that all we need to do is seek peace and comfort in Your arms.

Amen.

♟ FAMILY ACTIVITY

Create a scrapbook page with the heading "Rest in God". Each family member writes one burden they want to give to Jesus. Draw clouds and flowers on the page. At the end of the week, write how God gave peace in those areas on the page.

February 3
God Is Our Healer

"For I am the Lord, your healer." – Exodus 15:26

Have you ever felt so broken that you were convinced healing would never happen? The Bible teaches us that even in bad times, healing is possible.

When Israel left Egypt and traveled into the wilderness, they faced bitter water at Marah. God made the water drinkable and declared Himself their healer. This showed them that He cared not only about their physical needs but also about their hearts.

God's healing is complete. He heals bodies, minds, and spirits. Sometimes He brings physical healing immediately, other times slowly, and sometimes not until heaven. He always heals in ways that glorify Him.

Jesus' ministry was also full of healing. He opened the eyes of the blind, made the lame walk, and even raised the dead. These miracles were signs of God's kingdom breaking into the world. They revealed His compassion and power.

Most importantly, Jesus came to heal the greatest sickness of all: sin. Through His death and resurrection, He gives forgiveness and eternal life.

Families can trust God as healer in every situation. When someone is sick, pray for His touch. When hearts feel broken, ask Him for comfort. Healing may come through medicine, rest, encouragement, or simply His peace in the middle of pain. No matter how He works, He remains the Great Physician.

Go into this week with a spirit of healing. When someone in your family is hurting, lift them up through prayer. Pray with them for strength, and help them get through their sorrows.

Let's take a couple of minutes to go through today's Bible study questions:

1. How have you experienced God's healing in your life? Let each family member share their thoughts.
2. How can we as a family support one another when healing is needed?
3. Pick a specific example of healing in the Bible. Give each family member a chance to say what this example means to them.

PRAYER

Lord, you are our Healer. We thank You today for giving us peace and rest when our heart are weary.

Thank You for giving us peace and healing our hearts and spirit.

Forgive us when we forget to seek out Your wisdom in times of need.

Teach us to always put our trust in Your power and Your timing.

In Jesus' name, amen.

FAMILY ACTIVITY

In your scrapbook, make a page titled "Prayers for Healing". Give each family member a chance to write down their special prayer for healing. Leave enough space on the page so that you can add prayers through the year.

February 4
God Provides Daily Bread

"Give us this day our daily bread." – Matthew 6:11

When someone mentions "our daily bread" as part of Bible study, what is the first thing you think of? Do you think of food and shelter, or provisions in other ways?

In today's family Bible study, we receive a powerful reminder that God provides for our needs according to His will. He knows what we need, but we also have to trust that He will provide for us.

Israel learned this lesson in the wilderness. When they hungered, God gave manna each morning. They were told not to store it up for the next day. If they tried, it spoiled. God wanted them to trust Him for each new day's provision (Exodus 16:19-20). In the same way, we are not meant to carry the weight of tomorrow's worries. Jesus said, "Do not be anxious about tomorrow, for tomorrow will be anxious for itself" (Matthew 6:34).

Daily bread also points us to Jesus Himself. In John 6:35 He declared, "I am the bread of life; whoever comes to me shall not hunger, and whoever believes in me shall never thirst." God does more than provide food for our bodies. He provides salvation for our souls.

Families today need this reminder. It is easy to feel stressed about the future: bills, school, health, or jobs. Jesus invites us to pray for today's needs and to trust His Father's care. Gratitude is another part of this prayer. When we thank God for what we have, we see that every meal, every paycheck, and every blessing is His gift.

Let's reflect on today's Bible lesson for a couple of minutes with the following questions:

1. What does Jesus mean by "daily bread" in the Lord's Prayer?
2. How did God provide for Israel in the wilderness?
3. Why does God want us to depend on Him day by day instead of worrying about the future?
4. What is one way our family can practice gratitude for His provision this week?

PRAYER

Provider God, thank You for giving us everything we need each day. Thank You for food on our table, clothes to wear, and a home to live in. Forgive us when we worry about tomorrow or forget to thank You for today. Teach our family to trust You for daily needs and to share with others out of what You provide. In Jesus' name, amen.

FAMILY ACTIVITY

On a scrapbook page titled "Daily Bread," write Matthew 6:11 at the top. Throughout the week, each family member writes down one way God provided for them that day. At the end of the week, read the list aloud and add it to your scrapbook as a reminder of His faithfulness.

February 5
God Gives Courage

"Overhearing what they said, Jesus told him, "Don't be afraid; just believe." –
Mark 5:36

Have you ever been so afraid of something that might or could happen that you couldn't think about anything else? Perhaps it was a test on a subject you are not good at, or a situation at work that caused a lot of tension and uncertainty.

Today's Bible lessons teaches us that courage is not the absence of fear. Rather, it is how we decide to move forward from this fear that defines our faith in God.

It is the decision to trust God and obey Him even when you feel afraid.

In other words: Just believe in your Heavenly Father and that He will provide courage when you need it most.

Let's revisit the story of David and Goliath. Goliath was a big guy that could have easily crushed David, who was much smaller than he was.

David, though, didn't allow fear to take over his mind. Plus, he used the most basic of weapons: his sling and rocks.

Anyone else might have thought they would be doomed with so little protection, but David believed, and he defeated a danger so big and powerful.

Families often face "Goliath problems" of their own. The important thing is that we work together to raise one another up and help each other to keep our faith strong through prayer and Bible study.

So, let's make it our goal this week to be unshakeable in our faith when we face challenges.

Let's take a couple of minutes to discuss today's Bible study questions:

1. Have you faced a "Goliath" size problem in your life recently? How did it make you feel?
2. What is the most important lesson from today's Bible study?
3. Which example of someone who found courage through God is your favorite in the Bible, and why?

✐ PRAYER

Lord, thank You for being with us wherever we go. Thank You for giving us strength and courage through Your Word. Forgive us when we let fear stop us from obeying You. Teach our family to rely on Your promises and to live with courage each day. In Jesus' name, amen.

♟ FAMILY ACTIVITY

On a scrapbook page, write "Be Strong and Courageous" across the top. Each family member writes one situation where they need God's courage this week. Leave space for notes about how God helped. Add this page to your scrapbook as a record of answered prayers.

February 6

God Is The Inspiration

"We also have the prophetic message as something completely reliable, and you will do well to pay attention to it, as to a light shining in a dark place, until the day dawns and the morning star rises in your hearts. Above all, you must understand that no prophecy of Scripture came about by the prophet's own interpretation of things. For prophecy never had its origin in the human will, but prophets, though human, spoke from God as they were carried along by the Holy Spirit." – 2 Peter 1:19-21

Have you ever picked up your Bible and wondered: What inspired the words on every page?

Today's Bible lesson reminds us that every word in Scripture has one source: Our Heavenly Father.

Every time we page through our Bible or read specific sections, we are getting messages inspired by God. These messages remind us of stories spanning thousands of years ago, but even more amazing, they still teach us truth and reason today.

We read many stories about families in the Bible too, from Joseph and his brothers to Moses and Aaron and more. Every piece of the puzzle helps us learn valuable lessons.

Lessons about forgiveness among family members, lessons about supporting one another and even lessons about how important it is to not let jealousy get in the way of a family's daily life.

Make it a priority this week to take examples of Biblical families and what they teach us, even today, about living faith-built lives, inspired by the love our Heavenly Father has for us.

Let's reflect for a couple of minutes on today's Bible lesson:

1. What does it mean for you that God inspired every word in the Bible?
2. What are some of the lessons that Biblical families still teach us today?
3. Why is Bible study so important for families?

PRAYER

Heavenly Father, thank you for every incredible lesson in the Bible.

We are in awe of each truth that we find inside.

Thank you for teaching families how to serve You, and how to support one another.

Help us to always seek out Your Word, in good and bad times.

Amen.

FAMILY ACTIVITY

Use one of your scrapbook pages to draw a picture of a Biblical family with a positive, beautiful message. You could draw Noah and his family, or perhaps Joseph and his brothers making peace. At the top of the page, you can write: A Biblical Family To Remember.

February 7

God Always Answers Those Who Call To Him

"Call to me and I will answer you and tell you great and unsearchable things you do not know." – Jeremiah 33:3

Have you ever wondered why we pray? Do we do this only to get what we want in life or to get something for personal gain?

Prayer is about much more than that.

Today's Bible lesson focuses on a core truth of our Christian lives: When we pray to our Heavenly Father, we do not simply just fire off requests. We seek out His Wisdom and His Will, ask for His guidance and strength to overcome any challenge in our lives.

And when we truly yearn for truth and ask for it through our prayers, amazing things can happen.

Think about Hezekiah who was very sick and close to death. He prayed to God and his prayers were answered. There is also Hannah, who was a childless woman but still prayed to God and received the blessing of motherhood.

Both examples show people who were facing troubled, but still held onto faith and their devotion to God.

So, what does today's verse mean for families?

It is a reminder that when we pray together and seek out wisdom, peace and guidance from our Heavenly Father, He will answer our call. Even if we pray for something we might feel is so small or insignificant, He hears our prayers.

Let's reflect further on today's lesson for a couple of minutes with the following questions:

1. Think about a time when God answered your prayers. What did you pray for or about, and what was the guidance that you received?
2. What does praying together mean for you as a family?
3. What is one thing that your family needs guidance for at the moment? Discuss for a couple of minutes what you need.
4. What is an example in the Bible of someone who prayed and had their prayers answered?

✐ PRAYER

Heavenly Father, thank you for the incredible prayer. Thank you for today's Bible lesson that reminds us that when we call to You in prayer, You hear us and You know what we need.

Teach us to have patience when we pray, and help us to learn from examples in the Bible that teach us how to pray non-stop in faith.

Amen.

♟ FAMILY ACTIVITY

Choose a blank page in your family Bible study scrapbook. Paint the palms of your hands and press them down gently on the page, making sure there is enough space underneath each hand for writing down words. Let the page dry, then give each family member the opportunity to write down underneath their handprints about a time when their prayers were answered. Create an extra page if you would like to add more handprints with notes on answered prayers.

February 8

God Teaches Us To Forgive Others

"Then Peter came to Jesus and asked, "Lord, how many times shall I forgive my brother or sister who sins against me? Up to seven times?" Jesus answered, "I tell you, not seven times, but seventy-seven times." – Matthew 18:21-22

How often have you struggled with forgiveness? Perhaps someone treated you unkindly. Perhaps it was someone at school who pushed you out of the way during a sports match, or someone at work who told lies to make it seem like your work was their own.

When someone hurts us, it can be easy to immediately feel we have to "push back" and retaliate. This would just be so easy, right?

Not quite.

Today's Bible lessons teach us to always have a sense of forgiveness, even when circumstances are hard. Jesus gave the example of seventy-seven times, meaning in other words, always.

Think about Joseph. His brothers sold him into slavery. He was taken to a foreign land. And despite these hardships, he managed to show his brothers forgiveness.

Would you have done the same if you were in his shoes?

Also, think about when Jesus was on the cross: "Jesus said, "Father, forgive them, for they do not know what they are doing." And they divided up his clothes by casting lots. - Luke 23:34

Jesus showed compassion even when he was suffering. He spoke words of forgiveness because He knew the people around Him couldn't fully understand His purpose.

Families need to make forgiveness a priority too in everyday life. It's no secret that our home, our family unit, is often where we are most vulnerable, where we let our guard down. So, let's make it a priority this week to be slow to anger and to forgive one another. Forgive a sibling who played with a toy without asking or borrowed a shirt that wasn't theirs.

When we show this kindness, we truly reflect the love God has for us.

Now, let's reflect on today's lesson for a couple of minutes with the following questions:

1. What does God teach us about forgiveness?
2. How can we make forgiving part of how we interact with family members?
3. What does the story of Joseph teach us about forgiving someone who wronged us?
4. Why is forgiveness so important for our spiritual lives?

PRAYER

Heavenly Father, thank you for teaching us about forgiveness.

Thank you for setting the example of forgiveness from a Heavenly Father and helping us understand how important it is to forgive others.

Teach us this week to calm our thoughts and guard our minds against anger.

Help is to forgive without resentment.

Amen.

FAMILY ACTIVITY

Draw a big cross on a blank page of your Bible study scrapbook. Let each family member write down what it means to them to be forgiven by God. Then, say a prayer together thanking God for His mercy and teaching us why forgiveness is so important.

February 9
God Teaches Us to be Generous

"A generous person will prosper; whoever refreshes others will be refreshed." –
Proverbs 11:25

What does generosity mean to you? Is it giving someone money? Donating items to those in need?

These are certainly generous gestures, but it is important to remember that generosity is also making time to listen to others when they need support. It is showing encouragement when someone close to us is going through a difficult time.

Generosity is about more than just giving away tangible things. It's about having a giving spirit that is open to giving blessings. It can be something as simple as spending time with a friend that needs moral support, or helping a colleague who is struggling with a project at work.

God teaches us that we get a reward of our own when we are generous of others: That we are refreshed. It feels good being generous to others, and it does the soul good to embrace a kind, giving attitude.

A beautiful example of generosity in the Bible is the widow's offering (Mark 12:41-44). Although the widow had almost nothing to give, she still gave what little she had. And Jesus praised her for her generosity!

We might think that small acts of generosity are not really worthwhile, but the fact is, they are. A kind word can mean the world for someone in need of fellowship, and a big brother or sister helping their younger sibling with homework can be a wonderful experience.

So, let's embrace this kindness this week. Let's bring generosity into our hearts.

Let's reflect for the next couple of minutes with some questions about today's Bible lesson:

1. What does it mean to be refreshed when we are generous?
2. Can you think of an example in the Bible of someone who showed generosity?
3. How can we notice God's generosity in daily life?
4. How can our family practice generosity this week?

PRAYER

Heavenly Father, thank you for teaching about the gift of generosity through Your own examples that we find in the Bible.

Help us to not shy away from being generous this week. Help us to be kind and gentle to those who need it the most.

Amen.

FAMILY ACTIVITY

Draw a picture of a tree with big green leaves on a page of your scrapbook with the heading "Giving Tree". Write on each leaf how you as a family can be generous this week, and add more leaves over time to show that generosity should never run out.

God Loves Us Always

"Your faithfulness continues through all generations; you established the earth, and it endures." – Psalm 119:90

Faithfulness means keeping promises, never failing, and always being true. God is perfectly faithful. His love never ceases. His mercies are fresh each day. His promises never change.

The Bible tells the story of God's faithfulness from beginning to end. He kept His promise to Noah by never flooding the earth again. He kept His promise to Abraham by making him the father of many nations. He kept His promise to Israel by bringing them into the promised land. Most importantly, He kept His promise to send a Savior, fulfilled in Jesus Christ.

Even when people failed, God remained faithful. Second Timothy 2:13 says, "If we are faithless, he remains faithful—for he cannot deny himself." His faithfulness is not based on our actions but on His character.

Families can find hope in God's faithfulness during uncertain times. Life changes, but God does not. People may break promises, but He never will. His Word is reliable, and His care is steady.

God's faithfulness also teaches us how to live. He calls us to be faithful in our commitments, in our words, and in our love. Families can reflect His faithfulness by showing up for each other, keeping promises, and staying true to God's commands.

Let's reflect for a couple of moments on today's Bible lesson:

1. What does today's Bible verse teach us about God's faithfulness?
2. How has God shown His faithfulness in the Bible?
3. How has He shown faithfulness in your life?
4. How can our family reflect God's faithfulness in our daily choices?

🕮 PRAYER

Faithful God, thank You for keeping every promise. Thank You for mercies that are new every morning. Forgive us when we forget Your faithfulness or fail to keep our own promises. Teach our family to trust Your Word and to live in a way that reflects Your character.

Amen.

⛄ FAMILY ACTIVITY

Start a "Faithfulness Journal" in your scrapbook. Each week, write down one way God has shown His faithfulness to your family. Over time, you will build a record of His goodness that strengthens your faith.

February 11

God Gives Us Strength

"I can do all this through him who gives me strength." – Philippians 4:13

Have you ever felt like you do not have any strength left in your heart to face the day ahead?

Often, life can come with challenges that make us feel tapped out. These can be small things such as studying all night for a test, or bigger problems like financial worries or even strife among family members.

Feeling absolutely depleted can impact our spiritual lives too, making us feel low and hopeless.

Today's Bible study lesson reminds us that even when we feel weak or like we cannot go on, our true Source of strength will never leave us.

God provides the strength and courage that we need. Even when it feels like we are in hopeless situations, it is important to remember that we are not without hope.

So many people in the Bible proved this point. Job, for instance, lost everything he had, and went through a very hard time. He could have easily just given up, lost his faith and stopped praying. All was not lost though. Despite struggling, he found healing. In Job 42:10, we read the following: The Lord restored the fortunes of Job when he prayed for his friends, and the Lord gave Job twice as much as he had before.

Job returned to his Source of strength, and enjoyed a prosperous blessed long life. He went through a bad patch, but his faith and prayer took him forward.

Families can learn from Job's example. When bad things happen, we should never forget that God is with us, and that He can help and heal us.

Next time you or someone in your family faces a bad situation, come together in prayer and remind one another to seek out strength from our Heavenly Father.

Let's reflect for a couple of minutes with the following questions:

1. What does it mean when we say God is our true source of strength?
2. What does the example of Job teach us about trust and faith?
3. How can we as a family support one another through faith when times are tough?

✐ PRAYER

Heavenly Father, You are our true source of strength.

Thank you for making us strong when we are facing challenges.

Bless us this week when we struggle and help us to stay true to our faith and prayers.

Amen.

⛪ FAMILY ACTIVITY

Draw a picture in your scrapbook of a trophy, with the heading "God is our Source of Strength". Let each family member write a truth on the trophy about strength, such as "God gave me strength to get through a difficult test". Add more words to the trophy during the week to remind you of how faithful our Heavenly Father is.

February 12

God Takes Away Our Guilt

"as far as the east is from the west, so far has he removed our transgressions from us."
– Psalm 103:12

Have you ever done something so bad that you felt there was no turning back? Perhaps you kicked a soccer ball through a neighbor's window, or you bumped into someone's car in a parking lot and drove off.

Maybe you used God's name in vain when swearing at someone in traffic, or ignored God's teachings in the Bible and sinned.

Situations like these can cause a lot of guilt. It can make us feel so removed from a place of forgiveness that life might seem hopeless.

The good news is that you are never far away from God's grace. Think about a guy like Jonah in the Bible. He ignored God's command to go to Nineveh and fled ... and ended up being swallowed by a whale!

Did he just become whale food and that was the end of his journey? No, not at all. He prayed for forgiveness, and was saved.

If you feel guilt at the moment about something that happened, reach out in prayer to your Heavenly Father. Being caught in guilt's grip can feel like you are in the belly of the whale, but God's forgiveness will free you.

Pray together as a family this week for strength when you feel remorse for something that happened in your life. Pray for forgiveness and guidance.

And remember to forgive yourself too.

Let's reflect for a couple of moments on today's Bible lesson with the following questions:

1. What does the story of Jonah teach us about forgiveness?
2. What does it mean to be cleansed of all sin?
3. What are some ways our family can help one another seek out forgiveness?

✒ PRAYER

Heavenly Father, thank you for teaching us about forgiveness.

Thank you for teaching us that we are never far removed from your grace.

Forgive us when we doubt whether we can ever break free from guilt, and help us to stay strong in faith and prayer.

Amen.

♟ FAMILY ACTIVITY

Draw a picture of the whale in Jonah's story on a page on the lefthand side in your scrapbook. Draw a picture of Jonah inside the whale's belly, praying with his eyes closed. Draw a picture on the right side of Jonah looking happy and walking to Nineveh, with the sun shining above him.

February 13

God Teaches Us To Help Those In Need

"There will always be poor people in the land. Therefore I command you to be openhanded toward your fellow Israelites who are poor and needy in your land." –
Deuteronomy 15:11

Kindness is about more than being a good person. Today's Bible lesson reminds us that helping those in need was already mentioned early on in the Bible.

Acts 9:36-42 tells us about Tabitha (also called Dorcas in Greek) who was known for here generosity: In Joppa there was a disciple named Tabitha (in Greek her name is Dorcas); she was always doing good and helping the poor. About that time she became sick and died, and her body was washed and placed in an upstairs room. Lydda was near Joppa; so when the disciples heard that Peter was in Lydda, they sent two men to him and urged him, "Please come at once!"

Peter went with them, and when he arrived he was taken upstairs to the room. All the widows stood around him, crying and showing him the robes and other clothing that Dorcas had made while she was still with them.

Peter sent them all out of the room; then he got down on his knees and prayed. Turning toward the dead woman, he said, "Tabitha, get up." She opened her eyes, and seeing Peter she sat up. 41 He took her by the hand and helped her to her feet. Then he called for the believers, especially the widows, and presented her to them alive. 42 This became known all over Joppa, and many people believed in the Lord.

Any skill that you may have, such as preparing extra food or making clothes for the needy, can help provide relief for those in need in your community.

Is there a charity that your church perhaps supports that you can help with? Or does your school do any charity drives? If you are unsure, ask friends or community members which organizations they know that need extra help.

As families, you can work together doing charitable work, such as clothing drives, putting together food parcels or collecting books for schools that cannot afford them.

This week, open your heart to God's call to support those in need. Pray that you will not miss out on providing relief where you can.

Let's reflect on today's lesson with the following questions:

1. What is a good example of helping those in need that we find in the Bible?
2. Why is it important for families to help those in need?

📖 PRAYER

Heavenly Father, thank you for teaching us how important it is to help those in need.

Open our hearts this week to recognize those that need our assistance the most, and help us to use our talents to serve others.

Amen.

⛪ FAMILY ACTIVITY

On a scrapbook page, write "How We Can Serve Those In Need". Draw various small pictures, such as baskets of food, clothes or books. Discuss how these can meaningfully enhance people's lives, and give thanks to God for the lessons we receive about being generous to others.

Nothing Can Separate Us From God's Love

"Though the mountains be shaken and the hills be removed, yet my unfailing love for you will not be shaken nor my covenant of peace be removed," says the Lord, who has compassion on you." – Isaiah 54:10

Valentine's Day is often a day that we associate with chocolates, flowers and hearts. A day where we might exchange goofy greeting cards and other tokens of affection.

Today's Bible lesson is a sort of love letter for you and your family too.

It is a reminder that nothing can separate us from God's love. Isaiah 54:10 offers an incredible truth: God's love for us, His children, is neverending. It is one of the most powerful examples of love that never fails.

There are many examples in the Bible of God's love for his children. From the start, He loved His children like a father would. He guided Biblical heroes like Moses, Joshua and David, provided assurance to Mary, and through Jesus lovingly inspired disciples.

Today, we can reflect His unconditional love through kindness, friendship and acts of service to others. We can show love through sharing the Gospel with others, by joining our communities in prayer at church and together reflecting on examples of love in the Bible.

Let us remember on Valentine's Day today the words of 1 Corinthians 13:4-7: Love is patient, love is kind. It does not envy, it does not boast, it is not proud. It does not dishonor others, it is not self-seeking, it is not easily angered, it keeps no record of wrongs. Love does not delight in evil but rejoices with the truth. It always protects, always trusts, always hopes, always perseveres.

Here are some reflection questions for today's Bible lesson:

1. What does it mean that God has compassion for us?
2. How can we reflect His neverending love in our communities?
3. Read 1 Corinthians 13 in full. What does this book in the Bible teach us about love?
4. What are some practical ways our family can reflect God's love this week?

PRAYER

Heavenly Father, thank you for teaching us what love is. Thank you for blessing us with neverending love, even when we feel like we do not deserve it.

Forgive us, Father, for the times that we struggled with showing love and support for one another.

Teach us to be patient and kind, and open our hearts so that we can show love and compassion to others.

Amen.

FAMILY ACTIVITY

Use pink carton to cut out a large pink heart. Write "God is Love" in the middle, then stick the heart in your scrapbook. Use today's Scripture as inspiration and cut out more hearts with affirmation about God's love for us written on them.

February 15
God Is Our Protector

"The Lord will keep you from all evil; he will keep your life. The Lord will keep your going out and your coming in from this time forth and forevermore." – Psalm 121:7–8

Protection is something every family longs for. Parents want to keep their children safe from harm. Children want to feel secure in their homes and schools. Psalm 121 assures us that God Himself is our Protector. He watches over us in every season of life, guarding us day and night.

Israel often traveled dangerous roads on their way to Jerusalem for worship. Psalm 121 was a song of trust sung on those journeys. It reminded them that God does not sleep or grow weary. He never takes His eyes off His people.

The Bible gives many examples of God's protection. He protected Noah and his family in the ark. In the lion's den, he kept Daniel safe. He shielded Paul from difficulties and shipwrecks. While God's protection does not imply that His people are immune to adversity, it does imply that He is there to protect them and maintain their faith.

Today's families are at risk from a variety of physical, mental, and spiritual threats. God's assurance of protection ought to bring solace and tranquility. Every day, parents can ask God to keep their kids safe. Even in times of fear, children can remember that God is always with them.

Let's take a couple of minutes to work through the following questions:

1. What can we learn about God's protection from Psalm 121?
2. In the Bible, how did God safeguard His people?
3. What threats do modern families face, and how can we have faith in God to protect them?
4. In what way does Jesus offer us the best protection available?

PRAYER

Protector God, thank You for watching over our lives. Thank You for guarding us day and night. Forgive us when we let fear control us instead of trusting You. Keep our family safe in Your care, both in body and spirit. Thank You for Jesus, who gives us eternal protection. In His name we pray, amen.

FAMILY ACTIVITY

On a scrapbook page, write "God Is Our Protector." Each family member draws a shield and writes inside one area where they trust God for protection. Decorate the shields with colors or symbols of strength. Place the page in your scrapbook as a reminder of His care.

February 16
God Gives Peace

"And the peace of God, which surpasses all understanding, will guard your hearts and your minds in Christ Jesus." – Philippians 4:7

Have you ever wondered what real peace looks like? Is it being happy all the time and not having a worry in the world? Or is it something even better?

Peace is something everyone wants, but it often feels hard, and sometimes impossible, to get. Sometimes, when we have moments of peace, life can suddenly be disrupted by stress or challenges. Kids might struggle with school work, adults might struggle with navigating interpersonal relationships.

Despite all of this, peace is possible.

Philippians 4:7 promises that God offers peace beyond understanding, a peace that guards our hearts and minds through Christ Jesus.

It's amazing, right?

Paul wrote these words while in prison. Even when he was in chains, he felt God's peace because he trusted in Christ.

So, what does today's Bible lesson mean for families?

First and foremost, we must help each other to seek out peace from God. We must pray together for peace constantly, and never lose sight of the powerful fact that we can find rest and assurance in the presence of God.

Let's take a couple of minutes now to talk about today's Bible study:

1. What does God's peace look like?
2. How can families seek out His peace in everyday life?
3. What can we do as a family when we feel anxious or worried?

✎ PRAYER

Heavenly father, thank You for giving us peace beyond understanding. Thank You that Your presence guards our hearts and minds. Forgive us when we let fear or worry rule our thoughts. Teach our family to focus on You and to live in Your peace each day. Amen.

♟ FAMILY ACTIVITY

Create a scrapbook page titled "Peace of God". Each family member writes or draws one situation where they need God's peace this week. At the end of the week, write how God answered or gave comfort.

February 17
God Protects Us From Trouble

"You are my hiding place; you will protect me from trouble and surround me with songs of deliverance." – Psalm 32:7

Have you ever been in so much trouble that it felt like you couldn't get any rest?

In yesterday's Bible lesson, we learned how God gave us peace. Our blessings do not stop there: God is also our safe place where we can be safe from trouble and worry.

Think about a time when you were younger when you seeked out safety. Did it mean seeking out a quiet place like your bedroom that made you feel secure? Or was it being in your family's presence that gave you that feeling of being protected?

Often, families pray for safekeeping during the day. These prayers are not simply words: they are an affirmation of trust in God's holy plan for us and that He will protect us from trouble.

This can be from harm and from personal hurt. It could be protecting us while traveling to school or work, or giving us a place of refuge against the worries of everyday life and challenges.

There are many examples of being saved from troubles in the Bible, In Psalm 107:6, we read the following: Then they cried out to the Lord in their trouble, and he delivered them from their distress.

Families might often feel like certain situations cannot be overcome, but the fact is, when we reach out to our Heavenly Father and ask Him to save us, He hears our call.

Let's stand strong this week and remind each other every day that God is our safe place that will always protect us from sorrow and hurt.

Take a couple of minutes to go over today's reflection questions:

1. What does it mean that God protects us from trouble?
2. How has God helped you and your family in the past from difficult times and sorrows?
3. What are some ways our family can pray when we are facing troubles?

PRAYER

Heavenly Father, thank you for being our safe place when we are facing troubles in life.

Please help us to never lose sight of the fact that you are our Heavenly Protector.

Amen.

FAMILY ACTIVITY

Use one page in your scrapbook to draw a picture of a big house with your family in it. At the top of the page, write "God protects us from trouble".

February 18

God Is Holy

"You shall be holy, for I the Lord your God am holy." – Leviticus 19:2

Holiness means being set apart, pure, and without sin. God is perfectly holy. Every part of His character is pure, righteous, and good. Because He is holy, He calls His people to live holy lives.

In the Old Testament, God's holiness was displayed in the tabernacle and the temple. Only the high priest could enter the Most Holy Place, and only with sacrifice. This showed that God's presence is pure and cannot be approached casually.

Isaiah saw a vision of God's holiness. Angels cried out, "Holy, holy, holy is the Lord of hosts; the whole earth is full of his glory" (Isaiah 6:3). In response, Isaiah confessed his sin and received cleansing. Holiness always reveals our need for forgiveness.

Through Jesus, we are made holy. Hebrews 10:10 says, "We have been sanctified through the offering of the body of Jesus Christ once for all." His sacrifice cleanses us and sets us apart as God's children. Families should live in a way that reflects His holiness: choosing honesty, purity, forgiveness, and love.

Holiness is not about perfection we achieve. It is about walking daily in obedience to God's Word, relying on His Spirit to shape us. Families can pursue holiness together by setting apart time for prayer, worship, and serving others.

Let's spend a couple of minutes discussing the following questions:

1. What does it mean that God is holy?
2. Why does God call His people to holiness?
3. How does Jesus make us holy before God?
4. How can our family reflect holiness in daily life?

📖 PRAYER

Holy God, thank You for showing us Your perfect character. Thank You that through Jesus we are cleansed and set apart for You. Forgive us when we choose sin instead of holiness. Teach our family to live in obedience to Your Word and to reflect Your holiness in our home. Amen.

⛪ FAMILY ACTIVITY

On a scrapbook page, write "Set Apart for God." Each family member writes one way they can live differently for God this week—speaking truth, showing kindness, or resisting temptation. At the end of the week, add notes about what you learned.

February 19
God Gave Us Victory

"Where, O death, is your victory? Where, O death, is your sting? The sting of death is sin, and the power of sin is the law. But thanks be to God! He gives us the victory through our Lord Jesus Christ. Therefore, my dear brothers and sisters, stand firm. Let nothing move you. Always give yourselves fully to the work of the Lord, because you know that your labor in the Lord is not in vain." – 1 Corinthians 15:55-58

Have you ever run a race and won? How did that make you feel? Were you on top of the world, more sure of yourself than ever?

Feeling like you have won in life can be a great feeling, but as Christians it is important that we remember the ultimate victory was won for us through Jesus Christ.

This victory was not to get medals or prestige. It was a triumph over sin.

So, what does this mean in modern times?

For you and your family, it is a reminder to be thankful to God for cleansing His children of all sin, for freeing us from the clutches of sin, and for giving us that assurance of eternal life by his side.

The victory of Jesus and the cross remains as much an affirmation today as it meant for the people that were present at the crucifixion and experienced how Jesus rose again after three days.

Whenever we might feel far removed from grace, we simply need to reach out in prayer and Bible study to seek out the messages that we can still return to today for spiritual guidance.

Make today's Bible lesson a priority in your spiritual life. Embrace the gift of victory over sin, and live a life blessed with forgiveness.

Let's take a couple of minutes to go over the following questions:

1. What does today's Bible lesson teach us about God's victory?
2. How did Jesus pave the way for sin to be conquered?
3. How can our family remind one another of how we are victorious thanks to Jesus Christ?

PRAYER

Heavenly Father, thank you for crowning us with victory over sin.

Thank you for reminding us today that the gift of Jesus Christ and the cross still blesses us today.

Help us to never lose sight of Your love for us.

Amen.

FAMILY ACTIVITY

Draw a picture on a page in your Scrapbook of a big cross. Above the cross, write the words "God gave us victory". Let each family write an affirmation on this page of how they will embrace this victory in the coming week.

February 20

God Is Our Shield

"We wait in hope for the Lord; he is our help and our shield." – Psalm 33:20

It is incredible how many things we are protected from every day. Not only physical harm, but also unseen threats that could hurt our hearts and souls.

This is the protection that our Heavenly Father gives to us. He is our Shield and our Savior, always present in our lives.

A beautiful example of God protecting his children is Daniel 3:16-18: Shadrach, Meshach and Abednego replied to him, "King Nebuchadnezzar, we do not need to defend ourselves before you in this matter. If we are thrown into the blazing furnace, the God we serve is able to deliver us from it, and he will deliver us from Your Majesty's hand. But even if he does not, we want you to know, Your Majesty, that we will not serve your gods or worship the image of gold you have set up.

The three friends were indeed saved thanks to their faith. Can you imagine facing a huge furnace and having that level of faith? It is proof that your trust in God can truly be your salvation.

Families can also look to the example of Noah and his family. They were given protection in the ark when the great flood raged on, and had sanctuary when the waters receded. Stepping into unknown territory can be scary, but when you trust in your Creator, you can overcome any situation.

Your family might face many problems in life, sometimes not ark-sized problems but still situations where you might feel unsure.

Always remember that your Heavenly Father is your shield and Protector. Put your hope in Him, always.

Let's now reflect on today's lesson for a couple of minutes:

1. What does today's lesson teach us about God being our Shield?
2. How has God shielded your family in the past when you faced problems?
3. How can our family remind each other to ask God for help?

PRAYER

Helper God, thank You for being our Shield and Protector.

Thank You that You never stop taking care of us.

Forgive us when we try to do everything on our own.

Teach our family to call on You for help in every situation.

Amen.

FAMILY ACTIVITY

On a scrapbook page titled "God Is Our Shield," each family member writes one way they need God's protection this week. Leave space to add notes later about how He answered.

February 21

God Shows Us The Way

"Whether you turn to the right or to the left, your ears will hear a voice behind you, saying, "This is the way; walk in it." – Isaiah 30:21

When was the last time you needed to make a big decision, but you were not sure if you were heading in the right direction?

Perhaps it was what you needed to study after school, or whether you should accept a job at a company you interviewed at.

In the Bible, there are lots of examples of people that needed to make decisions about the future. Take Moses, for instance. He was given the task to set in motion rescuing his people from the Pharaoh. He felt that he wasn't the right guy for the job and that he wouldn't know what to say.

Despite these worries, God showed Moses the way to help his people. An unimaginable task suddenly became possible, thanks to the grace and guidance Moses received from God.

Families who feel like they are facing a crossroad, such as moving to a new town, might feel like they are facing a mammoth task that they are super unsure about. However, trusting in God like Moses did can make a big difference.

When we trust our Heavenly Father to show us the way, we will always know that we are not flying blind into the unknown.

He is with us, He knows what is best for us, and He will never lead us on the wrong paths.

Let us reflect on today's lesson for a couple of minutes:

1. What does it mean when we say God shows us the way?
2. How does God help us to make the right decisions?
3. What does the story of Moses teach us about trusting God to put us on the right path?
4. How can our family practice seeking His guidance each day?

✎ PRAYER

Lord, thank You for being our guide. Thank You for instructing us through Your Word, answering us in prayer, and leading us by Your Spirit.

Forgive us when we rely on our own wisdom. Teach our family to follow You step by step.

Amen.

♟ FAMILY ACTIVITY

Draw a winding path on a scrapbook page. Along the path, each family member writes one area where they need God's guidance. Add arrows or footprints to symbolize His leading.

February 22
God Is Our Provider

"And my God will supply every need of yours according to his riches in glory in Christ Jesus." – Philippians 4:19

Provision is one of God's constant blessings. Philippians 4:19 reminds us that He supplies every need according to His riches in glory. His care is not limited or uncertain.

And His blessings for us never run out.

In the Old Testament, we read about the Israelites receiving manna in the wilderness, and water from a rock and quail for food. They were taken care of in the most divine and wonderful way, all thanks to their Heavenly Father.

Then in the New Testament, Jesus fed thousands with a few loaves and fish. Imagine how amazing it was for people to receive these blessings that might have seemed impossible at the start.

All of these stories remind us that God is able to provide in miraculous ways. Even if we think something is not possible, we are reminded constantly that through God, anything and everything is possible.

What we need to remember is that anything we receive through God's grace is according to His will.

Sometimes, we might pray for something when the time to receive it is not right. Or there might be something better coming your way at the best moment.

Therefore, it is important to trust in both God's Will and His plan for us. We've learned in this book about guidance, and when we trust in this guidance and God's provision accordingly, families can truly live a wonderful life.

Let's reflect on today's Bible lesson for a couple of minutes:

1. What did we learn today about how God provides for His children?
2. How has God provided for you and your family in the past?
3. How can families practice patience when they pray for a specific blessing in life?

PRAYER

Provider God, thank You for supplying every need. Thank You for daily bread, clothing, shelter, and all Your blessings. Forgive us when we complain or forget to give thanks. Teach our family to depend on You and to share generously with others. Amen.

FAMILY ACTIVITY

On a scrapbook page titled "God Provides," each family member draws or writes one way God has provided recently. At the bottom, write Philippians 4:19. Use the page as a reminder to trust His provision daily.

February 23

God Is Gracious

"The Lord is gracious and merciful, slow to anger and abounding in steadfast love." –
Psalm 145:8

Grace means receiving kindness we do not deserve. Psalm 145:8 describes God as gracious, merciful, patient, and loving. His grace is greater than our failures and stronger than our weaknesses.

God's grace is shown throughout the Bible. He gave Israel another chance after they disobeyed. He gave David forgiveness after his sins. He gave Peter restoration after his denial. Most of all, He gave Jesus as a gift of grace to the world. Ephesians 2:8-9 says, "For by grace you have been saved through faith. And this is not your own doing; it is the gift of God."

Grace is not earned. It is freely given. Families should remember this when dealing with one another. Parents can show grace by forgiving mistakes. Children can show grace by being kind to siblings. Grace creates a home filled with love and patience.

Living in God's grace also means sharing it with others. Families can extend grace to neighbors, friends, and even strangers. This reflects God's heart to a world in need of His love.

Let's take a couple of minutes to reflect on today's Bible lesson:

1. What does Psalm 145:8 teach us about God's character?
2. How is grace different from mercy?
3. How has God shown grace in your life?
4. How can our family show grace to one another this week?

📖 PRAYER

Gracious God, thank You for giving us kindness we do not deserve. Thank You for the gift of salvation in Jesus. Forgive us when we are slow to show grace to others. Teach our family to reflect Your grace in our words and actions. Amen.

♟ FAMILY ACTIVITY

On a scrapbook page, write "God Is Gracious." Each family member shares one way they can show grace this week. Decorate the page with words like "kindness," "forgiveness," and "love."

February 24
God Is Compassionate

"The Lord is good to all, and his mercy is over all that he has made." – Psalm 145:9

One of the big truths that we learn about in the Bible is that God has compassion for His children.

What does compassion mean though?

Simply put, compassion describes feeling deep care for someone in need and acting to help them. Psalm 145:9 describes God as compassionate toward all He has made. His mercy covers creation and especially His children.

When we read our Bibles, we are sure to come across examples of how Jesus showed compassion in many ways.

He fed the hungry, healed the sick, and comforted the brokenhearted. Matthew 9:36 says, "When he saw the crowds, he had compassion for them, because they were harassed and helpless, like sheep without a shepherd." His heart was moved to act.

As Christians, it is important that we always open our hearts to others and show compassion. It can be towards someone that is struggling financially or emotionally, or even someone who is dealing with mental health issues.

What we need to remember is that compassion is more than feeling sorry for someone. It means stepping in to help, encourage, or pray. It means showing love through action. First John 3:18 says, "Let us not love in word or talk but in deed and in truth".

Compassion begins at home, within our families. Parents show compassion when they listen patiently when their children need their help. And kids show how they care when they help their siblings or parents.

Let's set an example for others, beginning today, by making compassion a part of our family's faith and caring for others without fail, as our Heavenly Father taught us.

Let's take a moment to consider today's Bible lesson:

1. What did we learn about God's compassion for His children today?
2. How can we as a family show compassion to one another?
3. What is an example in the Bible about compassion?

📖 PRAYER

Compassionate God, thank You for caring for us and for all creation. Thank You for Jesus, who showed compassion to the hurting and the lost. Forgive us when we are selfish or slow to act. Fill our family with compassion and teach us to love others through our actions. Amen.

⚜ FAMILY ACTIVITY

On a scrapbook page, write "God Is Compassionate." Each family member suggests one act of compassion your family can do this week, such as visiting someone, sharing food, or writing a note of encouragement. Add pictures or notes afterward to record what you did.

God Helps Us With Prayer

"In the same way, the Spirit helps us in our weakness. We do not know what we ought to pray for, but the Spirit himself intercedes for us through wordless groans. And he who searches our hearts knows the mind of the Spirit, because the Spirit intercedes for God's people in accordance with the will of God. And we know that in all things God works for the good of those who love him, who have been called according to his purpose." – Romans 8:26-28

Have you ever sat down to pray, and then realized that you are at a loss for words? That you didn't know where to start?

Sometimes, we might feel like we are praying the same thing over and over again. We could feel like we are just always praying for strength, protection, courage and give thanks in the same monotone words.

Today's Bible lesson reminds us of an important lesson in Scripture: God helps us with our prayers.

A wonderful example of this is the Our Father prayer (Matthew 6:9-13). It is more than just Scripture that we learn at church or school. It is a reminder of how to pray: giving praise to God, asking forgiveness for our sins, and protecting us from sins, to mention a few.

In our family unit, we can also think about what our loved ones need prayers for.

It can be a family member who is sick, a child who is struggling to fit in at school or a parent that is having a tough time with financial worries.

We can then ask God to guide our prayers to help those in our family with specific needs, and to also open our hearts and prayers to neighbors or others that we know that we can pray for.

Always remember: God doesn't expect us to pray perfect prayers every time. He is always there to guide us, and to help us realize what we need to pray for.

Let's take a couple of minutes to reflect on today's Bible lesson:

1. What did we learn today about how God helps us with prayer?
2. How does the Our Father prayer help us to understand praying?
3. What does our family need the most at the moment in our spiritual lives? How can we address these things in prayer?

✎ PRAYER

Heavenly Father, thank you for teaching us to pray.

Guide our thoughts and hearts this week when we pray, and help us to pray when we feel we do not have the right words to start with.

Amen.

♟ FAMILY ACTIVITY

Create a special page in your scrapbook with the heading: Prayer List. Write down who you as a family would like to pray for this week, and if there is anything specific you need prayer for, such as a specific situation or worry, add that is well. Revisit this page often as a reminder of how your prayers can make a difference for your family and others.

February 26
God Is Our Redeemer

"For I know that my Redeemer lives, and at the last he will stand upon the earth." –
Job 19:25

Have you ever wondered what the word redeem means in a spiritual context>

In an everyday context, redeem can mean to purchase something again, saving, or liberating. In the Bible, this word gets a deeper meaning.

Job is a great example of this. Despite the pain he was going through, he said that his Redeemer is alive. This reality directs us to Jesus, who saves us from sin and mortality.

God's redemption is also shown in how He saved Israel from bondage in Egypt, freeing them with great power. He saved Ruth's life by giving her Boaz as her kinsman-redeemer, symbolizing Jesus' ultimate act of redemption.

Jesus is our Savior as He atoned for our sins by sacrificing His blood.

First Peter 1:18–19 says, "You were ransomed from the futile ways inherited from your forefathers, not with perishable things such as silver or gold, but with the precious blood of Christ." His death and resurrection secured freedom for all who believe.

Families can rejoice in this redemption daily. It means we no longer live under guilt or fear. We belong to God as His children, bought at a price.

Like Job, we can say, "I know that my Redeemer lives," even in the face of hardship.

Living as redeemed people means choosing obedience, gratitude, and worship. Families should reflect the Redeemer's love in their words, actions, and attitudes.

Let's reflect for a couple of minutes on today's Bible lesson:

1. What does it mean to be redeemed?
2. How did God redeem His people in the Old Testament?
3. How does Jesus redeem us through His sacrifice?
4. How should our family live as people who are redeemed?

PRAYER

Redeeming God, thank You for buying us back through the blood of Jesus. Thank You that we belong to You as Your children. Forgive us when we forget the price that was paid. Teach our family to live in gratitude, obedience, and worship. Amen.

FAMILY ACTIVITY

On a scrapbook page, draw a large cross. Around it, each family member writes one blessing that comes from redemption (forgiveness, freedom, eternal life, hope). Title the page "Our Redeemer Lives."

God Rescues Us When We Are in Trouble

"The righteous cry out, and the Lord hears them; he delivers them from all their troubles." – Psalm 34:17

Have you ever been in a situation where you needed someone to come save you? Perhaps you got injured at school, or your car broke down on the way to work.

In those moments, we often seek out those closest to us to come help, but when we are facing a crisis, we must also remember to not lose sight of our Heavenly Savior.

Psalm 34:17 reminds us that when the righteous cry out, the Lord hears and delivers them. Families can take hope in this promise, knowing God is powerful to save.

Throughout the Bible, God delivered His people again and again. He delivered Israel from Pharaoh's army by parting the Red Sea. Can you imagine being stuck on a shore with your enemy fast approaching, and then seeing the sea part right in front of you? What an amazing sight that must have been!

The greatest deliverance came through Jesus. He delivered us from the power of sin and death. Colossians 1:13 says, "He has delivered us from the domain of darkness and transferred us to the kingdom of his beloved Son."

Deliverance does not always mean our problems evaporate into thin air immediately. What it does mean is that God will help us when the time is right, and every time He is delivered, His name is exalted and His children are blessed.

Through prayer, families can practice asking God to save them. They can call out to Him, trusting His timing and power, rather than becoming anxious.

Let's take a couple of minutes to reflection on today's lesson:

1. What does it mean that God rescues us in times of trouble? Does it mean our problems will simply go away?
2. What does God's miracle at the Red Sea parting teach us about deliverance?
3. What is one area where our family needs to pray for God's deliverance?

PRAYER

Heavenly Father, thank you for saving us when we are in trouble. Thank you for hearing our voices when we are scared or uncertain in life.

Open our hearts this week and help us to always remember that You are our Source of strength.

Amen

FAMILY ACTIVITY

Create a page in your family Bible study scrapbook with the heading, God Saves Us. Let each family member write down a short paragraph recounting a time when God saved them, and how it made them feel. Give thanks to God for these times of salvation and sanctuary.

February 28

God Is Our Teacher

"Teach me your way, O Lord, that I may walk in your truth; unite my heart to fear your name." – Psalm 86:11

Have you ever had a teacher at school who you admired for their knowledge and grasp of certain subjects? Or was the "teacher" you admired a mentor at work who helped you when you struggled with a new project?

A good teacher not only gives knowledge but also shows how to live it out. And the best example of such a Teacher is, of course, our Heavenly Father!

Psalm 86:11 asks God to teach His way so that we may walk in truth.

He teaches through His Word, which reveals His commands and promises. He teaches through His Spirit, who guides believers in righteousness. He also teaches through experiences, shaping us through trials and blessings alike.

Jesus was called Teacher many times. He taught with authority, explaining the kingdom of God through parables, miracles, and personal example. Families today can learn from His teaching by reading the Gospels together and applying His words.

Learning from God requires humility. We must be willing to admit we do not know everything and to submit to His wisdom. Proverbs 1:7 says, "The fear of the Lord is the beginning of knowledge; fools despise wisdom and instruction."

Families who embrace God's teaching grow in unity, obedience, and joy. His lessons bring life and direction for every step.

So, let's open our hearts this week to the teachings we receive in the Bible. Think about the Ten Commandments and what they teach us. Or the many miracles, such as manna in the desert or the Red Sea parting that we discussed earlier this month that teaches us the importance of faith.

Let's reflect on today's Bible lesson for a couple of minutes:

1. What does Psalm 86:11 teach us about God as our Teacher?
2. How does God teach us through His Word, Spirit, and experiences?
3. What can we learn from Jesus' teaching in the Gospels?
4. How can our family be more teachable before God?

🕮 PRAYER

Teacher God, thank You for giving us Your Word and Your Spirit to guide us. Thank You for showing us truth through Jesus. Forgive us when we resist Your lessons or ignore Your wisdom. Teach our family to walk in Your ways and to fear Your name. Amen.

♟ FAMILY ACTIVITY

On a scrapbook page titled "Taught by God," each family member writes one lesson they have learned from God recently. Decorate the page with open books or scrolls to symbolize learning.

February 29
God Is Eternal

"Before the mountains were brought forth, or ever you had formed the earth and the world, from everlasting to everlasting you are God." – Psalm 90:2

Everything in this world has a beginning and an end. People are born and die, nations rise and fall, and even mountains eventually crumble. Psalm 90:2 declares that God is eternal, existing from everlasting to everlasting.

God has no beginning and no end. He is the same yesterday, today, and forever. This truth should bring families comfort and security. In a world of constant change, God remains steady.

The Bible reveals God's eternal nature through His promises. He promised Abraham descendants as numerous as the stars, and that promise continues today. He promised David an everlasting kingdom, fulfilled in Jesus. His Word endures forever, never failing or fading.

Jesus also shares this eternal nature. Revelation 1:8 records His words: "I am the Alpha and the Omega... who is and who was and who is to come, the Almighty." Families who trust in Jesus have the promise of eternal life with Him.

Knowing God is eternal should shape the way we live. Instead of clinging to temporary things, families can focus on eternal values: faith, love, obedience, and service. Our time on earth is brief, but our hope in Christ lasts forever.

Let's take a couple of minutes to reflect on today's Bible lesson:

1. What does Psalm 90:2 teach us about God's eternal nature?
2. How does God's eternity bring us comfort in a changing world?
3. What promises has God made that last forever?
4. How can our family focus more on eternal values this week?

PRAYER

Eternal God, thank You for being the same from everlasting to everlasting. Thank You that Your promises never fail and that in Jesus we have eternal life. Forgive us when we focus only on temporary things. Teach our family to live with eternity in view. Amen.

FAMILY ACTIVITY

On a scrapbook page, draw an infinity symbol. Inside, write the words "From Everlasting to Everlasting." Around it, each family member writes one eternal truth about God or His promises. Title the page "God Is Eternal."

MARCH

March 1

God Is Our Creator

"In the beginning, God created the heavens and the earth." – Genesis 1:1

The Bible begins with the beautiful declaration that God created everything. Before there was light, land, or life, there was God. He spoke the universe into existence by His power and wisdom. This truth shapes the way we see the world and ourselves.

We are part of our Heavenly Father's plan for mankind, and every we meet was designed with the same life and their own unique purpose.

What today's Bible lesson teaches us, is that creation was not random. Every part of the universe reflects God's order and design. The stars, oceans, animals, and plants all reveal His glory. Psalm 19:1 says, "The heavens declare the glory of God, and the sky above proclaims his handiwork".

Families can look around at nature and be reminded that God is the Creator of it all. Something as simple as taking a walk through a park can serve as proof of Go's greatness.

God also created people in His image. We are able to think, love, create, and make decisions because we are built in His image. It also implies that every human life has value and dignity.

Knowing that the One who created the world also gave his life to save it allows families to celebrate.

Now, let's take a moment or two to consider today's Bible study:

1. What can we learn about God's might from Genesis 1:1?
2. What does it mean to be created in God's image?
3. How should knowing God is Creator shape the way we live?
4. What parts of creation remind you most of God's glory?

✐ PRAYER

Creator God, thank You for making the heavens, the earth, and everything in them. Thank You for creating us in Your image and giving us life. Forgive us when we fail to honor You with our choices. Teach our family to live with gratitude and obedience to You each day. In Jesus' name, amen.

♟ FAMILY ACTIVITY

On a scrapbook page titled "God Our Creator," each family member draws or pastes a picture of their favorite part of creation, such as stars, animals, trees, oceans. Give praise to God for His incredible creations and how we are part of this beautiful story.

March 2

God Is Our Father

"See what kind of love the Father has given to us, that we should be called children of God; and so we are." – 1 John 3:1

When you think of God as not just our Creator but also as our Heavenly Father, what image immediately comes to mind? Do you imagine a Biblical Father dressed in clothing we would typically see in kids' Bible story books? Or do you picture Him in another way?

The assurance that God is our Father can be found throughout the Bible.

A beautiful example of this is Isaiah 64:8: "Yet you, Lord, are our Father. We are the clay, you are the potter; we are all the work of your hand."

It is an unforgettable declaration that God is both our loving Creator and our Father. We are His children.

First John 3:1 invites us to see the kind of love that makes us His children. Through Jesus, we are adopted into God's family.

A good father provides, protects, and guides. God does all these perfectly. Matthew 7:11 says, "If you then, who are evil, know how to give good gifts to your children, how much more will your Father who is in heaven give good things to those who ask him!" Families can trust that God cares more than any earthly parent.

He asks His children to address Him as "Abba, Father" (Romans 8:15). Families can pray to Him because they know He hears them lovingly.

At the same time, God disciplines His children for their good. Hebrews 12:6 says, "For the Lord disciplines the one he loves." Discipline is not punishment to harm but guidance to grow. Families should see His correction as proof of His love.

Jesus shows us the Father's love in action. He cleared the path for us to become God's children by dying and rising. Families ought to feel secure in the knowledge that the Father loves, cares for, and accepts them.

Let's take a moment to consider the lesson from today's Bible study:

1. How does God provide and protect like a Father?
2. Why is discipline an important part of God's love?
3. How can our family consistently live as God's children?

PRAYER

Heavenly Father, thank You for loving us and calling us Your children. Thank You for providing for us, protecting us, and guiding us. Forgive us when we forget Your love. Teach our family to live in obedience and joy as Your children. Amen.

FAMILY ACTIVITY

On a scrapbook page titled "Children of God," write 1 John 3:1 at the top. Each family member draws themselves holding God's hand to symbolize being part of His family.

God Is Our King

"The Lord sits enthroned forever; he has established his throne for justice." –
Psalm 9:7

In the last couple of days, we've revisited several truths. God is our Creator, He is our Father and He created us with a perfect plan in mind.

Today, we are reminded that He is also our King. Psalm 9:7 affirms that He reigns forever on a throne of justice. His authority is absolute, and His kingdom never ends.

Unlike fallible, imperfect earthly leaders, God's kingship is perfect. He rules with justice, righteousness, and Godly wisdom. He knows what His Children need, and provides for us like no other king could.

His reign is eternal, and we as a family are called to submit to His rule. This means obeying His Word, honoring His commands, and seeking His will above our own.

Jesus spoke often about the kingdom of God. He taught that it is both present and future. Present, because God rules in the hearts of believers now. Future, because one day His kingdom will be fully revealed when He returns. Families should live with anticipation of this coming kingdom.

Families who belong to the King can rest secure, knowing He reigns forever.

Even more so, we need to always remember that we are serving the one true King, the Leader who has since the beginning of time set the example of what true leadership looks like.

Let's make this heavenly example part of our daily lives. Whether we are leaders at school or in positions of power at work, let's draw inspiration from God our King.

Now, take a couple of moments to reflect about the lessons we've learned today:

1.   What does God being our King mean for us as His children?
2.   How is God's rule different from the leadership of earthly leaders?
3.   What does Jesus teach us about the kingdom of God?

📖 PRAYER

King of kings, thank You for ruling with justice and righteousness. Thank You that Your kingdom is everlasting. Forgive us when we resist Your authority or live for ourselves. Teach our family to honor You as King in our words, choices, and actions.

Amen.

👪 FAMILY ACTIVITY

On a scrapbook page titled "God Our King," draw a crown. Inside the crown, each family member writes down what it means to have God as our King, our Father and our Creator.

March 4
God Is Our Savior

"For unto you is born this day in the city of David a Savior, who is Christ the Lord." –
Luke 2:11

Think for a moment about a time when you received what you felt was the best news ever. Perhaps it was hearing that you got a promotion at work, or that you were chosen for a top sports team at school.

How did this good news make you feel? On top of the world and that life couldn't get any better?

Now, imagine how the announcement of Jesus' birth affected those who were there to witness the declaration that a Savior was born. And how this news would continue to resonate for centuries to come. It truly was the most powerful "good news" that the world received and can still reflect on today.

Today's Bible lesson reminds us that Jesus was born to rescue His people from sin and death.

It is important that our family never forgets that salvation is at the heart of the gospel. We are saved, and therefore should make this blessing part of our daily prayers when we give thanks to our Heavenly Savior.

The second truth that we must hold close to our hearts is that Jesus is our Savior because He took our place. Through His death on the cross, He bore the punishment for sin. Through His resurrection, He defeated death and opened the way to eternal life. Acts 4:12 says, "There is salvation in no one else, for there is no other name under heaven given among men by which we must be saved."

This salvation is not something to take for granted. Being saved changes everything: our identity, our future, and our purpose. As redeemed people, families are called to worship, obey, and share the good news with others.

So, let's make it our goal this week to live anew as saved people.

Our salvation was lovingly prepared for us, and we can, every day, live this truth through everything that we do.

Let's reflect for a couple of minutes on the lessons we learned in today's Bible study:

1. What does it mean for our family that Jesus is our Savior?
2. What makes the salvation that we received so extraordinary?
3. How can we share the good news of salvation with others?

PRAYER

Savior Jesus, thank You for rescuing us from sin and death. Thank You for taking our place on the cross and rising again to give us eternal life. Forgive us when we take Your salvation lightly. Teach our family to rejoice in You daily and to live in gratitude and obedience.

Amen.

FAMILY ACTIVITY

On a scrapbook page, draw a cross at the center and write Luke 2:11 underneath. Around the cross, each family member writes one way salvation has changed their life.

March 5

God Teaches Us to Rejoice

"Then Jesus told them this parable: "Suppose one of you has a hundred sheep and loses one of them. Doesn't he leave the ninety-nine in the open country and go after the lost sheep until he finds it? And when he finds it, he joyfully puts it on his shoulders and goes home. Then he calls his friends and neighbors together and says, 'Rejoice with me; I have found my lost sheep.' I tell you that in the same way there will be more rejoicing in heaven over one sinner who repents than over ninety-nine righteous persons who do not need to repent." –
Luke 15:3-7

Have you ever known someone who completely strayed from their faith and seemed "lost"? Perhaps it was someone who made friends with people who were on the wrong path, or perhaps even someone who chose to pursue goals that were not what God intended for them.

Did this person get back on the right track, and what was your reaction? Were you happy for them and did you share their joy?

Today's Bible lesson serves as a reminder of two important things: That God saves those who strayed, and that we should rejoice when people find their way back to God.

Does this perhaps sound easier said than done?

When we know someone who we might feel have "lost the plot" and strayed, it can be almost a knee-jerk reaction to immediately judge them.

This is not what we should be doing, though. If we can help someone get back on the right path through prayer and inspiration through faith, we should do so with glad and giving hearts. And when they have found their way back, we should rejoice with them.

Put yourself in the shoes of someone who was or still is lost. How would you feel if those around judged and turned their backs to you? Would you yearn for guidance through prayer and Scripture?

As a family, we need only to look at the examples God has put in place for us about forgiveness and rejoicing to understand what our roles in our communities and congregations are.

And if one of us in our family circle should stray, let us pray for guidance to provide support, and rejoice when that person finds their way back.

Let's reflect for a couple of minutes on today's Bible study:

1. What does it mean to rejoice when someone who was lost has found their way back?
2. How should we help someone who is on the wrong path?
3. What does the Bible teach us about how God saves people who strayed?

PRAYER

Heavenly Father, thank you for teaching us to rejoice when someone was lost but found their way back to You.

Open our hearts this week and guide us to help those around us who need to get back on the right path.

Fill our hearts, minds and prayers with the right words, and guide us to have a loving spirit, inspired by the kindness that You teach us in the Bible.

Amen.

FAMILY ACTIVITY

Create a scrapbook page with the title, Rejoice. Let each family member write down the name of someone who was lost but found their way back to God, and how they rejoice these miracles.

March 6
God Teaches Us to be Gentle

"Let your gentleness be evident to all. The Lord is near." – Philippians 4:5

What does it mean to be gentle?

Does it mean being meek and mild, and to not cause any conflict?

One thing is certain: Having a gentle heart does not mean weakness. It means treating those around us, our family, our neighbors, our friends, with kindness, respect and love.

And what better example is there of gentleness than what we learn from Jesus in the Bible. There are so many stories that show how Jesus' kind approach touched so many lives.

He healed the sick, fed the hungry, and lovingly taught His disciples. Even when He was crucified for our sins, He still asked for forgiveness for those around them, because He knew they did not understand what they were doing.

So, what can we as a family learn from being gentle, like Jesus?

First, we need to pray to God to open our hearts and help us.

We are human, fallible, and need His guidance to instill a spirit of gentle calmness in our hearts.

So often, when we are tired or struggling, it might feel like a difficult task to handle others with patience and respect. We might lash out, due to our own frustrations, and regret our actions soon after.

Luckily, with the guidance of our Heavenly Father, we can soften our hearts and learn to be gentle with others, and ourselves.

Something as simple as being gentle with a younger sibling, or being attuned to the needs of adult family members can help us to give them support they need.

Let's make it our goal this week to be gentle like Jesus, and to embrace kind loving hearts.

Now, let's take a couple of minutes to reflect on today's Bible lesson:

1. What does it mean to be gentle like Jesus?
2. What examples of being gentle do we see in the Bible?
3. How can we as a family become more gentle with one another and others?

PRAYER

Heavenly Father, thank you for teaching us to be gentle. Thank you for teaching us kindness and being pure of heart.

Forgive us for those times when we struggled to be gentle with others, and ourselves.

Open our hearts this week and help us to have gentle hearts for those around us.

Amen.

FAMILY ACTIVITY

On a scrapbook page, draw a big heart. Make the title of this page "Let's be gentle like Jesus". Let each family member write in the heart what they've learned about being gentle. Then, make a border of extra hearts around the big heart.

March 7
God Is Faithful

"Let us hold fast the confession of our hope without wavering, for he who promised is faithful." – Hebrews 10:23

When we read through the Bible, we often read about God's faithfulness, which is also the topic of today's lesson.

So, what does this beautiful quality of God's character look like?

Faithfulness means keeping promises and staying true. God is perfectly faithful. He never breaks His word, never abandons His people, and never fails in His purposes. Hebrews 10:23 calls us to hold fast to our hope because the One who promised is faithful.

God's faithfulness is seen throughout history. He promised Noah He would never again flood the earth, and He kept that promise. He promised Abraham descendants as numerous as the stars, and He fulfilled it. He promised a Savior, and Jesus came in the fullness of time.

Even when His people were unfaithful, God remained faithful. Second Timothy 2:13 says, "If we are faithless, he remains faithful—for he cannot deny himself." His faithfulness depends on His character, not our performance.

Families can rest in God's promises today. Life is uncertain, but God is steady.

God is certain, and He is always faithful, no matter what situations we might find ourselves in.

People may disappoint, but God never will. His Word is trustworthy, and His love endures forever.

What can we as a family learn from this faithfulness?

First, we should pray for guidance from God to help us become more attuned to keeping our word, to show consistency in love, and to reflect God's steadfast character in our relationships. A faithful home is built on trust and truth, and through prayer and faith, we can make our house a place of truth and promises that hold.

Let's make it our goal this week to embrace a spirit of faithfulness, like we are taught in the Bible.

Now, let's reflect for a couple of minutes on today's Bible lesson:

1. What does Hebrews 10:23 teach us about God's faithfulness?
2. How has God shown faithfulness in the Bible?
3. How has He shown faithfulness in your life?
4. How can our family reflect God's faithfulness in our words and actions?

PRAYER

Faithful God, thank You for keeping every promise. Thank You for showing Your love and mercy every day. Forgive us when we waver in our hope. Teach our family to trust Your Word and to live in a way that reflects Your faithfulness. Amen.

FAMILY ACTIVITY

Start a "Faithfulness Timeline" in your scrapbook. Write down key moments when God has been faithful to your family, such as answers to prayer, provision, protection. Leave space to keep adding to it throughout the year.

God Teaches us to Accept One Another

"Accept one another, then, just as Christ accepted you, in order to bring praise to God.." – Romans 15:7

Have you ever struggled to accept someone? Perhaps someone in your school, your group of friends, or maybe someone at work?

Personality clashes can often make it difficult to relate to people from different backgrounds than our own.

We can feel this struggle in faith as well, when we might interpret a Bible verse or Bible lesson in a certain way, then feel someone with a different opinion is just simply wrong/

Today's Bible lesson ties in strongly with our previous lesson about being gentle. Today, we are reminded of how God teaches us to accept one another to honor Him.

Acceptance and love go hand in hand. When we show how we accept someone for who they are, we not only show them grace but also forgiveness for any time they might have wronged us.

Unconditional acceptance means we embrace God's example of acceptance. Think about it this way: Every person on earth has been uniquely created, and each person is unconditionally loved by God.

In the same way, we can demonstrate kind and loving hearts to others, accepting them as they are and providing support when they need it.

As a family, we can also strengthen this mindset of acceptance among each other. Brothers and sisters might be different from one another, parents might have different types of personalities, but together you are part of one family, on earth and as part of God's family.

Therefore, let the knowledge of being part of a spiritual family guide you this week when it comes to acceptance. Accept one another as brothers and sisters, and praise God for the beautiful gift of acceptance.

Now, let's take a couple of minutes to reflect on today's lesson:

1. What does unconditional acceptance mean?
2. What are some examples of acceptance in the Bible?
3. How can we as a family support one another when it comes to accepting others?

PRAYER

Heavenly Father, thank you for the gift of acceptance.

Teach us this week how to honor you by accepting others, and open our hearts to be kind and gentle to others.

Amen.

FAMILY ACTIVITY

Write "Acceptance" on top of a scrapbook page. Let each family member write in a little speech bubble what they learned today about acceptance, and how they would like to make this part of their daily lives.

March 9
God Is Our Reliable Father

"He will not let your foot slip—he who watches over you will not slumber;" –
Psalm 121:3

In today's Bible lesson, we look at another core truth about God: His reliability.

Our Heavenly Father never sleeps, and He is always watching over us.

This is such a powerful truth that we can always hold on to. Often, when we are experiencing times of sorrow or struggle, we might feel all alone. We might look into ourselves, searching for hope and sanctuary.

However, our faith teaches us to look beyond ourselves and look towards God. The Bible provides so many examples of how God never wavered from taking care of His children. When Moses was just a baby, He kept him safe as his basket floated on the river. God knew He had a special purpose and protected Him every step of the way.

Then, there is the story of David who was given the courage to stand up and defeat Goliath with a simple tool and an abundance of faith in God.

Think of a moment when God also prevented you from "slipping". Was it helping you overcome a difficult situation at school, or keeping you from a situation at work that could have had bad consequences?

Every day, we are protected by our reliable Heavenly Father. He keeps us safe through life's struggles, and guides us to walk the right paths.

Let's make it our goal this week to open our hearts and minds to God's impact on our lives. Let's give praise to our almighty Father who never slumbers and is always in our corner.

Remind one another that God is also present in our family network, always watching and guiding us. He hears our prayers, and will lovingly help us according to His will

Let's reflect on today's Bible lesson for a couple of minutes:

1. What does it mean that God never slumbers?
2. What is an example of God's reliability in the Bible?
3. How does God bless our family through His reliability?

PRAYER

Heavenly Father, thank you for being our reliable King who never sleeps.

Thank you for the knowledge that you are always watching over us.

Open our hearts this week, and help us to always embrace and mirror Your reliability.

Amen.

FAMILY ACTIVITY

Create a page in your Bible study scrapbook with the title "Our God is a Reliable God". Let each family member draw a box on the page, in which they write down a time when they experienced the reliability of God. Give praise to God for these wonderful memories.

March 10
God Is Our Light

"The Lord is my light and my salvation; whom shall I fear?" – Psalm 27:1

Light makes all the difference in darkness. It brings clarity, comfort and direction. Psalm 27:1 says God is light and salvation and removes fear and brings hope.

God's light is throughout Scripture. He led Israel with a pillar of fire by night. He filled the temple with His glory. He sent Jesus as the Light of the World. John 8:12 says, "I am the light of the world. Whoever follows me will not walk in darkness, but will have the light of life."

Light reveals what is hidden. Families can trust God's light to expose lies, guide decisions and bring truth. His Word is also light. Psalm 119:105 says, "Your word is a lamp to my feet and a light to my path."

Living in God's light means rejecting sin and walking in holiness. 1 John 1:7 says, "If we walk in the light, as he is in the light, we have fellowship with one another, and the blood of Jesus his Son cleanses us from all sin." Families should seek to live in His light daily, confessing sin and choosing righteousness.

Let's look at today's Bible lesson for a couple of minutes:

1. What does it mean for God to be our light?
2. How does Jesus fulfill this truth as the Light of the World?
3. How does God's Word shine as a lamp in our lives?
4. How can our family live in the light each day?

PRAYER

Light of the world, thank You for shining in our darkness. Thank You for guiding us with truth and hope. Forgive us when we hide in sin or fear. Teach our family to walk in Your light and to reflect it to others. Amen.

FAMILY ACTIVITY

On a scrapbook page, draw a candle or lantern. Around the light, each family member writes one way God has guided them recently. Title the page "The Lord Is Our Light."

God Gives Us the Gift of Love

"If I speak in the tongues of men or of angels, but do not have love, I am only a resounding gong or a clanging cymbal. If I have the gift of prophecy and can fathom all mysteries and all knowledge, and if I have a faith that can move mountains, but do not have love, I am nothing. If I give all I possess to the poor and give over my body to hardship that I may boast, but do not have love, I gain nothing." –
1 Corinthians 13:1-3

The Bible is filled with beautiful references of love. One that we certainly know is that of Mark 12:30-31: Love the Lord your God with all your heart and with all your soul and with all your mind and with all your strength.' The second is this: 'Love your neighbor as yourself.' There is no commandment greater than these.

And then there is Proverbs 17:17: A friend loves at all times, and a brother is born for a time of adversity.

God is our true Source of love. He loves all of His children equally and gave us the gift of love so that we can bestow it on others as well.

Today's main Bible verse also reminds us how important the spiritual gift of love is. It truly is everything!

There are several ways that we can show love to those around us. Helping those in need, sharing food with friends, helping out with chores at home and even just listening when someone needs our support are all ways to show love.

We also need to show compassion for ourselves too in small ways, such as self-care, not dwelling on negative thoughts and taking care of our mental health. As a family, we need to show love to each other through the way we interact, and the way we obey our parents or guide our children.

Most importantly, we need to give thanks to the Heavenly Father that loves and protects us, and ask for His guidance to help us have loving hearts.

Always remember: God loves us, and by embracing the example He gave us, we honor and obey Him.

Let's reflect on today's Bible lesson for a couple of minutes:

1. What does it mean when we say God is our true Source of Love?
2. How can we show love to those around us?
3. In our family, how can we practice having more loving hearts?
4. What does Proverbs 17:17 teach us about love and friendship?

📖 PRAYER

Heavenly Father, thank you for the gift of love.

Thank you for teaching us to love, and for giving us a true example of what unconditional love looks like.

Help us this week to open our hearts to love: to show love and embrace a loving mindset.

Amen.

⛪ FAMILY ACTIVITY

On a scrapbook page titled "God Teaches Us To Love," each family member draws a heart that they can write about how they have shown love to others. Add more hearts throughout the year to fill up the page.

March 12

God Teaches Us to be Selfless

"When Jesus saw his mother there, and the disciple whom he loved standing nearby,
he said to her, "Woman, here is your son," and to the disciple, "Here is your mother."
From that time on, this disciple took her into his home." – John 19:26–27

Throughout our recent Bible studies, we have reflected on many gifts God has given us: love, grace, forgiveness, salvation, and hope. Each of these gifts reveals something about God's heart and His purposes for His people.

Today, we are reminded of another powerful lesson: **selflessness**.

These words from John are spoken while Jesus is on the cross, in the middle of intense suffering. Yet even then, His focus is not on Himself. Instead, He cares for His mother and ensures she will not be left alone. Jesus places her into the care of His disciple, showing us that love rooted in God always looks outward.

This moment teaches us that selflessness is not about recognition or convenience. It flows from obedience and love. Jesus demonstrates that serving others is part of honoring God, even when it costs us something. His life, and His death, was never centered on self, but always on fulfilling the Father's will.

As families, this truth challenges us to look beyond our own wants and frustrations. God calls us to care for one another with humility, patience, and compassion. When we choose to put others first, we reflect the heart of Christ and honor God in our daily lives.

Let's take a couple of minutes to discuss the following questions:

1. What does Psalm 103:8 teach us about God's patience?
2. How do we see God's patience in Bible stories?
3. Why is patience important in family life?
4. How can our family practice patience with one another this week?

PRAYER

Patient God, thank You for being slow to anger and full of love. Thank You for giving us time to repent and grow. Forgive us when we lose patience quickly. Teach our family to reflect Your patience in our home and in our relationships. Amen.

FAMILY ACTIVITY

On a scrapbook page, write **"Patience in Action."** Each family member writes one situation where they often lose patience. Leave space to add notes at the end of the week about how God helped in those moments.

March 13

God Is Just

"For the Lord is a God of justice; blessed are all those who wait for him." –
Isaiah 30:18

Justice means doing what is right and fair. Isaiah 30:18 reminds us that the Lord is a God of justice. He cannot ignore sin or wrongdoing. His character demands righteousness.

The Bible shows God's justice in many ways. He judged Egypt with plagues for oppressing Israel. He judged kings of Israel and Judah who led people into idolatry. He will one day bring perfect justice to the world through Jesus Christ.

God's justice is not cruel or harsh. It is righteous and fair. At the same time, His justice is balanced with mercy. The cross is the clearest picture of both. God's justice demanded punishment for sin, and His mercy provided Jesus as the substitute. Romans 3:26 says God is "just and the justifier of the one who has faith in Jesus."

Families should care about justice because God does. This means treating others with fairness, honesty, and kindness. It means standing up for what is right, even when it is difficult. Micah 6:8 says, "He has told you, O man, what is good... to do justice, and to love kindness, and to walk humbly with your God."

Justice also means trusting God to make things right. Families may not always see fairness in this world, but they can wait for the God of justice to bring perfect judgment in His time.

Let's spend the next couple of minutes discussing the following questions:

1. What does Isaiah 30:18 teach us about God's justice?
2. How do we see both justice and mercy at the cross?
3. Why should families care about justice?
4. How can we practice justice in our daily lives?

PRAYER

Righteous God, thank You for being a God of justice. Thank You that Your judgments are always fair and true. Forgive us when we treat others unfairly or ignore what is right. Teach our family to live with integrity, to love kindness, and to walk humbly with You. Amen.

FAMILY ACTIVITY

On a scrapbook page titled "God Is Just," write Micah 6:8. Each family member writes one way they can act justly this week, at school, at work, or at home.

March 14

God Is Near

"The Lord is near to all who call on him, to all who call on him in truth." –
Psalm 145:18

God is not far away. Psalm 145:18 reminds us that He is near to all who call on Him. Families can take great comfort in knowing that the Creator of the universe listens when they pray.

Throughout Scripture, God shows His nearness. He walked with Adam and Eve in the garden. He guided Israel with a pillar of cloud and fire. He spoke to Elijah in a gentle whisper. Most importantly, He came near through Jesus, who is called Immanuel, "God with us."

The Holy Spirit also makes God's nearness real. Jesus promised that the Spirit would live within believers, guiding, comforting, and empowering them. Families who trust in Jesus can be certain that God is always with them.

God's nearness brings peace and courage. Families who remember this promise can face challenges with confidence.

Calling on God "in truth" means praying sincerely and trusting His Word. Families should avoid empty words or prayers without faith. God is near to those who call honestly, humbly, and faithfully.

Let's take a couple of minutes to discuss the following questions:

1. What does Psalm 145:18 teach us about God's nearness?
2. How did God show His nearness in the Old Testament?
3. How does Jesus fulfill the promise of "God with us"?
4. How can our family call on God in truth this week?

✎ PRAYER

Near God, thank You for being close to us. Thank You that You hear our prayers and know our hearts. Forgive us when we treat You as distant or forget to call on You. Teach our family to live with the confidence of Your presence every day. Amen.

♟ FAMILY ACTIVITY

On a scrapbook page, draw a picture of your family. Around the picture, write promises of God's nearness (Psalm 145:18, Joshua 1:9, Matthew 28:20). Title the page "God Is Near."

God Is Our Peace

"For he himself is our peace, who has made us both one and has broken down in his flesh the dividing wall of hostility." – Ephesians 2:14

Peace is more than the absence of conflict. It is wholeness, harmony, and unity. Ephesians 2:14 declares that Jesus Himself is our peace. He not only gives peace but embodies it.

Through His death, Jesus brought peace between humanity and God. Sin created separation, but Jesus broke down the wall of hostility by taking sin's penalty. Romans 5:1 says, "Since we have been justified by faith, we have peace with God through our Lord Jesus Christ."

Jesus also brings peace between people. In Ephesians 2, Paul speaks of Jews and Gentiles being united in Christ. Families can learn from this truth. God's peace heals divisions, reconciles relationships, and creates unity.

The world offers temporary peace through distractions or compromises. Jesus offers lasting peace through His presence. John 14:27 says, "Peace I leave with you; my peace I give to you." Families can trust that His peace endures through every season.

Living in God's peace means choosing forgiveness, patience, and love. It means remembering that Jesus is greater than fear or conflict. Families who live in His peace become witnesses of His love to others.

Let's take the next couple of minutes to discuss the following questions:

1. What does Ephesians 2:14 teach us about peace in Christ?
2. How does Jesus bring peace between us and God?
3. How does His peace bring unity between people?
4. How can our family live in the peace of Christ this week?

📖 PRAYER

Prince of Peace, thank You for breaking down the walls of hostility. Thank You for giving us peace with God and with one another. Forgive us when we live in conflict or let fear steal our peace. Fill our family with Your Spirit so we may live in Your peace and share it with others. Amen.

♟ FAMILY ACTIVITY

On a scrapbook page titled "Christ Our Peace," draw a wall with a cross breaking through it. Inside the broken wall, each family member writes one way they can live in peace this week.

Strength That Comes From the Lord

"The Lord is the strength of his people; he is the saving refuge of his anointed." –
Psalm 28:8

There are moments in life when effort alone is not enough. No matter how determined we are, weariness eventually sets in. Our plans may fall short, our patience may thin, and our confidence may waver. Scripture reminds us that this is not a flaw—it is a reminder of where true strength is found.

God does not call His people to rely on themselves. From the beginning, He has revealed Himself as the source of strength for those who belong to Him. When His people faced battles they could not win alone, God went before them. When they were weary from the journey, He sustained them. When they cried out in fear or weakness, He answered with power and faithfulness.

This kind of strength is not loud or boastful. It is steady and rooted in trust. It strengthens hearts that feel uncertain and restores those who feel worn down. God's strength does not remove every challenge, but it carries His people through them with purpose and hope.

As a family, learning to depend on God's strength reshapes how we respond to difficulty. Instead of rushing to solve everything on our own, we turn first to prayer. Instead of giving in to frustration, we wait on the Lord. When we trust Him as our refuge, we learn that His strength is sufficient for every season of life.

Let us discuss the following questions for a couple of minutes:

1. What does it mean that the Lord is the strength of His people?
2. Can you think of examples in the Bible where God strengthened someone who felt weak or afraid?
3. Why do you think God allows us to experience weakness at times?
4. Where does our family need to rely more fully on God's strength right now?

PRAYER

Faithful God, You are the strength of Your people and our refuge in every season. Thank You for carrying us when we feel weary and uncertain. Forgive us for the times we depend on our own ability instead of trusting You. Teach our family to lean on Your strength and to seek You first in every challenge. Amen.

FAMILY ACTIVITY

On a scrapbook page, draw a large tree with deep roots. Each family member writes on one branch a situation where they need God's strength this week. Near the roots, write the words **"The Lord is our strength."** At the end of the week, add notes about how God provided help, peace, or endurance during those moments.

Learning to Walk in God's Ways

"Make me to know your ways, O Lord; teach me your paths." – Psalm 25:4

Learning is part of every season of life. From childhood into adulthood, growth happens when instruction is given and received. Scripture reveals that God Himself takes on the role of teacher, patiently guiding His people according to His truth and wisdom.

This verse from Psalm 25 is a humble request. David does not ask God to bless his own plans or confirm his own understanding. Instead, he asks to be taught God's ways. This reminds us that true wisdom begins when we surrender our own direction and seek the Lord's instruction.

God teaches His people so they may walk in paths that lead to life, faithfulness, and obedience. His teaching is never rushed or careless. He shapes hearts over time, forming character and discernment through His Word and through daily dependence on Him.

For families, this means choosing to listen before acting and seeking God's guidance before making decisions. It means allowing Scripture to shape our values and letting God correct us when we drift. When God teaches, He does so with purpose: leading His people closer to Him and strengthening their walk of faith.

A family that desires to learn from God grows in unity and spiritual depth. As His instruction becomes central in the home, hearts are shaped to trust Him more fully and follow Him more faithfully.

Let us take the next couple of minutes to discuss the following questions together:

1. What does it mean to ask God to teach us His ways instead of following our own?
2. How does God guide His people throughout Scripture?
3. Why is it important to listen and obey when God teaches us?
4. What is one area where our family needs God's guidance right now?

⬙ PRAYER

Faithful Teacher, thank You for guiding Your people with wisdom and truth. Thank You for teaching us paths that lead to life. Forgive us when we rely on our own understanding instead of seeking You. Teach our family to listen, to obey, and to walk in Your ways. Amen.

⬙ FAMILY ACTIVITY

On a scrapbook page, draw an open book with a path leading out from its pages. Write the title **"Walking in God's Ways"** at the top. Each family member writes one lesson they believe God is teaching them right now. Leave space to add notes later about how these lessons shape your family's walk with Him.

The Lord Restores What Is Broken

"He sent out his word and healed them, and delivered them from their destruction." –
Psalm 107:20

God's healing often begins with His Word. Long before a wound is seen on the outside, God knows the places within us that need restoration. Scripture shows us that healing is not only an act of power but an expression of God's faithfulness and mercy toward His people.

Throughout the Bible, God restores those who cry out to Him. When His people were weary, fearful, or broken, He did not turn away. Instead, He spoke truth, brought deliverance, and guided them back to life. His Word carried healing because it carried His presence.

Jesus fulfilled this truth perfectly. Every healing He performed revealed God's authority and compassion. Yet even more powerful than physical healing was the restoration He brought to hearts that had been separated from God. Through Jesus, forgiveness is given, hope is renewed, and lives are made whole.

As families, we are reminded that healing does not always come in the same way or on the same timeline. Sometimes God restores immediately. At other times, He strengthens us to endure while He works. In every case, He remains near. Trusting Him means believing that His Word is enough to sustain, restore, and carry us forward.

Let us take a few moments to reflect together on the following questions:

1. What does it mean that God sends His Word to heal and deliver?
2. How do we see God restoring people throughout Scripture?
3. Why is it important to trust God's timing when we pray for healing?
4. How can our family encourage one another while waiting on God's restoration?

✎ PRAYER

Restoring Lord, thank You for speaking life and healing over Your people. Thank You for Your Word that brings hope and deliverance. Forgive us when we become discouraged or impatient while waiting for restoration. Teach our family to trust You fully and to rest in Your faithful care. Amen.

♟ FAMILY ACTIVITY

On a scrapbook page, write the title **"Restored by the Lord."** Draw an image of light breaking through darkness or cracks being filled with gold. Each family member writes one area where they are trusting God to restore or heal. Leave space to record how God brings peace, strength, or renewal in the days ahead.

Trusting God With Our Daily Needs

"Therefore do not be anxious, saying, 'What shall we eat?' or 'What shall we drink?' or 'What shall we wear?'... for your heavenly Father knows that you need them all." –
Matthew 6:31–32

Worry often begins when we focus too closely on what we lack. Jesus speaks directly to this tendency in Matthew 6, reminding His listeners that God is fully aware of every need His children face. Nothing required for daily life escapes the notice of our Heavenly Father.

Jesus is not telling us that needs do not exist. Instead, He teaches that fear does not belong in the lives of those who trust God. Anxiety shifts our focus away from God's faithfulness and places it on uncertainty. Trust brings our hearts back to the truth that God provides according to His wisdom and care.

Throughout Scripture, God proves Himself attentive and faithful. He sustained His people in times of scarcity and abundance alike. He provided not only food and shelter, but guidance, protection, and peace. His provision was never random, it was always purposeful.

For families, this teaching invites a daily posture of trust. When concerns about finances, responsibilities, or the future arise, we are reminded to bring them before God in prayer. Choosing trust over worry strengthens faith and teaches children that dependence on God is not weakness, but wisdom.

God's provision may not always look the way we expect, but it is always sufficient. When we seek Him first, our hearts learn to rest in His care, confident that He knows what we need before we even ask.

Let us take a few moments to talk through the following questions together:

1. Why do you think Jesus tells us not to worry about daily needs?
2. How does trusting God change the way we handle uncertainty?
3. Can you think of times when God provided in ways you did not expect?
4. What worries can our family give to God today?

PRAYER

Faithful Father, thank You for knowing our needs before we speak them. Thank You for caring for every detail of our lives. Forgive us when worry takes hold of our hearts instead of trust. Teach our family to rely on You daily and to rest in Your faithful provision. Amen.

FAMILY ACTIVITY

On a scrapbook page, write the title **"God Knows What We Need."** Each family member writes or draws one concern they are tempted to worry about. Next to it, write a short prayer of trust. Leave space to add notes later about how God provided peace, guidance, or help.

The Lord Pays the Price for Our Freedom

"You were bought with a price; do not become slaves of men." – 1 Corinthians 7:23

Scripture speaks plainly about the cost of our freedom. It was not earned through effort or good behavior. It was purchased. This verse reminds us that God Himself paid the price so His people could live free from sin and bondage.

Redemption means being claimed and restored. God did not look away from humanity's brokenness. He acted. Through Christ, He stepped in where we could not, taking upon Himself what we could never repay. Our freedom rests entirely on His work, not ours.

Because God paid the price, our lives now belong to Him. This does not lead to fear or burden, but to freedom rightly understood. We are no longer ruled by sin, guilt, or the need to prove ourselves. We belong to the Lord, who redeems with purpose and love.

For families, this truth shapes identity. Children learn they are valued and claimed by God. Adults are reminded that their worth does not come from performance or approval. Living as God's redeemed people means walking in gratitude, obedience, and trust, responding to what He has already done.

Let us take a few minutes to talk together about the following:

1. What does it mean to be "bought with a price"?
2. Why is it important to remember that our freedom came at a cost?
3. How does belonging to God bring true freedom?
4. How can our family live in gratitude for what God has done?

✎ PRAYER

Redeeming God, thank You for paying the price we could never pay. Thank You for freeing us through Your mercy and grace. Forgive us when we forget who we belong to or take our freedom lightly. Help our family live in grateful obedience, honoring You with our lives. Amen.

♟ FAMILY ACTIVITY

On a scrapbook page, write the title **"Bought With a Price."** Draw an open chain or a simple cross. Each family member writes one way they want to live in gratitude for God's redeeming work. Leave space to return later and reflect on how remembering this truth shapes daily choices.

March 21
God Leads Us Forward

"The Lord will guide you continually and satisfy your desire in scorched places, and make your bones strong; and you shall be like a watered garden, like a spring of water, whose waters do not fail." – Isaiah 58:11

There are seasons in life when the way ahead feels unclear. Decisions weigh heavily, circumstances shift unexpectedly, and it becomes difficult to know which step to take next. Scripture reminds us that God does not leave His people to figure these moments out alone. He leads, even when the path feels dry or uncertain.

God's guidance is not rushed or careless. He walks with His people through both abundance and hardship, shaping their steps with purpose. Isaiah describes this guidance as steady and sustaining, like water in a dry place. God does not merely point the way forward; He provides strength for the journey itself.

Throughout the Bible, God led His people step by step. Sometimes He guided them through open doors, and other times through waiting. His direction was not always easy, but it was always faithful. When His people listened and followed, they found that His way led to life.

For families, trusting God's guidance means learning to pause, pray, and listen. It means choosing obedience even when answers are not immediate. God's leadership brings growth, resilience, and quiet confidence. When we allow Him to lead, we discover that He is faithful to provide direction and strength for every season.

Let us take a few minutes to talk through the following questions together:

1. What does it mean to trust God's guidance when the path feels unclear?
2. How have we seen God lead His people in Scripture?
3. Why is patience important when waiting for God's direction?
4. Where does our family need God's guidance right now?

PRAYER

Guiding Lord, thank You for leading Your people with faithfulness and care. Thank You for walking with us through every season, even when the way forward feels uncertain. Forgive us when we rush ahead without seeking You. Teach our family to trust Your direction and to follow You with obedient hearts. Amen.

FAMILY ACTIVITY

On a scrapbook page, draw a winding path leading toward a horizon. Write the title **"Led by the Lord"** at the top. Along the path, each family member writes one decision or situation where they are trusting God to lead them. Leave space to add notes later about how God provided direction, clarity, or peace.

March 22

God Shapes Our Hearts

*"I will give you a new heart and put a new spirit within you; I will remove from you
your heart of stone and give you a heart of flesh." – Ezekiel 36:26*

Change does not usually happen all at once. Most of the time, it happens quietly and gradually, often in ways we do not immediately notice. Scripture reminds us that God is deeply involved in this process, shaping the hearts of His people so they may reflect His will.

This promise from Ezekiel was spoken to people who had wandered far from God. Instead of turning away from them, God promised renewal. He spoke of replacing hardened hearts with hearts that are alive, responsive, and willing to follow Him. This work was something only God could do.

God still works this way today. He softens hearts that have grown weary, stubborn, or fearful. He brings conviction where change is needed and comfort where healing must begin. Rather than forcing transformation, He patiently reshapes hearts through His Word, His Spirit, and daily obedience.

For families, this truth offers hope. Growth does not depend on perfection, but on willingness. When we invite God to shape our hearts, our attitudes begin to change, our words become gentler, and our actions start to reflect His character. A family that allows God to work within them grows stronger in faith, humility, and love.

Let us take a few minutes to reflect together on the following questions:

1. What does it mean for God to give His people a new heart?
2. Why do hearts sometimes become hardened over time?
3. How does God shape our hearts through everyday experiences?
4. What is one area where our family can ask God to bring change?

✑ PRAYER

Renewing God, thank You for working patiently within us. Thank You for shaping our hearts with wisdom and love. Forgive us when we resist change or harden our hearts toward Your truth. Help our family to remain open to Your work and willing to follow where You lead. Amen.

⬣ FAMILY ACTIVITY

On a scrapbook page, draw a heart being gently molded, like clay in careful hands. Write the title **"God Shapes Our Hearts."** Each family member writes one attitude or habit they are asking God to change. Leave space to add reflections later about how God brings growth over time.

March 23
Learning to Wait on the Lord

"The Lord is good to those who wait for him, to the soul who seeks him." –
Lamentations 3:25

Waiting is rarely easy. It can feel uncomfortable and uncertain, especially when answers seem delayed or circumstances remain unchanged. Yet Scripture reminds us that waiting is not wasted time when it is placed in God's hands.

This verse from Lamentations speaks to God's goodness, even in seasons of hardship. Written during a time of great sorrow, it points to a quiet truth: God remains faithful, even when life feels unsettled. Waiting becomes an act of trust, not passivity, as hearts turn toward Him instead of giving in to fear or frustration.

Throughout the Bible, God often worked while His people waited. Promises unfolded over time, not all at once. In those moments, waiting shaped faith, deepened dependence, and taught God's people to seek Him more fully.

For families, learning to wait on the Lord can change how challenges are faced. Instead of rushing for quick solutions, we learn to pause and pray. Instead of growing discouraged, we learn to hope. Waiting together teaches patience, strengthens faith, and reminds us that God's timing is guided by wisdom and love.

Let us take a few minutes to talk through the following questions together:

1. Why is waiting often difficult for us?
2. How does waiting on the Lord strengthen our faith?
3. What are some examples in the Bible where God worked during a time of waiting?
4. Where might our family need to practice patience and trust right now?

PRAYER

Patient and faithful God, thank You for Your goodness in every season. Thank You for being near to those who seek You, even while they wait. Forgive us when impatience replaces trust. Help our family to wait with hope, confidence, and faith in Your perfect timing. Amen.

FAMILY ACTIVITY

On a scrapbook page, write the title **"Waiting With Hope."** Draw an hourglass or a growing plant. Each family member writes one situation where they are waiting on God. Leave space to add reflections later about how God showed His faithfulness during that time.

God Responds When His People Cry Out

"God heard their groaning, and God remembered his covenant with Abraham, with Isaac, and with Jacob." – Exodus 2:24

This verse comes from a quiet but powerful moment in Scripture. God's people were suffering in Egypt, worn down by years of hardship. There is no recorded speech in this verse, no long prayer, only groaning. And yet, God heard.

What stands out is not the volume of their cry, but God's response. He heard, He remembered, and He moved. God's faithfulness did not depend on perfect words or strong faith. It rested on His covenant and His character.

God still responds this way. He hears the prayers that come easily and the ones that come through tears. He listens when His people do not know what to say and when prayer feels heavy. God's care is not distant or delayed by indifference. He is attentive to the cries of His people.

For families, this truth brings reassurance. There will be seasons when prayers feel weak or unfinished. Children may struggle to express what they feel. Adults may carry burdens quietly. God hears them all. Teaching this truth helps families turn toward God honestly, trusting that He responds with faithfulness and care.

Let us take a few minutes to talk through the following questions together:

1. Why do you think God responded even when His people only groaned?
2. What does this verse tell us about God's faithfulness?
3. How does it help to know God hears us even when words are hard to find?
4. How can our family bring our concerns to God honestly this week?

PRAYER

Faithful God, thank You for hearing the cries of Your people. Thank You for remembering Your promises and responding with compassion. Forgive us when we believe our prayers are too small or unclear for You. Help our family to come to You honestly, trusting that You hear and care. Amen.

FAMILY ACTIVITY

On a scrapbook page, write the title **"God Hears Us."** Draw simple lines or symbols representing prayers rising upward. Each family member writes or draws one concern they want to bring to God, even if it feels hard to explain. Leave space to add notes later about how God brought comfort, clarity, or help.

March 25

Held Secure by the Lord

"The eternal God is your dwelling place, and underneath are the everlasting arms." –
Deuteronomy 33:27

Security is something every heart longs for. We want to know that we are safe, supported, and not facing life on our own. Scripture reminds us that true security is not found in circumstances or stability, but in God Himself.

This verse paints a quiet but powerful picture. God is described as both a dwelling place and a support beneath us. He surrounds His people and sustains them at the same time. Even when the ground beneath life feels unsteady, God remains firm and unchanging.

Throughout the Bible, God proved Himself to be a refuge for His people. When they wandered, He remained their home. When they were weak, He carried them. His presence was not temporary or conditional: it was constant. God's everlasting arms did not fail, even when His people did.

For families, this truth brings peace. It reminds us that no matter what changes around us, God holds us steady. Children learn that they are not alone. Adults are reminded that they are supported beyond their own strength. Living with this assurance allows families to face challenges with calm trust, knowing they are held by the Lord.

Let us take a few minutes to talk through the following questions together:

1. What does it mean for God to be our dwelling place?
2. How does the image of God's "everlasting arms" bring comfort?
3. Why is it important to remember God's faithfulness during uncertain times?
4. How can our family rest more fully in God's care this week?

PRAYER

Everlasting God, thank You for being our refuge and our support. Thank You for holding us steady when life feels uncertain. Forgive us when we search for security apart from You. Help our family to rest in Your care and trust in Your unchanging faithfulness. Amen.

FAMILY ACTIVITY

On a scrapbook page, write the title **"Held by God."** Draw open arms or a shelter. Each family member writes one thing that makes them feel uncertain and one reason they can trust God instead. Leave space to add reflections later about how God provided peace or reassurance.

March 26
God Keeps Us From Falling

"To him who is able to keep you from stumbling and to present you blameless before the presence of his glory with great joy..." – Jude 1:24

There are moments when faith feels steady and confident, and others when it feels fragile. Scripture acknowledges this reality and points us to a comforting truth: God Himself is the One who keeps His people standing. Our security does not rest on perfect steps, but on His faithful care.

This verse reminds us that God is actively involved in preserving His people. He does not watch from a distance, waiting to see if we succeed or fail. He strengthens, steadies, and guards those who belong to Him. Even when the path is uneven, God remains present, providing what is needed to endure.

God's keeping power is not rooted in our consistency, but in His. Throughout Scripture, His people stumbled, doubted, and wandered. Yet God continued to guide them, correct them, and draw them back. His purpose was never to shame them, but to restore and sustain them.

For families, this truth brings reassurance. Growth in faith does not happen without missteps. Children learn. Adults learn. In every stage, God's grace remains at work. Trusting that God keeps us from falling allows families to move forward with humility, confidence, and gratitude, knowing that He is faithful to finish what He begins.

Let us take a few minutes to talk through the following questions together:

1. What does it mean that God keeps His people from stumbling?
2. Why is it comforting to know our faith rests in God's faithfulness, not our perfection?
3. How have we seen God's patience with His people in the Bible?
4. How can our family rely more fully on God when faith feels difficult?

PRAYER

Faithful God, thank You for guarding our steps and keeping us in Your care. Thank You for Your patience when we struggle and Your strength when we feel weak. Forgive us when we rely on ourselves instead of trusting You. Help our family to walk forward with confidence, knowing that You are holding us steady. Amen.

FAMILY ACTIVITY

On a scrapbook page, write the title **"Kept by God."** Draw a path with guiding handrails or footprints being steadied. Each family member writes one way they have seen God help them stay faithful or grow stronger. Leave space to add reflections later about how God continued to guide your family.

Depending on God Day by Day

"The young lions suffer want and hunger; but those who seek the Lord lack no good thing." – Psalm 34:10

This verse draws a striking comparison. Even the strongest creatures can experience lack, while those who seek the Lord are cared for in ways that go beyond strength or ability. God's provision is not based on power, effort, or status, it flows from the relationship with Him.

Seeking the Lord is not a one-time act. It is a daily posture of trust. When families turn their hearts toward God, they begin to see how faithfully He supplies what is truly needed. His care is not always dramatic, but it is steady. Often, His provision shows up in ordinary ways, through daily bread, timely help, and the strength to face another day.

God's definition of "good" is wiser than ours. He knows what will grow faith, shape character, and draw His people closer to Him. At times, that means giving generously. At other times, it means teaching contentment and dependence. In every season, God remains attentive to those who seek Him.

For families, this truth invites a shift in focus. Instead of measuring life by what is missing, we learn to recognize what God has already provided. Gratitude grows when we acknowledge His care, and trust deepens when we remember that He has never failed to provide what truly matters.

Let us take a few minutes to talk through the following questions together:

1. What does it mean to seek the Lord in our daily lives?
2. Why do you think God connects provision with seeking Him?
3. How has our family seen God provide in quiet or unexpected ways?
4. How can we practice gratitude for God's provision this week?

PRAYER

Faithful Provider, thank You for caring for those who seek You. Thank You for meeting our needs with wisdom and love. Forgive us when we focus on what we lack instead of trusting Your care. Help our family to seek You daily and to recognize Your provision with grateful hearts. Amen.

FAMILY ACTIVITY

On a scrapbook page, write the title **"God Provides What Is Good."** Each family member writes one thing they are thankful for that God has provided recently, big or small. Leave space to add more entries throughout the week as you notice God's care in daily life.

March 28
God Watches Over Our Lives

"The Lord watches over you—the Lord is your shade at your right hand." –
Psalm 121:5

There is comfort in knowing that God is attentive. Scripture reminds us that God does not simply create and then step back. He watches over His people with care that is constant and personal. His attention never drifts, and His presence never fades.

This verse describes God as a protective shade: close, steady, and always present. Shade does not draw attention to itself, yet it quietly guards from harm. In the same way, God's watchful care is often unseen, but it is always at work.

Throughout Scripture, God is shown as One who keeps watch. He guarded His people during long journeys, watched over them in times of rest, and remained faithful during seasons of uncertainty. Even when His people were unaware, God was present, guiding events according to His will.

For families, this truth brings reassurance. God sees every moment: busy days and quiet nights, joyful seasons and difficult ones. Nothing is hidden from His care. Remembering that God watches over us helps families live with confidence rather than fear, trusting that their lives rest securely in His hands.

Let us take a few minutes to reflect together on the following questions:

1. What does it mean that God watches over His people?
2. How does knowing God is always attentive bring comfort?
3. Can you think of examples in the Bible where God watched over His people?
4. How can our family rest more fully in God's care this week?

PRAYER

Watchful God, thank You for caring for us with steady and faithful attention. Thank You for being near in every moment of our lives. Forgive us when we forget Your presence or allow fear to take hold. Help our family to trust Your care and to rest in the knowledge that You are always watching over us. Amen.

FAMILY ACTIVITY

On a scrapbook page, write the title **"The Lord Watches Over Us."** Draw an eye, a shelter, or a shaded tree. Each family member writes one situation where they are thankful for God's watchful care. Leave space to add notes later about moments when God's protection or guidance became clear.

March 29

God Is Our Judge

"For we must all appear before the judgment seat of Christ." – 2 Corinthians 5:10

Judgment means God evaluates every person's life. Second Corinthians 5:10 reminds us that all will stand before Christ's judgment seat. Families should understand both the seriousness and the hope in this truth.

God is a righteous Judge. His decisions are always fair and true. Unlike human judges who may make mistakes, God sees every heart, thought, and action. Psalm 7:11 says, "God is a righteous judge."

For believers, judgment is not condemnation. Romans 8:1 says, "There is therefore now no condemnation for those who are in Christ Jesus." Jesus took the punishment for sin on the cross. For His people, judgment is about reward and accountability. Families should live faithfully, knowing their choices matter to God.

Judgment also reminds us of urgency. Those who reject Christ face eternal separation from God. Families should pray for and share the gospel with others, pointing them to salvation in Jesus.

Living in light of God's judgment means living with integrity, honesty, and obedience. Families who remember this truth will choose words and actions that honor Him.

Let's take two to three minutes to discuss the following questions as a family:

1. What does 2 Corinthians 5:10 teach us about judgment?
2. How does Jesus change judgment for believers?
3. Why is God's judgment always fair?
4. How can our family live with eternity in view?

✐ PRAYER

Righteous Judge, thank You that Jesus took our punishment on the cross. Thank You that believers face no condemnation. Forgive us when we forget that our choices matter. Teach our family to live with faithfulness, integrity, and hope in Your coming kingdom. Amen.

⚠ FAMILY ACTIVITY

On a scrapbook page, write "Living with Eternity in View." Each family member writes one way they can live faithfully this week. Add 2 Corinthians 5:10 at the bottom.

March 30

God Is Our Friend

"No longer do I call you servants... but I have called you friends." – John 15:15

Friendship with God is a beautiful gift. In John 15:15, Jesus told His disciples they were not merely servants but friends. This shows His closeness, love, and trust.

God's friendship is unique. He is still Lord and King, yet He draws near in intimacy. Abraham was called God's friend because of his faith. Moses spoke with God "face to face, as a man speaks to his friend" (Exodus 33:11). Through Jesus, all believers are welcomed into this friendship.

Friendship with God means knowing His heart. Jesus said, "For all that I have heard from my Father I have made known to you." He shares His Word and His will with His friends. Families can grow in this friendship through Scripture, prayer, and obedience.

Friendship also means loyalty. True friends stand by one another. God promises never to leave or forsake His people. Families can rest in His faithful presence.

This friendship changes the way we live. Families should approach God not with fear but with reverence and love, enjoying His presence daily.

Let's spend the next couple of minutes discussing the following questions as a family:

1. What does John 15:15 teach us about friendship with God?
2. Who in the Bible was called a friend of God?
3. How does Jesus invite us into this friendship?
4. How can our family grow closer to God as His friends?

PRAYER

Faithful Friend, thank You for calling us into a relationship with You. Thank You for revealing Your heart through Jesus. Forgive us when we treat Your friendship lightly. Teach our family to walk closely with You and to enjoy Your presence. Amen.

FAMILY ACTIVITY

On a scrapbook page, write "God Our Friend." Each family member writes one way they enjoy time with God: through prayer, singing, reading, or serving. Decorate the page with bright colors to celebrate His friendship.

March 31

God Is Steadfast in All Seasons

"Great are the works of the Lord, studied by all who delight in them." – Psalm 111:2

As this month comes to a close, Scripture invites us to pause and consider the work of God. Psalm 111 reminds us that God's actions are not hidden or careless. They are intentional, faithful, and worthy of reflection. Those who seek Him begin to notice His hand at work more clearly.

God's faithfulness is not limited to moments of great change or crisis. It is woven into ordinary days and quiet routines. His works are seen in provision that arrives at the right time, strength given when needed, and guidance offered when the way forward feels uncertain.

Throughout the Bible, God's people were encouraged to remember what He had done. Remembering strengthened their trust and renewed their faith. When they looked back on His works, they were reminded that the same God who acted before would remain faithful in the days ahead.

For families, reflecting on God's works builds gratitude and confidence. Taking time to notice what God has done, both seen and unseen, helps anchor faith. As we move forward into a new season, we do so with the assurance that God's steadfast care does not change.

Let us take a few minutes to reflect together on the following questions:

1. Why is it important to remember and reflect on God's works?
2. What are some ways God has been faithful to our family this month?
3. How does looking back help us trust God with what lies ahead?
4. How can we make remembering God's works a regular family practice?

📖 PRAYER

Faithful Lord, thank You for the many ways You work in our lives. Thank You for Your steady presence through every season. Forgive us when we rush past Your blessings without noticing them. Help our family to remember Your faithfulness and to trust You as we move forward. Amen.

🎄 FAMILY ACTIVITY

On a scrapbook page, write the title **"Remembering God's Faithfulness."** Divide the page into sections for each family member. In each section, write or draw one way God has been faithful this month. Leave space to return later and add reflections as new seasons unfold.

APRIL

April 1

God Is Our Hope

"Blessed be the God and Father of our Lord Jesus Christ! According to his great mercy,
he has caused us to be born again to a living hope through the resurrection of Jesus
Christ from the dead." – 1 Peter 1:3

Hope is more than wishful thinking. True hope is confident expectation rooted in God's promises. First Peter 1:3 tells us that through the resurrection of Jesus, believers are given a living hope. This hope is alive, secure, and unshakable.

Hope in the Bible is often tied to God's promises of deliverance. Abraham hoped in God's word that he would become the father of many nations, even when he and Sarah were old. Israel hoped for the Messiah, and God fulfilled that hope in Jesus. Families today can hope in God's promises for forgiveness, provision, guidance, and eternal life.

Jesus' resurrection is the foundation of our hope. Because He rose from the dead, we can be certain of eternal life. Romans 6:4 says, "Just as Christ was raised from the dead by the glory of the Father, we too might walk in newness of life." This gives families strength to face difficulties knowing that the future is secure.

Hope also changes daily life. Families who live with hope do not give in to despair. They face trials with confidence, pray with expectation, and encourage one another with God's promises. Hebrews 10:23 says, "Let us hold fast the confession of our hope without wavering, for he who promised is faithful."

Let's discuss the below questions for the next two to three minutes:

1. What does 1 Peter 1:3 teach us about living hope?
2. How does Jesus' resurrection give us confidence for the future?
3. What promises of God give you hope today?
4. How can our family encourage one another with hope?

✎ PRAYER

God of hope, thank You for giving us a living hope through Jesus' resurrection. Thank You that our future is secure in You. Forgive us when we give in to despair or forget Your promises. Teach our family to live with confidence, joy, and endurance as we rest in Your hope. Amen.

♟ FAMILY ACTIVITY

On a scrapbook page, write "Our Living Hope." Each family member writes one promise of God they are hoping in. Add bright colors and a sunrise drawing to symbolize hope through Jesus' resurrection.

April 2

God Remains Faithful When We Look to Him

"But as for me, I will look to the Lord; I will wait for the God of my salvation; my God will hear me." – Micah 7:7

There are moments when the world feels unsettled and answers seem distant. In those times, Scripture does not tell us to look inward for strength or clarity. Instead, it calls us to look toward the Lord. This verse from Micah reflects a quiet resolve, a decision to trust God even when circumstances are uncertain.

Looking to the Lord is an act of faith. It means choosing to believe that God sees, hears, and remains attentive, even when situations do not change right away. Micah spoke these words during a time of moral failure and instability among God's people, yet his confidence rested in God's unchanging character.

God's faithfulness does not depend on human faithfulness. He remains steady when people falter. He listens when His people call, and He responds according to His wisdom and purpose. Throughout Scripture, those who turned their eyes toward God found hope renewed and faith strengthened.

For families, this truth encourages a shared posture of trust. When challenges arise, choosing together to look to God shapes hearts and homes. It teaches children and adults alike that hope is not found in perfect circumstances, but in a faithful God who hears and responds to His people.

Let us take a few minutes to reflect together on the following questions:

1. What does it mean to truly look to the Lord in difficult moments?
2. Why is it comforting to know that God hears us?
3. How have we seen God remain faithful even when situations were hard?
4. How can our family choose to look to God more intentionally this week?

📖 PRAYER

Faithful God, thank You for hearing those who look to You. Thank You for remaining steady when life feels uncertain. Forgive us when we look elsewhere for hope or assurance. Help our family to fix our eyes on You and to trust Your faithfulness each day. Amen.

♟ FAMILY ACTIVITY

On a scrapbook page, write the title **"Looking to the Lord."** Draw a simple horizon or upward arrow. Each family member writes one situation where they are choosing to look to God instead of relying on their own understanding. Leave space to add notes later about how God provided reassurance, guidance, or peace.

God Rejoices Over His People

"The Lord your God is in your midst, a mighty one who will save; he will rejoice over you with gladness; he will quiet you by his love; he will exult over you with loud singing." – Zephaniah 3:17

This verse offers a picture of God that is both powerful and tender. He is described as mighty and saving, yet also joyful and gentle. Scripture reveals that God does not merely tolerate His people or keep them at a distance. He is present among them, actively involved, and filled with delight.

God's joy is not based on human perfection. It flows from His covenant love and faithfulness. Even when His people struggled or wandered, God remained committed to them. His rejoicing reflects His grace, not their performance.

The verse also speaks of God bringing quietness. His love calms anxious hearts and settles troubled spirits. In a world filled with noise, pressure, and uncertainty, God's presence brings rest. He does not shout condemnation; He sings over His people with joy.

For families, this truth reshapes how God is viewed. He is not distant or impatient. He is near, strong, and loving. Teaching children that God delights in His people builds confidence rooted in Him rather than in achievement. As families rest in God's love, they learn to live with gratitude, humility, and trust.

Let us take a few minutes to reflect together on the following questions:

1. What stands out to you about how this verse describes God?
2. Why is it important to know that God delights in His people?
3. How does God's love bring peace and quiet to our hearts?
4. How can our family live with greater confidence in God's presence this week?

PRAYER

Loving God, thank You for being near to us and for delighting in Your people. Thank You for Your strength that saves and Your love that brings peace. Forgive us when we forget Your kindness or view You through fear instead of truth. Help our family to rest in Your love and to trust Your faithful care. Amen.

FAMILY ACTIVITY

On a scrapbook page, write the title **"Delighted in by God."** Draw musical notes, hearts, or a joyful scene. Each family member writes one reason they are thankful for God's love and presence. Leave space to add reflections later about how this truth brings peace or confidence during the week.

April 4

God Gives Strength to Stand Firm

*"God, the Lord, is my strength; he makes my feet like the deer's; he makes me tread on
my high places." – Habakkuk 3:19*

Life does not always feel steady. There are seasons when circumstances shift quickly, when confidence feels shaken, and when it becomes difficult to stand firm. Scripture reminds us that stability does not come from favorable conditions, but from the Lord who gives strength.

Habakkuk spoke these words after acknowledging fear, loss, and uncertainty. Nothing around him suggested ease or comfort. Yet he declared that God Himself was his strength. Like a deer moving securely across steep ground, God enables His people to stand and move forward even when the path is uneven.

God's strength does not remove every obstacle, but it equips His people to walk faithfully through them. He gives balance when footing feels unsure and courage when the climb feels steep. His strength is not hurried or fragile, it is steady, dependable, and sufficient.

For families, this truth offers encouragement. There will be times when challenges arise without warning. Trusting God's strength teaches families to remain grounded instead of fearful. As hearts learn to rely on Him, confidence grows, not in circumstances, but in the God who sustains His people through every season.

Let us take a few minutes to reflect together on the following questions:

1. What does this verse tell us about where true strength comes from?
2. Why do you think God is compared to steady footing in difficult places?
3. How can trusting God's strength help us face challenges calmly?
4. Where does our family need God's strength to stand firm right now?

✎ PRAYER

Strong and faithful God, thank You for giving strength when our footing feels unsure. Thank You for sustaining us through difficult seasons. Forgive us when fear causes us to doubt Your care. Help our family to rely on You and to walk forward with confidence rooted in Your strength. Amen.

♟ FAMILY ACTIVITY

On a scrapbook page, write the title **"Standing Firm With God."** Draw a mountain path or sturdy footprints. Each family member writes one challenge where they are trusting God to give strength and stability. Leave space to add reflections later about how God provided courage, balance, or perseverance.

April 5
God Brings Light to Our Path

"Send out your light and your truth; let them lead me; let them bring me to your holy
hill and to your dwelling!" – Psalm 43:3

There are times when the way forward feels unclear. Decisions wait to be made, questions remain unanswered, and direction feels distant. Scripture reminds us that God does not leave His people to navigate life alone. He sends His light and His truth to lead them.

Light reveals what cannot be seen in darkness. Truth steadies the heart when uncertainty presses in. Together, they guide God's people toward Him, not simply toward solutions, but toward deeper fellowship with Him. God's guidance is never random; it draws hearts closer to His presence.

Throughout Scripture, God's light was connected to His holiness and truth. He guided His people through wilderness journeys, corrected them when they wandered, and restored them when they turned back to Him. His light was not meant to dazzle, but to direct.

For families, trusting God's light shapes daily life. It teaches patience when answers take time and humility when correction is needed. As families seek God's truth together, they learn to walk with confidence, not because they see the entire path, but because they trust the One who leads them.

Let us take a few minutes to reflect together on the following questions:

1. Why do we need both God's light and His truth?
2. How does God's truth guide us when we feel unsure?
3. What does it mean to let God lead us instead of rushing ahead?
4. Where is our family asking God for direction right now?

PRAYER

Guiding God, thank You for sending Your light and truth to lead us. Thank You for directing our steps and drawing us closer to You. Forgive us when we rely on our own understanding instead of seeking You. Help our family to follow Your guidance with trust and obedience. Amen.

FAMILY ACTIVITY

On a scrapbook page, write the title **"Led by God's Light."** Draw a lantern or pathway. Each family member writes one decision or situation where they are asking God for guidance. Leave space to add reflections later about how God provided clarity or peace.

April 6

God Invites Us to Rest in Him

"It is in vain that you rise up early and go late to rest, eating the bread of anxious toil;
for he gives to his beloved sleep." – Psalm 127:2

Busyness often convinces us that everything depends on our effort. We push ourselves to do more, fix more, and control outcomes, believing rest can come later. Scripture gently corrects this thinking by reminding us that God is at work even when we are not.

This verse does not praise laziness, but it exposes anxiety-driven striving. God never intended His people to live weighed down by constant worry. He provides for those He loves, not only through labor, but through rest. Sleep itself is described as a gift, evidence that God remains in control while His people lay down their burdens.

Throughout Scripture, God showed care for His people by calling them to pause. He commanded Sabbath rest, not as a restriction, but as a reminder of trust. Rest declares that God sustains life, not human effort alone.

For families, this truth reshapes daily rhythms. Choosing rest means setting aside fear, releasing pressure, and trusting God with what remains unfinished. When families learn to rest in Him, their hearts grow calmer, their faith deepens, and their home becomes a place shaped by trust rather than anxiety.

Let us take a few minutes to reflect together on the following questions:

1. Why do you think God connects rest with trust in Him?
2. How can worry make it difficult to rest?
3. What does this verse teach us about God's care for His people?
4. How can our family create space to rest in God this week?

📖 PRAYER

Caring God, thank You for providing for us even when we rest. Thank You for reminding us that our lives are held in Your hands. Forgive us when anxiety drives our decisions or steals our peace. Help our family to trust You more deeply and to rest in Your faithful care. Amen.

♟ FAMILY ACTIVITY

On a scrapbook page, write the title **"Resting in God's Care."** Draw a pillow, a peaceful scene, or folded hands. Each family member writes one worry they are choosing to release to God. Leave space to return later and reflect on how God brought peace or reassurance.

April 7

God Renews Us Day by Day

"Therefore we do not lose heart. Though outwardly we are wasting away, yet inwardly we are being renewed day by day." – 2 Corinthians 4:16

Some days leave us tired in ways that sleep does not fix. Bodies grow weary, patience runs thin, and discouragement can creep in quietly. Scripture does not pretend this does not happen. Instead, it reminds us that God is doing a deeper work, one that continues even when strength feels low.

Paul speaks honestly here. He acknowledges that life takes a toll. Yet he points to something stronger than exhaustion. While outward strength fades, God is renewing the hearts of His people from within. This renewal is not sudden or dramatic. It happens slowly, faithfully, and often without notice.

God's renewing work shows itself over time. It appears in steadier faith, softened hearts, and the ability to keep going when giving up would be easier. God does not waste weakness. He uses it to draw His people closer to Himself and to teach them dependence on His strength rather than their own.

For families, this truth brings relief. Not every day needs to feel successful or strong. God is still at work in ordinary moments and difficult seasons. Trusting His daily renewal allows families to move forward with humility, hope, and confidence that God is shaping something lasting within them.

Let us take a few minutes to reflect together on the following questions:

1. What does it mean to be renewed on the inside, even when we feel worn out?
2. Why do you think God often works slowly rather than all at once?
3. How can this verse encourage us on difficult days?
4. What might God be renewing in our family right now?

✎ PRAYER

Faithful God, thank You for working within us even when we feel weak or tired. Thank You for renewing our hearts day by day. Forgive us when we focus only on what feels heavy and forget that You are at work. Help our family to trust You and to rest in the renewal You provide. Amen.

♟ FAMILY ACTIVITY

On a scrapbook page, write the title **"Renewed Little by Little."** Draw a simple image such as a growing leaf or a candle being relit. Each family member writes one area where they are trusting God to bring quiet renewal. Leave space to add reflections later about how God brought strength, patience, or encouragement.

April 8
God Steadies the Faithful

"My steps have held fast to your paths; my feet have not slipped." – Psalm 17:5

Faith is not always loud or dramatic. Often, it looks like quiet faithfulness, one step taken after another, even when the road feels long or uncertain. This verse reflects a steady confidence, not in personal strength, but in God's guidance and care.

The psalmist does not claim perfection. Instead, he acknowledges that remaining steady comes from walking in God's paths. Stability is not something we create for ourselves; it is something God provides as we follow Him. When He directs our steps, He also gives the ability to stand firm.

Throughout Scripture, God's people were often called to walk forward without seeing the entire journey. They relied on God to keep them steady along the way. Even when challenges pressed in, God remained faithful to guard their steps and keep them from falling away.

For families, this truth offers reassurance. Life moves quickly, and it is easy to feel off balance. Trusting God to steady our steps reminds us that faithfulness grows through daily obedience, not perfection. As families choose to follow God together, they can trust Him to keep them grounded and secure.

Let us take a few minutes to reflect together on the following questions:

1. What does it mean to walk in God's paths?
2. Why do you think steadiness in faith matters more than speed?
3. How has God helped you stay grounded during difficult times?
4. How can our family walk faithfully with God this week?

📖 PRAYER

Steady and faithful God, thank You for guiding our steps and keeping us from slipping. Thank You for walking with us through every season. Forgive us when we rush ahead or grow distracted from Your ways. Help our family to follow You with trust and faithfulness each day. Amen.

♟ FAMILY ACTIVITY

On a scrapbook page, write the title **"Steady Steps With God."** Draw a set of footprints or stepping stones. Each family member writes one way they want to walk faithfully with God this week. Leave space to return later and note how God helped guide and steady those steps.

April 9

God Sees What We Cannot

"For the Lord sees not as man sees: man looks on the outward appearance, but the
Lord looks on the heart." – 1 Samuel 16:7

We often judge situations by what is visible. We notice results, behavior, and appearances, and we draw conclusions based on what seems obvious. Scripture reminds us that God's sight reaches much deeper. He sees what is hidden: motives, intentions, and the quiet places of the heart.

This verse was spoken when Samuel was sent to anoint Israel's next king. Those who looked strong and impressive were passed over, while God chose David, the one no one expected. God's choice was not based on outward strength, but on the heart He saw within.

God still works this way. He is not impressed by image or performance. He pays attention to sincerity, humility, and faithfulness, even when they go unnoticed by others. What feels small or unseen to us is never overlooked by Him.

For families, this truth invites honesty before God. It reminds us that character matters more than appearance and that God values hearts that seek Him, even imperfectly. When families focus on pleasing God rather than impressing others, faith becomes more genuine and less driven by pressure.

Let us take a few minutes to reflect together on the following questions:

1. Why do you think God focuses on the heart instead of outward appearance?
2. How does this verse challenge the way we judge situations or people?
3. What might God see in our hearts right now?
4. How can our family encourage honesty and sincerity before God?

📖 PRAYER

All-knowing God, thank You for seeing beyond what is visible. Thank You for caring about our hearts and not just our actions. Forgive us when we focus too much on appearances or compare ourselves to others. Help our family to live honestly before You and to seek hearts that please You. Amen.

♟ FAMILY ACTIVITY

On a scrapbook page, write the title **"God Sees the Heart."** Draw a large heart in the center. Each family member writes one quality they want God to grow in their heart, such as faithfulness, humility, patience, or trust. Leave space to return later and reflect on how God shapes these qualities over time.

April 10
God Is Our Father

"As a father shows compassion to his children, so the Lord shows compassion to those who fear him." – Psalm 103:13

God reveals Himself as Father, showing His compassion and care for His children. Psalm 103:13 compares His love to a father's, but His compassion is perfect and unchanging.

A good father provides, protects, and guides. God does all these things for His children. Jesus taught His disciples to pray, "Our Father in heaven" (Matthew 6:9), reminding us of the closeness we have with Him.

God's fatherhood also means discipline. Hebrews 12:6 says, "The Lord disciplines the one he loves." Discipline is not punishment to harm but correction to grow. Families should understand that God's correction is proof of His love.

Through Jesus, we are adopted into God's family. John 1:12 says, "To all who did receive him... he gave the right to become children of God." Families should live in confidence knowing they belong to the Father forever.

Being children of God also means reflecting His character. Families should show compassion, patience, and love to one another, following the Father's example.

Let's discuss the following questions for two or three minutes as a family:

1. What does Psalm 103:13 teach us about God as Father?
2. How does Jesus teach us to approach God in prayer?
3. Why is God's discipline an act of love?
4. How can our family live as children of God this week?

PRAYER

Heavenly Father, thank You for loving us with compassion and care. Thank You for adopting us as Your children through Jesus. Forgive us when we forget Your love or resist Your correction. Teach our family to live in obedience and joy as Your children. Amen.

FAMILY ACTIVITY

On a scrapbook page titled "Children of God," each family member draws themselves in a family circle with God at the center. Write John 1:12 under the drawing.

April 11

God Stands Firm When Everything Shifts

"The counsel of the Lord stands forever, the plans of his heart to all generations." –
Psalm 33:11

Life has a way of reminding us how little stays the same. Schedules change. Plans fall through. People grow, move, or disappoint us. Even good seasons don't last forever. When that happens, it's easy to feel unsteady, as if the ground beneath us keeps shifting.

This verse pulls our attention back to something solid. God's plans do not shift the way ours do. They are not rushed, revised, or weakened by time. What He purposes is not temporary. It does not depend on circumstances lining up just right. God's counsel stands, whether life feels calm or completely unsettled.

That does not mean we always understand what God is doing. Often, His people in Scripture were confused, afraid, or unsure of what came next. They asked questions. They waited longer than they wanted to. Yet over time, it became clear that God had not lost control or forgotten His promises. He was working, even when it didn't look like it.

For families, this truth matters more than we may realize. When life feels unpredictable, we don't need all the answers to feel secure. We need to remember who God is. His wisdom does not wear out. His purposes do not fail. Trusting that allows us to loosen our grip on control and rest in the knowledge that God is steady, even when everything else feels uncertain.

Let us take a few minutes to talk together about the following:

1. What kinds of changes make us feel the most unsettled?
2. Why is it reassuring to know that God's plans do not change?
3. How does this verse help when we don't understand what God is doing?
4. Where does our family need to trust God's wisdom right now?

📖 PRAYER

Steady and faithful God, thank You for being constant when life feels unstable. Thank You that Your plans do not depend on our understanding. Forgive us when fear makes us cling too tightly to our own ideas. Help our family to trust You, even when the way forward feels unclear. Amen.

⛪ FAMILY ACTIVITY

On a scrapbook page, write the title **"What Stays the Same."** Draw something strong and simple, like a rock or a straight line. Each family member writes one thing about God that never changes. Leave space to add notes later when your family sees His faithfulness more clearly.

April 12

Learning to Be Still Before God

"But I have calmed and quieted my soul, like a weaned child with its mother; like a weaned child is my soul within me." – Psalm 131:2

Stillness does not come naturally. Most days are filled with noise: conversations, responsibilities, worries, and plans that keep moving through our minds. Even when things are quiet on the outside, our thoughts often are not. This verse describes something different: a soul that has learned to rest.

The image here is gentle and personal. A weaned child no longer cries out for what it wants, but rests calmly, trusting the one who cares for it. In the same way, this psalm speaks of a heart that is no longer driven by anxiety or striving, but settled in God's presence.

This kind of calm does not come from having everything figured out. It grows from trust. It forms over time as God's people learn that He is faithful, attentive, and enough. Stillness before God is not about doing nothing: it is about letting go of the need to control and choosing to trust instead.

For families, learning to be still before God creates space for peace. It teaches children that they do not have to carry every worry and reminds adults that God is at work even when they pause. When a home learns to quiet its heart before God, faith deepens and relationships grow steadier.

Let us take a few minutes to talk together about the following:

1. Why do you think it is difficult to quiet our hearts before God?
2. What does this verse suggest about trust and peace?
3. How does stillness help us listen to God more clearly?
4. What might it look like for our family to practice stillness this week?

PRAYER

Gentle and faithful God, thank You for inviting us to rest in Your presence. Thank You for calming our hearts when life feels overwhelming. Forgive us when we rush, worry, or strive instead of trusting You. Help our family learn to be still before You and to rest in Your care. Amen.

FAMILY ACTIVITY

On a scrapbook page, write the title **"Quiet Before God."** Draw a peaceful image such as a seated child, a calm lake, or folded hands. Each family member writes one thing they are choosing to release to God. Leave space to return later and reflect on how God brought peace or reassurance.

April 13
God Teaches Us to Listen

"Whoever has ears to hear, let them hear." – Matthew 11:15

Listening sounds simple, but it is often harder than we expect. We are quick to speak, quick to respond, and quick to move on. Jesus' words here slow us down. They are not about physical hearing, but about attention of the heart.

When Jesus spoke these words, many people were listening to Him, yet not truly hearing what He was saying. Some were distracted. Others had already decided what they believed. Jesus reminded them that hearing God requires humility and willingness, not just presence.

God still speaks through His Word, through prayer, and through the quiet prompting of His Spirit. But listening takes intention. It means setting aside assumptions and allowing God to shape understanding over time. Often, what God teaches unfolds gradually, not all at once.

For families, learning to listen to God together builds spiritual awareness. It encourages patience, reflection, and obedience. When a family values listening, both to God and to one another, it creates space for wisdom, understanding, and growth rooted in faith.

Let us take a few minutes to talk together about the following:

1. What does it mean to truly listen to God?
2. Why is it sometimes easier to hear words than to respond to them?
3. How can we tell the difference between listening and just waiting to speak?
4. What might help our family listen more carefully to God this week?

PRAYER

Speaking God, thank You for making Your truth known. Thank You for inviting us to listen and to learn. Forgive us when we rush past Your words or ignore Your guidance. Help our family to listen with open hearts and to respond with obedience and trust. Amen.

FAMILY ACTIVITY

On a scrapbook page, write the title **"Learning to Listen."** Draw an ear, an open Bible, or a quiet scene. Each family member writes one way they want to listen more carefully, to God or to others, this week. Leave space to add reflections later about what they noticed when they slowed down to listen.

April 14

God Responds With Kindness

"The Lord is gracious and merciful, slow to anger and abounding in steadfast love." –
Joel 2:13

Kindness is often quiet. It does not draw attention to itself, yet it has the power to change hearts and restore hope. Scripture reminds us that God's response toward His people is marked by kindness, even when they have fallen short.

This verse was spoken as a call to repentance, not condemnation. God invited His people to turn back to Him, not out of fear, but because of who He is. His grace and mercy are not earned. They flow from His character. He is patient, not quick to anger, and His love does not run dry.

God's kindness does not ignore sin or pretend brokenness does not exist. Instead, it creates space for repentance and renewal. When God shows kindness, it is meant to draw His people closer, not push them away. Again and again in Scripture, His kindness leads to restoration.

For families, this truth matters deeply. Homes are places where grace is needed daily. Remembering how God responds to His people helps families choose patience over harshness and understanding over quick judgment. As God shows kindness, families learn to reflect that same spirit toward one another.

Let us take a few minutes to talk together about the following:

1. Why do you think God responds to repentance with kindness instead of anger?
2. How does God's patience change the way we see our own failures?
3. What does God's kindness look like in everyday life?
4. How can our family show kindness more intentionally this week?

✐ PRAYER

Gracious God, thank You for responding to us with patience and kindness. Thank You for inviting us back to You instead of turning us away. Forgive us when we forget Your grace or fail to show it to others. Help our family to reflect Your kindness in our words and actions. Amen.

♟ FAMILY ACTIVITY

On a scrapbook page, write the title **"Kindness at Work."** Draw small acts of care, such as helping hands or shared meals. Each family member writes one way they can show kindness to someone this week. Leave space to return later and note how choosing kindness made a difference.

God Is Faithful When We Feel Unsure

"Commit your way to the Lord; trust in him, and he will act." – Psalm 37:5

Uncertainty has a way of slowing us down. When we don't know how things will turn out, it's tempting to hold tightly to our own plans or try to control every outcome. This verse invites us to do something different: to place our way, our direction, and our concerns into God's hands.

Committing our way to the Lord is not about having everything figured out. It is about choosing trust when clarity is missing. God does not ask His people to see the whole path ahead. He asks them to place their confidence in Him and to walk forward one step at a time.

Scripture shows that God acts in response to trust. His work is not always immediate or obvious, but it is faithful. When His people release control and depend on Him, He moves according to His wisdom and timing. What He does may not look like what we expected, but it is never careless or empty.

For families, this truth speaks into everyday decisions and worries. From small choices to larger concerns, learning to commit each step to God builds faith together. It teaches children and adults alike that trust is not passive: it is an active decision to rely on God's faithfulness, even when the way forward feels uncertain.

Let us take a few minutes to talk together about the following:

1. What does it mean to commit our way to the Lord?
2. Why is trust difficult when outcomes are unclear?
3. How have we seen God act when we placed our trust in Him?
4. What is one situation our family needs to commit to God right now?

PRAYER

Faithful God, thank You for inviting us to place our trust in You. Thank You for acting with wisdom and care in our lives. Forgive us when fear causes us to cling to our own plans. Help our family to commit our way to You and to trust You with what we cannot control. Amen.

FAMILY ACTIVITY

On a scrapbook page, write the title **"Committed to God."** Draw a simple path or arrow pointing forward. Each family member writes one decision or concern they are choosing to place in God's hands. Leave space to return later and note how God brought guidance, peace, or clarity.

April 16
God Calms the Anxious Heart

"When I am afraid, I put my trust in you." – Psalm 56:3

Fear shows up in many ways. Sometimes it is loud and obvious. Other times it sits quietly beneath the surface, shaping our thoughts and reactions without us realizing it. Scripture does not shame fear. Instead, it shows us what to do with it.

This short verse is honest. It does not say if fear comes, but when. The response is simple but powerful—trust. Rather than pretending fear does not exist, the psalmist turns directly to God. Trust becomes a choice made in the middle of fear, not after it disappears.

God does not ask His people to face anxious moments alone. He invites them to bring their fear to Him. Over and over in Scripture, we see that trust does not remove every challenge, but it changes how those challenges are carried. Fear no longer has the final word.

For families, this truth matters in everyday moments. Children feel fear just as deeply as adults do, even if they express it differently. Learning to say, "We will trust God," creates a shared response that brings calm and confidence. When fear rises, trust reminds the family where safety is truly found.

Let us take a few minutes to talk together about the following:

1. What kinds of situations tend to make us feel afraid or anxious?
2. Why do you think God invites us to trust Him when we are afraid?
3. How does trust change the way fear affects us?
4. How can our family practice trusting God during anxious moments?

PRAYER

Trustworthy God, thank You for inviting us to come to You when we are afraid. Thank You for being steady when our hearts feel unsettled. Forgive us when fear takes over and we forget to trust You. Help our family learn to place our confidence in You, no matter what we face. Amen.

FAMILY ACTIVITY

On a scrapbook page, write the title **"Choosing Trust Over Fear."** Draw a heart or a simple shield. Each family member writes one fear or worry they are choosing to place in God's hands. Leave space to return later and note how trusting God brought peace or courage.

April 17

God Is Faithful

"Know therefore that the Lord your God is God, the faithful God who keeps covenant and steadfast love with those who love him." – Deuteronomy 7:9

Faithfulness means keeping promises and staying true. Deuteronomy 7:9 calls God the faithful God who keeps covenant and steadfast love. Families can trust that every word He has spoken will come true.

Throughout history, God has been faithful. He kept His promise to Abraham by giving him many descendants. He kept His promise to Israel by leading them into the promised land. He kept His promise of a Savior by sending Jesus.

Even when people are unfaithful, God remains faithful. Second Timothy 2:13 says, "If we are faithless, he remains faithful—for he cannot deny himself." His faithfulness is based on His character, not on our actions.

Jesus also revealed God's faithfulness. He fulfilled the prophecies, never failed in obedience, and promised to be with His people always.

Faithfulness calls for response. Families should live in trust, holding firmly to God's Word, and reflecting His faithfulness by keeping their own promises. A faithful home builds trust, peace, and love.

Let's discuss the following questions together as a family:

1. What does Deuteronomy 7:9 teach us about God's faithfulness?
2. How has God shown faithfulness in the Bible?
3. How has God been faithful to our family?
4. How can we reflect His faithfulness in our daily lives?

📖 PRAYER

Faithful God, thank You for keeping every promise. Thank You for loving us even when we are unfaithful. Forgive us when we doubt Your Word or fail to keep our promises. Teach our family to trust You completely and to reflect Your faithfulness in our home. Amen.

♟ FAMILY ACTIVITY

On a scrapbook page, write "God's Faithfulness." Each family member lists one way God has been faithful in their life. Decorate the page with rainbows to symbolize His covenant promise.

April 18
God Carries Us Through Every Season

"Even to your old age I am he, and to gray hairs I will carry you. I have made, and I will bear; I will carry and will save." – Isaiah 46:4

Some days require more strength than we have. Not because something dramatic happens, but because life itself feels heavy. Responsibilities pile up, worries linger, and energy fades. Scripture speaks directly into those moments with a promise that is both steady and deeply reassuring: God carries His people.

This verse does not describe a God who helps only when asked or supports only when we are strong. It describes a God who bears the weight Himself. From beginning to end, He remains faithful to carry what His people cannot.

What stands out is the certainty in God's words. I have made. I will bear. I will carry. This is not temporary help or conditional care. It is a lifelong promise rooted in God's character. He does not grow tired or withdraw when the journey becomes long.

For families, this truth offers comfort across generations. Children learn that they are not expected to face life alone. Adults are reminded that strength does not come from holding everything together. God carries His people through changing seasons, through weariness, and through moments when faith feels quiet but still present.

Let us take a few minutes to talk together about the following:

1. What does it mean to be carried by God?
2. Why is it comforting to know God carries us over time, not just in emergencies?
3. How does this verse change the way we think about weakness?
4. Where might our family need to rely on God's strength right now?

PRAYER

Faithful God, thank You for carrying us when we feel weak or overwhelmed. Thank You for Your steady care through every season of life. Forgive us when we try to carry everything on our own. Help our family to trust You and to rest in the strength You provide. Amen.

FAMILY ACTIVITY

On a scrapbook page, write the title **"Carried by God."** Draw open arms or a pathway supported from beneath. Each family member writes one situation where they are trusting God to carry them. Leave space to return later and reflect on how God provided strength, help, or peace.

April 19

God Is Holy

"Exalt the Lord our God, and worship at his holy mountain; for the Lord our God is holy!" – Psalm 99:9

Holiness means being set apart, pure, and perfect. Psalm 99:9 calls us to exalt God because He is holy. Families should recognize that holiness defines God's nature and shapes how we live before Him.

Isaiah 6 gives a vivid picture of God's holiness. Angels around His throne cried, "Holy, holy, holy." Isaiah responded with humility, confessing his unclean lips. God then cleansed him, showing that holiness reveals our sin and God's mercy.

Through Jesus, God's holiness is revealed and shared with His people. Hebrews 10:10 says, "We have been sanctified through the offering of the body of Jesus Christ once for all." Holiness is not about being perfect by ourselves but being set apart for God's purposes.

Families can live holy lives by choosing purity in words, honesty in actions, and kindness in relationships. Holiness means living differently because we belong to God.

Holiness also shapes worship. Families should approach God with reverence, acknowledging His greatness, while rejoicing in His mercy.

Let's discuss the following questions as a family:

1. What does it mean that God is holy?
2. How did Isaiah respond to God's holiness?
3. How does Jesus make us holy?
4. How can our family reflect holiness in daily life?

PRAYER

Holy God, thank You for revealing Your glory and purity. Thank You for cleansing us through Jesus. Forgive us when we choose sin over obedience. Teach our family to live holy lives and to honor You in our home. Amen.

FAMILY ACTIVITY

On a scrapbook page, write "Set Apart for God." Each family member writes one action or habit they want to dedicate to God this week.

April 20

Learning to Leave the Outcome With God

"Do not say, 'I will repay evil'; wait for the Lord, and he will deliver you." –
Proverbs 20:22

There is something in us that wants resolution right away. We want situations to be settled, wrongs to be made right, and loose ends tied up quickly. Waiting can feel uncomfortable, especially when we believe something needs to be fixed now.

This verse reminds us that not every outcome belongs in our hands. God asks His people to wait, not because He is indifferent, but because He sees more than we do. What feels urgent to us may require patience, wisdom, or restraint that only God can provide.

Waiting on the Lord is not passive. It takes trust to step back and allow God to work in His time and His way. Scripture shows again and again that God acts with purpose, even when His people cannot yet see how things will unfold.

For families, this truth matters in everyday moments. Conflicts, disappointments, and unanswered questions are part of life together. Choosing to wait on God teaches restraint, humility, and faith. It reminds everyone in the home that God is just, attentive, and fully capable of handling what we cannot.

Let us take a few minutes to talk together about the following:

1. Why is it difficult to wait when something feels unresolved?

2. What does this verse suggest about trusting God with outcomes?

3. How can waiting protect us from acting out of frustration or fear?

4. Where does our family need to leave the outcome with God right now?

PRAYER

Faithful God, thank You for reminding us that You are in control. Thank You for seeing what we cannot and acting with wisdom and justice. Forgive us when impatience leads us to take matters into our own hands. Help our family learn to wait on You and to trust You with every outcome. Amen.

FAMILY ACTIVITY

On a scrapbook page, write the title **"Trusting God With the Outcome."** Draw an open hand releasing something. Each family member writes one situation they are choosing to place in God's care. Leave space to return later and reflect on how waiting on God brought peace, clarity, or resolution.

April 21
Learning to Lay Ourselves Down

"He must increase, but I must decrease." – John 3:30

These words are short, but they carry weight. John the Baptist spoke them at a moment when attention was shifting away from him and toward Jesus. Instead of resisting that change, he accepted it. His joy came from knowing his role was never about himself, but about pointing others to Christ.

This verse reminds us that life with God is not centered on being noticed, praised, or proven right. It is centered on surrender. Decreasing does not mean losing value; it means letting God take His rightful place. When He increases, our lives begin to align with His purposes rather than our own desires.

Throughout Scripture, God worked powerfully through people who were willing to step back and trust Him to lead. Their obedience mattered more than their recognition. Their faithfulness mattered more than their position.

For families, this truth can reshape everyday life. Decreasing might look like listening instead of insisting, serving instead of demanding, or choosing patience over pride. When a family learns to let God increase, relationships grow healthier and faith becomes less about self and more about honoring Him.

Let us take a few minutes to talk together about the following:

1. What do you think it means for God to increase in our lives?
2. Why can it be hard to let go of recognition or control?
3. How does decreasing ourselves make room for God to work?
4. What is one way our family can choose humility this week?

📖 PRAYER

Holy God, thank You for reminding us that life is not about lifting ourselves up, but about honoring You. Forgive us when pride or self-interest takes center stage. Help our family learn to step back, trust You more fully, and allow You to increase in every area of our lives. Amen.

⚶ FAMILY ACTIVITY

On a scrapbook page, write the title **"Letting God Increase."** Draw an arrow pointing upward and another pointing downward. Each family member writes one way they want God to have more room in their life. Leave space to return later and reflect on how choosing humility changed attitudes or actions.

April 22
Pausing to Consider God's Ways

"This is what the Lord Almighty says: 'Give careful thought to your ways.'" –
Haggai 1:7

Life moves quickly. Days fill up before we realize it, and routines begin to run on their own. In the middle of that pace, this verse feels like an interruption. God calls His people to stop and think, not about others, but about themselves.

When these words were spoken, God's people were busy, but distracted. They were active, but not attentive to what mattered most. God did not accuse or shame them. Instead, He invited them to reflect. To look honestly at where their choices were leading and whether their lives were aligned with His purposes.

God still invites this kind of pause. Reflection is not about guilt; it is about clarity. It helps us notice patterns we've ignored and priorities that may have quietly shifted. When we stop long enough to consider our ways, we give God room to redirect our hearts.

For families, this kind of reflection is valuable. It creates space for meaningful conversations and shared growth. Pausing together helps everyone learn that faith is not just about staying busy, but about walking intentionally with God, one choice at a time.

Let us take a few minutes to talk together about the following:

1. Why do you think God asks His people to stop and reflect?
2. What does it mean to consider our ways honestly before God?
3. How can reflection help us grow in faith?
4. What is one area where our family might need to pause and seek God's direction?

📖 PRAYER

Wise God, thank You for inviting us to slow down and reflect. Thank You for caring about the direction of our lives. Forgive us when we rush ahead without seeking You. Help our family learn to pause, listen, and walk more closely in Your ways. Amen.

♟ FAMILY ACTIVITY

On a scrapbook page, write the title **"Considering Our Ways."** Draw a pause symbol or a crossroads. Each family member writes one habit, choice, or routine they want to bring before God. Leave space to return later and reflect on how God provided guidance or clarity.

April 23
Trusting God With What Takes Time

"Though it linger, wait for it; it will certainly come and will not delay." –
Habakkuk 2:3

Waiting is rarely comfortable. When answers take longer than expected, it can feel as though nothing is happening at all. Scripture speaks honestly about this tension and reminds us that God's work is not rushed, even when it feels delayed.

This verse was given during a time of uncertainty. God did not promise immediate resolution, but He did promise faithfulness. What He had spoken would come to pass, even if it required patience. Waiting, in this sense, was not wasted time, it was part of the process.

God often works in ways that unfold slowly. Growth happens beneath the surface long before it becomes visible. Trust is formed in the waiting, not just in the outcome. Scripture shows that God's timing is intentional, shaped by wisdom rather than urgency.

For families, this truth offers reassurance. Not every prayer is answered right away. Not every situation changes quickly. Learning to wait together teaches patience and deepens faith. When families trust God with what takes time, they learn that His promises are steady, even when the journey feels long.

Let us take a few minutes to talk together about the following:

1. Why is waiting often difficult for us?
2. What does this verse teach us about God's timing?
3. How can waiting strengthen our trust in God?
4. Where is our family being asked to wait right now?

✑ PRAYER

Faithful God, thank You for reminding us that Your promises are sure. Thank You for working even when we do not see immediate change. Forgive us when impatience leads to discouragement. Help our family trust You fully and wait with hope, knowing You are faithful. Amen.

⚱ FAMILY ACTIVITY

On a scrapbook page, write the title **"Waiting With Trust."** Draw an hourglass, a growing vine, or a road stretching forward. Each family member writes one situation where they are choosing to trust God's timing. Leave space to return later and reflect on how God showed His faithfulness along the way.

April 24

Learning to Receive Each Day From God

"In the day of prosperity be joyful, and in the day of adversity consider: God has made the one as well as the other." – Ecclesiastes 7:14

Not every day feels the same. Some arrive with ease and encouragement, while others feel heavy before they even begin. Scripture reminds us that God is present in both kinds of days, not just the ones we would choose for ourselves.

This verse invites honesty. It does not pretend that adversity feels good or that difficulty should be ignored. Instead, it calls God's people to consider, to remember that no day is outside of God's awareness or control. Both joy and hardship are held within His purposes.

God does not waste difficult days. He uses them to shape faith, deepen dependence, and teach humility. At the same time, He invites His people to receive good days with gratitude, recognizing them as gifts rather than guarantees.

For families, this truth brings balance. It teaches children that faith is not tied only to happy moments and reminds adults that hard seasons do not mean God has stepped away. Receiving each day from God, whatever it holds, helps a family walk forward with steadiness and trust.

Let us take a few minutes to talk together about the following:

1. Why is it sometimes easier to trust God on good days than on hard ones?
2. What does it mean to "consider" God's hand during adversity?
3. How can gratitude and trust exist at the same time?
4. What kind of day is our family facing right now, and how can we place it in God's hands?

✎ PRAYER

Faithful God, thank You for being present in every kind of day. Thank You for moments of joy and for Your nearness in times of difficulty. Forgive us when we forget You are at work in both. Help our family receive each day from You with trust, humility, and gratitude. Amen.

⚑ FAMILY ACTIVITY

On a scrapbook page, write the title **"Receiving Today From God."** Divide the page into two sections labeled Joy and Challenge. Each family member writes one thing they are thankful for today and one thing they are trusting God with. Leave space to return later and reflect on how God met you in both.

April 25

God Invites Us to Seek Him First

"You will seek me and find me, when you seek me with all your heart." –
Jeremiah 29:13

Seeking God is not the same as searching for answers. Often, we want clarity, solutions, or reassurance before we are willing to slow down and turn to Him. Scripture reminds us that God invites His people to seek Him, not just what He can provide.

This verse speaks to intention. Seeking God with the whole heart means coming honestly, without holding anything back. It is not about saying the right words or knowing exactly what to ask. It is about drawing near with sincerity and trust, believing that God desires to be found.

God has always responded to those who seek Him. Throughout Scripture, He met people in moments of longing, confusion, and hope. He did not hide Himself from those who came with open hearts. Instead, He revealed His presence in ways that shaped their faith and direction.

For families, this truth sets a simple but meaningful focus. Life is full of distractions, schedules, and competing priorities. Choosing to seek God together, through prayer, conversation, and time in His Word, builds a foundation that keeps faith centered on relationship, not routine.

Let us take a few minutes to talk together about the following:

1. What does it mean to seek God with your whole heart?
2. Why is it sometimes easier to seek answers than to seek God Himself?
3. How have you experienced God when you have sought Him sincerely?
4. What would it look like for our family to seek God more intentionally?

PRAYER

Faithful God, thank You for inviting us to seek You and for promising that You will be found. Thank You for meeting us with patience and grace. Forgive us when distractions pull our hearts away from You. Help our family learn to seek You first, trusting that You will guide us as we draw near. Amen.

FAMILY ACTIVITY

On a scrapbook page, write the title **"Seeking God Together."** Draw a heart or a simple compass. Each family member writes one way they want to seek God more intentionally this week. Leave space to return later and reflect on how drawing closer to God shaped your family's days.

April 26
God Walks With Us Through Each Step

"The Lord himself goes before you and will be with you; he will never leave you nor forsake you." – Deuteronomy 31:8

Some days feel straightforward, and others feel uncertain before they even begin. Decisions wait to be made, responsibilities press in, and the future can feel unclear. Scripture speaks into this reality with reassurance: God does not send His people forward alone.

This verse was spoken at a moment of transition, when the path ahead carried both promise and fear. God's words did not remove the challenges, but they offered something better: His presence. He goes ahead, He remains near, and He does not step away when the journey becomes difficult.

God's presence does not mean every step feels confident. It means His people are never abandoned in their uncertainty. Throughout Scripture, God walked with His people through change, obedience, and waiting. His faithfulness was not tied to ease, but to relationship.

For families, this truth brings quiet confidence. Whether facing small daily choices or larger transitions, God's presence steadies the heart. Teaching children that God walks with them helps shape courage rooted in trust rather than fear. As families move forward together, they do so knowing God is already there.

Let us take a few minutes to talk together about the following:

1. Why is it comforting to know that God goes before us?
2. How does God's presence change the way we face uncertainty?
3. What transitions or decisions is our family facing right now?
4. How can we remind one another that God is with us each day?

PRAYER

Faithful God, thank You for going before us and staying with us. Thank You for Your presence in every step we take. Forgive us when fear causes us to forget that You are near. Help our family walk forward with trust, confident that You will not leave us. Amen.

FAMILY ACTIVITY

On a scrapbook page, write the title **"Walking With God."** Draw footprints along a path. Each family member writes one situation where they are trusting God to walk with them. Leave space to return later and reflect on how God provided courage, guidance, or peace.

April 27

God Teaches Us What Truly Matters

"So teach us to number our days that we may get a heart of wisdom." – Psalm 90:12

Time moves quickly. Days fill up before we notice, and weeks pass without pause. This verse gently calls God's people to slow down, not to fear time, but to understand it. To number our days is not about counting hours, but about living with awareness.

Moses wrote these words while reflecting on God's eternity and human frailty. Compared to God, our days are brief. That truth is not meant to discourage us, but to guide us. When we recognize that time is a gift, our priorities begin to shift.

God uses this awareness to shape wisdom. Wisdom is not just knowledge or experience; it is learning what deserves our attention and devotion. Numbering our days helps us focus less on what is urgent and more on what is lasting: faithfulness, obedience, love, and trust in God.

For families, this truth encourages intentional living. It invites meaningful conversations, thoughtful choices, and shared time rooted in what matters most. When a family learns to see each day as a gift from God, even ordinary moments take on deeper significance.

Let us take a few minutes to talk together about the following:

1. What does it mean to "number our days"?
2. Why do you think wisdom is connected to how we view time?
3. How can being aware of time help us live more faithfully?
4. What is one way our family can use our time more intentionally?

PRAYER

Eternal God, thank You for the days You give us. Thank You for reminding us that our time belongs to You. Forgive us when we rush through life without considering what matters most. Help our family grow in wisdom and learn to use each day in ways that honor You. Amen.

FAMILY ACTIVITY

On a scrapbook page, write the title **"Using Our Days Wisely."** Draw a calendar page or a simple clock. Each family member writes one way they want to use their time more intentionally this week. Leave space to return later and reflect on how focusing on what matters brought growth or peace.

April 28
God Delights in Obedient Hearts

"To obey is better than sacrifice, and to listen than the fat of rams." – 1 Samuel 15:22

Obedience is often misunderstood. It can sound heavy or restrictive, as if God is asking something burdensome. Scripture shows us something different. Obedience is not about doing more for God: it is about listening to Him and responding with trust.

This verse was spoken at a moment when outward religious actions were present, but hearts were not fully aligned with God's instruction. God made it clear that what mattered most was not ritual or appearance, but a willing heart that listened and followed.

God values obedience because it reflects trust. When His people obey, they show that they believe His ways are good, even when they do not fully understand them. Obedience is not perfection; it is a posture of humility and willingness before God.

For families, this truth shapes everyday choices. Obedience can look like honesty when it is uncomfortable, patience when it is difficult, or choosing what is right when it costs something. When families learn to listen to God together, obedience becomes a response of love rather than obligation.

Let us take a few minutes to talk together about the following:

1. Why do you think God values obedience over outward actions?
2. How does listening to God help us obey Him?
3. What makes obedience difficult at times?
4. What is one area where our family can practice obedience this week?

✍ PRAYER

Holy God, thank You for caring more about our hearts than our outward actions. Thank You for guiding us with wisdom and love. Forgive us when we listen halfheartedly or choose our own way instead of Yours. Help our family learn to listen carefully and to obey You with willing hearts. Amen.

♟ FAMILY ACTIVITY

On a scrapbook page, write the title **"Listening and Obeying."** Draw an ear and a heart side by side. Each family member writes one way they want to listen more closely to God this week. Leave space to return later and reflect on how obedience shaped your family's choices.

April 29

God Gives Courage to Move Forward

"Wait for the Lord; be strong, and let your heart take courage; wait for the Lord!" –
Psalm 27:14

Courage is often mistaken for boldness or fearlessness. In Scripture, courage looks quieter. It shows up in waiting, trusting, and continuing to move forward even when confidence feels thin. This verse speaks directly to moments when strength feels hard to find.

The call to courage here is tied to waiting on the Lord. That connection matters. Courage does not come from pushing harder or pretending fear is not there. It comes from placing hope in God and believing He will act in His time.

Waiting can feel passive, but it requires strength. It asks us to resist panic, to hold steady when answers are delayed, and to trust that God is at work even when nothing seems to be changing. In that waiting, God strengthens the heart.

For families, this truth is deeply practical. There are seasons when decisions linger, problems persist, or the next step feels uncertain. Learning to wait together, and to take courage from God, helps a family move forward without fear controlling their choices. Courage grows when trust is shared and God remains at the center.

Let us take a few minutes to talk together about the following:

1. What situations make it difficult for us to feel courageous?
2. Why do you think courage is connected to waiting on God?
3. How does trusting God help strengthen the heart?
4. Where does our family need courage to keep trusting God right now?

PRAYER

Faithful God, thank You for strengthening our hearts when we wait on You. Thank You for giving courage when fear tries to take over. Forgive us when impatience weakens our trust. Help our family learn to wait with hope and to move forward with courage that comes from You. Amen.

FAMILY ACTIVITY

On a scrapbook page, write the title **"Courage From God."** Draw a heart or a shield. Each family member writes one situation where they are asking God for courage. Leave space to return later and reflect on how God provided strength, peace, or reassurance.

April 30

God Completes What He Begins

"For the Lord will not forsake his people, for his great name's sake, because it has pleased the Lord to make you a people for himself." – 1 Samuel 12:22

As this month comes to a close, it is natural to look back and notice unfinished things. Growth that feels slow. Prayers that are still unanswered. Changes that are still in progress. Scripture reminds us that God is not discouraged by what is incomplete. He remains faithful to His people because of who He is.

This verse speaks from a place of assurance. God's commitment does not depend on human consistency or performance. He chose His people, and He does not abandon what He has chosen. His faithfulness flows from His character, not from our success.

Throughout Scripture, God remained with His people through failure, growth, correction, and restoration. He did not walk away when progress was uneven. Instead, He continued to guide, teach, and sustain. What God begins, He carries forward with patience and purpose.

For families, this truth brings comfort and hope. Faith is not built in a single day. Neither are relationships, habits, or understanding. God is at work beyond what we can see, and He does not give up midway. Trusting Him with unfinished places allows families to move forward with confidence and gratitude.

Let us take a few minutes to talk together about the following:

1. Why is it reassuring to know that God does not forsake His people?

2. How does this verse change the way we see unfinished growth?

3. Where have we seen God's faithfulness over time?

4. What unfinished area can our family place in God's care today?

🕮 PRAYER

Faithful God, thank You for staying with Your people and never walking away from Your work. Thank You for Your patience and steady care in every season. Forgive us when we become discouraged by what feels incomplete. Help our family trust You with what is still unfolding and rest in Your faithfulness. Amen.

♟ FAMILY ACTIVITY

On a scrapbook page, write the title **"God Is Still Working."** Draw an open circle or a path that continues beyond the page. Each family member writes one area where they are trusting God to continue His work. Leave space to return later and reflect on how God's faithfulness became clear over time.

MAY

May 1
God Sustains Us One Day at a Time

"Your mercy, O Lord, is in the heavens; your faithfulness reaches to the clouds." –
Psalm 36:5

There is something reassuring about knowing that God's care does not start and stop with our effort. This verse lifts our eyes upward, reminding us that God's mercy and faithfulness are far greater than what we can measure or manage.

God's mercy is not limited by circumstances or seasons. It does not shrink when life feels heavy or when we fall short. His faithfulness stretches beyond what we can see, steady and dependable, holding each day in place.

Scripture often points us away from ourselves and toward who God is. When we focus on His faithfulness, we are reminded that our lives are sustained by His grace, not by our ability to keep everything together. Each day becomes something received, not something earned.

For families, this truth brings calm and perspective. Children learn that God is reliable. Adults are reminded that they are not carrying life alone. As a new month begins, trusting God's mercy one day at a time allows a family to walk forward with gratitude rather than pressure.

Let us take a few minutes to talk together about the following:

1. What does this verse tell us about God's mercy and faithfulness?
2. Why is it helpful to remember that God sustains us daily?
3. How does focusing on God's faithfulness change our outlook?
4. What is one way our family can rely on God more intentionally this month?

PRAYER

Faithful God, thank You for Your mercy that surrounds us and Your faithfulness that never fades. Thank You for sustaining us each day by Your grace. Forgive us when we rely on our own strength instead of trusting You. Help our family begin this month with confidence rooted in who You are. Amen.

FAMILY ACTIVITY

On a scrapbook page, write the title **"Held by God's Faithfulness."** Draw clouds, a wide sky, or open hands. Each family member writes one way they have seen God's faithfulness in the past and one way they are trusting Him in the days ahead. Leave space to return later and reflect on how God continued to sustain your family.

May 2
God Is Faithful to Finish His Work

"He who calls you is faithful; he will surely do it." – 1 Thessalonians 5:24

Some days begin with energy and confidence. Others begin with questions about growth, direction, or whether we are truly moving forward. Scripture reminds us that faith is not sustained by our consistency, but by God's faithfulness.

This verse shifts the focus away from human effort and back to God's character. God is the One who calls His people, and He is also the One who remains faithful to complete what He has begun. The weight does not rest on us to hold everything together.

God's faithfulness shows up quietly. It is seen in steady growth, gentle correction, and ongoing care. Even when progress feels slow or uneven, God continues His work. He does not abandon what He has called into being.

For families, this truth brings reassurance. Growth in faith, relationships, and character does not depend on perfection. God remains faithful through ordinary days and imperfect moments. Trusting Him to finish His work allows a family to walk forward with hope rather than pressure.

Let us take a few minutes to talk together about the following:

1. What does this verse teach us about God's faithfulness?
2. Why is it comforting to know that God finishes what He starts?
3. How does this truth change the way we view our own growth?
4. Where does our family need to trust God's faithfulness right now?

✐ PRAYER

Faithful God, thank You for calling us and staying with us. Thank You for finishing the work You begin in our lives. Forgive us when we place too much pressure on ourselves instead of trusting You. Help our family rest in Your faithfulness and walk forward with confidence in Your care. Amen.

⛪ FAMILY ACTIVITY

On a scrapbook page, write the title **"God Is Still Working."** Draw a simple line that continues beyond the page. Each family member writes one area where they are trusting God to continue His work. Leave space to return later and reflect on how God's faithfulness became clearer over time.

May 3
God Teaches Us to Depend on Him

"I am the vine; you are the branches. Whoever abides in me and I in him, he it is that bears much fruit, for apart from me you can do nothing." – John 15:5

Dependence is not something we naturally seek. We are often taught to be independent, capable, and self-sufficient. Yet Jesus speaks plainly here. Life that bears fruit does not come from effort alone. It comes from staying connected to Him.

This image is simple but honest. A branch does not struggle to produce fruit by trying harder. It remains connected to the vine. Once it is separated, it withers, no matter how healthy it once looked. Jesus uses this picture to remind His followers where true life and strength are found.

God does not ask His people to prove themselves. He invites them to remain close to Him. Dependence is not weakness, it is the place where growth begins. When hearts stay rooted in Christ, fruit follows in God's time and by His power.

For families, this truth reshapes daily faith. It reminds parents and children alike that spiritual growth is not about performance. Prayer, obedience, patience, and love grow naturally when a family stays connected to Christ together. Dependence on God creates space for humility, trust, and lasting fruit.

Let us take a few minutes to talk together about the following:

1. What does it mean to stay connected to Jesus?
2. Why do you think dependence on God can feel difficult at times?
3. How does this verse change the way we think about growth and success?
4. What helps our family stay rooted in Christ each day?

PRAYER

Faithful God, thank You for reminding us that life and growth come from You. Thank You for inviting us to remain close to Christ. Forgive us when we rely on our own strength instead of depending on You. Help our family stay rooted in You and trust You to bring fruit from our lives. Amen.

FAMILY ACTIVITY

On a scrapbook page, write the title **"Staying Connected to Christ."** Draw a vine with branches. Each family member writes one habit or choice that helps them stay close to Jesus, such as prayer, reading Scripture, or showing love to others. Leave space to return later and reflect on how staying connected shaped your family's week.

May 4

God Honors a Willing Heart

"The sacrifices of God are a broken spirit; a broken and contrite heart, O God, you will not despise." – Psalm 51:17

God has never been impressed by appearances alone. Throughout Scripture, He consistently turns His attention toward the heart. This verse reminds us that what God values most is not perfection, strength, or outward success, but humility and honesty before Him.

A willing heart does not pretend to have everything together. It comes openly, aware of its need for God's mercy and guidance. This kind of heart listens, repents, and learns. God does not reject weakness brought to Him: He receives it.

God's work often begins in quiet moments of surrender. When pride is set aside and hearts soften, space is made for God to shape, restore, and lead. Growth rooted in humility lasts longer than growth driven by performance.

For families, this truth changes the atmosphere of faith at home. It reminds everyone that mistakes are not the end of the story. A home shaped by humility becomes a place where forgiveness is practiced, grace is extended, and hearts are continually turned back toward God.

Let us take a few minutes to talk together about the following:

1. What does it mean to come to God with a willing and humble heart?
2. Why do you think God values humility so deeply?
3. How does honesty before God help us grow?
4. How can our family create space for humility and grace at home?

✐ PRAYER

Merciful God, thank You for welcoming humble hearts. Thank You for not turning away from us when we come honestly before You. Forgive us when pride or fear keeps us from surrendering fully. Help our family walk humbly with You and trust You to shape our hearts. Amen.

⚖ FAMILY ACTIVITY

On a scrapbook page, write the title **"A Willing Heart."** Draw a simple heart or open hands. Each family member writes one way they want to come honestly before God this week. Leave space to return later and reflect on how humility brought growth, healing, or peace.

Pouring Our Hearts Out Before God

"Trust in him at all times, O people; pour out your heart before him; God is a refuge for us." – Psalm 62:8

There are moments when words come easily in prayer, and others when they do not. Sometimes prayers are polished and confident. Other times they are quiet, emotional, or unfinished. Scripture reminds us that God invites His people to come honestly, just as they are.

This verse does not call for perfect words or carefully arranged thoughts. It calls for trust. To pour out the heart is to bring everything, joy, fear, confusion, gratitude, into God's presence without holding back. God is not unsettled by honest prayer. He welcomes it.

God is described here as a refuge, a place of safety rather than judgment. When His people come to Him openly, they are not turned away. Instead, they find shelter in His faithfulness. Trust grows as hearts learn that God listens and cares deeply.

For families, this truth shapes how prayer is practiced at home. It teaches children that prayer is not about sounding right, but about being real. It reminds adults that God already knows what is in the heart and still invites conversation. A family that learns to pray honestly together grows in trust, humility, and dependence on God.

Let us take a few minutes to talk together about the following:

1. What does it mean to pour out your heart before God?
2. Why is honesty important in prayer?
3. How does knowing God is a refuge change the way we pray?
4. How can our family practice more honest prayer together?

PRAYER

Faithful God, thank You for inviting us to come to You with open hearts. Thank You for being a refuge where we are safe to speak honestly. Forgive us when we hide our fears or try to sound stronger than we are. Help our family trust You fully and bring everything to You in prayer. Amen.

FAMILY ACTIVITY

On a scrapbook page, write the title **"Honest Prayer."** Draw an open heart or open hands. Each family member writes one thing they want to bring honestly before God this week, whether a joy, a worry, or a question. Leave space to return later and reflect on how God provided comfort, peace, or clarity.

May 6
Holding Fast to God's Word

"I have treasured the words of his mouth more than my portion of food." – Job 23:12

There are moments when God feels distant, when answers are unclear and prayers seem to linger unanswered. Job spoke these words during a season like that. Even in confusion and suffering, he held tightly to what he knew about God: His word.

This verse does not come from a place of comfort or ease. It comes from deep trust. Job valued God's words above physical provision, not because life was easy, but because God's truth remained steady when everything else felt uncertain.

God's Word nourishes the heart in ways nothing else can. It reminds His people who He is when circumstances suggest otherwise. Holding fast to His Word is an act of faith, especially when understanding is limited and emotions are strained.

For families, this truth encourages consistency. God's Word is not only for moments of clarity, but for seasons of uncertainty. Reading, remembering, and trusting Scripture together helps anchor the home in truth that does not change, even when life does.

Let us take a few minutes to talk together about the following:

1. Why do you think Job valued God's words so highly?
2. How can God's Word strengthen us during difficult seasons?
3. What makes it challenging to hold onto truth when life feels hard?
4. How can our family treasure God's Word more intentionally?

PRAYER

Faithful God, thank You for giving us Your Word to guide and sustain us. Thank You for truth that remains steady when life feels uncertain. Forgive us when we neglect Your Word or look elsewhere for strength. Help our family treasure what You have spoken and trust You through every season. Amen.

FAMILY ACTIVITY

On a scrapbook page, write the title **"Treasuring God's Word."** Draw a heart around an open Bible. Each family member writes one verse or truth from Scripture that has encouraged them. Leave space to return later and add reflections about how God used His Word during the week.

God Watches Over Our Steps

"The Lord will keep your going out and your coming in from this time forth and forevermore." – Psalm 121:8

Most days are made up of small movements: leaving home, returning again, handling ordinary responsibilities. Scripture reminds us that none of these moments escape God's attention. He watches over both the beginning and the end of each day.

This verse speaks of steady care rather than dramatic rescue. God's protection is constant, not occasional. Whether His people are stepping into the unknown or settling back into the familiar, He remains present. His watchfulness does not depend on circumstance or success.

God's care stretches beyond a single moment. The promise here is ongoing. From now on and forever, God remains faithful. His protection is rooted in His character, not in our awareness of it. Even when His care goes unnoticed, it is never absent.

For families, this truth brings quiet reassurance. Children learn that God is with them wherever they go. Adults are reminded that daily routines are held within God's care. Trusting God with both the coming and going of life allows a family to live with peace rather than anxiety.

Let us take a few minutes to talk together about the following:

1. What does it mean that God watches over our daily steps?
2. Why is it comforting to know God's care is constant?
3. How does this verse change the way we view ordinary days?
4. How can our family trust God more with our daily routines?

PRAYER

Watchful God, thank You for caring for us in every moment of our days. Thank You for guarding our steps and surrounding our lives with Your presence. Forgive us when worry causes us to forget Your care. Help our family trust You with each coming and going, resting in Your faithful protection. Amen.

FAMILY ACTIVITY

On a scrapbook page, write the title **"God Watches Over Us."** Draw a simple path, doorway, or set of footsteps. Each family member writes one place or activity they want to place in God's care this week. Leave space to return later and reflect on how God's presence brought peace or confidence.

May 8
God Sees the Whole Way Ahead

"I know, O Lord, that the way of man is not in himself, that it is not in man who walks to direct his steps." – Jeremiah 10:23

There are times when we want clarity more than anything else. We want to know what comes next, how things will turn out, and whether we are making the right choices. Scripture gently reminds us that full understanding was never meant to rest on our shoulders.

This verse speaks with humility. It acknowledges that direction does not come from human wisdom alone. Even with good intentions, we are limited in what we can see and understand. God, however, sees the full path: every step, every turn, and every outcome.

Trusting God with direction requires surrender. It means admitting that we do not always know the best way forward and choosing to rely on God's guidance instead. This kind of trust grows slowly, shaped by prayer, obedience, and patience over time.

For families, this truth brings relief. Parents are not expected to have every answer. Children are not expected to understand everything immediately. When a family looks to God for direction together, uncertainty becomes a place where faith can grow rather than fear.

Let us take a few minutes to talk together about the following:

1. Why do you think God does not give us the full picture all at once?
2. What does this verse teach us about human limitation and God's wisdom?
3. How does relying on God change the way we face decisions?
4. Where does our family need to ask God for direction right now?

✎ PRAYER

Wise God, thank You for seeing what we cannot see. Thank You for guiding our steps with care and purpose. Forgive us when we try to rely only on our own understanding. Help our family trust You more fully and follow Your leading, even when the way forward is unclear. Amen.

⚨ FAMILY ACTIVITY

On a scrapbook page, write the title **"God Directs Our Steps."** Draw a winding path or a compass. Each family member writes one decision or situation they are placing in God's hands. Leave space to return later and reflect on how God provided guidance, clarity, or peace.

May 9
The Lord Hears the Cry of His People

"I waited patiently for the Lord; he inclined to me and heard my cry." – Psalm 40:1

Waiting can be one of the hardest parts of faith. When prayers feel unanswered and situations remain unchanged, it is easy to wonder if God is listening. Scripture offers reassurance: God does hear, and He does respond, even when the timing feels slow.

This verse speaks from experience, not theory. The psalmist waited, not because waiting was easy, but because he trusted God's character. God's response was not rushed, yet it was personal. He inclined Himself, He paid attention and acted with care.

God's listening is not passive. He does not overlook the cries of His people or grow weary of their prayers. His timing reflects wisdom, not indifference. When He responds, it is purposeful and rooted in love.

For families, this truth brings comfort during seasons of waiting. Children learn that prayer is not ignored, even when answers take time. Adults are reminded that persistence in prayer is an act of trust. As families wait together, faith deepens, and hope remains anchored in God's faithfulness.

Let us take a few minutes to talk together about the following:

1. Why is waiting on God sometimes difficult?
2. What does this verse show us about how God responds to prayer?
3. How can patience strengthen our trust in God?
4. Where might our family need to wait on the Lord right now?

✎ PRAYER

Listening God, thank You for hearing the cries of Your people. Thank You for inclining Your ear toward us with care and compassion. Forgive us when impatience weakens our trust. Help our family wait faithfully, confident that You hear us and will respond in Your perfect time. Amen.

⛪ FAMILY ACTIVITY

On a scrapbook page, write the title **"Waiting and Trusting."** Draw an ear, a heart, or hands folded in prayer. Each family member writes one prayer they are waiting on God to answer. Leave space to return later and reflect on how God showed His faithfulness during the waiting.

May 10
Noticing the Work of the Lord

"How great are your works, O Lord! Your thoughts are very deep!" – Psalm 92:5

It is easy to move through the day without stopping to notice what God is doing. Life stays busy, routines take over, and attention is often pulled toward what feels urgent rather than what is meaningful. This verse invites us to pause and look again.

The psalmist does not rush past God's work. He reflects on it. God's works are described as great, and His thoughts as deep, beyond quick understanding or surface observation. This reminds us that God is always at work, even when His actions are quiet or unfolding slowly.

Noticing God's work takes intention. It means paying attention to His faithfulness in small things: provision that came at the right time, protection we didn't see until later, lessons learned through difficulty, or peace given in unexpected moments. God's work is often clearer in reflection than in the moment.

For families, learning to notice God's work together builds gratitude and awareness. It teaches children to look beyond circumstances and helps adults slow down and recognize God's presence. A family that reflects on what God has done grows in faith, humility, and trust.

Let us take a few minutes to talk together about the following:

1. What are some ways God has been at work in our lives recently?
2. Why do you think it can be hard to notice God's work right away?
3. What does this verse teach us about God's wisdom and care?
4. How can our family become more attentive to what God is doing each day?

✎ PRAYER

Great and faithful God, thank You for the work You are doing in our lives, even when we do not always notice it. Thank You for Your wisdom and care that go deeper than we understand. Forgive us when we rush past Your blessings or forget to reflect on Your faithfulness. Help our family slow down, pay attention, and live with grateful hearts. Amen.

⚜ FAMILY ACTIVITY

On a scrapbook page, write the title **"Where We See God at Work."** Divide the page into sections labeled Provision, Protection, Growth, and Answered Prayer. Each family member writes or draws one example of God's work they have noticed recently. Leave space to add more throughout the week.

May 11

God Teaches Us to Live With Gratitude

"Give thanks to the Lord, for he is good, for his steadfast love endures forever." –
Psalm 107:1

Gratitude does not always come easily. It is often shaped by circumstances, strong when life feels smooth, weaker when challenges arise. Scripture, however, anchors gratitude not in what is happening around us, but in who God is. He is good, and His love does not run out.

This verse calls God's people to give thanks because of His character, not because everything feels right. God's steadfast love remains firm through joy, struggle, obedience, and failure. Gratitude, then, becomes an act of faith. It is a way of remembering what does not change when much else does.

Throughout Scripture, God's people were reminded to look back and give thanks. Remembering God's faithfulness helped them trust Him again in the present. Gratitude kept their hearts from becoming hardened by worry or distracted by discontent.

For families, practicing gratitude shapes the atmosphere of the home. It encourages contentment, patience, and humility. When families learn to thank God together, especially in ordinary moments, they grow more aware of His presence and more confident in His enduring love.

Let us take a few minutes to talk together about the following:

1. Why does God call His people to give thanks even during difficult times?
2. What does this verse teach us about God's love?
3. How can gratitude change our attitude and perspective?
4. What are some ways our family can practice gratitude daily?

✎ PRAYER

Good and faithful God, thank You for Your steadfast love that never ends. Thank You for Your goodness in every season of life. Forgive us when we focus more on what is lacking than on what You have given. Help our family grow in gratitude and learn to give thanks in all circumstances. Amen.

♟ FAMILY ACTIVITY

On a scrapbook page, write the title **"Grateful Hearts."** Each family member writes or draws three things they are thankful for today. Encourage everyone to include both big and small blessings. Leave space to add more throughout the week as reminders of God's enduring goodness.

May 12

Learning to Rest in God's Care

"Be still before the Lord and wait patiently for him." – Psalm 37:7

Stillness is not something most of us choose easily. We are used to filling silence with activity and waiting with worry. Scripture invites God's people into something different, not inactivity, but trust. Being still before the Lord is a posture of the heart, not simply a lack of movement.

This verse connects stillness with patience. It reminds us that waiting on God is not wasted time. When we are still, we stop trying to manage everything ourselves and allow God to work in ways we cannot see. Stillness creates space for trust to grow.

God does not rush His purposes. Throughout Scripture, He worked through seasons of waiting, shaping hearts while circumstances unfolded slowly. Those moments of stillness often prepared His people for what came next, even when they did not realize it at the time.

For families, learning to rest in God's care brings peace into daily life. It teaches children that they do not need to have everything figured out and reminds adults that control is not the same as security. When a family practices stillness together, it becomes easier to listen, trust, and move forward with confidence in God.

Let us take a few minutes to talk together about the following:

1. Why is it difficult to be still and wait patiently?
2. What does stillness before God look like in everyday life?
3. How can waiting help us grow in trust?
4. Where might our family need to practice stillness right now?

✧ PRAYER

Faithful God, thank You for inviting us to be still before You. Thank You for caring for us while we wait. Forgive us when impatience or worry takes over. Help our family learn to rest in Your care and trust Your timing in every season. Amen.

▲ FAMILY ACTIVITY

On a scrapbook page, write the title **"Still Before the Lord."** Draw a calm scene such as water, a quiet room, or folded hands. Each family member writes one area where they are choosing to wait patiently on God. Leave space to return later and reflect on how God brought peace or clarity during the waiting.

May 13

God Draws Near to Those Who Fear Him

"The friendship of the Lord is for those who fear him, and he makes known to them his covenant." – Psalm 25:14

This verse speaks of a closeness that grows out of reverence. To fear the Lord is not to be afraid of Him, but to honor Him with humility and trust. Scripture tells us that God responds to this kind of heart by drawing near.

God does not reveal Himself casually. Throughout Scripture, He shared His ways with those who approached Him with respect and obedience. This verse reminds us that knowing God is not merely about learning facts, but about relationship. God makes Himself known to those who desire to walk closely with Him.

Reverence slows us down. It helps us listen more carefully and depend less on our own understanding. When hearts are rightly aligned toward God, He gives clarity, direction, and assurance according to His will.

For families, this truth shapes how faith is practiced at home. Teaching children to respect God's holiness while trusting His goodness builds a balanced view of who He is. As families grow in reverence together, their understanding of God deepens, not through effort alone, but through relationship shaped by trust and obedience.

Let us take a few minutes to talk together about the following:

1. What does it mean to fear the Lord in a healthy way?
2. Why do you think God draws near to those who honor Him?
3. How does reverence help us grow closer to God?
4. What can our family do to show respect and trust toward God this week?

📖 PRAYER

Holy and faithful God, thank You for inviting us into a close relationship with You. Thank You for revealing Your ways to those who honor You. Forgive us when we approach You casually or forget Your holiness. Help our family grow in reverence, trust, and a deeper knowledge of who You are. Amen.

⛪ FAMILY ACTIVITY

On a scrapbook page, write the title **"Growing Closer to God."** Draw a heart and a pathway leading toward it. Each family member writes one way they want to honor God more intentionally: through obedience, prayer, or trust. Leave space to return later and reflect on how drawing near to God shaped your family's week.

May 14

The Lord Lifts Those Who Are Weak

"The Lord upholds all who are falling and raises up all who are bowed down." –
Psalm 145:14

There are seasons when strength feels out of reach. Not because of one dramatic moment, but because the weight of ordinary life slowly presses in. Scripture speaks gently into those moments, reminding us that God notices when His people are struggling to stand.

This verse paints a quiet picture of God's care. He does not ignore those who are slipping or bowed down. He upholds them. He lifts them. God's help is not reserved for the strong; it is given to those who are weary and in need of support.

God's faithfulness is often revealed in small acts of sustaining grace. He steadies those who feel unsteady and gives relief to those who are weighed down. His help may not always look dramatic, but it is constant and purposeful.

For families, this truth brings reassurance and honesty. Everyone has moments of weakness, children and adults alike. Learning to bring those moments to God builds trust and humility. When a family depends on God together, weakness becomes a place where faith grows rather than a source of shame.

Let us take a few minutes to talk together about the following:

1. What does this verse teach us about how God responds to weakness?
2. Why is it comforting to know that God lifts those who are bowed down?
3. How does relying on God change the way we face difficult days?
4. How can our family support one another while trusting God's help?

PRAYER

Faithful God, thank You for lifting us when we feel weak and worn down. Thank You for seeing us when we struggle and for holding us steady. Forgive us when we try to carry everything on our own. Help our family rely on You and trust Your faithful care each day. Amen.

FAMILY ACTIVITY

On a scrapbook page, write the title **"Lifted by the Lord."** Draw hands lifting something gently. Each family member writes one area where they need God's help or strength right now. Leave space to return later and reflect on how God provided support, encouragement, or peace.

May 15

Learning to Trust God With Tomorrow

"Do not boast about tomorrow, for you do not know what a day may bring." –
Proverbs 27:1

There is a natural desire to plan ahead. We think about what needs to be done, what might go wrong, and how to prepare for what comes next. Scripture does not say planning is wrong, but it gently reminds us of our limits. We do not control tomorrow: God does.

This verse calls us to humility. It reminds us that each day is given, not guaranteed. Trusting God with tomorrow does not mean ignoring responsibility; it means holding plans loosely and placing confidence in God rather than outcomes.

God alone sees what lies ahead. What feels uncertain to us is already known to Him. When His people learn to trust Him with the future, anxiety begins to loosen its grip. Faith grows as hearts rest in the truth that God will be present in whatever tomorrow brings.

For families, this truth shapes everyday conversations and attitudes. Children often worry about what is coming next, and adults do too, even if they hide it better. Learning to trust God together, one day at a time, builds peace, patience, and confidence rooted in His faithfulness rather than in plans or predictions.

Let us take a few minutes to talk together about the following:

1. Why do you think it is easy to worry about tomorrow?
2. What does this verse teach us about our need for humility?
3. How does trusting God with the future bring peace today?
4. What concerns about tomorrow can our family place in God's hands right now?

📕 PRAYER

Faithful God, thank You for holding tomorrow in Your hands. Thank You for reminding us that our lives depend on You, not on our plans. Forgive us when worry about the future steals our peace. Help our family trust You one day at a time and rest in Your care for what lies ahead. Amen.

♟ FAMILY ACTIVITY

On a scrapbook page, write the title **"Trusting God With Tomorrow."** Draw a calendar page with tomorrow circled or an open road ahead. Each family member writes one concern about the future they are choosing to give to God. Leave space to return later and reflect on how trusting God brought peace or clarity.

May 16
Passing Faith Along at Home

"You shall teach them to your children, talking of them when you are sitting in your house, and when you are walking by the way, and when you lie down, and when you rise." – Deuteronomy 11:19

Faith in Scripture is not meant to stay contained within formal moments. It is woven into everyday life: spoken, observed, and lived out in ordinary rhythms. This verse paints a picture of faith being shared naturally, as part of daily conversation and family routine.

God did not instruct parents to teach faith only at specific times or in perfect settings. Instead, He placed faith in the flow of life, at the table, on the road, at the beginning and end of each day. This kind of teaching happens through presence, consistency, and example.

Passing faith along does not require flawless knowledge or carefully planned lessons. It grows through honest conversations, prayer in real moments, and children watching adults rely on God in both joy and difficulty. God uses faith lived out imperfectly but sincerely.

For families, this truth brings freedom. Faith does not have to feel forced or formal. When God is spoken of naturally and trusted openly, the home becomes a place where faith is learned through relationship. Over time, these shared moments shape hearts in lasting ways.

Let us take a few minutes to talk together about the following:

1. Why do you think God wanted faith taught in everyday moments?
2. What are some natural times our family already talks together?
3. How can our actions teach faith as much as our words?
4. What is one simple way we can talk about God more naturally at home?

PRAYER

Faithful God, thank You for placing faith within the rhythms of everyday life. Thank You for calling families to share Your truth through words and actions. Forgive us when we separate faith from daily living. Help our family speak of You naturally, trust You openly, and pass faith along with love and sincerity. Amen.

FAMILY ACTIVITY

On a scrapbook page, write the title **"Faith in Our Everyday Life."** Divide the page into sections labeled Morning, Mealtime, On the Go, and Evening. Each family member writes one way faith can be shared during those moments. Leave space to add reflections later about how these conversations grew over time.

May 17
God Remains Faithful Through Family Trials

"The Lord was with Joseph, and he became a successful man, and he was in the house of his Egyptian master." – Genesis 39:2

Joseph's life changed quickly and painfully. Betrayed by his brothers and taken far from home, he found himself alone in a foreign land. Yet this verse offers a quiet but powerful truth: the Lord was with Joseph. God's presence did not depend on Joseph's circumstances or the faithfulness of his family.

This moment in Joseph's story comes before restoration, before reunion, and before understanding. God's faithfulness was already at work long before the outcome was clear. Even in hardship, God remained present, guiding and sustaining Joseph through every season.

For families, this truth is comforting. Not every family season is peaceful or predictable. There are moments of misunderstanding, separation, and disappointment. Joseph's story reminds us that God does not withdraw when family relationships are strained. He remains close, working patiently beyond what we can see.

God's faithfulness often shows itself quietly. It may appear through endurance, growth in character, or unexpected opportunities. Like Joseph, families may not immediately see how God is working, but His presence never leaves. Trust grows as families learn to look for God's faithfulness even in difficult chapters.

Let us take a few minutes to talk together about the following:

1. What does this verse tell us about God's presence in hard situations?
2. Why do you think God stayed with Joseph even when his family failed him?
3. How does knowing God is present bring comfort during family challenges?
4. Where might our family need to trust that God is still with us?

✎ PRAYER

Faithful God, thank You for staying with Your people through every season of life. Thank You for being present even when family relationships are strained or painful. Forgive us when hardship makes us doubt Your nearness. Help our family trust that You are always with us, working with purpose and care. Amen.

⛄ FAMILY ACTIVITY

On a scrapbook page, write the title **"God Is With Us."** Draw a simple house or a heart surrounded by light. Each family member writes one situation where they need to remember that God is present. Leave space to return later and reflect on how God showed His faithfulness over time.

God Helps Us to Be Brave

"Fear not, for I am with you; be not dismayed, for I am your God; I will strengthen you." – Isaiah 41:10

Strength is something we all need, especially when life feels overwhelming. Isaiah 41:10 reminds us that God Himself gives strength to His people. Families should take comfort in His promise to hold them up when they feel weak.

The Bible shows God giving strength in many ways. He gave Joshua courage to lead Israel into the Promised Land. He gave David power to defeat Goliath. He gave Paul endurance to preach the gospel despite persecution.

God's strength is not only physical. It includes courage, patience, and perseverance. Isaiah 40:29 says, "He gives power to the faint, and to him who has no might he increases strength." Families should remember that God strengthens them for every challenge.

Paul learned this truth deeply. In 2 Corinthians 12:9, God told him, "My grace is sufficient for you, for my power is made perfect in weakness." Weakness is not failure, it is an opportunity for God's strength to be revealed.

Living in God's strength means admitting our need and trusting His supply. Families should pray daily for strength to face trials, resist temptation, and serve faithfully.

Let's discuss the following questions for the next two to three minutes:

1. What does Isaiah 41:10 teach us about God's strength?
2. What examples of God's strength do we see in Scripture?
3. What does it mean for God's power to be made perfect in weakness?
4. Where does our family need His strength this week?

✍ PRAYER

Mighty God, thank You for promising to strengthen us. Thank You for being near when we feel weak. Forgive us when we try to live in our own power. Teach our family to rely on You for every need. Amen.

⚑ FAMILY ACTIVITY

On a scrapbook page, draw a tree with deep roots. Each family member writes on a branch one area where they need God's strength. Title the page "God Our Strength."

May 19
Finding Shelter in the Faithfulness of God

"For you have been a stronghold for me, a shelter from the storm." – Psalm 61:3

Life does not always unfold gently. There are moments when circumstances feel overwhelming and steady ground seems hard to find. Scripture does not deny the presence of storms. Instead, it points us to where true safety is found: in God Himself.

This verse speaks of God as a stronghold, a place of protection and refuge. A stronghold is not temporary shelter; it is a secure place built to withstand pressure. When God's people run to Him, they find stability that does not shift with circumstances.

God's faithfulness becomes especially clear in difficult seasons. He does not always remove the storm right away, but He provides shelter within it. His presence steadies hearts, guards faith, and reminds His people that they are not facing hardship alone.

For families, this truth offers reassurance and grounding. Children need to know where safety lies when emotions run high or situations feel uncertain. Adults need the reminder as well. When a family learns to turn to God as their refuge, trust grows and fear loses its hold.

Let us take a few minutes to talk together about the following:

1.   What does it mean for God to be a shelter or stronghold?
2.   Why is it important to run to God during difficult times?
3.   How have you seen God provide refuge in hard moments?
4.   How can our family turn to God more quickly when challenges arise?

PRAYER

Faithful God, thank You for being our shelter and stronghold. Thank You for guarding us when life feels uncertain. Forgive us when fear causes us to look elsewhere for safety. Help our family learn to run to You, trusting Your presence to steady our hearts in every season. Amen.

FAMILY ACTIVITY

On a scrapbook page, write the title **"God Our Shelter."** Draw a house, fortress, or umbrella. Each family member writes one situation where they are trusting God to protect and sustain them. Leave space to return later and reflect on how God provided peace, strength, or reassurance.

Placing Our Plans in God's Hands

"The plans of the heart belong to man, but the answer of the tongue is from the Lord."
– Proverbs 16:1

Most of us plan without thinking much about it. We plan our days, our weeks, our responses, even our words. Planning itself is not the problem. Scripture makes room for that. What this verse gently reminds us is that plans are not the same thing as control.

We may decide what we hope will happen, but God is the One who determines how things unfold. That can feel uncomfortable. We like certainty. We like knowing how things will turn out. Yet God, in His wisdom, keeps the final outcome in His hands.

This truth invites humility. It reminds us that even our best intentions need to be surrendered to God. Sometimes He affirms our plans. Other times He redirects them. And sometimes He simply asks us to wait and trust Him with what we cannot predict.

For families, this shows up in everyday ways. Plans change. Expectations shift. Things don't always go the way we hoped. Learning to acknowledge God in the middle of that teaches children, and adults, that trust is not about getting the result we want, but about believing God is still at work when plans fall apart.

Let us take a few minutes to talk together about the following:

1. Why do you think we like to hold tightly to our plans?
2. How does this verse help us think differently about control?
3. What is a time when a change in plans turned out to be for good?
4. What plans does our family need to place more fully in God's hands right now?

✐ PRAYER

Faithful God, thank You for caring about every part of our lives, even the plans we make. Thank You for guiding outcomes with wisdom we cannot see. Forgive us when we cling too tightly to our own expectations. Help our family trust You with our plans, our words, and what comes next. Amen.

♟ FAMILY ACTIVITY

On a scrapbook page, write the title **"Trusting God With Our Plans."** Draw a list or calendar with an eraser beside it. Each family member writes one plan they are willing to surrender to God this week. Leave space to return later and reflect on how trusting God changed your perspective, even if the outcome wasn't what you expected.

May 21
Remembering That the Lord Is With Us

"Then Haggai, the messenger of the Lord, spoke to the people with the Lord's message, 'I am with you, declares the Lord.'" – Haggai 1:13

God's words in this verse are simple, but they carry deep weight. The people had been discouraged. Progress was slow, obedience felt costly, and motivation had faded. In the middle of that weariness, God did not begin with correction or instruction. He began with reassurance: I am with you.

Sometimes faith falters not because God's people stop believing, but because they forget they are not alone. God knew this about His people then, and He knows it now. His presence is not reserved for moments of success or confidence. He draws near when hearts are tired and unsure.

God's promise to be with His people did not remove their responsibility, but it changed how they faced it. Knowing God was present gave them courage to continue. His presence did not make the work easy, but it made obedience possible.

For families, this truth speaks gently but powerfully. There are seasons when parenting feels heavy, conversations are hard, or spiritual growth feels slow. Remembering that God is with us reshapes those moments. Faith becomes less about pressure and more about perseverance, grounded in God's faithful presence.

Let us take a few minutes to talk together about the following:

1. Why do you think God reminded His people that He was with them?
2. How does God's presence change the way we face difficult responsibilities?
3. When have you needed reassurance that God was near?
4. How can our family remind one another that God is with us this week?

PRAYER

Faithful God, thank You for staying with Your people in every season. Thank You for reminding us that we are not alone when faith feels difficult. Forgive us when discouragement causes us to forget Your nearness. Help our family move forward with confidence, trusting that You are with us always. Amen.

FAMILY ACTIVITY

On a scrapbook page, write the title **"God Is With Us."** Draw a simple house, heart, or path. Each family member writes one situation where they need to remember God's presence. Leave space to return later and reflect on how knowing God was near brought courage, peace, or perseverance.

May 22

Learning to Be Still Before a Holy God

"But the Lord is in his holy temple; let all the earth keep silence before him." –
Habakkuk 2:20

This verse does not rush the reader forward. It calls for stillness. In a world filled with noise, opinions, and constant movement, Scripture pauses us and reminds us where God is, and who He is.

Habakkuk wrote during a time of confusion and injustice. Questions were unanswered, and God's ways were difficult to understand. Yet this verse does not explain everything. Instead, it re-centers the heart. God is in His holy temple. He is not absent. He is not unaware. He reigns.

Silence before God is not empty or passive. It is an act of reverence. It acknowledges that God is greater than our understanding and wiser than our conclusions. In silence, trust grows, not because every question is resolved, but because God remains sovereign.

For families, this truth invites a different posture toward faith. Not every moment requires explanation or instruction. Sometimes faith is practiced by pausing together: quieting hearts, listening, and remembering who God is. A home that learns reverence becomes a place where humility and awe shape daily life.

Let us take a few minutes to talk together about the following:

1. Why do you think Scripture calls for silence before God?
2. What does this verse teach us about God's holiness and authority?
3. Why is it hard to be still and quiet before God?
4. How can our family practice reverence and stillness together?

✐ PRAYER

Holy God, thank You for reminding us of Your greatness and authority. Thank You for being present and reigning, even when we do not understand everything. Forgive us when noise and busyness crowd out reverence. Help our family learn to be still before You, honoring You with quiet trust and humility. Amen.

♟ FAMILY ACTIVITY

On a scrapbook page, write the title **"Still Before the Lord."** Create a simple design using calm images such as a candle, temple, or quiet sky. As a family, spend one minute in silence together before writing. Each person then writes one word that describes how remembering God's holiness shapes their faith.

May 23

The Lord Preserves What Belongs to Him

"But in Mount Zion there shall be those who escape, and it shall be holy, and the house of Jacob shall possess their own possessions." – Obadiah 1:17

This short verse comes from a small book, but it carries a strong message of hope. It speaks of preservation, of God keeping what belongs to Him, even when circumstances seem uncertain or hostile. God's people were not forgotten, overlooked, or erased. They were protected according to His promise.

Obadiah spoke during a time when God's people felt threatened and displaced. The future looked fragile. Yet God declared that there would be a place of safety, a space set apart, where His purposes would stand. What God promised to His people would not be lost.

God's preservation is not always loud or immediate. Sometimes it unfolds quietly, over time. But Scripture reminds us that God remains faithful to what He has established. What He declares holy, He guards. What He promises, He keeps.

For families, this truth brings reassurance. There are seasons when stability feels uncertain: when routines change, challenges arise, or the future feels unclear. Remembering that God preserves His people helps families trust that their lives are held securely in His care, even when circumstances shift.

Let us take a few minutes to talk together about the following:

1. What does this verse teach us about God's faithfulness to His people?
2. Why is it comforting to know that God preserves what belongs to Him?
3. How does God's protection look different from what we might expect?
4. Where does our family need to trust God's keeping power right now?

✏ PRAYER

Faithful God, thank You for preserving what belongs to You. Thank You for guarding Your people and keeping Your promises secure. Forgive us when fear causes us to doubt Your care. Help our family trust that You are at work, protecting and sustaining us according to Your will. Amen.

♟ FAMILY ACTIVITY

On a scrapbook page, write the title **"Kept by the Lord."** Draw a circle around your family's name or a simple symbol of protection. Each family member writes one thing they are thankful God has preserved: faith, relationships, provision, or peace. Leave space to return later and reflect on how God's faithfulness became evident over time.

May 24
Finding Refuge Under the Care of God

"The Lord repay you for what you have done, and a full reward be given you by the Lord, the God of Israel, under whose wings you have come to take refuge." – Ruth 2:12

This verse was spoken during a quiet conversation, not a dramatic moment. Ruth had walked a hard road, leaving her homeland, losing security, and stepping into an uncertain future. Yet her faith was recognized. She had chosen to seek refuge under the care of the Lord.

The image here is tender and powerful. God is described as One who shelters, like wings covering what is fragile. Refuge does not mean the absence of hardship. It means protection, belonging, and care in the middle of uncertainty. Ruth's story shows that God sees faith expressed through trust and obedience, even when the path is unfamiliar.

God often works through ordinary faithfulness. Ruth did not know how her story would unfold, but she trusted God enough to keep walking forward. God honored that trust, not because she earned His care, but because He is faithful to those who seek Him.

For families, this truth offers reassurance. There are seasons when decisions feel risky and outcomes unclear. Choosing to trust God's care, together, creates a sense of safety that does not depend on circumstances. A family that seeks refuge in God learns to rest, knowing they are held under His watchful care.

Let us take a few minutes to talk together about the following:

1. What does it mean to take refuge under God's care?
2. Why do you think God values quiet faithfulness like Ruth's?
3. How does trusting God bring peace during uncertain seasons?
4. Where does our family need to seek God's refuge right now?

🪧 PRAYER

Caring God, thank You for being our refuge and shelter. Thank You for watching over those who trust in You. Forgive us when fear causes us to rely on our own strength. Help our family rest under Your care, confident that You see us and will provide according to Your will. Amen.

⛄ FAMILY ACTIVITY

On a scrapbook page, write the title **"Under God's Wings."** Draw wings, a shelter, or a heart surrounded by protection. Each family member writes one situation where they are choosing to trust God's care instead of giving in to worry. Leave space to return later and reflect on how God provided peace, guidance, or reassurance.

May 25

Strength That Comes From the Lord Alone

"Do not be grieved, for the joy of the Lord is your strength." – Nehemiah 8:10

These words were spoken to God's people at a moment of deep emotion. They had just heard God's law read aloud and were overwhelmed by how far they had fallen short. Instead of allowing sorrow to consume them, God reminded them where true strength was found, not in their resolve, but in His joy.

The joy of the Lord is not shallow happiness. It is rooted in who God is: faithful, merciful, and present with His people. This joy does not ignore repentance or hardship. It follows forgiveness and restoration. It strengthens hearts that might otherwise remain weighed down by guilt or fear.

God's joy gives endurance. When His people remember His goodness and faithfulness, they find renewed strength to continue walking in obedience. This strength does not come from pretending everything is fine, but from trusting that God is at work even after failure.

For families, this truth offers freedom. Homes are filled with mistakes, learning moments, and growing pains. Remembering that strength comes from the Lord's joy helps families move forward with hope rather than discouragement. It teaches both children and adults that God's grace restores and strengthens, allowing joy to shape the days ahead.

Let us take a few minutes to talk together about the following:

1. What do you think it means that God's joy gives us strength?
2. Why is it important to remember God's joy after moments of failure or regret?
3. How does focusing on God's faithfulness renew our hearts?
4. How can our family choose joy rooted in God rather than in circumstances?

📘 PRAYER

Joy-giving God, thank You for strengthening Your people through Your joy. Thank You for restoring us with grace rather than leaving us in discouragement. Forgive us when we dwell on failure instead of trusting Your mercy. Help our family find strength in who You are and walk forward with renewed hope. Amen.

☰ FAMILY ACTIVITY

On a scrapbook page, write the title **"Strength Through God's Joy."** Draw a heart or a sun breaking through clouds. Each family member writes one way they have seen God's goodness recently, even in a challenging season. Leave space to return later and reflect on how remembering God's joy brought renewed strength.

Remembering the Mercy of Our God

"Who is a God like you, pardoning iniquity and passing over transgression for the remnant of his inheritance? He does not retain his anger forever, because he delights in steadfast love." – Micah 7:18

This verse begins with a question, and it is meant to slow us down. Who is a God like You? Micah was pointing God's people back to something they easily forgot: God's mercy is unmatched.

God is described here not as holding tightly to anger, but as delighting in steadfast love. That does not mean sin is ignored or taken lightly. It means mercy has the final word. God chooses forgiveness and restoration because love is part of who He is.

Throughout Scripture, God showed patience with His people even when they failed repeatedly. He corrected them, but He did not abandon them. His mercy made room for repentance and renewal. This verse reminds us that God's heart is inclined toward compassion.

For families, this truth is deeply grounding. Homes are places where mistakes happen, words are misused, and patience is tested. Remembering God's mercy shapes how forgiveness is practiced at home. When families reflect God's mercy, grace becomes a regular part of daily life rather than a rare response.

Let us take a few minutes to talk together about the following:

1. What does this verse teach us about God's character?
2. Why is it important to remember that God delights in steadfast love?
3. How does God's mercy change the way we respond to failure?
4. How can our family reflect God's mercy toward one another this week?

✒ PRAYER

Merciful God, thank You for Your steadfast love and forgiveness. Thank You for not holding onto anger but inviting us into restoration. Forgive us when we forget Your mercy or fail to show it to others. Help our family live in light of Your grace and reflect Your compassion each day. Amen.

♟ FAMILY ACTIVITY

On a scrapbook page, write the title **"Living in God's Mercy."** Draw a heart or an open circle. Each family member writes one way they can show mercy or forgiveness this week. Leave space to return later and reflect on how choosing grace strengthened your family relationships.

May 27

Living as People Who Love Truth and Peace

"Therefore love truth and peace." – Zechariah 8:19

These words come from a season when God's people were rebuilding: physically, spiritually, and relationally. Life had not been simple, and trust needed to be restored. In the middle of that work, God gave clear instruction, not a long list of rules, but a guiding call: love truth and peace.

Truth and peace belong together. Truth without peace can become harsh. Peace without truth can become shallow. God calls His people to hold both closely, allowing honesty and wholeness to shape how they live and relate to one another.

Loving truth means walking honestly before God and others, even when it is uncomfortable. Loving peace means seeking unity, patience, and reconciliation rather than conflict or control. These are not passive qualities. They require intentional choices shaped by obedience to God.

For families, this verse speaks directly into everyday life. Homes are built through conversations, corrections, and countless small interactions. When truth and peace are valued together, trust grows. Children learn that honesty matters and that relationships are protected through gentleness and care. A family shaped by truth and peace reflects God's heart in practical ways.

Let us take a few minutes to talk together about the following:

1. Why do you think God connects truth and peace in this verse?

2. What can happen when one is present without the other?

3. How do truth and peace help strengthen relationships at home?

4. What is one way our family can practice truth and peace together this week?

🔖 PRAYER

God of truth and peace, thank You for guiding Your people with wisdom and care. Thank You for showing us how to live in ways that honor You and strengthen relationships. Forgive us when we choose conflict over peace or avoid truth out of fear. Help our family love truth and peace, reflecting Your character in our home. Amen.

👪 FAMILY ACTIVITY

On a scrapbook page, write the title **"Truth and Peace in Our Home."** Divide the page into two sections labeled Truth and Peace. Each family member writes one way they can practice honesty and one way they can promote peace this week. Leave space to return later and reflect on how these choices shaped your family's interactions.

May 28
Speaking Faithfully About the Lord Together

"Then those who feared the Lord spoke with one another. The Lord paid attention and heard them, and a book of remembrance was written before him of those who feared the Lord and esteemed his name." – Malachi 3:16

This verse offers a quiet but meaningful picture. God's people were talking with one another about Him: sharing concern, hope, and reverence. Their conversations were not overlooked. Scripture tells us that the Lord listened and remembered.

Faith is often strengthened through shared words. When God's people speak openly about who He is and what He has done, encouragement grows. These conversations may not feel dramatic or public, but God values them deeply. He pays attention to hearts that honor Him together.

Malachi reminds us that God notices more than actions. He notices speech shaped by reverence and trust. Words spoken in faith, especially during uncertain or difficult times, become part of a testimony God remembers.

For families, this truth highlights the importance of everyday conversation. Talking about God does not have to be formal or scripted. It can happen during meals, car rides, or moments of reflection. When families speak about the Lord together, faith becomes part of daily life, and children learn that God is central to both belief and conversation.

Let us take a few minutes to talk together about the following:

1. Why do you think God values conversations that honor Him?
2. How can talking about God strengthen faith within a family?
3. What are some natural moments when our family could speak about God more often?
4. How does knowing God listens change the way we talk about Him?

PRAYER

Attentive God, thank You for listening to Your people and remembering those who honor You. Thank You for caring about the words we share and the faith we express together. Forgive us when we neglect to speak of You in our daily lives. Help our family talk about You naturally, with reverence and gratitude, trusting that You are near and listening. Amen.

FAMILY ACTIVITY

On a scrapbook page, write the title **"Talking About the Lord."** Draw speech bubbles or a simple table scene. Each family member writes one thing they are thankful to God for or one way they have seen Him at work recently. Leave space to add more throughout the week as conversations continue.

May 29
God Is Righteous

"For the Lord is righteous; he loves righteous deeds; the upright shall behold his face."
– Psalm 11:7

Righteousness means being perfectly good, pure, and just. Psalm 11:7 declares that the Lord is righteous and loves righteous deeds. Families should rejoice in knowing that everything God does is right.

The Bible shows God's righteousness throughout history. He judged Pharaoh's oppression, punished Israel's idolatry, and upheld justice through His law. Unlike people, who are easily swayed, God's righteousness never changes.

The problem is that humanity is not righteous. Romans 3:10 says, "None is righteous, no, not one." Left to ourselves, we fall short of God's standard. But the good news is that Jesus gives His righteousness to those who believe. Second Corinthians 5:21 says, "For our sake he made him to be sin who knew no sin, so that in him we might become the righteousness of God."

Families who trust Jesus are declared righteous before God. This truth should lead to gratitude and holy living. Righteousness is not about earning God's love but responding to it with obedience.

Righteous living in the family means honesty, fairness, kindness, and respect. God loves righteous deeds, and when families live in this way, they reflect His character to the world.

Let us take a few minutes to talk together about the following:

1. What does Psalm 11:7 teach us about God's righteousness?
2. Why does humanity fall short of righteousness?
3. How does Jesus give us His righteousness?
4. What righteous deeds can our family practice this week?

PRAYER

Righteous God, thank You for being perfectly good and just. Thank You for giving us the righteousness of Jesus. Forgive us when we live in sin. Teach our family to walk in righteousness and to reflect Your character. Amen.

FAMILY ACTIVITY

On a scrapbook page titled "Living Righteously," each family member writes one action of honesty or kindness they will do this week.

May 30

Turning Our Hearts Back to the Lord

"For thus says the Lord to the house of Israel: 'Seek me and live.'" – Amos 5:4

These words were spoken during a time when God's people were busy with religious activity but drifting in their hearts. God did not begin with a long explanation. He offered a simple invitation: seek Me. Life, real life, was found there.

Seeking God is more than routine. It is not about keeping up appearances or going through motions. It is about turning the heart toward Him with sincerity and humility. God's call through Amos reminds us that life flows from relationship with Him, not from habits alone.

God speaks this invitation because He desires restoration, not distance. Even when His people wandered, He called them back. Seeking God meant realigning priorities, listening again, and choosing obedience rooted in trust.

For families, this truth is grounding. It reminds us that faith is not something to perform, but something to pursue. In busy seasons, it is easy for hearts to drift even while routines continue. Choosing to seek God together, through prayer, conversation, and obedience, brings renewal and life into the home.

Let us take a few minutes to talk together about the following:

1. What does it mean to truly seek the Lord?
2. Why do you think God connects seeking Him with life?
3. How can routines distract us from genuine faith?
4. What is one way our family can seek God more intentionally right now?

PRAYER

Living God, thank You for inviting Your people to seek You and find life. Thank You for calling us back when our hearts drift. Forgive us when we rely on routine instead of relationship. Help our family seek You with sincerity, trusting that life and renewal are found in You alone. Amen.

FAMILY ACTIVITY

On a scrapbook page, write the title **"Seeking the Lord Together."** Draw a heart turned upward or a path leading forward. Each family member writes one simple way they want to seek God this week, through prayer, obedience, listening, or gratitude. Leave space to return later and reflect on how seeking God brought renewed life and focus.

May 31

Setting Our Hearts to Seek the Lord

"For Ezra had set his heart to study the Law of the Lord, and to do it and to teach his statutes and rules in Israel." – Ezra 7:10

This verse does not describe a moment of emotion or inspiration. It describes a decision. Ezra set his heart. Before teaching, before leading, before acting, his heart was deliberately turned toward the Lord.

Ezra's example reminds us that faith begins internally before it is seen outwardly. Studying God's Word, living it out, and sharing it with others flowed from a heart already committed. His faith was not rushed or accidental. It was shaped by intention and reverence for God.

God often works through people who quietly decide to seek Him first. Ezra's faithfulness did not depend on circumstances being easy. He aligned his heart with God's Word and trusted that obedience would shape everything that followed.

For families, this truth offers a meaningful way to reflect as the month ends. Faith is not built only through big moments, but through steady decisions. When a family chooses to set their hearts toward the Lord, again and again, faith grows naturally, shaping conversations, choices, and relationships over time.

Let us take a few minutes to talk together about the following:

1. What does it mean to "set your heart" toward the Lord?
2. Why do you think Ezra focused on obedience before teaching others?
3. How do our heart decisions shape daily life in a family?
4. What is one way our family can intentionally seek God as we move forward?

📖 PRAYER

Faithful God, thank You for calling Your people to seek You with intention. Thank You for showing us, through Scripture, how a heart devoted to You shapes every part of life. Forgive us when our attention is divided or our priorities drift. Help our family set our hearts toward You, trusting You to guide and shape us each day. Amen.

⚜ FAMILY ACTIVITY

On a scrapbook page, write the title **"Setting Our Hearts Toward God."** Draw a heart with an arrow pointing upward. Each family member writes one way they want to seek God more intentionally, through prayer, obedience, learning, or trust. Leave space to revisit this page later and reflect on how choosing God shaped the days ahead.

JUNE

June 1
God Is Our Creator

"For by him all things were created, in heaven and on earth, visible and invisible." –
Colossians 1:16

The Bible begins with creation and continues to affirm that God made everything. Colossians 1:16 reminds us that all things were created by Christ and for Christ. This truth means life has order, meaning, and purpose.

Creation reveals God's power. The stars, oceans, mountains, and animals all testify that He is mighty and wise. Psalm 19:1 says, "The heavens declare the glory of God, and the sky above proclaims his handiwork." Families can look at the night sky or a blooming flower and see His handiwork.

Creation also reveals God's care. He made people in His image, giving them dignity and responsibility. Genesis 1:27 says, "So God created man in his own image." Families should remember that every person reflects God's image and should be treated with respect.

Jesus is the Creator as well as the Redeemer. John 1:3 says, "All things were made through him." This truth shows that the One who made the world also came to save it.

Families who see God as Creator should live with gratitude and stewardship. Gratitude means giving thanks for life, food, and daily blessings. Stewardship means caring for creation, using resources wisely, and treating others with honor.

Let us take a few minutes to talk together about the following:

1. What does Colossians 1:16 teach us about Christ as Creator?
2. How does creation show God's power and wisdom?
3. What does it mean to be made in God's image?
4. How can our family live as grateful stewards of His creation?

PRAYER

Creator God, thank You for making the heavens, the earth, and all living things. Thank You for creating us in Your image. Forgive us when we fail to honor You. Teach our family to live with gratitude and to care for what You have made. Amen.

FAMILY ACTIVITY

On a scrapbook page titled "God Our Creator," each family member draws or pastes a picture of something in creation that reminds them of God's greatness. Write Colossians 1:16 underneath.

Seeking the Lord With a Willing Heart

"If you seek him, he will be found by you, but if you forsake him, he will cast you off forever." – 1 Chronicles 28:9

These words were spoken from a father to a son, at a moment filled with responsibility and transition. David was preparing Solomon for leadership, but more importantly, he was pointing him toward God. Before speaking of tasks or achievements, David spoke of the heart. Faith, he reminded Solomon, begins with seeking the Lord.

Seeking God is not casual or occasional. Scripture presents it as an intentional pursuit. It involves the will as much as the emotions. God does not hide Himself from those who seek Him sincerely. He desires to be known, and He responds to hearts that turn toward Him with reverence and trust.

This verse also speaks honestly about choice. God does not force devotion. He invites it. Seeking Him brings relationship and guidance, while turning away leads to distance. The weight of the verse reminds us that faith is not neutral; it is shaped by daily decisions about where the heart is directed.

Throughout Scripture, those who sought the Lord wholeheartedly experienced His faithfulness. They were not always spared from difficulty, but they were never abandoned. God revealed Himself to them in ways that strengthened their trust and clarified their purpose.

For families, this truth carries lasting significance. Faith is not inherited automatically. It is modeled, encouraged, and chosen. When parents and caregivers seek the Lord openly, children learn that God is worth pursuing. A home shaped by a willing heart becomes a place where faith grows through example rather than pressure.

Let us take a few minutes to talk together about the following:

1. What does it mean to seek the Lord with your whole heart?
2. Why do you think God values willingness more than perfection?
3. How do daily choices shape the direction of our faith?
4. What helps or distracts our family from seeking God consistently?
5. How can we encourage one another to seek the Lord more faithfully?

📖 PRAYER

Faithful God, thank You for inviting us to seek You and promising that You will be found. Thank You for caring about the direction of our hearts. Forgive us when distractions pull us away from You. Help our family seek You with sincerity, trust You with obedience, and grow in faith together. Amen.

⛪ FAMILY ACTIVITY

On a scrapbook page, write the title **"A Willing Heart for God."** Draw a heart with an open door. Each family member writes one way they want to seek the Lord more intentionally, through prayer, listening, obedience, or trust. Leave space to return later and reflect on how choosing to seek God shaped your family's days.

June 3

Learning to Know the Lord, Not Just About Him

"Let us know; let us press on to know the Lord; his going out is sure as the dawn." –
Hosea 6:3

This verse is an invitation rather than a command. It does not urge God's people to accomplish something impressive, but to pursue something essential: knowing the Lord. Hosea spoke these words to people who were familiar with religious practices but distant in their hearts. God desired more than routine, He desired relationship.

Knowing the Lord is different from knowing information about Him. It is built through trust, obedience, listening, and time spent in His presence. This kind of knowing grows slowly, shaped by experience and faithfulness rather than quick understanding.

The phrase press on suggests perseverance. There are seasons when God feels near and others when He seems quiet. Hosea reminds us that God's faithfulness is steady, like the sunrise. Even when we do not feel it, God remains constant and reliable.

Throughout Scripture, those who truly knew the Lord learned to rely on His character rather than their circumstances. Their faith deepened not because life was easy, but because they continued to seek Him when answers were unclear. God revealed Himself faithfully to those who pressed on.

For families, this truth reshapes spiritual growth. Faith is not rushed or forced. It develops as families continue to seek God together, through prayer, Scripture, questions, and honest conversations. A home that values knowing God becomes a place where faith is lived, not just taught.

Let us take a few minutes to talk together about the following:

1. What does it mean to truly know the Lord?
2. Why is it sometimes easier to know about God than to know Him personally?
3. What does it look like to "press on" in faith during difficult seasons?
4. How can our family grow in knowing God more deeply together?

✎ PRAYER

Faithful God, thank You for inviting us to know You and promising that You are steady and sure. Thank You for revealing Yourself to those who seek You. Forgive us when we settle for routine instead of relationship. Help our family press on in knowing You, trusting Your faithfulness in every season. Amen.

⚜ FAMILY ACTIVITY

On a scrapbook page, write the title **"Growing in Knowing God."** Draw a sunrise or an open Bible. Each family member writes one way they want to grow closer to God. through prayer, listening, obedience, or trust. Leave space to return later and reflect on how continuing to seek God shaped your family's faith.

June 4

God Is Merciful

"But because of his great love for us, God, who is rich in mercy ..." – Ephesians 2:4

Mercy is compassion shown to those who deserve judgment. Ephesians 2:4 tells us that God is rich in mercy. Families can celebrate that His mercy flows out of His great love.

Scripture is filled with mercy. God spared Nineveh when they repented. He forgave David after his sin. Jesus showed mercy to the sick, the outcasts, and the sinners He met.

The cross is the greatest act of mercy. Instead of punishing humanity, God punished His Son in their place. Titus 3:5 says, "He saved us, not because of works done by us in righteousness, but according to his own mercy."

Mercy also calls us to act. Jesus said, "Blessed are the merciful, for they shall receive mercy" (Matthew 5:7). Families should be quick to forgive, kind to the weak, and compassionate toward those in need.

Living in mercy creates a home filled with kindness and patience. It also reflects God's character to the world.

Let us take a few minutes to talk together about the following:

1. What does Ephesians 2:4 teach us about God's mercy?
2. What examples of mercy are seen in the Bible?
3. How does the cross show God's greatest mercy?
4. How can our family show mercy this week?

PRAYER

Merciful God, thank You for compassion that covers our sins. Thank You for showing kindness we do not deserve. Forgive us when we are harsh. Teach our family to live with mercy and to reflect Your love. Amen.

FAMILY ACTIVITY

On a scrapbook page titled "God's Mercy," each family member writes one act of mercy they will show this week. Decorate the page with hearts.

Learning to Receive Each Day as God's Gift

"Every good gift and every perfect gift is from above, coming down from the Father of lights." – Ecclesiastes 3:13

Much of life is spent moving quickly from one responsibility to the next. In the process, it is easy to overlook the simple truth Scripture reminds us of: each day, with its work and its rest, is given by God. This verse draws attention to something easily forgotten, that enjoyment itself is a gift from the Lord.

Ecclesiastes speaks honestly about the rhythm of life. There is effort, repetition, and sometimes weariness. Yet God does not present daily life as meaningless. He allows His people to experience satisfaction in ordinary moments as part of His kindness. Receiving life as a gift reshapes how we live it.

This perspective requires humility. When we recognize that good things come from God, gratitude replaces entitlement. Work becomes purposeful rather than burdensome. Rest becomes something to receive, not something to earn. God's hand is seen not only in major milestones, but in quiet, everyday blessings.

Scripture does not promise that every day will be easy, but it does remind us that God is present in each one. His gifts often arrive wrapped in ordinary moments: shared meals, meaningful conversations, steady provision, and the ability to keep going even when life feels repetitive.

For families, this truth brings balance. It teaches children to recognize God's goodness in daily life and reminds adults to slow down and give thanks. When a family learns to receive each day as a gift from God, contentment grows, and faith becomes woven into everyday living.

Let us take a few minutes to talk together about the following:

1. What does it mean to receive everyday life as a gift from God?
2. Why is it sometimes hard to notice God's goodness in ordinary moments?
3. How does gratitude change the way we approach work and rest?
4. What are some simple gifts from God our family has experienced recently?

✒ PRAYER

Generous God, thank You for the gifts You give each day. Thank You for allowing us to find meaning and joy in ordinary moments. Forgive us when we rush past Your blessings or take them for granted. Help our family receive each day with gratitude, trusting that You are the source of every good gift. Amen.

⚜ FAMILY ACTIVITY

On a scrapbook page, write the title **"Gifts From God Today."** Divide the page into sections for Morning, Afternoon, and Evening. Each family member writes one simple blessing they noticed during each part of the day. Leave space to return later and reflect on how recognizing God's gifts shaped your family's attitude and gratitude.

Trusting God When We Feel Inadequate

"And the angel of the Lord appeared to him and said to him, 'The Lord is with you, O mighty man of valor.'" – Judges 6:12

These words were spoken to Gideon at a time when he felt anything but strong. He was hiding, fearful, and unsure of his place in God's plan. Yet God addressed him not according to how Gideon saw himself, but according to what God knew to be true.

God often speaks to His people in ways that challenge their self-understanding. Gideon saw weakness and limitation. God saw someone He would use. This moment reminds us that God's call is not based on confidence, ability, or status. It is grounded in His presence and purpose.

What made Gideon capable was not bravery or experience, but the simple truth spoken first: The Lord is with you. God's presence changes how weakness is understood. When God is with His people, fear does not have the final word.

Throughout Scripture, God repeatedly chose those who felt unqualified. In doing so, He showed that strength comes from Him, not from human ability. God's work is often accomplished through those who rely on Him rather than on themselves.

For families, this truth offers encouragement. Children and adults alike face moments of insecurity and self-doubt. Learning to see ourselves through God's promises rather than our fears builds faith and resilience. A family that trusts God's presence learns that inadequacy is not an obstacle when God is near.

Let us take a few minutes to talk together about the following:

1. Why do you think Gideon struggled to see himself the way God did?
2. What does this verse teach us about God's presence?
3. How can God's promises change how we view our weaknesses?
4. When has our family needed to trust God despite feeling unprepared or unsure?

✎ PRAYER

Faithful God, thank You for being with Your people even when we feel weak or uncertain. Thank You for seeing beyond our fears and calling us according to Your purpose. Forgive us when self-doubt keeps us from trusting You. Help our family rely on Your presence and walk forward with faith, knowing You are with us. Amen.

♟ FAMILY ACTIVITY

On a scrapbook page, write the title **"God Is With Us."** Draw a simple figure standing with a light beside it. Each family member writes one situation where they feel unsure or unprepared and then writes the words "The Lord is with me." Leave space to return later and reflect on how trusting God's presence brought courage or peace.

June 7

Trusting God's Hand in Quiet Moments

"But the Lord was gracious to them and had compassion on them and turned toward them, because of his covenant with Abraham, Isaac, and Jacob." – 2 Kings 13:23

This verse appears in the middle of a difficult chapter in Israel's history. The people were experiencing consequences of long-standing disobedience, and circumstances had not improved quickly. Yet Scripture pauses to remind us of something steady and unchanging: God's compassion.

God's response was not driven by the people's consistency, but by His covenant. He remained gracious not because they deserved it, but because He is faithful to His promises. Even when progress was slow and the situation remained hard, God had not turned away.

God's compassion often works quietly. It does not always remove difficulty immediately. Instead, it sustains, preserves, and keeps hope alive over time. This verse reminds us that God's faithfulness is not fragile. It endures through long seasons, even when change feels delayed.

For families, this truth brings reassurance. There are times when growth feels slow and prayers seem unanswered. Remembering God's compassion helps families remain patient and hopeful. God's care is not dependent on perfect faith or quick results. He remains faithful to His promises, even in ordinary and unseen moments.

God's covenant faithfulness also shapes how families treat one another. When God shows patience and compassion, His people are called to reflect that same grace at home. Faith grows as families learn to trust God's steady care rather than immediate outcomes.

Let us take a few minutes to talk together about the following:

1. What does this verse teach us about God's compassion?
2. Why is it important to remember God's faithfulness during slow or difficult seasons?
3. How does God's covenant shape His response to His people?
4. How can our family practice patience and compassion with one another this week?

✎ PRAYER

Gracious God, thank You for Your compassion that does not fail. Thank You for remaining faithful to Your promises, even when progress feels slow. Forgive us when discouragement causes us to doubt Your care. Help our family trust Your steady hand and reflect Your patience and grace in our home. Amen.

♣ FAMILY ACTIVITY

On a scrapbook page, write the title **"Held by God's Compassion."** Draw open hands or a heart surrounded by light. Each family member writes one area where they are trusting God's patience and care. Leave space to return later and reflect on how God's faithfulness became clearer over time.

June 8

Resting in the Steadfast Love of the Lord

"He brought me to the banqueting house, and his banner over me was love." –
Song of Songs 2:4

This verse uses warm and welcoming imagery to describe God's care. A banqueting house is a place of provision, safety, and belonging. The banner raised over God's people is not one of judgment or demand, but love. Scripture reminds us that God's relationship with His people is marked by commitment and affection.

God's love is not distant or reluctant. It covers, protects, and identifies those who belong to Him. A banner was a sign of ownership and unity. To be under God's banner means to live under His faithful care, knowing that His love defines our identity more than any circumstance.

This kind of love invites rest. God does not call His people to strive endlessly for His attention. He welcomes them into His presence and provides what they need. His love is steady, not dependent on performance or perfection.

Throughout Scripture, God showed His love through provision, patience, and protection. Even when His people wandered, His love remained a constant covering. This verse reminds us that God's care surrounds His people in both joy and difficulty.

For families, this truth brings reassurance and security. Children need to know they are loved and protected. Adults need the reminder as well. When a family rests in the love of the Lord, fear loses its grip, and trust grows. God's love becomes the foundation on which daily life is built.

Let us take a few minutes to talk together about the following:

1. What does it mean to live under God's banner of love?
2. Why is it important to remember that God's love is steady and faithful?
3. How does knowing we are loved by God bring peace and security?
4. How can our family reflect God's love in the way we treat one another?

PRAYER

Loving God, thank You for covering Your people with steadfast love. Thank You for welcoming us into Your presence and providing for our needs. Forgive us when we forget Your care or doubt Your affection. Help our family rest in Your love and reflect it in our words and actions each day. Amen.

FAMILY ACTIVITY

On a scrapbook page, write the title **"Under God's Banner of Love."** Draw a banner, heart, or table set for a meal. Each family member writes one way they have experienced God's love recently. Leave space to return later and reflect on how remembering God's love brought peace, gratitude, or reassurance.

June 9

Trusting the God Who Does Not Change

"God is not man, that he should lie, or a son of man, that he should change his mind."
– Numbers 23:19

These words were spoken in a surprising setting. They came through a man who was hired to curse God's people, yet God made His truth clear anyway. The message is simple and steady: God does not change. His character, His promises, and His purposes remain firm.

People change their minds. Circumstances shift. Words are sometimes spoken without follow-through. God is different. What He says, He means. What He promises, He fulfills. This verse reminds us that God's faithfulness is not affected by mood, pressure, or uncertainty.

Because God does not change, His people can trust Him completely. His truth is reliable, even when situations feel unstable. When God speaks, His words stand firm. This gives confidence not in outcomes we can see, but in the character of the One who is speaking.

Throughout Scripture, God proved Himself faithful across generations. His promises carried forward despite human failure, doubt, or delay. God remained true to His word, showing that His faithfulness is rooted in who He is, not in how people respond.

For families, this truth brings security. Children need to know that God is dependable. Adults need the reminder too. When a family learns to trust God's unchanging nature, fear loses its power. Faith becomes anchored, not in circumstances, but in the steadfast character of God.

Let us take a few minutes to talk together about the following:

1. Why is it important to know that God does not change?
2. How does God's faithfulness differ from human promises?
3. What does this verse teach us about trusting God's word?
4. How can our family rely on God's truth when life feels uncertain?

🕮 PRAYER

Faithful God, thank You for being unchanging and trustworthy. Thank You for keeping Your word and remaining true in every generation. Forgive us when doubt causes us to question Your promises. Help our family place our confidence in who You are, trusting that Your truth will always stand. Amen.

⛪ FAMILY ACTIVITY

On a scrapbook page, write the title **"God Is Faithful and Unchanging."** Draw a rock or anchor. Each family member writes one promise from God they are trusting right now. Leave space to return later and reflect on how God's faithfulness became clear over time.

June 10

Remembering What the Lord Has Done

"Only fear the Lord and serve him faithfully with all your heart. For consider what great things he has done for you." – 1 Samuel 12:24

These words were spoken as a reminder, not a warning. Samuel called God's people to pause and look back before moving forward. Remembering what God had already done was meant to strengthen faith and shape obedience.

God knows how easily His people forget. When life becomes busy or difficult, it is easy to focus on what is missing instead of what God has already provided. Scripture repeatedly calls God's people to remember, not out of nostalgia, but to renew trust and gratitude.

Looking back on God's faithfulness helps steady the heart. Past provision, answered prayers, and moments of guidance become reminders that God has been at work all along. Remembering does not erase current challenges, but it gives perspective and hope.

Serving the Lord with faithfulness flows naturally from remembrance. When God's goodness is kept in view, obedience becomes a response of gratitude rather than obligation. Fear of the Lord grows not from anxiety, but from reverence shaped by trust.

For families, this truth is deeply practical. Homes are shaped by the stories that are told and remembered. When families take time to recall what God has done, both big and small, faith becomes rooted in real experience. Children learn that God's faithfulness is not abstract, but personal and enduring.

Let us take a few minutes to talk together about the following:

1. Why is it important to remember what God has done?
2. How can forgetting God's faithfulness affect our trust?
3. What are some ways God has shown faithfulness to our family?
4. How can remembering God's work help us serve Him faithfully?

✎ PRAYER

Faithful God, thank You for the great things You have done for Your people. Thank You for Your steady care and guidance through every season. Forgive us when we forget Your goodness or take it for granted. Help our family remember Your faithfulness and serve You with grateful and willing hearts. Amen.

♟ FAMILY ACTIVITY

On a scrapbook page, write the title **"Remembering God's Faithfulness."** Create a list or timeline. Each family member writes one moment when they saw God's care, provision, or guidance. Leave space to add more memories over time, building a record of God's work in your family's life.

June 11
Honoring God Even When Answers Are Missing

"The Lord gave, and the Lord has taken away; blessed be the name of the Lord." –
Job 1:21

These words were spoken at one of the lowest moments recorded in Scripture. Job had lost nearly everything: family, security, and stability. Yet his response did not begin with explanations or demands. It began with worship.

Job did not pretend his loss was small or painless. Scripture is honest about his grief. What stands out is not a lack of sorrow, but a refusal to turn away from God. In the middle of confusion and pain, Job acknowledged that God remained worthy of honor.

This verse reminds us that faith is not measured by understanding. Job did not know why these things had happened, and he would wrestle deeply with God in the chapters that followed. Still, he chose to bless the Lord. His faith rested not in circumstances, but in the character of God.

God does not ask His people to deny hardship. He invites them to remain faithful even when answers are delayed. Job's response shows that reverence for God can exist alongside sorrow. Trust does not require clarity; it requires surrender.

For families, this truth is important and tender. There are moments when questions arise and answers do not come easily. Teaching children that God is worthy of trust even in hard seasons builds a faith that is honest and resilient. A family that honors God through uncertainty learns to lean on Him rather than turning away.

Let us take a few minutes to talk together about the following:

1. Why do you think Job chose to honor God even in great loss?
2. What does this verse teach us about faith during difficult times?
3. How can sorrow and trust exist at the same time?
4. How can our family honor God when we don't understand what is happening?

📖 PRAYER

Faithful God, thank You for being worthy of honor in every season. Thank You for remaining near to Your people in times of loss and confusion. Forgive us when pain tempts us to pull away from You. Help our family trust You even when answers are missing and choose to honor Your name with humility and faith. Amen.

⚶ FAMILY ACTIVITY

On a scrapbook page, write the title **"Trusting God in Every Season."** Draw a tree with changing seasons around it. Each family member writes one situation where they are choosing to trust God, even without full understanding. Leave space to return later and reflect on how God provided strength, comfort, or clarity over time.

June 12

Standing Faithful When Pressure Is Strong

"But Daniel resolved that he would not defile himself..." – Daniel 1:8

Daniel's story begins far from comfort and familiarity. He was taken from his home, placed in a foreign culture, and pressured to conform in ways that challenged his faith. Before any public test or miracle, Scripture highlights a quiet but powerful moment: Daniel resolved in his heart to remain faithful to God.

This verse reminds us that faithfulness often begins internally. Daniel's resolve was not loud or dramatic. It was a settled decision made before the pressure reached its peak. He chose obedience not because it was easy, but because honoring God mattered more than convenience or acceptance.

God honored Daniel's faithfulness in ways that went beyond what Daniel could have predicted. His obedience influenced others, preserved his integrity, and positioned him to witness God's power in future trials. What began as a private decision shaped a public testimony.

God still works this way. He strengthens those who quietly choose obedience when no one else is watching. Faithfulness under pressure is not about proving strength, but about trusting God enough to stand firm.

For families, this truth is especially relevant. Children and adults face pressure to fit in, compromise values, or stay silent about faith. Learning to resolve together, to honor God in small, unseen choices, builds courage and integrity. A family that chooses faithfulness prepares itself to stand strong when challenges arise.

Let us take a few minutes to talk together about the following:

1. What does it mean to "resolve" to honor God?
2. Why are quiet decisions often the most important ones?
3. How can faithfulness in small things prepare us for bigger challenges?
4. Where might our family need to stand firm in obedience right now?

📖 PRAYER

Faithful God, thank You for strengthening those who choose to honor You. Thank You for seeing our quiet decisions and using them for Your purposes. Forgive us when pressure causes us to compromise. Help our family resolve to obey You with courage and trust, even when it is difficult. Amen.

♟ FAMILY ACTIVITY

On a scrapbook page, write the title **"Resolved to Honor God."** Draw a shield or a firm foundation. Each family member writes one value or choice they want to protect in their walk with God. Leave space to return later and reflect on how God gave strength to remain faithful.

Remembering the Lord in Ordinary Life

"You shall remember the Lord your God, for it is he who gives you power to get wealth." – Deuteronomy 8:18

This verse was spoken as a warning rooted in care. God knew how easily His people could forget Him once life became stable and comfortable. When needs were met and routines settled, the temptation would be to believe success came from their own effort rather than from God's provision.

God did not deny the value of work or responsibility. Instead, He reminded His people where ability and opportunity truly come from. Strength, skill, and provision are not self-generated. They are gifts given by God, meant to lead hearts toward gratitude rather than pride.

Forgetting God rarely happens all at once. It often happens quietly, when daily life feels manageable and dependence seems unnecessary. This verse calls God's people back to awareness, to remember Him not only in need, but also in abundance.

Remembering the Lord reshapes how ordinary life is lived. Meals become moments of gratitude. Work becomes stewardship. Success becomes humility. When God is remembered, everyday life is placed back into its proper order, with Him at the center.

For families, this truth is especially important. Children learn what matters by watching what is acknowledged and thanked for. When families consistently remember God's role in provision, growth, and opportunity, faith becomes woven into daily living rather than reserved for special occasions.

Let us take a few minutes to talk together about the following:

1. Why do you think God warned His people about forgetting Him?

2. How can comfort and routine make it easier to rely on ourselves?

3. What does it look like to remember God in everyday moments?

4. How can our family practice gratitude for God's provision this week?

PRAYER

Providing God, thank You for every ability, opportunity, and blessing You give. Thank You for sustaining us in both ordinary and challenging seasons. Forgive us when we forget Your role in our daily lives. Help our family remember You with gratitude and humility, trusting You as the source of all that we have. Amen.

FAMILY ACTIVITY

On a scrapbook page, write the title **"Remembering the Lord."** Divide the page into sections labeled Home, Work/School, and Daily Needs. Each family member writes one way they see God's provision in those areas. Leave space to return later and add new reminders of God's faithfulness.

Remembering the Cost of Our Salvation

"For you know that it was not with perishable things such as silver or gold that you were redeemed from the empty way of life handed down to you from your ancestors, but with the precious blood of Christ, a lamb without blemish or defect." –
1 Peter 1:18–19

This passage asks us to slow down and remember what truly matters. Peter reminds believers that their salvation was not secured through anything temporary or human-made. No amount of wealth, effort, or tradition could accomplish what only Christ could do.

The verse points directly to the cost. Salvation was not abstract or symbolic. It required the willing sacrifice of Jesus, described here as a spotless lamb. This language echoes the Old Testament sacrifices, but it also makes clear that Christ's offering was final and complete.

Peter contrasts what is perishable with what is eternal. Silver and gold lose value. Traditions fade. Human systems change. But what Christ accomplished through His sacrifice remains forever. This truth reshapes how believers view their lives, their priorities, and their hope.

Remembering the cost of salvation guards against taking grace lightly. It does not produce guilt, but gratitude. When God's people remember what was given for them, obedience becomes a response of love rather than obligation.

For families, this truth invites thoughtful conversation. Children need to understand that salvation is not earned or inherited, it is given. Adults are reminded that faith is grounded not in feelings or effort, but in what Christ has already done. A family that remembers the cost of salvation learns to live with humility, thankfulness, and reverence before God.

Let us take a few minutes to talk together about the following:

1. Why does Peter emphasize what did not redeem us?
2. What does this verse teach us about the value of Christ's sacrifice?
3. How does remembering the cost of salvation shape the way we live?
4. How can our family show gratitude for what Christ has done for us?

✐ PRAYER

Holy God, thank You for the precious gift of salvation through Jesus Christ. Thank You that our redemption was secured not by human effort, but by His perfect sacrifice. Forgive us when we forget the cost of grace or take it lightly. Help our family live with gratitude and reverence, honoring You in response to what You have done for us. Amen.

⛪ FAMILY ACTIVITY

On a scrapbook page, write the title **"The Cost of Our Salvation."** Draw a cross or a simple lamb symbol. Each family member writes one reason they are thankful for what Jesus has done. Leave space to return later and add reflections as your family continues to grow in understanding and gratitude.

June 15
Living Differently Because We Belong to the Lord

"For at one time you were darkness, but now you are light in the Lord. Walk as children of light." – Ephesians 5:8

This verse speaks plainly about change, not a small adjustment, but a complete shift in identity. Paul does not say believers simply moved toward the light. He says they are light in the Lord. This change is not self-made; it is the result of belonging to Christ.

Light reveals what is true. It exposes what was hidden and makes the way forward clear. When God brings people into His light, He changes how they see, how they choose, and how they live. Walking as children of light means letting God's truth shape daily actions, not just beliefs.

Paul's words remind us that faith affects everyday life. Being children of light influences how we speak, how we treat others, and how we respond when no one is watching. This is not about perfection, but about direction, choosing to live in a way that reflects who we now belong to.

God does not call His people to walk in light on their own strength. He calls them to walk in the Lord. Obedience flows from relationship. As believers remain close to Christ, His light guides their steps and shapes their character.

For families, this truth is deeply practical. Homes are places where habits are formed and values are practiced. When a family understands that they belong to the Lord, daily choices begin to reflect that identity. Walking in the light together creates an atmosphere of honesty, grace, and growing faith.

Let us take a few minutes to talk together about the following:

1. What does it mean to be "light in the Lord"?
2. How does belonging to Christ change the way we live?
3. Why is walking in the light a daily choice?
4. How can our family reflect God's light in our home this week?

PRAYER

Gracious God, thank You for bringing us out of darkness and into Your light. Thank You for changing who we are through Christ. Forgive us when we forget our identity or choose paths that do not reflect Your truth. Help our family walk as children of light, honoring You in our words, actions, and choices each day. Amen.

FAMILY ACTIVITY

On a scrapbook page, write the title **"Walking as Children of Light."** Draw a lamp, candle, or sun. Each family member writes one choice or habit that helps them live in God's light. Leave space to return later and reflect on how choosing light shaped your family's week.

June 16
Staying Close to God When Life Feels Unsteady

"Keep yourselves in the love of God, waiting for the mercy of our Lord Jesus Christ that leads to eternal life." – Jude 1:21

This verse was written to believers who were living in confusing times. Voices competed for attention, truth was challenged, and faith required discernment. Jude's encouragement is simple but grounding: stay close to God's love.

Notice what the verse does not say. It does not tell believers to create God's love or earn it. God's love is already there. What Jude calls for is attentiveness: a choice to remain near, to not drift, and to keep returning to what is true.

Staying in God's love often looks ordinary. It shows up in daily trust, quiet obedience, and choosing faithfulness when distractions pull hard. It means remembering who God is when circumstances feel uncertain or unsettled.

The verse also reminds us to wait. Waiting here is not passive. It is hopeful. God's mercy through Jesus is sure, even if the present moment feels incomplete. Faith learns to live between what God has already done and what He has promised to finish.

For families, this encouragement matters deeply. Life does not slow down, and faith can easily become crowded out. Choosing to stay close to God together, through prayer, conversation, and shared trust, helps faith remain steady. A family that stays near to God's love finds strength not in certainty, but in belonging.

Let us take a few minutes to talk together about the following:

1. What do you think it means to "stay close" to God's love?
2. What kinds of things cause faith to drift over time?
3. Why is waiting part of trusting God?
4. What helps our family stay connected to God during busy or uncertain seasons?

📖 PRAYER

Faithful God, thank You for Your steady and unfailing love. Thank You for inviting us to remain close to You, even when life feels unsettled. Forgive us when we drift or become distracted. Help our family return to You often, trusting Your mercy and resting in Your care. Amen.

⛪ FAMILY ACTIVITY

On a scrapbook page, write the title **"Staying Close to God."** Draw a heart near a flame or a small group gathered together. Each family member writes one habit or moment that helps them stay connected to God. Leave space to return later and reflect on how staying close brought peace, clarity, or reassurance.

June 17
Learning to Live Changed Lives

"For perhaps this is why he was parted from you for a while, that you might have him
back forever." – Philemon 1:15

This verse comes from a very personal letter. Paul was writing about a broken relationship, a painful separation, and the hope of restoration. He did not pretend the situation was easy or ideal. Instead, he pointed to the possibility that God had been at work even in what felt like loss.

Philemon reminds us that God often works quietly through real-life situations—conflict, distance, and waiting. What looks like disruption from our point of view may be part of a larger story God is shaping with care and purpose.

The verse does not say that the separation was good, but it suggests that God can redeem even difficult chapters. God's work does not erase the past, but it can transform the future. Restoration becomes possible because God remains involved.

Living a changed life often means seeing situations differently over time. Faith grows as we learn to trust that God can bring good from what we do not understand. This kind of trust is not quick or easy, but it is deeply rooted.

For families, this truth brings hope. Relationships are not always smooth. Mistakes happen. Seasons of distance or misunderstanding may come. Remembering that God can work through broken moments helps families choose patience, forgiveness, and hope instead of giving up.

Let us take a few minutes to talk together about the following:

1. Why do you think God sometimes allows difficult seasons to happen?
2. How does this verse help us see separation or hardship differently?
3. What does it mean to trust God with broken or unfinished situations?
4. Where might our family need to hope for restoration right now?

✐ PRAYER

Faithful God, thank You for working even in situations we do not understand. Thank You for bringing hope where relationships feel broken or strained. Forgive us when we lose patience or doubt Your purposes. Help our family trust You with every season, believing that You are always at work for restoration and good. Amen.

♟ FAMILY ACTIVITY

On a scrapbook page, write the title **"God at Work in Our Story."** Draw puzzle pieces or a timeline. Each family member writes one situation, past or present, where they are trusting God to bring understanding or restoration. Leave space to return later and reflect on how God continues to work over time.

Turning Our Hearts Fully Toward the Lord

"If my people who are called by my name humble themselves, and pray and seek my face and turn from their wicked ways, then I will hear from heaven and will forgive their sin and heal their land." – 2 Chronicles 7:14

These words were spoken to God's people at a moment of celebration, not crisis. The temple had just been completed, prayers had been offered, and God responded with a reminder that faith must continue beyond special moments. What mattered most was the posture of the heart.

God's invitation begins with humility. Before action, before change, before healing, God calls His people to humble themselves. Humility acknowledges dependence. It admits that help, forgiveness, and restoration must come from God rather than from human effort.

Prayer and seeking God's face are not rushed acts. They involve turning attention fully toward Him, listening as much as speaking. God was not asking for empty words, but for hearts willing to return to Him honestly and completely.

This verse also speaks of turning. Repentance is not just regret; it is redirection. God promises to respond when His people turn back to Him. Forgiveness and healing flow from relationship restored, not from perfection achieved.

For families, this truth carries lasting value. Homes experience tension, mistakes, and seasons of drift just like individuals do. Learning to humble ourselves together, pray together, and seek God together builds a culture of honesty and grace. A family that turns toward God finds renewal not because they do everything right, but because they trust the One who restores.

Let us take a few minutes to talk together about the following:

1. Why do you think God begins with humility in this verse?
2. What does it mean to truly seek God's face?
3. How does repentance lead to healing and restoration?
4. What is one way our family can turn our hearts more fully toward God right now?

PRAYER

Restoring God, thank You for inviting Your people to return to You. Thank You for listening when hearts humble themselves and seek You. Forgive us when pride or distraction pulls us away from You. Help our family turn toward You with sincerity, trusting Your forgiveness and healing grace. Amen.

FAMILY ACTIVITY

On a scrapbook page, write the title **"Turning Our Hearts to God."** Draw a heart with an arrow pointing upward or a path turning toward light. Each family member writes one way they want to seek God more intentionally this week. Leave space to return later and reflect on how turning toward God brought peace, clarity, or renewal.

June 19
Choosing Faithfulness in Everyday Relationships

"Strive for peace with everyone, and for the holiness without which no one will see the Lord." – Hebrews 12:14

This verse speaks to the daily, often unseen work of faith. It does not describe a single moment or spiritual milestone. Instead, it points to a way of living that takes intention, effort, and reliance on God.

Striving for peace does not mean avoiding truth or pretending conflict does not exist. It means choosing humility, patience, and grace in how we relate to others. Peace requires effort because relationships are complex and hearts are imperfect. God calls His people to pursue peace anyway.

Holiness, as described here, is not about appearing religious or set apart for show. It is about belonging to God and allowing His ways to shape everyday choices. Holiness shows itself in how words are spoken, how forgiveness is practiced, and how love is extended even when it is costly.

The verse ties peace and holiness together. Faithfulness to God affects how His people treat one another. Walking closely with the Lord changes relationships, not through control or pressure, but through obedience rooted in reverence for God.

For families, this truth is deeply practical. Home is where patience is tested and grace is needed most. Choosing peace and holiness together shapes a home where faith is lived honestly. Children learn that following God matters not only in belief, but in how people love, forgive, and reconcile each day.

Let us take a few minutes to talk together about the following:

1. Why do you think Scripture calls peace something we must strive for?
2. How does holiness affect the way we treat others?
3. What makes choosing peace difficult in close relationships?
4. How can our family pursue peace while remaining faithful to God?

✒ PRAYER

Holy God, thank You for calling us to live in peace and faithfulness. Thank You for shaping our hearts through Your presence and truth. Forgive us when pride or impatience disrupts relationships. Help our family pursue peace, walk in holiness, and honor You in the way we treat one another each day. Amen.

▲ FAMILY ACTIVITY

On a scrapbook page, write the title **"Choosing Peace and Faithfulness."** Draw linked hands or a circle representing unity. Each family member writes one relationship or situation where they want God's help to choose peace and obedience. Leave space to return later and reflect on how God worked through those efforts.

June 20

Turning Back to the Lord With Honest Hearts

"Yet even now," declares the Lord, "return to me with all your heart." – Joel 2:12

These words were spoken during a time of great loss and alarm. The people were facing consequences they could not ignore. Yet God's message was not one of rejection. It was an invitation. Even now, God said, return to Me.

What stands out is God's timing. He did not say it was too late. He did not wait for conditions to improve. He spoke in the middle of difficulty and called for the heart. God has always been more concerned with genuine repentance than outward appearance.

Returning to God with the whole heart is not about perfection. It is about honesty. It means coming without excuses, without pretending, and without holding anything back. God welcomes hearts that are willing to turn toward Him, even when they are weary or unsure.

This verse reminds us that God's mercy is active, not delayed. He invites His people back again and again. His desire is restoration, not distance. No matter how far someone feels they have drifted, God's invitation still stands.

For families, this truth is deeply reassuring. There are moments when routines slip, attitudes harden, or faith feels distant. Learning to return to God together, openly and sincerely, builds humility and trust. A family that practices turning back to God learns that grace is always available.

Let us take a few minutes to talk together about the following:

1. What does it mean to return to God with your whole heart?
2. Why do you think God says "even now"?
3. What makes it hard to admit when we need to turn back to God?
4. How can our family practice honest repentance and renewal together?

✎ PRAYER

Merciful God, thank You for inviting us to return to You again and again. Thank You for meeting us with grace instead of rejection. Forgive us when pride or fear keeps us from turning back to You. Help our family come to You with honest hearts, trusting Your mercy and love. Amen.

⛊ FAMILY ACTIVITY

On a scrapbook page, write the title **"Returning to God."** Draw a heart with a path leading back to it. Each family member writes one area where they want to turn their heart more fully toward God. Leave space to return later and reflect on how God brought renewal, peace, or clarity.

June 21
Learning to Be Faithful in Daily Devotion

"Now these Jews were more noble than those in Thessalonica; they received the word with all eagerness, examining the Scriptures daily to see if these things were so." –
Acts 17:11

This verse describes ordinary faith lived with sincerity. The people in Berea were not praised for status or influence, but for their posture toward God's Word. They listened carefully, received the truth willingly, and took time to examine Scripture for themselves.

What stands out is consistency. Their devotion was not occasional or reactive. They returned to God's Word daily, allowing it to shape understanding and guide belief. Faith was not something they accepted blindly or ignored casually; it was something they engaged with thoughtfully.

God honors hearts that seek truth with humility. The Bereans did not rely solely on what they were told. They measured teaching against Scripture, showing respect for God's authority above all else. This kind of faith grows steady and grounded over time.

Daily devotion does not require long study sessions or perfect discipline. It begins with eagerness: a willingness to listen, learn, and return to God's Word again and again. God works through this faithfulness, shaping hearts through small, consistent choices.

For families, this truth is especially practical. Faith is built through habits, not just moments. When families make space for God's Word regularly, even briefly, it teaches children that Scripture matters. Over time, devotion becomes part of everyday life rather than a separate activity.

Let us take a few minutes to talk together about the following:

1. What do you notice about the way the Bereans approached God's Word?
2. Why do you think daily devotion helps faith grow stronger?
3. What can make it difficult to spend time in Scripture regularly?
4. How can our family build simple, faithful habits around God's Word?

✐ PRAYER

Faithful God, thank You for giving us Your Word and inviting us to know You through it. Thank You for honoring hearts that seek truth with humility and eagerness. Forgive us when distractions crowd out time with You. Help our family develop faithful habits that keep us rooted in Your truth each day. Amen.

▲ FAMILY ACTIVITY

On a scrapbook page, write the title **"Growing Through God's Word."** Draw an open Bible or a growing plant. Each family member writes one simple way they can engage with Scripture regularly, reading, listening, asking questions, or reflecting. Leave space to return later and note how these small habits shaped your family's faith.

June 22

Learning What True Love Really Means

"In this is love, not that we have loved God but that he loved us and sent his Son to be the propitiation for our sins." – 1 John 4:10

This verse gently but firmly redefines love. It shifts the focus away from human effort and places it fully on God's action. Love did not begin with people reaching for God. It began with God reaching toward us.

Scripture makes clear that love is not measured by intention or feeling alone. It is revealed through sacrifice. God's love took shape in a specific, costly way: the sending of His Son. This was not a reaction to human goodness, but an expression of God's mercy toward sinners.

By placing God's love first, this verse removes comparison and pressure. Love is not something we prove to God. It is something we receive. Everything else, obedience, gratitude, devotion, flows from that starting point.

God's love also clarifies how His people are called to live. When love is received humbly, it reshapes how others are treated. It produces patience, forgiveness, and compassion, not as obligations, but as responses to grace already given.

For families, this truth is foundational. Children learn what love looks like by what they see and hear at home. When God's love is understood as undeserved and freely given, homes become places where grace is practiced more readily. Faith grows not through pressure to perform, but through gratitude for what God has already done.

Let us take a few minutes to talk together about the following:

1. What stands out to you about how this verse defines love?
2. Why is it important to remember that God loved us first?
3. How does receiving God's love change the way we treat others?
4. How can our family reflect God's love in everyday situations?

📖 PRAYER

Loving God, thank You for loving us before we ever reached for You. Thank You for showing Your love through the sacrifice of Jesus. Forgive us when we forget the depth of Your grace or try to earn what You freely give. Help our family live in response to Your love, reflecting it with humility, gratitude, and care for one another. Amen.

⛪ FAMILY ACTIVITY

On a scrapbook page, write the title **"Loved First by God."** Draw a heart with a cross at the center. Each family member writes one way they have experienced God's love or one way they want to show that love to others this week. Leave space to return later and reflect on how understanding God's love shaped your family's actions.

June 23
Learning to Trust God's Ways

"This God—his way is perfect; the word of the Lord proves true; he is a shield for all those who take refuge in him." – 2 Samuel 22:31

These words were spoken by David after a long journey marked by danger, waiting, and deliverance. They were not written in the middle of ease, but after years of seeing God prove faithful again and again. Looking back, David did not focus on his own decisions or strength. He focused on God's ways.

Calling God's way "perfect" does not mean life felt simple or pain-free. It means that, over time, David saw that God's plans were trustworthy, even when they were hard to understand in the moment. God's word proved true not because circumstances were easy, but because God remained faithful through them all.

This verse reminds us that trust is often formed in hindsight. God's people may question, struggle, or feel unsure along the way, but refuge is found by continuing to rely on Him. God does not promise an easy path, but He does promise to be a shield for those who turn to Him.

God's word stands firm even when emotions shift or situations change. Trusting God's way requires humility, accepting that His understanding is greater than ours and His timing wiser than we prefer.

For families, this truth encourages patience and faith. Children and adults alike face moments when God's ways do not make immediate sense. Learning to trust God together, especially during uncertainty, builds a shared confidence that He is faithful. A family that takes refuge in God learns to rest in His character, not just outcomes.

Let us take a few minutes to talk together about the following:

1. What does it mean to say that God's way is perfect?
2. Why can trusting God feel difficult when we don't understand what He is doing?
3. How does God's word give us confidence during uncertain times?
4. What is one area where our family needs to trust God's way right now?

✐ PRAYER

Faithful God, thank You for being trustworthy in all Your ways. Thank You for proving Your word true through every season of life. Forgive us when doubt or fear makes it hard to trust You. Help our family take refuge in You, believing that Your ways are good and Your promises never fail. Amen.

⚜ FAMILY ACTIVITY

On a scrapbook page, write the title **"Trusting God's Way."** Draw a path leading forward or a shield for protection. Each family member writes one situation where they are choosing to trust God, even if the outcome is unclear. Leave space to return later and reflect on how God showed His faithfulness over time.

June 24

Listening and Responding to God's Word

"But he said, 'Blessed rather are those who hear the word of God and keep it!'" –
Luke 11:28

These words of Jesus gently redirect attention. They remind us that closeness to God is not about position, familiarity, or outward connection. What matters most is hearing God's Word and responding to it with obedience.

Hearing God's Word involves more than listening with our ears. It requires attention, humility, and openness. God's Word often challenges assumptions, corrects attitudes, and invites change. Hearing well means allowing God to speak honestly into our lives.

Keeping God's Word is not about perfection. It is about direction. Obedience grows through daily choices, small adjustments, and willingness to respond when God's truth becomes clear. Faith takes shape when God's Word moves from hearing into action.

Jesus' statement reminds us that blessing is connected to obedience rooted in trust. God's Word is not given to burden His people, but to guide them. When His Word is kept, it brings clarity, growth, and peace over time.

For families, this truth shapes everyday faith. Children learn not only by what is read aloud, but by what is lived out. When families listen to God's Word together and seek to obey it sincerely, faith becomes visible and practical. God's truth moves from pages into daily life.

Let us take a few minutes to talk together about the following:

1. What does it mean to truly hear God's Word?
2. Why is obedience sometimes harder than listening?
3. How does keeping God's Word shape our daily choices?
4. What is one way our family can better live out what God teaches us?

PRAYER

Speaking God, thank You for giving us Your Word to guide and teach us. Thank You for inviting us not only to hear, but to obey with trust and humility. Forgive us when we listen without responding. Help our family receive Your Word openly and live it out faithfully in our everyday lives. Amen.

FAMILY ACTIVITY

On a scrapbook page, write the title **"Hearing and Living God's Word."** Draw an ear and a pair of hands. Each family member writes one truth from Scripture they want to put into practice this week. Leave space to return later and reflect on how obeying God's Word shaped your family's actions and attitudes.

June 25

Making Room for One Another in God's Presence

"But when Jesus saw it, he was indignant and said to them, 'Let the children come to me; do not hinder them, for to such belongs the kingdom of God.'" – Mark 10:14

This moment with Jesus is brief, but it speaks volumes. Children were being pushed aside, not out of cruelty, but out of assumption. Others believed Jesus had more important things to do. Jesus corrected that thinking immediately. He made room.

Jesus did not treat children as interruptions. He welcomed them openly and deliberately. In doing so, He revealed something about God's heart. God does not measure worth by productivity, maturity, or status. He delights in drawing His people near, young and old alike.

This verse reminds families that God's presence is not reserved for a certain age or stage of faith. Children belong in moments of prayer, learning, and worship. Their questions, energy, and growing understanding matter to God.

Making room for one another begins at home. Families are shaped by what they allow space for: conversation, patience, listening, and shared faith. When a home reflects God's welcoming heart, every family member knows they are seen, valued, and invited to grow.

For parents and caregivers, this passage is also a gentle reminder. Spiritual growth does not require perfection or quiet compliance. It grows best in an environment of invitation and grace. A family that makes room for one another learns together how to come to God with trust and openness.

Let us take a few minutes to talk together about the following:

1. Why do you think Jesus cared so deeply about welcoming children?
2. What does this verse teach us about God's heart for families?
3. How can we make sure everyone in our family feels included and valued?
4. What is one way our family can make more room for faith conversations at home?

PRAYER

Welcoming God, thank You for inviting each of us into Your presence. Thank You for showing us that every person matters to You. Forgive us when we rush past one another or overlook small moments. Help our family reflect Your open heart, making room for patience, love, and shared faith as we grow together. Amen.

FAMILY ACTIVITY

On a scrapbook page, write the title **"Everyone Belongs."** Draw a table, open door, or group gathered together. Each family member writes one way they feel welcomed at home and one way they can help others feel included. Leave space to return later and add reflections as your family grows in unity.

June 26

Choosing Unity in the Way We Love One Another

"Complete my joy by being of the same mind, having the same love, being in full accord and of one mind." – Philippians 2:2

Families share more than a last name. They share daily life: meals, conversations, disagreements, laughter, and quiet moments. This verse speaks into those shared spaces, reminding believers that unity is not automatic. It is something that is chosen and nurtured.

Paul connects unity with love. Being of one mind does not mean thinking the same way about everything. It means choosing care over conflict and understanding over pride. Unity grows when love shapes responses, especially when opinions differ or patience runs thin.

God values unity because it reflects His character. He calls His people to live in harmony not by ignoring differences, but by responding to one another with humility. Unity is strengthened when hearts are aligned with God's purposes rather than personal preferences.

In family life, unity is often tested in small, ordinary moments. Tone of voice, willingness to listen, and readiness to forgive all matter. Choosing unity may mean slowing down, apologizing first, or letting go of the need to be right.

When families seek unity together, joy grows. Home becomes a place of safety rather than tension. Children learn what it looks like to love well, and adults are reminded that unity is built through grace-filled choices made day after day.

Let us take a few minutes to talk together about the following:

1. What does unity look like in everyday family life?
2. Why can it be hard to choose unity during disagreements?
3. How does love help keep families connected?
4. What is one way our family can work toward greater unity this week?

✒ PRAYER

God of peace, thank You for calling Your people to live in love and unity. Thank You for shaping our hearts through Your truth. Forgive us when pride or impatience creates distance between us. Help our family choose unity, reflect Your love, and grow together in understanding and grace. Amen.

♟ FAMILY ACTIVITY

On a scrapbook page, write the title **"Growing Together in Unity."** Draw interlocking shapes or hands joined together. Each family member writes one action they can take to strengthen unity in the home, listening, forgiving, encouraging, or serving. Leave space to return later and reflect on how choosing unity shaped your family's relationships.

June 27
Learning Faithfulness in the Small Things at Home

"Beloved, it is a faithful thing you do in all your efforts for these brothers, strangers as they are." – 3 John 1:5

This short verse speaks quietly, but it carries weight. John was writing to commend faithfulness that showed up in practical ways. The actions were not flashy or public. They were steady, consistent, and rooted in love.

Faithfulness often looks like showing up when no one applauds. It is found in everyday care: helping, serving, and choosing to do what is right even when it goes unnoticed. God values this kind of faithfulness deeply.

In family life, faithfulness is built through small, repeated choices. It shows up in keeping promises, offering help without being asked, and choosing patience when it would be easier to withdraw. These small acts shape trust and stability over time.

God uses quiet faithfulness to strengthen relationships. It reflects His own character: steady, dependable, and loving. When His people live faithfully in ordinary moments, His presence is made visible through their actions.

For families, this verse offers encouragement. Faith does not require dramatic gestures to matter. Homes are shaped by consistent love and care practiced day after day. A family that values faithfulness learns to serve one another with sincerity, reflecting God's heart in the simplest moments.

Let us take a few minutes to talk together about the following:

1. What does faithfulness look like in everyday family life?
2. Why are small, consistent actions important in building trust?
3. How does serving one another reflect God's character?
4. What is one simple way our family can practice faithfulness this week?

✎ PRAYER

Faithful God, thank You for valuing the quiet acts of love and service we offer each day. Thank You for teaching us that faithfulness matters, even when it feels small. Forgive us when we overlook opportunities to serve one another. Help our family live faithfully, reflecting Your steady love in all that we do. Amen.

♟ FAMILY ACTIVITY

On a scrapbook page, write the title **"Faithful in the Small Things."** Draw small hearts or hands serving one another. Each family member writes one small act of faithfulness they can practice this week—helping, encouraging, or following through on a commitment. Leave space to return later and reflect on how these small choices strengthened your family.

June 28
Finding Strength Together When God Calls Us Forward

"Yet now be strong... declares the Lord. Work, for I am with you." – Haggai 2:4

These words were spoken to people who felt discouraged. They were rebuilding, but what stood before them felt small compared to what once was. God did not deny their weariness. Instead, He spoke directly into it, reminding them that His presence mattered more than their resources or confidence.

God's instruction was simple and reassuring: Be strong... for I am with you. Strength did not come from enthusiasm or ability. It came from knowing that God was present in the work He had called them to do.

Families experience similar moments. There are seasons when responsibilities feel heavy, progress feels slow, or energy feels thin. This verse reminds us that God does not wait for perfect conditions before He walks with His people. He is present in the rebuilding, the learning, and the trying again.

God's presence does not remove effort, but it changes how effort is carried. When families trust that God is with them, they can keep going even when things feel unfinished. Faith grows as families learn to rely on God's nearness rather than their own strength.

For children especially, this message is powerful. Knowing that God is with their family through challenges builds confidence and peace. A family that moves forward together, trusting God's presence, learns that strength is shared and hope is sustained.

Let us take a few minutes to talk together about the following:

1. Why do you think God reminded His people that He was with them?
2. What does this verse teach us about where true strength comes from?
3. How can knowing God is with us help during hard or tiring seasons?
4. Where does our family need God's strength and presence right now?

PRAYER

Faithful God, thank You for being with Your people when the work feels hard. Thank You for giving strength that does not depend on our energy alone. Forgive us when discouragement makes us forget Your presence. Help our family move forward together, trusting that You are with us every step of the way. Amen.

FAMILY ACTIVITY

On a scrapbook page, write the title **"God Is With Us as We Move Forward."** Draw a path with footprints or a family standing together. Each family member writes one challenge they are facing and the words "God is with us." Leave space to return later and reflect on how trusting God's presence gave strength and hope.

Choosing Faithful Love in Our Family

"Where you go I will go, and where you lodge I will lodge. Your people shall be my people, and your God my God." – Ruth 1:16

These words were spoken during a moment of deep loss. Ruth had every reason to turn back. She was widowed, far from home, and facing an uncertain future. Yet she chose to stay, not because it was easy, but because she was committed to Naomi, and to the God Naomi served.

Ruth's choice was an act of faithful love. She did not know what lay ahead, but she trusted enough to walk forward anyway. Her decision was quiet and personal, made without promises of comfort or reward. God honored that faithfulness in ways Ruth could not have imagined at the time.

This verse reminds us that love is often shown through commitment. Faithful love stays when circumstances change. It chooses presence over convenience and loyalty over self-protection. God often works through these kinds of steady, unseen decisions.

In family life, faithful love looks very similar. It shows up in staying connected through hard seasons, choosing patience when emotions are tender, and remaining present when life feels uncertain. These choices shape relationships more deeply than words ever could.

For families, Ruth's story teaches that faith and love grow together. When families choose to walk together, trusting God and supporting one another, God weaves something meaningful out of ordinary faithfulness. What begins as a simple decision to stay can become part of a much bigger story God is writing.

Let us take a few minutes to talk together about the following:

1. Why do you think Ruth chose to stay even when the future was uncertain?
2. What does faithful love look like in everyday family life?
3. How does trusting God help us remain committed to one another?
4. Where might our family need to choose patience or loyalty right now?

PRAYER

Faithful God, thank You for showing us what committed love looks like. Thank You for walking with families through uncertain seasons. Forgive us when we choose comfort over faithfulness. Help our family stay connected, trusting You as we walk forward together in love and obedience. Amen.

FAMILY ACTIVITY

On a scrapbook page, write the title **"Choosing Faithful Love."** Draw two paths joining into one. Each family member writes one way they can show faithful love at home, through patience, encouragement, or staying present. Leave space to return later and reflect on how choosing faithfulness strengthened your family.

God Is Worthy of Praise

"Great is the Lord, and greatly to be praised, and his greatness is unsearchable." –
Psalm 145:3

God is worthy of praise not only for what He does, but for who He is. Psalm 145:3 reminds us that His greatness is beyond measure. Families should make praise a daily practice, not just something for Sunday worship.

The Bible is filled with calls to praise. The psalms overflow with songs of thanksgiving. Angels worship Him day and night, crying "Holy, holy, holy." Revelation 4:11 declares, "Worthy are you, our Lord and God, to receive glory and honor and power."

God is worthy of praise because He created everything. He is worthy because He saves His people through Jesus. He is worthy because He sustains life daily. Families should look at blessings like food, health, and love and respond with thanksgiving.

Praise shifts focus from problems to God's greatness. It strengthens faith and brings joy. Families who practice praise will find their home filled with peace and gratitude.

Living in praise means more than singing. Romans 12:1 calls believers to present their bodies as living sacrifices. Obedience, service, and love are acts of worship that honor God.

Let us take a few minutes to talk together about the following

1. What does Psalm 145:3 teach us about God's greatness?
2. Why is He worthy of praise for both who He is and what He does?
3. How does praise strengthen faith and joy?
4. How can our family practice daily praise?

✎ PRAYER

Worthy God, thank You for being great and mighty. Thank You for creating, saving, and sustaining us. Forgive us when we forget to praise You. Teach our family to live with thankful hearts and to worship You in all we do. Amen.

♟ FAMILY ACTIVITY

On a scrapbook page, write "Praising God." Each family member writes one reason they are thankful today. Decorate with music notes and bright colors.

JULY

July 1
Remembering Who Walks With Our Family

"I will walk among you and will be your God, and you shall be my people." –
Leviticus 26:12

These words were spoken as a promise, not a command. God was reminding His people that obedience and relationship were never meant to be separated. At the heart of His covenant was presence: God choosing to walk with His people.

God did not promise a distant relationship. He promised nearness. To walk among His people meant shared life, daily awareness, and steady guidance. This was not about special moments only, but about ordinary days lived with God nearby.

For families, this promise speaks into daily routines. God is not only present during prayer or worship, but in meals, conversations, challenges, and rest. He walks with families through both calm days and difficult ones.

Belonging to God shapes identity. "You shall be my people" is a statement of care and commitment. Families do not walk alone or define themselves by circumstances. They are held by God's promise and presence.

As a new month begins, this verse offers reassurance. Whatever lies ahead, God is not watching from afar. He walks with His people. A family that remembers this truth can move forward with confidence, humility, and peace.

Let us take a few minutes to talk together about the following:

1. What does it mean that God walks among His people?
2. How does knowing God is near affect our family's daily life?
3. Why is belonging to God important for families?
4. How can our family be more aware of God's presence this month?

PRAYER

Present God, thank You for choosing to walk with Your people. Thank You for being near to our family in every season. Forgive us when we forget Your presence in ordinary moments. Help our family walk with You each day, trusting Your guidance and resting in Your care. Amen.

FAMILY ACTIVITY

On a scrapbook page, write the title **"God Walks With Us."** Draw footprints or a family walking together. Each family member writes one moment in daily life where they want to remember God's presence—at school, work, meals, or bedtime. Leave space to return later and reflect on how being aware of God's nearness changed your days.

July 2
Learning to Rely on God's Power as a Family

"Not by might, nor by power, but by my Spirit, says the Lord of hosts." –
Zechariah 4:6

This verse was spoken during a time of rebuilding. God's people were facing a task that felt bigger than their strength and resources. Instead of urging them to try harder, God reminded them where true help comes from: His Spirit.

God knew they would be tempted to rely on what they could see and measure. But progress was not going to come through effort alone. It would come through dependence. This verse gently shifts the focus away from human ability and back to God's work.

Families experience similar moments. There are responsibilities that feel overwhelming and problems that cannot be solved by effort alone. This verse reminds us that God does not expect families to carry everything in their own strength. His Spirit supplies wisdom, patience, and endurance when strength runs low.

Relying on God's Spirit teaches humility. It invites prayer before action and trust before control. When families learn to pause and depend on God, they discover that His help often comes quietly but faithfully.

For families, this truth brings relief. God's work in a home does not depend on perfection or constant effort. It depends on His presence. A family that relies on God's Spirit learns to move forward with peace, even when the path feels uncertain.

Let us take a few minutes to talk together about the following:

1. Why do we sometimes rely on our own strength instead of God's help?
2. What does it mean to depend on God's Spirit in daily life?
3. How can prayer help us shift from control to trust?
4. Where does our family need God's strength right now?

PRAYER

Mighty God, thank You for reminding us that Your work is done through Your Spirit. Thank You for being present when our strength feels small. Forgive us when we rely only on ourselves. Help our family depend on You, trusting that You will provide what we need each day. Amen.

FAMILY ACTIVITY

On a scrapbook page, write the title **"Not by Our Strength."** Draw a small figure supported by a larger hand or light. Each family member writes one area where they want to rely more on God instead of themselves. Leave space to return later and reflect on how trusting God's Spirit brought peace or clarity.

Remembering That God Does Not Change

"For I the Lord do not change; therefore you, O children of Jacob, are not consumed."
– Malachi 3:6

This verse was spoken as reassurance. God's people had wandered, doubted, and failed in many ways, yet God reminded them of something steady and unshaken: His own character. He does not change. His faithfulness does not wear out.

Life changes constantly. Routines shift, relationships grow, and seasons come and go. For families, change can feel unsettling. This verse reminds us that while circumstances change, God remains the same. His promises do not weaken, and His care does not fade.

God's unchanging nature is not harsh or rigid. It is protective. Because He remains faithful, His people are not consumed by their failures. God's mercy continues because His character remains firm.

For families, this truth brings security. Children need to know that love can be dependable. Adults need the reminder too. God's consistency becomes the anchor that steadies homes through uncertainty, mistakes, and growth.

Remembering that God does not change helps families respond to life with trust instead of fear. When God's character is kept in view, change becomes something that can be faced together, not something to be feared.

Let us take a few minutes to talk together about the following:

1. Why is it comforting to know that God does not change?
2. How does change affect our family emotionally or spiritually?
3. What does this verse teach us about God's faithfulness?
4. How can our family lean on God's unchanging nature during change?

PRAYER

Unchanging God, thank You for remaining faithful through every season. Thank You for holding Your people steady when life feels uncertain. Forgive us when fear causes us to forget who You are. Help our family trust Your constant love and rest in the security of Your promises. Amen.

FAMILY ACTIVITY

On a scrapbook page, write the title **"God Does Not Change."** Draw an anchor or a strong foundation. Each family member writes one thing that changes in life and one truth about God that never changes. Leave space to return later and reflect on how trusting God's faithfulness brought peace to your family.

July 4

Learning to Depend on God's Protection

"The hand of our God is for good on all who seek him, and the power of his wrath is against all who forsake him." – Ezra 8:22

This verse was spoken during a moment of vulnerability. God's people were preparing for a long journey, carrying families, possessions, and responsibility. Instead of relying on military protection, they chose to place their trust in God's care.

Depending on God's protection required faith. It meant believing that God's presence was enough, even when the road ahead felt uncertain. God honored that trust, not because His people were fearless, but because they chose to rely on Him rather than their own safeguards.

Families today also face journeys of many kinds: new seasons, difficult decisions, and moments of risk or uncertainty. This verse reminds us that God's care is not distant. His hand is actively at work for those who seek Him.

Trusting God's protection does not remove responsibility, but it reshapes where confidence is placed. Families are invited to pray, plan wisely, and still rest knowing that God's care goes beyond what can be controlled.

For families, this truth builds courage. Children learn that safety is not found only in visible measures, but in trusting God's presence. Adults are reminded that God watches over what matters most. A family that depends on God's protection learns to move forward with peace rather than fear.

Let us take a few minutes to talk together about the following:

1. Why was it hard for God's people to trust Him for protection?
2. What kinds of "journeys" does our family face right now?
3. How does trusting God change the way we handle fear or uncertainty?
4. What is one way our family can seek God's protection this week?

📖 PRAYER

Protecting God, thank You for watching over Your people with care and faithfulness. Thank You for being present in every journey we face. Forgive us when fear causes us to rely only on what we can see. Help our family trust Your hand, seeking You with confidence and resting in Your protection. Amen.

♟ FAMILY ACTIVITY

On a scrapbook page, write the title **"God's Hand Is Over Us."** Draw a road, a shield, or a guiding hand. Each family member writes one situation where they want to trust God's protection. Leave space to return later and reflect on how trusting God brought peace or reassurance.

July 5

Remembering Where Our Help Truly Comes From

"But I with the voice of thanksgiving will sacrifice to you; what I have vowed I will pay. Salvation belongs to the Lord." – Jonah 2:9

Jonah spoke these words from a place of desperation. He had run from God, made mistakes, and found himself overwhelmed. Yet in that moment, he remembered something true and unchanging: salvation belongs to the Lord.

This verse is not about Jonah's strength or resolve. It is about God's power to rescue. Jonah did not save himself. He called out, gave thanks, and acknowledged that help could only come from God. Even in failure, God remained merciful and attentive.

Families experience moments like this too. There are times when problems feel bigger than wisdom or effort. This verse reminds us that God is not surprised by those moments. He invites His people to turn back to Him, trusting that He alone can bring deliverance.

Thanksgiving appears alongside surrender in this verse. Gratitude does not wait for everything to be fixed. It grows from remembering who God is, even while waiting for His help. This kind of faith reshapes fear into trust.

For families, this truth brings reassurance. Help does not depend on getting everything right. God remains the source of rescue, guidance, and hope. A family that remembers where help comes from learns to face difficulties together with humility and trust.

Let us take a few minutes to talk together about the following:

1. Why do you think Jonah gave thanks even before he was rescued?
2. What does it mean that salvation belongs to the Lord?
3. When does our family most need God's help?
4. How can gratitude help us trust God during hard times?

✒ PRAYER

Saving God, thank You for being our help when we are overwhelmed. Thank You for hearing Your people even when we fall short. Forgive us when we forget where our help truly comes from. Help our family trust You, give thanks in every season, and rest in the knowledge that salvation belongs to You alone. Amen.

♟ FAMILY ACTIVITY

On a scrapbook page, write the title **"Our Help Comes From the Lord."** Draw waves or a lifeline. Each family member writes one situation where they need God's help or one moment when they are thankful for His rescue. Leave space to return later and reflect on how trusting God brought peace or deliverance.

July 6

Passing Faith Forward as a Family

"For I have chosen him, that he may command his children and his household after him to keep the way of the Lord." – Genesis 18:19

God spoke these words about Abraham, not because Abraham was perfect, but because God trusted him with something lasting. God's plan was not only about one person's faith, but about a household shaped by obedience and trust in Him.

This verse shows that faith was meant to be shared. God cared about what would be passed on: values, obedience, and knowledge of who He is. Faith was not intended to stop with one generation, but to continue through families who walk in God's ways together.

Keeping the way of the Lord involves daily life. It shows up in decisions, conversations, and examples set over time. Teaching faith is not only about instruction, but about living in a way that reflects trust in God's truth and character.

Families today carry that same opportunity. Children learn faith not only from what they are told, but from what they see practiced consistently. When families choose to follow God together, faith becomes part of everyday life rather than a separate activity.

This verse reminds families that their influence matters. God works through ordinary homes to shape future generations. A family that chooses to walk in God's ways leaves a legacy that reaches far beyond what they can see.

Let us take a few minutes to talk together about the following:

1. Why do you think God cared so much about Abraham's household?
2. How is faith passed on through everyday family life?
3. What helps children learn trust in God?
4. What is one way our family can live out our faith more intentionally?

✐ PRAYER

Faithful God, thank You for working through families to share Your truth. Thank You for trusting Your people with the responsibility of passing faith forward. Forgive us when we take this calling lightly or feel unprepared. Help our family walk in Your ways together, trusting You to shape hearts across generations. Amen.

♟ FAMILY ACTIVITY

On a scrapbook page, write the title **"Passing Faith Forward."** Draw a tree with branches or a path moving forward. Each family member writes one value or habit they want to pass on: prayer, kindness, trust, or obedience. Leave space to return later and reflect on how living out faith together shaped your family.

July 7

Growing Strong as We Remain Faithful to God

"But those who love the Lord shall be like the sun when it rises in its strength." –
Judges 5:31

This verse appears at the close of a song of praise after a hard-fought victory. It looks beyond the battle itself and points to a deeper truth: strength comes from loving the Lord, not from winning or striving alone.

The image of the rising sun speaks of steady strength, not sudden power. It grows brighter as it rises. In the same way, faithfulness to God often builds strength gradually. It is shaped through trust, obedience, and perseverance over time.

Loving the Lord does not mean life is free from difficulty. It means choosing faithfulness even when circumstances are challenging. God honors that love by giving strength that endures rather than fades.

For families, this verse offers encouragement. Strength in a home is not created by having everything figured out. It grows as families choose to love God together, through prayer, forgiveness, and daily faithfulness in ordinary moments.

Children learn that strength is connected to devotion, not dominance. Adults are reminded that faithfulness matters more than visible success. A family that loves the Lord grows steadily stronger, rooted in His presence and care.

Let us take a few minutes to talk together about the following:

1. What does it mean to love the Lord in everyday family life?
2. How is God's strength different from human strength?
3. Why does strength often grow slowly over time?
4. How can our family show love for God this week?

✒ PRAYER

Faithful God, thank You for strengthening those who love You. Thank You for growing our strength through steady faithfulness rather than sudden success. Forgive us when we look for strength in the wrong places. Help our family love You deeply and walk faithfully with You, trusting You to strengthen us day by day. Amen.

⛰ FAMILY ACTIVITY

On a scrapbook page, write the title **"Growing Strong in the Lord."** Draw a rising sun or a plant growing toward the light. Each family member writes one way they want to show love for God, through obedience, kindness, prayer, or trust. Leave space to return later and reflect on how loving God brought strength to your family.

Choosing to Walk Faithfully Within Our Home

"I will walk with integrity of heart within my house." – Psalm 101:2

This verse speaks quietly, but it carries weight. It is not about public appearance or reputation. It is about how life is lived behind closed doors, where words, attitudes, and choices are often unseen by others but fully known to God.

Walking with integrity of heart begins inside the home. It shapes how family members speak to one another, how conflicts are handled, and how forgiveness is offered. Integrity is not perfection—it is consistency between what is believed and how life is lived.

God cares deeply about what happens within the home. Faith is not meant to be performed only in public spaces. It is meant to be lived out in ordinary moments: at the table, in conversation, and during disagreement or disappointment.

For families, this verse is both an encouragement and a guide. It reminds parents that children learn faith by watching daily life. It reminds children that faith shapes choices even when no one else is watching. God honors hearts that desire to walk faithfully before Him at home.

Choosing integrity within the home builds trust and peace. When families commit to walking honestly and humbly before God, the home becomes a place of safety and growth. Faith becomes something lived together, not simply talked about.

Let us take a few minutes to talk together about the following:

1. What does it mean to walk with integrity at home?
2. Why can it be harder to live out faith with family than in public?
3. How does integrity shape trust within a household?
4. What is one way our family can choose faithfulness at home this week?

✎ PRAYER

Holy God, thank You for caring about the way we live within our homes. Thank You for inviting us to walk before You with honest hearts. Forgive us when our actions do not match our faith. Help our family live with integrity, reflecting Your truth and love in all that we do. Amen.

♟ FAMILY ACTIVITY

On a scrapbook page, write the title **"Walking Faithfully at Home."** Draw a house with a heart inside. Each family member writes one choice or habit that helps them live with integrity at home: kind words, honesty, patience, or forgiveness. Leave space to return later and reflect on how choosing faithfulness strengthened your family.

July 9
Building a Home That Reflects God's Wisdom

"By wisdom a house is built, and by understanding it is established; by knowledge the rooms are filled with all precious and pleasant riches." – Proverbs 24:3–4

This verse reminds us that a home is more than walls and routines. What truly builds a household is wisdom, understanding, and knowledge that come from God. These are not material riches, but lasting qualities that shape how family life is lived.

Wisdom guides decisions. It helps families choose words carefully, respond with patience, and seek God's ways rather than reacting out of frustration. Understanding allows family members to listen, empathize, and grow together even when differences arise.

The verse speaks of rooms being filled, not with possessions, but with what is "precious and pleasant." Peace, trust, forgiveness, and faith are the kinds of riches God desires for a home. These things grow when God's wisdom is welcomed into daily life.

Building this kind of home takes time. It is formed through countless small moments: prayers spoken, apologies offered, and grace extended. God is at work in these ordinary moments, shaping homes that reflect His care and truth.

For families, this verse offers hope and direction. A home built on God's wisdom becomes a place of security and growth. Children learn that faith shapes how life is lived, and adults are reminded that God provides what is needed to build something lasting.

Let us take a few minutes to talk together about the following:

1. What does it mean to build a home with wisdom?
2. How do understanding and patience help families grow stronger?
3. What kinds of "riches" matter most in a household?
4. How can our family invite God's wisdom into our home this week?

PRAYER

Wise God, thank You for caring about the way our homes are built. Thank You for offering wisdom, understanding, and knowledge to those who seek You. Forgive us when we rely on our own ways instead of Yours. Help our family build a home that reflects Your truth, peace, and love each day. Amen.

FAMILY ACTIVITY

On a scrapbook page, write the title **"Building Our Home With God's Wisdom."** Draw a house with labeled rooms. In each room, write a quality your family wants God to grow there, such as peace, kindness, patience, faith, or forgiveness. Leave space to return later and reflect on how God filled your home with what truly matters.

July 10
Learning to Walk Faithfully as We Grow Together

"And keep the charge of the Lord your God, walking in his ways and keeping his statutes." – 1 Kings 2:3

These words were spoken from a father to a son at a meaningful moment. David was passing on more than instruction: he was passing on a way of life shaped by faith. His encouragement focused not on success or comfort, but on faithfulness to God.

Walking in God's ways is not about knowing every answer. It is about choosing obedience one step at a time. This kind of faithfulness grows through daily decisions, often made quietly and without recognition. God honors hearts that desire to follow Him consistently.

For families, this verse speaks to shared direction. Faith is not only taught through words, but through example. Children learn what it means to walk with God by watching how trust, obedience, and humility are practiced at home.

Keeping God's ways requires attentiveness. It invites families to pause, seek God's guidance, and choose His wisdom over convenience. These choices shape character and strengthen relationships over time.

When families commit to walking faithfully together, faith becomes a shared journey. There will be missteps and learning along the way, but God remains patient and present. A family that walks in God's ways grows together under His care.

Let us take a few minutes to talk together about the following:

1. What does it mean to walk in God's ways as a family?
2. Why is faithfulness often shown in small, daily choices?
3. How do examples at home help shape faith?
4. What is one way our family can follow God more closely today?

PRAYER

Guiding God, thank You for showing us the path of faithfulness. Thank You for walking with our family as we grow and learn. Forgive us when we lose focus or choose our own way. Help our family walk in Your ways together, trusting Your wisdom and care each day. Amen.

FAMILY ACTIVITY

On a scrapbook page, write the title **"Walking in God's Ways Together."** Draw a path or footprints leading forward. Each family member writes one choice they want to make this week that reflects faithfulness to God. Leave space to return later and reflect on how walking together strengthened your family's faith.

July 11

Faith That Is Passed From One Heart to Another

"I am reminded of your sincere faith, a faith that dwelt first in your grandmother Lois and your mother Eunice and now, I am sure, dwells in you as well." – 2 Timothy 1:5

This verse gives us a glimpse into a family story shaped quietly by faith. Paul does not describe a dramatic moment or public achievement. Instead, he points to something steady and sincere: a faith that lived in one generation and was passed on to the next.

Faith in this passage is not forced or rushed. It dwelt in Lois and Eunice. It had a home in their lives. Through everyday teaching, example, and trust in God, that faith took root in Timothy as well. God worked through ordinary family faithfulness to shape a young believer.

This reminds families that faith is often formed slowly. It grows through repeated moments: prayers spoken, Scripture read, questions welcomed, and trust demonstrated during hard times. God uses consistency more often than perfection.

Parents and caregivers are encouraged here, but not burdened. This verse does not suggest control over outcomes. It highlights God's faithfulness in using willing hearts. Faith passed on is ultimately sustained by God, not by flawless parenting.

For families today, this truth brings hope. What is lived out faithfully before God leaves an imprint. A family that walks with God together may not see immediate results, but God is at work across generations, shaping hearts in ways that endure.

Let us take a few minutes to talk together about the following:

1. What stands out to you about Timothy's family faith?
2. How does faith show itself in everyday family life?
3. Why is consistency more important than perfection?
4. What is one way our family can live out faith for the next generation?

PRAYER

Faithful God, thank You for working through families across generations. Thank You for planting faith in hearts and helping it grow over time. Forgive us when we feel discouraged or inadequate. Help our family live sincerely before You, trusting You to use our faithfulness in ways that last. Amen.

FAMILY ACTIVITY

On a scrapbook page, write the title **"Faith That Lives in Our Family."** Draw a tree with roots and branches. Each family member writes one way faith has been shown in their family or one way they want to pass faith on through words or actions. Leave space to return later and reflect on how God continues to grow faith across generations.

Covering Our Family in Faithful Prayer

"Thus Job did continually." – Job 1:5

This short sentence carries deep meaning. It comes after Scripture describes how Job regularly prayed on behalf of his children. He did not wait for trouble or react only when something went wrong. He prayed continually, faithfully bringing his family before God.

Job understood something important: while he loved his children deeply, their lives ultimately rested in God's hands. Prayer was not a ritual for him, it was an act of trust. He placed his family under God's care again and again, acknowledging God's authority and mercy.

This verse reminds families that faith is often practiced quietly. There is no dramatic scene here, no public display, just steady obedience. God sees that kind of faithfulness. He honors prayer that is offered consistently and humbly.

For families today, this example is reassuring. Parents and caregivers cannot control every outcome, protect from every hardship, or guide every decision. But they can pray. Bringing family members before God is one of the most loving and faithful things a family can do.

Prayer shapes hearts even when results are unseen. A family that prays together, and for one another, learns to depend on God rather than fear what they cannot control. Faith grows in the quiet spaces where trust is practiced daily.

Let us take a few minutes to talk together about the following:

1. Why do you think Job prayed for his children regularly?
2. What does "continually" teach us about faithfulness?
3. How does prayer help families trust God with what they cannot control?
4. How can our family grow more consistent in praying for one another?

✍ PRAYER

Faithful God, thank You for inviting us to bring our family before You in prayer. Thank You for caring deeply about every person in our home. Forgive us when worry replaces trust or prayer is forgotten. Help our family remain faithful in prayer, continually placing one another in Your loving care. Amen.

♟ FAMILY ACTIVITY

On a scrapbook page, write the title **"Praying Continually for Our Family."** Draw a circle of names or hands joined together. Each family member writes one person in the family they want to pray for regularly. Leave space to return later and reflect on how prayer has shaped your family's faith and trust in God.

July 13

Living Under God's Blessing as a Family

"The Lord bless you and keep you; the Lord make his face to shine upon you and be gracious to you." – Numbers 6:24–25

These words were given by God as a blessing to be spoken over His people. They were not instructions to follow or goals to reach. They were a reminder of God's favor, care, and nearness resting on those who belong to Him.

God's blessing begins with His presence. To be kept by the Lord means to be watched over, guarded, and cared for in ways both seen and unseen. This blessing speaks reassurance into everyday life, reminding families that God is attentive to their needs.

The image of God's face shining reflects relationship. It points to grace, kindness, and peace flowing from God toward His people. This is not earned favor, but given grace. Families live under God's blessing not because they are perfect, but because He is faithful.

For families, this verse offers comfort and confidence. It reminds parents and children alike that God's care covers every part of life—busy days, quiet nights, joys, and struggles. God's blessing is not limited to special moments; it rests on everyday living.

Living with an awareness of God's blessing shapes how families treat one another. Gratitude grows. Peace deepens. Trust becomes steadier. A family that remembers God's blessing learns to live with hope, knowing they are held by His gracious care.

Let us take a few minutes to talk together about the following:

1. What does it mean to be blessed and kept by the Lord?
2. How does knowing God is gracious affect our family's attitude?
3. Why is it important to remember God's presence in daily life?
4. How can our family live with gratitude for God's blessing today?

✐ PRAYER

Gracious God, thank You for blessing and keeping Your people. Thank You for watching over our family with care and kindness. Forgive us when we forget Your nearness or take Your grace for granted. Help our family live each day aware of Your blessing, trusting Your protection and resting in Your peace. Amen.

♟ FAMILY ACTIVITY

On a scrapbook page, write the title **"Living Under God's Blessing."** Draw a family surrounded by light or hands held together. Each family member writes one way they have seen God's care or blessing recently. Leave space to return later and add new reminders of how God continues to watch over your family.

July 14
Learning to Trust God's Care as We Grow

"Like an eagle that stirs up its nest, that flutters over its young, spreading out its wings, catching them, bearing them on its pinions." – Deuteronomy 32:11

This verse paints a tender and powerful picture of how God cares for His people. The image is not one of distance or detachment, but of attentive, watchful involvement. God is described as guiding growth while staying close enough to protect.

An eagle stirs the nest to encourage its young to learn to fly. It is not done to harm, but to help them grow stronger. Yet even as the young learn, the eagle remains ready to catch them. This shows that growth and care are never separated in God's design.

Families experience seasons like this. Children grow, independence develops, and change becomes necessary. This verse reassures families that God remains present through every stage. He does not abandon His people while they grow: He carries them.

God's care allows space for learning while providing security. Trusting Him means believing that even uncomfortable transitions are guided by His wisdom. God knows when to encourage growth and when to provide protection.

For families, this truth brings peace. Parenting, caregiving, and growing together can feel uncertain. Remembering that God is both guiding and guarding helps families move forward with confidence. A family that trusts God's care learns to grow without fear, knowing they are always held by Him.

Let us take a few minutes to talk together about the following:

1. What does this verse teach us about how God cares for His people?
2. Why do you think growth sometimes feels uncomfortable?
3. How does knowing God is watching over us bring peace?
4. What is one area where our family needs to trust God during change?

PRAYER

Caring God, thank You for guiding Your people with wisdom and love. Thank You for staying near as we grow and change. Forgive us when fear makes it hard to trust You. Help our family rely on Your care, knowing You guide us and hold us every step of the way. Amen.

FAMILY ACTIVITY

On a scrapbook page, write the title **"Held by God as We Grow."** Draw an eagle, wings, or hands supporting something fragile. Each family member writes one change or new step they are facing and a short prayer trusting God's care. Leave space to return later and reflect on how God provided strength and peace during growth.

July 15
Choosing Faithfulness Together as a Family

"So Joshua made a covenant with the people that day, and put in place statutes and rules for them at Shechem." – Joshua 24:25

This verse comes at the close of a significant gathering. Joshua was not only addressing individuals; he was speaking to families and an entire community. The moment was about commitment, choosing to live under God's guidance together.

A covenant is more than a promise. It is a shared decision to walk in faithfulness over time. Joshua understood that faith was not meant to be occasional or private. It was meant to shape daily life, guiding how people lived, worshiped, and treated one another.

For families, this verse highlights the importance of shared direction. Faith grows stronger when it is practiced together rather than separately. When families choose to live according to God's ways, they create consistency and clarity for one another.

God's instructions were not given to restrict life, but to protect it. His guidance provided structure and purpose. Families who choose faithfulness are not choosing rigidity; they are choosing a path shaped by God's wisdom and care.

This verse reminds families that commitment to God is lived out over time. It is strengthened through shared prayer, obedience, and trust. A family that chooses faithfulness together learns to walk with God in unity and confidence.

Let us take a few minutes to talk together about the following:

1. What does it mean for a family to choose faithfulness together?
2. Why is shared commitment important for spiritual growth?
3. How do God's instructions help guide family life?
4. What is one way our family can renew our commitment to God today?

PRAYER

Faithful God, thank You for inviting families to walk with You together. Thank You for giving guidance that brings clarity and purpose. Forgive us when we drift or make faith an individual effort only. Help our family choose faithfulness daily, trusting Your wisdom as we grow together in obedience and love. Amen.

FAMILY ACTIVITY

On a scrapbook page, write the title **"Choosing Faithfulness Together."** Draw a group standing side by side or a path with many footprints. Each family member writes one commitment they want to make, such as prayer, kindness, obedience, or trust. Leave space to return later and reflect on how walking faithfully together shaped your family.

July 16

Holding Fast to the Love God Has Given

"Many waters cannot quench love, neither can floods drown it." –
Song of Solomon 8:7

This verse speaks of a love that endures. It is not fragile or temporary, and it is not undone by difficulty. The picture is strong and steady: love that remains even when circumstances are overwhelming.

Scripture reminds us that love is part of God's design. It is not merely a feeling, but a gift that reflects His own faithfulness. The kind of love described here is resilient because it is rooted in commitment and care, not convenience.

Families experience seasons that test love. Stress, change, misunderstanding, and weariness can feel like rising waters. This verse reassures us that love grounded in God is not easily swept away. God strengthens what He has established.

Holding fast to love requires trust in God's work. He is the One who sustains relationships through hardship. When families rely on God rather than emotion alone, love becomes steadier and deeper over time.

For families, this truth brings hope. Love does not have to disappear when things are hard. God's design for love is lasting. A family that entrusts its relationships to Him learns to remain connected, even through challenges that feel overwhelming.

Let us take a few minutes to talk together about the following:

1. What does this verse teach us about the strength of love?
2. Why do challenges sometimes make love feel harder?
3. How does trusting God help love endure in families?
4. What is one way our family can protect and strengthen love this week?

✎ PRAYER

Faithful God, thank You for the love You have placed within families. Thank You for sustaining love through every season. Forgive us when we rely only on our own strength. Help our family hold fast to the love You give, trusting You to keep it strong even when challenges arise. Amen.

♟ FAMILY ACTIVITY

On a scrapbook page, write the title **"Love That Endures."** Draw waves with an anchor or a heart protected by a shield. Each family member writes one way they can show steady love: through patience, forgiveness, or care. Leave space to return later and reflect on how God helped your family remain strong in love.

July 17
God Is Our Teacher

"I will instruct you and teach you in the way you should go; I will counsel you with my eye upon you." – Psalm 32:8

Teaching is more than giving information, it is guiding someone to live wisely. Psalm 32:8 promises that God Himself will instruct and teach His people. Families can trust that His guidance is personal and caring.

Throughout history, God has taught His people. He gave the law to Moses, showing Israel how to live. He sent prophets to call them back when they strayed. Jesus came as the ultimate Teacher, explaining God's kingdom and calling His followers to obedience.

Jesus' teaching amazed people because He spoke with authority. He used parables to help them understand spiritual truths. He also taught by example, living out love, service, and obedience to the Father.

The Holy Spirit continues God's teaching today. Jesus promised that the Spirit would remind His followers of all He had said (John 14:26). Families can rely on the Spirit to help them understand Scripture and apply it daily.

Living with God as teacher means humility. Families should admit that they need guidance. It means listening to Scripture, praying for wisdom, and practicing obedience. True learning is not only knowing but living.

Let us take a few minutes to talk together about the following:

1. What does Psalm 32:8 teach us about God's teaching?
2. How did Jesus reveal Himself as the great Teacher?
3. How does the Spirit continue to teach believers today?
4. How can our family listen and obey God's teaching this week?

PRAYER

Wise Teacher, thank You for guiding us with truth. Thank You for showing us Your way through Scripture and the Spirit. Forgive us when we ignore Your counsel. Teach our family to walk in obedience with humble hearts. Amen.

FAMILY ACTIVITY

On a scrapbook page, write "God Our Teacher." Each family member writes one lesson they learned from the Bible this week.

July 18

Choosing to Trust God When Our Family Is Hurting

"But the mother of the child said, 'As the Lord lives and as you yourself live, I will not leave you.'" – 2 Kings 4:30

These words were spoken by a mother in deep distress. Her child was unwell, and fear pressed in on every side. Yet instead of giving in to despair, she clung to the hope that God could intervene. Her determination was not loud faith, it was persistent trust.

This verse captures a moment of unwavering resolve. The mother refused to walk away from the help God could provide. Her words reflect confidence not in herself, but in the Lord who gives life and hears the cries of His people.

Families experience moments when pain feels close and answers feel far away. This verse reminds us that faith does not always look calm or composed. Sometimes faith looks like refusing to give up hope and choosing to stay close to where God is at work.

God honored this mother's persistence. He saw her pain and responded with compassion and power. Scripture reminds us that God is attentive to the cries of families and present in moments of fear and uncertainty.

For families today, this passage offers reassurance. Trusting God does not require perfect words or understanding. It requires staying near Him, even when emotions are heavy. A family that chooses to trust God together during hardship learns that His care does not fail when it is needed most.

Let us take a few minutes to talk together about the following:

1. Why do you think this mother refused to leave?
2. What does this verse teach us about trusting God during fear or pain?
3. How can families support one another during hard moments?
4. What situation does our family need to bring to God right now?

📖 PRAYER

Compassionate God, thank You for seeing the pain Your people carry. Thank You for being near to families in moments of fear and uncertainty. Forgive us when we lose hope or try to face hardship alone. Help our family cling to You with trust, believing that You are present and powerful even in our hardest moments. Amen.

🎄 FAMILY ACTIVITY

On a scrapbook page, write the title **"Holding On to Hope."** Draw hands reaching upward or a family standing together. Each family member writes one worry or concern they want to entrust to God. Leave space to return later and reflect on how God brought comfort, strength, or help during that season.

July 19

Trusting God to Care for Our Family

"For thus says the Lord God: Behold, I, I myself will search for my sheep and will seek them out." – Ezekiel 34:11

God spoke these words to people who felt scattered and neglected. Leaders had failed them, and they were unsure where help would come from. In response, God made a personal promise: I myself will search for my sheep. He did not delegate His care. He claimed it.

This verse reveals God's heart as a Shepherd. He notices when His people feel lost, overlooked, or worn down. God does not wait for His sheep to find their way back on their own. He goes after them with intention and care.

Families can relate to this kind of need. There are seasons when family members feel overwhelmed, disconnected, or unsure of the next step. This verse reminds us that God is attentive to each person within a family. No one is invisible to Him.

God's care is active, not passive. He seeks, gathers, and protects. Trusting God as Shepherd means believing that He sees what we cannot always fix and cares in ways that are deeper than our understanding.

For families, this truth brings reassurance. God's care does not depend on perfect leadership at home or flawless faith. He remains faithful to seek, guide, and restore. A family that trusts God's care learns to rest, knowing they are watched over by a Shepherd who does not forget His own.

Let us take a few minutes to talk together about the following:

1. What does this verse teach us about how God cares for His people?
2. Why is it comforting to know that God seeks out those who feel lost?
3. How does God's care help families during difficult seasons?
4. Where does our family need to trust God's shepherding right now?

PRAYER

Caring God, thank You for seeking out Your people with love and faithfulness. Thank You for watching over our family even when we feel uncertain or weary. Forgive us when we forget that You see and care for every need. Help our family trust You as our Shepherd, resting in Your guidance and protection. Amen.

FAMILY ACTIVITY

On a scrapbook page, write the title **"God Cares for Our Family."** Draw a shepherd with sheep or a family surrounded by protective arms. Each family member writes one area where they need God's care or guidance. Leave space to return later and reflect on how God showed His faithfulness over time.

July 20

Seeking God's Guidance for Our Family

"Then Manoah prayed to the Lord and said, 'O Lord, please let the man of God whom you sent come again to us and teach us what we are to do with the child who will be born.'" – Judges 13:8

This prayer was spoken by a father who knew he needed God's direction. Manoah was preparing for something new and unknown, and rather than relying on his own understanding, he asked God to teach him how to lead and care for his child.

This verse shows humility. Manoah did not assume he already knew what to do. He recognized that raising and guiding a child was a responsibility that required wisdom beyond his own. His first response was prayer.

Families today face similar moments. Parenting, decision-making, and leading a household often come with uncertainty. This verse reminds families that God welcomes questions and requests for guidance. He is not distant from family concerns, He invites them.

Seeking God's instruction acknowledges that children are gifts entrusted by Him. Families are not meant to figure everything out alone. God provides wisdom for each season, step by step, as families look to Him.

For families, this prayer becomes an example. It encourages turning to God not only when problems arise, but also when preparing for what lies ahead. A family that seeks God's guidance learns to walk forward with humility, trust, and confidence in His care.

Let us take a few minutes to talk together about the following:

1. Why do you think Manoah asked God for guidance instead of relying on himself?
2. What does this verse teach us about parenting and responsibility?
3. Why is it important for families to seek God's wisdom?
4. What is one area where our family needs God's guidance right now?

📖 PRAYER

Wise God, thank You for inviting families to seek Your guidance. Thank You for caring about every detail of our lives and responsibilities. Forgive us when we rely on our own understanding instead of turning to You. Teach our family to seek Your wisdom, trusting You to guide us faithfully. Amen.

♟ FAMILY ACTIVITY

On a scrapbook page, write the title **"Seeking God's Guidance Together."** Draw a family praying or a path with signposts. Each family member writes one decision or responsibility they want to bring before God. Leave space to return later and reflect on how God provided clarity or direction.

July 21
God Is Our Savior

"For the Son of Man came to seek and to save the lost." – Luke 19:10

The title "Savior" is one of the most precious names of God. Luke 19:10 tells us that Jesus came with a mission, to seek and save the lost. Families should rejoice that salvation is not something we earn, but something God gives through Jesus.

The Bible shows God as Savior from the very beginning. He saved Noah and his family from the flood. He saved Israel from slavery in Egypt. He saved Jonah from the fish and Daniel from the lions. These moments all pointed forward to Jesus, who would bring the greatest salvation of all.

Jesus saves from sin and death. On the cross, He took the punishment that humanity deserved. His resurrection proved that salvation is complete and eternal. Acts 4:12 declares, "There is salvation in no one else." Families should cling to this truth, only Jesus saves.

Being saved is more than escaping punishment. It means being adopted into God's family, given eternal hope, and receiving new life. Salvation also transforms how we live. Families should show gratitude by loving God and serving others.

Living with God as Savior means daily trust in Jesus, celebrating forgiveness, and sharing the gospel with others. A family rooted in salvation will shine His love into their community.

Let us take a few minutes to talk together about the following:

1. What does Luke 19:10 teach us about Jesus' mission?
2. How does the Bible show God as Savior throughout history?
3. Why is salvation only through Jesus?
4. How can our family show gratitude for salvation this week?

PRAYER

Saving God, thank You for sending Jesus to seek and save the lost. Thank You for rescuing us from sin and death. Forgive us when we forget the cost of salvation. Teach our family to live with gratitude and to share Your good news. Amen.

FAMILY ACTIVITY

On a scrapbook page, draw a cross. Around it, each family member writes one blessing that comes from being saved. Title the page "God Our Savior."

July 22

God Is Our Comforter

"As a mother comforts her child, so will I comfort you." – Isaiah 66:13

Comfort is more than words. It is presence, care, and assurance. Isaiah 66:13 shows God's heart, comparing His comfort to that of a mother for her child. Families should remember that God's comfort is gentle, personal, and real.

The Bible gives many examples of God's comfort. He comforted Hagar when she was alone in the wilderness. He comforted Elijah when he was discouraged, sending an angel with food and rest. Jesus comforted His disciples when they were afraid, promising peace and the Holy Spirit.

Second Corinthians 1:3-4 calls God "the Father of mercies and God of all comfort." He comforts us so that we can comfort others. Families should learn to receive His comfort and share it.

Comfort does not always remove pain, but it gives strength in the middle of it. Families may face grief, disappointment, or fear, but God's comfort meets them where they are. His Spirit reminds us of His promises, and His people encourage us with love.

Living with God as comforter means bringing burdens to Him, trusting His care, and encouraging others with the comfort we receive. Families should create a home where God's comfort is shared freely.

Let us take a few minutes to talk together about the following:

1. What does Isaiah 66:13 teach us about God's comfort?
2. How has God comforted His people in the Bible?
3. How does He use His Spirit and His people to comfort us today?
4. How can our family share God's comfort this week?

📖 PRAYER

Comforting God, thank You for caring for us like a loving parent. Thank You for meeting us in our pain with Your peace. Forgive us when we forget to turn to You. Teach our family to rest in Your comfort and to comfort others. Amen.

⛪ FAMILY ACTIVITY

On a scrapbook page, write "God Our Comforter." Each family member writes one way God has comforted them. Add Isaiah 66:13 at the bottom.

July 23

When Our Family Chooses to Walk in Truth

"I have no greater joy than to hear that my children are walking in the truth." – 3 John 1:4

This verse feels personal. It sounds like something spoken from the heart, not from a distance. It reminds us that what matters most is not success, recognition, or outward achievement, but lives shaped by God's truth.

Walking in truth does not mean getting everything right. It means choosing honesty, faithfulness, and obedience day by day. It shows up in small moments: how we speak to one another, how we admit when we are wrong, and how we choose what is right even when it is inconvenient.

In family life, truth is learned slowly. Children notice how adults handle frustration, how forgiveness is offered, and how faith is lived when things are hard. Long before they understand Scripture fully, they understand whether God's truth is real in the home.

This verse reminds us that faith is not something we can force. It grows as it is lived out consistently. When families choose truth, especially in ordinary moments, it creates an environment where trust can grow and God's presence is honored.

There is deep joy in knowing that truth is taking root. It is a quiet joy, often unseen by others, but known to God. A family that walks in truth together may stumble at times, but they remain pointed in the right direction, guided by God's Word and grace.

Let us take a few minutes to talk together about the following:

1. What do you think it means to "walk in the truth"?
2. Why do you think truth is learned through everyday life, not just words?
3. How can our actions show what we truly believe?
4. What is one way our family can choose truth today?

PRAYER

God of truth, thank You for guiding Your people with wisdom and grace. Thank You for caring about how we live, not just what we say we believe. Forgive us when our choices do not reflect Your truth. Help our family walk honestly before You, trusting Your Word to guide us each day. Amen.

FAMILY ACTIVITY

On a scrapbook page, write the title **"Walking in Truth Together."** Draw a simple path or a set of footprints. Each family member writes one small choice they want to make that reflects God's truth: being honest, asking forgiveness, showing kindness, or keeping a promise. Leave space to return later and reflect on how choosing truth shaped your family's week.

July 24

Trusting God With What We Cannot See

"As you do not know the way the spirit comes to the bones in the womb of a woman with child, so you do not know the work of God who makes everything." – Ecclesiastes 11:5

This verse reminds us of something we all experience but cannot explain. Life itself is formed in ways we cannot see or control. God is at work long before results are visible, doing things far beyond our understanding.

Family life often feels this way. We teach, correct, encourage, and pray, but we don't always see immediate change. Growth happens quietly. Faith takes root slowly. God works in places we can't reach and in ways we can't measure.

This verse invites families to release the pressure to control outcomes. We are not meant to see or manage every detail. God is already at work, shaping hearts and guiding lives in ways that are hidden for now.

Trust grows when families learn to rest in God's unseen work. It means continuing to love, pray, and walk faithfully even when progress feels unclear. God does not waste those moments. He uses them.

For families, this truth brings peace. We don't have to understand everything to trust God. We only need to remember that He is working, even when we cannot see it yet.

Let us take a few minutes to talk together about the following:

1. Why do you think God's work is often hidden from us?
2. What is hard about trusting God when we don't see results?
3. Where might God be working in our family right now without us noticing?
4. How can we practice patience as we trust God's work?

✏ PRAYER

God who sees all things, thank You for working in ways we cannot see or understand. Thank You for caring about our family even when progress feels slow. Forgive us when we try to control what belongs to You. Help our family trust Your work, believing that You are always present and faithful. Amen.

♟ FAMILY ACTIVITY

On a scrapbook page, write the title **"God Is Working, Even When We Can't See It."** Draw something growing underground, like roots or a seed beneath the soil. Each family member writes one area where they want to trust God more, even without seeing immediate results. Leave space to return later and reflect on how God was at work over time.

July 25

Learning to Live With Quiet Trust

*"But I will leave in your midst a people humble and lowly. They shall seek refuge in
the name of the Lord." – Zephaniah 3:12*

This verse does not describe loud faith or public recognition. It speaks about people who live quietly before God: humble, dependent, and trusting Him for refuge. It reminds us that God often works through hearts that are willing to rely on Him rather than stand out.

Seeking refuge in the Lord means knowing where to turn when life feels heavy. It means trusting God as a place of safety, not only in crisis, but in everyday life. This kind of trust is steady, not rushed or dramatic.

Families need this kind of refuge. Homes face stress, disappointment, misunderstandings, and seasons of uncertainty. This verse reminds us that God does not overlook quiet faith lived behind closed doors. He sees families who come to Him simply because they need Him.

Humility creates space for trust. When families admit they do not have all the answers, they are more open to God's guidance. Seeking refuge becomes a habit, not a last resort.

For families, this verse is comforting. God is near to those who depend on Him. A family that learns to seek refuge in the Lord finds stability that does not depend on circumstances, but on God's faithful presence.

Let us take a few minutes to talk together about the following:

1. What does it mean to seek refuge in the Lord?
2. Why can quiet trust be harder than visible strength?
3. How does humility help families rely on God?
4. Where does our family need God to be our refuge right now?

✒ PRAYER

Faithful God, thank You for being a place of refuge for Your people. Thank You for welcoming humble hearts and quiet trust. Forgive us when we rely on ourselves instead of turning to You. Help our family seek You daily, resting in Your care and trusting Your presence. Amen.

♟ FAMILY ACTIVITY

On a scrapbook page, write the title **"Finding Refuge in the Lord."** Draw a shelter, a safe place, or a family gathered together. Each family member writes one situation where they want to trust God rather than worry. Leave space to come back later and reflect on how God provided peace and steadiness.

July 26

Asking God to Stay Close to Our Family

"May the Lord our God be with us, as he was with our fathers. May he not leave us or forsake us." – 1 Kings 8:57

This verse is part of a prayer, not a lesson. It comes from a moment when God's people were settling into something new, and Solomon knew they would need more than structure or leadership. They would need God's presence to remain with them.

There is something honest about this request. It doesn't assume strength or success. It simply asks God to stay close. To not leave. To remain faithful, just as He had been before.

Families often need this same prayer. Not for everything to be easy, but for God to stay near. Life changes. Children grow. Responsibilities increase. The need for God's presence doesn't fade, it deepens.

This verse reminds families that God's nearness is not something to take for granted. It is something to ask for, rely on, and cherish. God's faithfulness in the past becomes the reason we trust Him in the present.

When families ask God to remain with them, they are admitting something important: they cannot walk forward well on their own. A family that seeks God's presence learns to face change with humility and quiet confidence, trusting that He will not forsake them.

Let us take a few minutes to talk together about the following:

1. Why is God's presence more important than having everything figured out?

2. When does our family most need to ask God to stay close?

3. How does remembering God's past faithfulness help us trust Him now?

4. What is one way our family can invite God into our daily life?

✎ PRAYER

Faithful God, thank You for being present with Your people through every generation. Thank You for not leaving or forsaking those who trust You. Forgive us when we rely on our own strength instead of seeking You. Help our family walk forward knowing You are with us, today and always. Amen.

♟ FAMILY ACTIVITY

On a scrapbook page, write the title **"God With Us."** Draw a simple house or a family gathered together. Each family member writes one moment in daily life where they want to remember God's presence: during meals, conversations, work, or rest. Leave space to return later and reflect on how being aware of God's nearness changed your family's days.

July 27
God Is Our Helper

"Behold, God is my helper; the Lord is the upholder of my life." – Psalm 54:4

Life is full of challenges. Children need help with learning and growing. Parents need help with wisdom and patience. Families need help with decisions, struggles, and fears. Psalm 54:4 reminds us that God is our helper and sustainer.

The Bible shows God's help in many ways. He gave Moses courage to lead Israel. He gave Hannah the child she prayed for. He gave David strength against Goliath. He gave Paul boldness to keep preaching even when he was imprisoned.

Jesus promised the Holy Spirit as our Helper. John 14:26 says the Spirit teaches us, reminds us of God's Word, and gives strength. Families can be encouraged that God never leaves them alone.

God's help often comes at the right time, not always when we expect it. His help may look like wisdom, comfort, or endurance. Families should learn to call on Him first in prayer and trust His answers.

Living with God as helper means humility: admitting we need Him. It also means gratitude, thanking Him for daily help and strength. Families who depend on God's help will find peace and confidence.

Let us take a few minutes to talk together about the following:

1. What does Psalm 54:4 teach us about God's help?
2. How has God helped His people in the Bible?
3. How does the Spirit help believers today?
4. How can our family rely on God's help this week?

PRAYER

Helping God, thank You for upholding our lives. Thank You for sending the Spirit as our Helper. Forgive us when we try to do everything alone. Teach our family to depend on You in every situation. Amen.

FAMILY ACTIVITY

On a scrapbook page, write "God Our Helper." Each family member writes one area where they need God's help. At the end of the week, add notes about how God answered.

July 28

Moving Forward Knowing God Is With Us

"My Spirit remains in your midst. Fear not." – Haggai 2:5

These words were spoken to people who felt discouraged. What they were rebuilding did not look impressive, and many wondered if their efforts even mattered. God did not criticize them or rush them. He reminded them of one simple truth: His Spirit was still with them.

This verse speaks gently into moments when families feel tired or unsure. Sometimes progress looks small. Sometimes faith feels quiet. God does not measure faithfulness by outward appearance. He reassures His people with His presence.

"My Spirit remains" is a steady promise. It means God has not stepped away, even when circumstances feel uncertain. Fear loses its grip when families remember they are not facing life alone.

Families often need this reminder. Changes, responsibilities, and disappointments can stir anxiety. This verse does not promise that everything will feel easy, but it does promise that God's presence remains unchanged.

For families, this brings calm confidence. God is not waiting for perfection or impressive results. He is present now. A family that moves forward trusting God's nearness can face the next step without fear, knowing He walks with them.

Let us take a few minutes to talk together about the following:

1. Why do you think God reminded His people that His Spirit remained?
2. What kinds of things cause fear in family life?
3. How does knowing God is with us change how we face challenges?|
4. What is one area where our family needs to let go of fear and trust God?

PRAYER

Faithful God, thank You for staying with Your people through every season. Thank You for reminding us that Your Spirit remains with us. Forgive us when fear takes over our thoughts. Help our family move forward trusting Your presence, confident that You are near and faithful. Amen.

FAMILY ACTIVITY

On a scrapbook page, write the title **"God Is With Us."** Draw a small group walking forward together. Each family member writes one situation where they need to remember God's presence instead of giving in to fear. Leave space to come back later and write how trusting God helped bring peace or courage.

July 29

God Is Our Protector

"But the Lord is faithful. He will establish you and guard you against the evil one." –
2 Thessalonians 3:3

Protection is something families think about often. Parents lock doors, install alarms, and guide children safely. But true protection comes from God, who guards His people from harm and the evil one.

The Bible shows God's protection again and again. He kept Noah safe in the ark, Daniel safe in the lions' den, and Shadrach, Meshach, and Abednego safe in the fiery furnace. Each story reminds us that God's care is greater than danger.

Jesus prayed for His disciples in John 17:15: "I do not ask that you take them out of the world, but that you keep them from the evil one." Families should remember that God's protection is not always about removing problems but about guarding hearts and faith.

Protection also comes through His Word. Psalm 119:11 says, "I have stored up your word in my heart, that I might not sin against you." Memorizing Scripture shields us from temptation.

Living with God as protector means praying for His covering, trusting His care, and encouraging one another to stay faithful. Families can rest knowing that God's hand is stronger than any enemy.

Let us take a few minutes to talk together about the following:

1. What does 2 Thessalonians 3:3 teach us about God's protection?
2. How has God protected His people in the Bible?
3. How did Jesus pray for His disciples' protection?
4. How can our family trust His protection this week?

✤ PRAYER

Protecting God, thank You for guarding us each day. Thank You for keeping us safe from the evil one. Forgive us when we rely on our own strength. Teach our family to trust Your protection and to stand firm in Your Word. Amen.

♟ FAMILY ACTIVITY

On a scrapbook page, draw a shield. Each family member writes one area of life where they want God's protection. Title the page "God Our Protector."

July 30
Resting in God's Blessing Over Our Family

"Now therefore may it please you to bless the house of your servant, so that it may continue forever before you." – 2 Samuel 7:29

This verse comes from a prayer, not a command. David was not asking for success or comfort. He was asking for God's blessing to rest over his household, not just for the moment, but for what lay ahead.

There is something simple and honest about this request. It acknowledges that the future is not fully known or controlled. David placed his family in God's hands, trusting that God's faithfulness would carry them forward.

Families today still need this same posture. We plan, provide, and care, but we cannot see every outcome. This verse reminds us that God's blessing is not something we earn or manage. It is something we ask for and receive with humility.

God's blessing is steady. It does not depend on perfect decisions or flawless faith. It rests on God's promise and character. When families trust God with what is ahead, they learn to live with peace instead of constant worry.

This verse invites families to pause and pray simply: Lord, bless this home. A family that rests in God's blessing does not have to strive for security. They trust that God is already at work, shaping what comes next.

Let us take a few minutes to talk together about the following:

1. Why do you think David prayed for God's blessing over his household?
2. What does God's blessing mean to our family?
3. Why can it be hard to trust God with the future?
4. How can our family rest more fully in God's care?

✎ PRAYER

Faithful God, thank You for blessing families with Your care and presence. Thank You for holding our future in Your hands. Forgive us when worry replaces trust. Help our family rest in Your blessing, confident that You are faithful today and in the days to come. Amen.

⛄ FAMILY ACTIVITY

On a scrapbook page, write the title **"God's Blessing Over Our Home."** Draw a simple house or open hands. Each family member writes one hope or prayer they want to place before God for the future. Leave space to return later and reflect on how God's faithfulness became clear over time.

July 31

Ending the Month With Our Hearts Turned to God

"O Lord, the God of Abraham, Isaac, and Israel, our fathers, keep forever such purposes and thoughts in the hearts of your people, and direct their hearts toward you." – 1 Chronicles 29:18

This verse is a prayer, spoken at the end of a season. David was not looking ahead with control or certainty. He was asking God to do something deeper than manage events: to guide hearts.

As a month comes to a close, families often reflect on what went well and what didn't. Plans were made. Some were kept. Others quietly fell away. This verse reminds us that what matters most is not a perfect record, but hearts that keep turning back to God.

Directing the heart is God's work. Families can encourage, teach, and model faith, but ultimately it is God who shapes what lasts inside us. This prayer releases the pressure to fix everything and places trust where it belongs.

For families, this is comforting. God sees what we cannot: the slow shaping of character, the quiet growth of trust, the lessons still taking root. He is faithful to guide hearts, even when progress feels uneven.

Ending the month this way helps families let go. We place our efforts, failures, and hopes into God's hands and trust Him to continue His work. What comes next does not rest on us alone, it rests with Him.

Let us take a few minutes to talk together about the following:

1. Why do you think David prayed for God to direct hearts?
2. What does it mean to have our hearts turned toward God?
3. What from this month do we want to release to God?
4. How can we begin the next month trusting God to guide our family?

📖 PRAYER

Faithful God, thank You for caring about the hearts of Your people. Thank You for guiding us patiently, even when we stumble. Forgive us when we try to control what belongs to You. As this month ends, we ask You to direct our hearts toward You and continue Your work in our family. Amen.

⛄ FAMILY ACTIVITY

On a scrapbook page, write the title **"He Directs Our Hearts."** Draw a simple heart with an arrow pointing upward. Each family member writes one hope or concern they want to place before God as the month ends. Leave space to return later and reflect on how God continued to guide your family forward.

AUGUST

August 1
Serving with Love

"Through love serve one another." – Galatians 5:13

Service is not simply about doing tasks. It is about showing love through action. Galatians 5:13 commands believers to serve one another through love. Families should understand that service flows from God's love in us, not from obligation.

Jesus gave the best example of serving with love. He washed His disciples' feet, a job usually done by servants. He said in John 13:14, "If I then, your Lord and Teacher, have washed your feet, you also ought to wash one another's feet." His act of love showed that service is humble, not proud.

The Bible repeatedly links love and service. First Corinthians 13 reminds us that service without love is meaningless. True service cares for people's needs with kindness and patience. Families should practice service with joy, not grudging hearts.

Serving with love also means serving those who cannot repay us. Jesus said in Luke 14:13-14 to invite the poor, the crippled, the lame, and the blind. This reflects God's love, which gives freely.

Living this way means serving at home, at school, at work, and in the community. Families should encourage each other to look for daily opportunities to show love through service.

Let us take a few minutes to talk together about the following:

1. What does Galatians 5:13 teach about serving with love?
2. How did Jesus show service through love in John 13?
3. Why is service without love meaningless?
4. How can our family serve others with love this week?

📖 PRAYER

Loving God, thank You for serving us through Jesus. Thank You for showing us love through His life and death. Forgive us when we serve with pride or selfishness. Teach our family to serve with love daily. Amen.

⚖ FAMILY ACTIVITY

On a scrapbook page, write "Serving with Love." Each family member writes one act of service they will do this week in love.

August 2
Serving with Humility

"Do nothing from selfish ambition or conceit, but in humility count others more significant than yourselves." – Philippians 2:3

Humility means putting others before yourself. Philippians 2:3 commands believers to act with humility, valuing others. Families should learn that service is not about recognition but about blessing others.

Jesus lived this truth. Philippians 2:6–7 says He took the form of a servant, humbling Himself even to death on a cross. The King of glory became a servant to save us. Families should be inspired by His example.

In John 13, Jesus washed His disciples' feet. This humble act shocked them, but He explained that true greatness comes from serving, not being served. Families should remember that humility is the heart of service.

Humility also means accepting tasks that seem small or unnoticed. Families should serve one another in chores, kindness, and encouragement, knowing God sees every act of humility.

Living with humble service creates peace in the home and reflects Christ to the world. A humble family shines brightly in a culture that often seeks pride and self-interest.

Let us take a few minutes to talk together about the following:

1. What does Philippians 2:3 teach about humility?
2. How did Jesus show humility in His life and death?
3. Why is humble service better than seeking recognition?
4. How can our family serve with humility this week?

✐ PRAYER

Humble Savior, thank You for serving us by giving Your life. Thank You for showing that greatness is found in humility. Forgive us when we act with pride. Teach our family to serve humbly and reflect Your heart. Amen.

♟ FAMILY ACTIVITY

On a scrapbook page, write "Serving with Humility." Each family member writes one humble act of service they will do this week without seeking attention.

August 3
Serving with Generosity

"Each one must give as he has decided in his heart, not reluctantly or under compulsion, for God loves a cheerful giver." – 2 Corinthians 9:7

Generosity is serving by giving freely of time, energy, and resources. Second Corinthians 9:7 reminds us that God loves a cheerful giver. Families should learn to serve with open hands, not tight fists.

The Bible gives many examples of generous service. The Good Samaritan gave time, care, and money to help a stranger. The early church shared possessions so that no one was in need. Jesus praised a widow who gave two small coins because she gave from her heart.

Generosity reflects God's character. He gave His Son for our salvation. Romans 8:32 reminds us that if He gave His Son, He will also give us what we need. Families should serve generously because they have already received much.

Generosity is not measured by size but by heart. Families can serve with a meal, a helping hand, or kind words. Small acts, when given cheerfully, honor God.

Living generously creates joy and unity. Families who give together grow closer to God and to each other.

Let us take a few minutes to talk together about the following:

1. What does 2 Corinthians 9:7 teach about generosity?
2. What examples of generosity are found in the Bible?
3. How does God's generosity inspire ours?
4. How can our family serve generously this week?

PRAYER

Generous God, thank You for giving us everything we need. Thank You for giving Jesus as the greatest gift. Forgive us when we hold back in fear. Teach our family to serve generously and joyfully. Amen.

FAMILY ACTIVITY

On a scrapbook page, write "Serving with Generosity." Each family member writes one way they will give time, resources, or kindness this week.

August 4
Serving with Joy

"Serve the Lord with gladness! Come into his presence with singing!" – Psalm 100:2

Joy changes how we serve. Psalm 100:2 calls us to serve the Lord with gladness, not grudging hearts. Families should remember that joyful service honors God and blesses others.

The Bible shows joyful service in many places. David danced before the Lord as he brought the ark. Paul and Silas sang in prison while serving God. The early believers rejoiced even when they were persecuted because they were counted worthy to serve Christ.

Joyful service comes from remembering who we serve. When families realize they serve the Lord, not only people, their hearts are filled with gladness. Colossians 3:23 says, "Whatever you do, work heartily, as for the Lord."

Joyful service also encourages others. A cheerful attitude makes work lighter and points people to God. Families should make joy part of their service, even in chores or hard tasks.

Living with joy means thanking God daily, choosing a grateful heart, and serving with songs and smiles. Families who serve joyfully reflect the goodness of God.

Let us take a few minutes to talk together about the following:

1. What does Psalm 100:2 teach about joyful service?
2. What examples of joyful service are found in Scripture?
3. How does remembering who we serve change our attitude?
4. How can our family serve joyfully this week?

✎ PRAYER

Joyful God, thank You for filling our hearts with gladness. Thank You for giving us reasons to rejoice. Forgive us when we serve with complaints. Teach our family to serve with joy and gratitude. Amen.

⚶ FAMILY ACTIVITY

On a scrapbook page, draw smiling faces. Each family member writes one way they will serve with joy this week. Title the page "Serving with Joy."

August 5
Serving with Obedience

"Whatever he says to you, do it." – John 2:5

At the wedding in Cana, Mary told the servants, "Whatever he says to you, do it." Jesus then turned water into wine, revealing His glory.

Families should remember that true service begins with obedience to God's commands. What does obedience look like, though?

Obedience means trusting God's Word even when it does not make sense. The servants at Cana obeyed Jesus and saw a miracle. Noah obeyed God by building the ark, and his family was saved. Abraham obeyed God's call to leave his home, and he became the father of many nations.

Obedience is not always easy. Sometimes it requires sacrifice or risk. Yet obedience always brings blessing. Jesus said in John 14:15, "If you love me, you will keep my commandments." Families show love by serving God through obedience.

Living with obedient service means reading the Bible, listening carefully, and acting on God's Word. Families should encourage each other to obey in small daily choices, like speaking kindly, forgiving, and telling the truth.

Obedience shows trust in God. Families who obey together will see His faithfulness and grow in faith, every day.

Let us take a few minutes to talk together about the following:

1. What does John 2:5 teach us about obedience?
2. What examples of obedience are seen in the Bible?
3. Why is obedience a sign of love for God?
4. How can our family practice obedience in daily life this week?

PRAYER

Obedient Lord, thank You for showing us the blessing of following Your commands. Thank You for giving us Jesus as the perfect example of obedience. Forgive us when we resist Your Word. Teach our family to obey with trust and love. Amen.

FAMILY ACTIVITY

On a scrapbook page, write "Serving with Obedience." Each family member writes one area where they will obey God this wee

August 6
Serving in Small Things

"Whoever is faithful in very little is also faithful in much." – Luke 16:10

When you think about the words "serving God", what is the first thing that comes to mind? Is it organizing big events at your church or community, or something closer to home, like helping your mom and dad with chores?

Many people want to do great things for God, but Luke 16:10 teaches us that faithfulness begins with small things. Families should understand that serving God in ordinary, unnoticed ways is just as important as serving Him in big tasks.

The Bible gives many examples of serving in small things. Ruth served Naomi by gathering leftover grain. David served his brothers by bringing them food before he faced Goliath. The boy with five loaves and two fish offered his small lunch, and Jesus used it to feed thousands.

Jesus noticed acts that seemed small. In Mark 12:41-44, He praised the widow who gave two small coins. He explained that her small gift was greater than large sums because she gave all she had.

Serving in small things shows faithfulness, humility, and love. Families should remember that God sees every act of service, even when no one else does.

Living with this mindset means doing chores cheerfully, helping siblings, listening with kindness, and saying encouraging words. Small acts build strong families and honor God.

Let us take a few minutes to talk together about the following:

1. What does Luke 16:10 teach us about small acts of service?
2. What small acts of service are seen in the Bible?
3. Why are small things important to God?
4. How can our family serve faithfully in small things this week?

✎ PRAYER

Faithful God, thank You for noticing every act of love, big or small. Thank You for using little things to do great work. Forgive us when we want recognition instead of serving humbly. Teach our family to be faithful in small acts of service. Amen.

♟ FAMILY ACTIVITY

On a scrapbook page, write "Serving in Small Things." Each family member writes one small act of service they will do daily this week.

Using Our Gifts For the Greater Good

"As each has received a gift, use it to serve one another, as good stewards of God's varied grace." – 1 Peter 4:10

What is your most treasured talent or gift? Is it the ability to sing beautifully in the church choir, or is it the skill to bake delicious foods that you can share among community members?

God gives every believer gifts to use for His glory. First Peter 4:10 reminds us to use those gifts to serve others. Families should recognize that everyone has something to offer in God's kingdom.

The Bible shows many different gifts. Some people teach, some encourage, some give, and some lead. Romans 12:6–8 lists these gifts, showing that each one is valuable. No one has all the gifts, but together the body of Christ is complete.

Even children have gifts to use. Timothy was young, yet Paul encouraged him to use his gifts for teaching and leading. Families should encourage children to serve with their talents, whether through singing, helping, or encouraging others.

Using gifts is not about pride but stewardship. God gave the gift, and families should use it for His glory. First Corinthians 12:7 says gifts are given "for the common good."

Living this way means asking, "How has God gifted me to serve?" Families should celebrate each member's gifts and look for ways to use them in church, home, and community.

Let us take a few minutes to talk together about the following:

1. What does 1 Peter 4:10 teach us about spiritual gifts?
2. How do gifts work together in the body of Christ?
3. Why is it important to use gifts with humility?
4. How can our family use our gifts to serve this week?

PRAYER

Generous God, thank You for giving each of us gifts. Thank You for calling us to use them for Your glory. Forgive us when we hide our gifts or use them for ourselves. Teach our family to serve faithfully with the gifts You provide. Amen.

FAMILY ACTIVITY

On a scrapbook page, write "Serving with Our Gifts." Each family member writes one gift they believe God has given them and how they can use it this week.

August 8

When Forgiveness Feels Hard TO DO

"Be kind to one another, tenderhearted, forgiving one another, as God in Christ forgave you." – Ephesians 4:32

Have you ever been so mad at someone that you just wanted to scream and shout? Perhaps it was a friend who said something mean, or a brother or sister that took a toy without asking.

Forgiveness is one of the hardest ways to serve others, yet it is also one of the most powerful. Ephesians 4:32 commands believers to forgive as God forgave them in Christ. Families should understand that forgiveness serves others by healing relationships and showing God's love.

The Bible gives many examples of forgiveness. Joseph forgave his brothers who sold him into slavery. Jesus forgave Peter after he denied Him. On the cross, Jesus prayed, "Father, forgive them," for those who crucified Him.

Forgiveness is not excusing wrong. It is releasing anger and choosing love. Families should remember that forgiveness reflects God's mercy toward us. Without forgiveness, bitterness grows, but with forgiveness, peace and joy return.

Forgiveness is also service because it blesses others. It frees them from guilt and opens the door for reconciliation. Families who forgive one another show the gospel in action.

Living this way means practicing forgiveness daily, not letting small hurts build into anger. Families should talk honestly, pray together, and choose forgiveness as a way to serve.

Let us take a few minutes to talk together about the following:

1. What does Ephesians 4:32 teach us about forgiveness?
2. What examples of forgiveness are in the Bible?
3. Why is forgiveness a form of service?
4. How can our family practice forgiveness this week?

✎ PRAYER

Forgiving God, thank You for forgiving us through Jesus. Thank You for showing mercy when we did not deserve it. Forgive us when we hold grudges. Teach our family to serve one another through forgiveness. Amen.

♟ FAMILY ACTIVITY

On a scrapbook page, write "Serving Through Forgiveness." Each family member writes one person they will forgive or one way they will show kindness this week.

August 9
Embrace Having Welcoming Hearts

"Show hospitality to one another without grumbling." – 1 Peter 4:9

When was the last time a new friend joined your friend group at school or a new colleague became part of your work team? Did you welcome them and make them feel like they belong?

Hospitality means welcoming others with kindness. First Peter 4:9 commands believers to show hospitality without complaining. Families should understand that hospitality is a way of serving both God and others.

The Bible celebrates hospitality. Abraham welcomed strangers who turned out to be angels. Lydia opened her home to Paul and the early church. Jesus often ate with people, using meals as moments of love and teaching.

Hospitality is not about having a perfect house or fancy meals. It is about a welcoming heart. Families should remember that opening their home is opening their lives. Even a simple meal or kind invitation is service that honors God.

Hospitality should be joyful, not grudging. Complaints spoil the gift. Families should see hospitality as a way to bless, not a burden. Hebrews 13:2 reminds us that in showing hospitality, some have entertained angels without knowing it.

Living with hospitality means inviting neighbors, encouraging friends, and making others feel welcome. Families should look for ways to open doors and hearts, and encourage each other to do so daily.

Let us take a few minutes to talk together about the following:

1. What does 1 Peter 4:9 teach us about hospitality?
2. What examples of hospitality are in the Bible?
3. Why is hospitality about the heart, not the house?
4. How can our family practice hospitality this week?

PRAYER

Welcoming God, thank You for inviting us into Your family through Jesus. Thank You for opening Your arms to us. Forgive us when we close our doors or hearts. Teach our family to serve with hospitality and kindness. Amen.

FAMILY ACTIVITY

On a scrapbook page, write "Serving with Hospitality." Each family member writes one way they will make someone feel welcome this week.

August 10
Encouraging Equals Strength

"Therefore encourage one another and build one another up, just as you are doing." –
1 Thessalonians 5:11

Encouragement is serving with words. First, Thessalonians 5:11 reminds believers to encourage and build one another up. Families should remember that encouragement strengthens hearts and reflects God's love.

The Bible shows the power of encouragement. Barnabas encouraged Paul and the early church, earning the nickname "son of encouragement." Paul often wrote letters to strengthen churches, reminding them of God's promises.

Encouragement can be as simple as kind words, a smile, or a note. Families should learn to use words to lift others, not tear them down.

Encouragement is service because it blesses others and points them to God's truth. It reminds people they are not alone and gives strength to keep going.

Living this way means looking for opportunities to encourage every day. Families should encourage one another at home and encourage friends, teachers, and neighbors. Encouragement multiplies joy and builds unity.

Let us take a few minutes to talk together about the following:

1. What does 1 Thessalonians 5:11 teach us about encouragement?
2. How is encouragement shown in the Bible?
3. Why are encouraging words a form of service?
4. How can our family encourage one another this week?

PRAYER

Encouraging God, thank You for lifting our hearts through Your Word. Thank You for reminding us of hope in Jesus. Forgive us when we use words to harm instead of help. Teach our family to serve through encouragement. Amen.

FAMILY ACTIVITY

On a scrapbook page, write "Serving by Encouraging." Each family member writes one encouraging word or Bible verse for another member of the family.

August 11

Faithfulness, Even When We struggle

"Moreover, it is required of stewards that they be found faithful." – 1 Corinthians 4:2

Faithfulness means being steady, reliable, and consistent in doing what God has asked. First Corinthians 4:2 reminds us that God looks for faithfulness in His servants. Families should understand that serving God faithfully is not about being perfect but about being steady and true.

The Bible gives examples of faithful servants. Joseph remained faithful in Egypt, even when imprisoned. Daniel remained faithful in prayer, even when threatened with the lions' den. Paul continued preaching faithfully, even when beaten or jailed. Each one shows that faithfulness is service that honors God regardless of circumstances.

Jesus described faithfulness in His parables. In Matthew 25, He praised the servants who used their talents wisely, calling them "good and faithful." Faithfulness is not measured by the size of the task but by the heart of obedience.

Serving with faithfulness means showing up, keeping promises, and living with integrity. Families can practice this by being dependable at home, in school, at work, and in church.

Living faithfully also means finishing what we start, even when it is hard, because in due season we will reap if we do not give up. Families who live faithfully bless others and honor God.

Let us take a few minutes to talk together about the following:

1. What does 1 Corinthians 4:2 teach about faithfulness?
2. What examples of faithfulness are found in the Bible?
3. Why does God value faithfulness more than size or success?
4. How can our family serve faithfully this week?

PRAYER

Faithful God, thank You for remaining true to every promise. Thank You for calling us to serve You with steady hearts. Forgive us when we give up or lose focus. Teach our family to be faithful in serving You and others. Amen.

FAMILY ACTIVITY

On a scrapbook page, write "Serving with Faithfulness." Each family member writes one responsibility they will commit to do faithfully this week.

August 12
Learning to Teach Faith Through Daily Life

*"And these words that I command you today shall be on your heart. You shall teach
them diligently to your children." – Deuteronomy 6:6–7*

This verse speaks to everyday life, not special moments. God did not ask families to teach faith only in formal settings. He placed faith right in the middle of ordinary days: conversations, routines, and shared time.

Teaching faith begins with the heart. God's Word must live within us before it can be passed on. Children notice what matters to us long before they understand what we say. Faith is learned through what is valued, repeated, and practiced.

Families often worry about saying the right thing or having all the answers. This verse releases that pressure. Teaching faith is not about perfect explanations. It is about consistency: returning to God's truth again and again in simple ways.

Faith is shaped in small moments. During meals. In the car. At bedtime. In questions asked and prayers whispered. God works through these ordinary spaces, forming trust and understanding over time.

For families, this verse is encouraging. God does not expect perfection, only faithfulness. A family that keeps God's Word close and speaks of it naturally creates a home where faith is woven into daily life.

Let us take a few minutes to talk together about the following:

1. Why do you think God placed faith teaching in everyday life?
2. What helps God's Word stay on our hearts?
3. How do children learn faith from what they see at home?
4. What is one simple way our family can talk about God this week?

✎ PRAYER

Faithful God, thank You for inviting families to share Your truth in everyday moments. Thank You for working through simple conversations and faithful hearts. Forgive us when we feel inadequate or overwhelmed. Help our family keep Your Word close and pass it on with love and patience. Amen.

⚶ FAMILY ACTIVITY

On a scrapbook page, write the title **"Faith in Everyday Moments."** Draw small scenes from daily life: a table, a car, a bed. Each family member writes one moment when they could talk about God or pray together. Leave space to return later and note how God used those moments.

Be Patient Like Abraham

"Be completely humble and gentle; be patient, bearing with one another in love." –
Ephesians 4:2

Does being patient make you feel frustrated, especially in situations where you want quick solutions for problems?

Patience is serving others by waiting, enduring, and showing gentleness. Ephesians 4:2 commands believers to live with humility, gentleness, and patience. Families should remember that patience is a form of love in action.

The Bible shows patience in many stories. Abraham waited years for the promise of a son. Joseph waited in prison before God raised him up. Simeon waited faithfully in the temple until he saw the baby Jesus. Each one shows patience as trust in God's timing.

Jesus also showed patience. He bore with His disciples' weaknesses and mistakes. He endured suffering on the cross for our sake. His patience reveals His love.

Serving with patience means listening without interrupting, forgiving repeated mistakes, and waiting calmly when things are slow. Families should remember that patience reflects God's patience toward us. Second Peter 3:9 says that God is patient, not wanting anyone to perish.

Living with patience creates peace in the home. Families who serve with patience show others that God's timing is good and His love is steady.

Let us take a few minutes to talk together about the following:

1. What does Ephesians 4:2 teach about patience?
2. What examples of patience are in Scripture?
3. How did Jesus show patience with His disciples?
4. How can our family practice patience this week?

PRAYER

Patient God, thank You for bearing with us in love. Thank You for waiting for us to grow and obey. Forgive us when we are impatient with others. Teach our family to serve with patience and to trust Your timing. Amen.

FAMILY ACTIVITY

On a scrapbook page, write "Serving with Patience." Each family member writes one way they will practice patience this week.

Receiving Family Life as a Gift From God

"Enjoy life with the wife whom you love, all the days of your vain life that he has given you under the sun." – Ecclesiastes 9:9

This verse is honest about life. It does not pretend everything is easy or ideal. It speaks from the middle of real life: days that feel ordinary, tiring, or uncertain. And in that place, God points His people back to a gift they already have: life together.

Family life is not meant to be rushed past or taken lightly. This verse reminds us that God gives relationships intentionally. They are not distractions from faith, but part of how faith is lived out day by day.

Enjoying life together does not mean every moment feels joyful. It means choosing to value the people God has placed in our care, even on hard days. It means paying attention, showing kindness, and being present instead of always looking ahead.

Families often feel pressure to do more, fix more, or be more. This verse gently slows us down. It reminds us that God gives life as it is, not as we wish it would be, and invites us to receive it with gratitude.

When families learn to see daily life as a gift from God, perspective changes. Small moments matter more. Patience grows. Thankfulness takes root. A family that receives life together as God's gift learns to live with greater peace and contentment.

Let us take a few minutes to talk together about the following:

1. Why do you think God calls family life a gift?

2. What makes it hard to enjoy ordinary days together?

3. How can gratitude change the way we see our family?

4. What is one simple moment today we can receive as a gift from God?

PRAYER

Giver of life, thank You for the people You have placed in our family. Thank You for ordinary days and shared moments. Forgive us when we rush past the gifts You give. Help our family receive life together with gratitude, patience, and trust in You. Amen.

FAMILY ACTIVITY

On a scrapbook page, write the title **"Life Together Is God's Gift."** Draw small everyday moments: a table, a walk, a shared activity. Each family member writes one ordinary thing they are thankful for today. Leave space to return later and add more reminders of God's gifts in daily life.

August 15

Celebrating Our Roles

"Two are better than one, because they have a good reward for their toil." –
Ecclesiastes 4:9

Do you often feel like you are doing everything on your own when it comes to your role in your spiritual community?

Serving God and others is not meant to be done alone. Ecclesiastes 4:9 reminds us that two are better than one. Families should remember that God designed His people to serve together.

The Bible shows teamwork in service. Moses had Aaron and Hur to hold up his arms in battle. Nehemiah and the people rebuilt the walls of Jerusalem together. The early church shared everything and served side by side.

Jesus sent His disciples out in pairs to preach and heal. He knew they needed encouragement and support. Serving together strengthens faith and builds unity.

Serving as a family is powerful. When each person contributes, the whole family is blessed. Families can work together in chores, community service, or church ministry. Each person's part matters.

Living this way means valuing teamwork, encouraging one another, and celebrating each role. Families who serve together grow closer to each other and to God.

Let us take a few minutes to talk together about the following:

1. What does Ecclesiastes 4:9 teach about serving together?
2. What examples of teamwork are seen in the Bible?
3. Why did Jesus send disciples out in pairs?
4. How can our family serve together this week?

✎ PRAYER

Uniting God, thank You for giving us each other to serve with. Thank You for blessing us when we work together. Forgive us when we try to do things alone. Teach our family to serve side by side with love and unity. Amen.

⚐ FAMILY ACTIVITY

On a scrapbook page, write "Serving Together." Each family member writes one way they will serve with the whole family this week.

August 16
Serving with Gratitude

"Whatever you do, in word or deed, do everything in the name of the Lord Jesus, giving thanks to God the Father through him." – Colossians 3:17

Pause for a moment and think about three things in life that you and your family are grateful for. What makes them so unique and how do they add value to your life?

Gratitude changes the way we serve. Colossians 3:17 reminds us to do everything with thanksgiving. Families should remember that serving with a thankful heart brings joy to God and to others.

The Bible shows many examples of gratitude in service. When Jesus healed ten lepers, only one returned to thank Him (Luke 17:11-19). That man's gratitude became part of his testimony. Paul often thanked God for the churches he served, showing that thanksgiving strengthens ministry.

Serving with gratitude means remembering what God has done. He saved us, provided for us, and blessed us with family and community. Gratitude turns service into worship.

Gratitude also guards against bitterness. Without it, serving can feel like a burden. With it, serving becomes a privilege. Families should learn to say "thank You" to God and to one another as they serve.

Living gratefully means starting each day with thanks, serving with a cheerful heart, and ending the day by remembering blessings. Families who serve with gratitude create joy that spreads.

Let us take a few minutes to talk together about the following:

1. What does Colossians 3:17 teach about gratitude?
2. What examples of gratitude are seen in the Bible?
3. How does gratitude change the way we serve?
4. How can our family serve with gratitude this week?

📖 PRAYER

Gracious God, thank You for every gift and blessing. Thank You for the chance to serve in Your name. Forgive us when we complain or forget to be thankful. Teach our family to serve with gratitude in all things. Amen.

♟ FAMILY ACTIVITY

On a scrapbook page, write "Serving with Gratitude." Each family member writes one blessing from the week and how they will serve God in response.

August 17

The Power of Prayer

"First of all, then, I urge that supplications, prayers, intercessions, and thanksgivings
be made for all people." – 1 Timothy 2:1

What is your favorite place at home to pray with your family? Is it at the dining room table, in the living room or outside in the garden?

What do you usually pray about and how do you pray for others?

Prayer is one of the greatest ways to serve others. First Timothy 2:1 urges believers to pray for all people. Families should remember that prayer is service because it brings others before God.

The Bible shows prayer as service many times. Moses prayed for Israel when they sinned. Samuel prayed for the people and said he would not stop interceding for them. Paul prayed constantly for the churches, even when he was far away.

Jesus prayed for His disciples and for all believers in John 17. Even now, He intercedes for us at the Father's right hand. Prayer is powerful because it connects us to God's work in others' lives.

Serving with prayer means taking time to pray for family, friends, leaders, neighbors, and even enemies. It means lifting burdens to God and trusting His wisdom.

Living with prayerful service strengthens faith and brings peace. Families who pray together not only serve others but also grow closer to God and each other.

Let us take a few minutes to talk together about the following:

1. What does 1 Timothy 2:1 teach about prayer?
2. How is prayer shown as service in the Bible?
3. How did Jesus pray for others?
4. How can our family serve others through prayer this week?

📖 PRAYER

Prayerful God, thank You for listening when we pray. Thank You for inviting us to bring others before You. Forgive us when we neglect prayer. Teach our family to serve with prayer and to trust Your answers. Amen.

♟ FAMILY ACTIVITY

On a scrapbook page, write "Serving with Prayer." Each family member writes one person or situation they will pray for this week.

August 18

Letting Our Lives Point Others to God

"Show yourself in all respects to be a model of good works, and in your teaching show integrity, dignity." – Titus 2:7

This verse is practical and grounded. It doesn't talk about big moments or public recognition. It points instead to everyday life: the kind of life that is watched closely by the people nearest to us.

Family members learn more from what they see than from what they hear. This verse reminds us that faith is lived out through actions, attitudes, and consistency. Integrity shows up in how promises are kept, how mistakes are handled, and how others are treated when no one else is watching.

Living as an example does not mean being perfect. It means being honest. It means letting faith shape responses, even when patience is thin or days feel long. God uses ordinary faithfulness to teach lasting lessons.

Families often underestimate the impact of small choices, but God works through these moments. A calm response, a sincere apology, or a quiet act of kindness can speak louder than words ever could.

For families, this verse offers gentle direction. Faith does not need to be loud to be meaningful. A home shaped by integrity and steady obedience becomes a place where God's truth is seen, not just spoken.

Let us take a few minutes to talk together about the following:

1. Why do actions often teach more than words?
2. What does integrity look like in everyday family life?
3. Why is honesty important when we make mistakes?
4. What is one way our family can live out our faith today?

📖 PRAYER

Faithful God, thank You for caring about how we live each day. Thank You for using ordinary faithfulness to shape hearts. Forgive us when our actions do not reflect what we believe. Help our family live with integrity, allowing our lives to point others toward You. Amen.

♟ FAMILY ACTIVITY

On a scrapbook page, write the title **"Living Our Faith."** Draw simple scenes from daily life: helping, listening, or working together. Each family member writes one small action they want to take this week that reflects God's truth. Leave space to return later and reflect on how living out faith affected your family.

August 19
Serving with Generosity

"You will be enriched in every way to be generous in every way, which through us will produce thanksgiving to God." – 2 Corinthians 9:11

When was the last time you were generous? Was it helping someone with a difficult class project or assisting someone at work with a project?

Generosity is serving by giving freely of what God has provided. Second Corinthians 9:11 reminds us that God enriches us so we can be generous. Families should see generosity as both a blessing received and a blessing shared.

The Bible gives examples of generous service. The early church shared everything so that no one was in need. The Good Samaritan gave his time, energy, and money to care for a stranger. Jesus fed crowds by multiplying a boy's small lunch.

God Himself is the source of generosity. He gave His Son for our salvation. Romans 8:32 says that if He gave His Son, He will also give us everything we need. Families should mirror His generosity by serving with open hands.

Generosity is not about how much is given but the heart behind it. Families can serve generously with time, encouragement, meals, or money. Every generous act points to God's goodness.

Living with generosity means trusting God to provide, sharing freely, and being cheerful in giving. Families who serve generously show His love in practical ways.

Let us take a few minutes to talk together about the following:

1. What does 2 Corinthians 9:11 teach about generosity?
2. What examples of generosity are found in Scripture?
3. How does God's generosity inspire ours?
4. How can our family serve generously this week?

PRAYER

Generous God, thank You for blessing us in every way. Thank You for giving Jesus as the greatest gift. Forgive us when we hold back out of fear. Teach our family to serve with generosity and joy. Amen.

FAMILY ACTIVITY

On a scrapbook page, write "Serving with Generosity." Each family member writes one way they will give this week, such as time, help, or resources.

August 20

The Importance Of Faith

"For we walk by faith, not by sight." – 2 Corinthians 5:7

How often have you heard people say seeing is believing? Today's Bible verse is all about looking beyond those basic principles of trust.

Faith means trusting God even when we cannot see the outcome. Second Corinthians 5:7 reminds us that service must be rooted in faith. Families should remember that serving God often requires trusting Him without knowing every detail.

The Bible shows many examples of serving with faith. Noah built the ark before the rain came. Abraham left his home without knowing where God would lead. Peter stepped out of the boat to walk toward Jesus. Each act of service was done by faith.

Faithful service means obeying God's call even when it feels risky or uncertain. Families should trust that God rewards those who serve Him faithfully. Hebrews 11 is filled with people who served by faith, showing us that faith pleases God.

Serving with faith also means trusting God for strength, resources, and fruit. Families may not always see results immediately, but faith reminds them that God is working.

Living with faith means stepping forward in obedience, praying for guidance, and encouraging one another to trust God's promises.

Let us take a few minutes to talk together about the following:

1. What does 2 Corinthians 5:7 teach about faith?
2. What examples of serving with faith are in the Bible?
3. Why does serving require trust in God?
4. How can our family serve God by faith this week?

✎ PRAYER

Faithful God, thank You for guiding us even when we cannot see the full plan. Thank You for rewarding faith. Forgive us when we doubt or fear. Teach our family to serve with faith and to walk by trust in You. Amen.

⛄ FAMILY ACTIVITY

On a scrapbook page, write "Serving with Faith." Each family member writes one area where they will trust God in serving this week.

August 21

Why Serving with Our Time Matters

"Look carefully then how you walk, not as unwise but as wise, making the best use of the time, because the days are evil." – Ephesians 5:15–16

Time is one of the most valuable gifts God gives us. Ephesians 5:15-16 calls believers to walk wisely, making the best use of their time. Families should remember that how we spend our time shows what we value most.

The Bible reminds us that time is short. Psalm 90:12 says, "Teach us to number our days that we may get a heart of wisdom." James 4:14 compares life to a mist that appears and then vanishes. Because time is brief, families must use it well.

Serving with time means giving moments to God and others. Jesus gave His time to teach, heal, and listen. He stopped to help the needy and welcomed children. Even when tired, He still gave time to serve.

Families today are busy with school, work, and activities, but serving with time requires setting priorities. It may mean visiting someone in need, helping at church, or simply listening to a family member. Time given in love honors God.

Living wisely with time means not wasting it on selfish pursuits but investing it in God's kingdom. Families who serve with their time will find joy in eternal rewards.

Let us take a few minutes to talk together about the following:

1. What does Ephesians 5:15-16 teach us about time?
2. How does Jesus show the importance of giving time?
3. Why is time one of the most valuable ways to serve?
4. How can our family serve others with our time this week?

📖 PRAYER

Eternal God, thank You for the gift of time. Thank You for giving us each day as a chance to serve You. Forgive us when we waste our days on selfish things. Teach our family to use time wisely and to serve others faithfully. Amen.

♟ FAMILY ACTIVITY

On a scrapbook page, write "Serving with Time". Each family member writes one way they will use time this week to serve God or others.

August 22

Learning to Be Thankful in the Life We're Given

"And let the peace of Christ rule in your hearts, to which indeed you were called in one body. And be thankful." – Colossians 3:15

This verse doesn't ask us to pretend life is easy. It speaks into real life, where peace can feel fragile and gratitude doesn't always come naturally. God invites His people to let Christ's peace guide their hearts, even when circumstances are unsettled.

Peace here is not about everything going smoothly. It's about letting Christ have the final word in our thoughts and responses. When peace rules the heart, it steadies us. It keeps us from reacting only out of frustration or fear.

Families feel this tension often. Busy days, disagreements, and worries can crowd out thankfulness. This verse gently calls families back to what anchors them: Christ's peace, given by God, not created by effort.

Gratitude grows when peace leads. When families slow down enough to notice God's presence, thankfulness follows. It doesn't erase problems, but it changes how they are carried.

For families, this verse is a quiet reminder. God has called His people to live together, bound by Christ's peace. A family that learns to pause, trust God's peace, and practice thankfulness grows stronger in patience, unity, and faith.

Let us take a few minutes to talk together about the following:

1. What does it mean to let Christ's peace rule our hearts?
2. Why can thankfulness be hard during busy or stressful days?
3. How does peace help families handle conflict or worry?
4. What is one thing our family can thank God for today?

📖 PRAYER

God of peace, thank You for giving us peace through Christ. Thank You for being present in the middle of our busy and imperfect days. Forgive us when worry or frustration takes over. Help our family let Your peace guide our hearts and grow in thankfulness for what You provide each day. Amen.

♟ FAMILY ACTIVITY

On a scrapbook page, write the title **"Letting Peace Lead Our Hearts."** Draw a heart or a calm scene. Each family member writes one situation where they want to respond with peace instead of frustration, and one thing they are thankful for today. Leave space to return later and reflect on how choosing peace shaped your family's day.

Our Treasure Can Help Others

"For where your treasure is, there your heart will be also." – Matthew 6:21

Do you own a treasure that could serve a higher purpose in life? Perhaps it is knowledge or even extra resources that could help others.

Money and possessions are not bad in themselves, but how we use them shows where our heart is. Matthew 6:21 reminds us that our treasure reveals our priorities. Families should understand that serving with treasure means giving generously for God's work and helping others.

The Bible gives many examples of generous giving. Abraham gave a tenth to Melchizedek. The widow gave two coins, which Jesus praised. The early church sold possessions to care for those in need.

Jesus warned against storing treasures on earth, which do not last. Instead, He told His followers to store treasures in heaven through acts of generosity and service. Families should learn that eternal rewards are greater than temporary possessions.

Serving with treasure does not require wealth. It requires willingness. Second Corinthians 9:7 reminds us to give cheerfully. Even small gifts, when given from the heart, honor God.

Living with this attitude means budgeting for generosity, sharing with others, and remembering that everything belongs to God. Families who give together will see God's faithfulness.

Let us take a few minutes to talk together about the following:

1. What does Matthew 6:21 teach about treasure?
2. What examples of generous giving are in Scripture?
3. Why should families invest in eternal treasures?
4. How can our family serve God with treasure this week?

PRAYER

Generous Lord, thank You for providing all we need. Thank You for blessing us so we can give to others. Forgive us when we cling to possessions. Teach our family to serve with our treasure and to value eternal rewards. Amen.

FAMILY ACTIVITY

On a scrapbook page, write "Serving with Treasure". Each family member writes one way they will give or share this week.

August 24
Treating Our Family With Kindness

"But if anyone does not provide for his relatives, and especially for members of his household, he has denied the faith and is worse than an unbeliever." – 1 Timothy 5:8

When it comes to your household, are you slow to anger, or do you often feel the push and pull of different personalities?

Service begins at home. First Timothy 5:8 reminds us of the responsibility to care for family. Families should understand that serving one another in love is one of the clearest ways to honor God.

The Bible shows service within families. Joseph cared for his father and brothers in Egypt. Ruth cared for Naomi faithfully. Mary and Martha served Jesus and their household. Each example shows that love expressed at home is valuable to God.

Serving family may include helping with chores, encouraging siblings, showing respect, or caring for parents. These daily acts, though simple, are powerful ways to live out faith.

Jesus also honored family. On the cross, He made sure His mother Mary would be cared for by John. This shows that service to family is part of God's will.

Living with this focus means treating family members with kindness, forgiveness, and care. A family that serves one another becomes strong and joyful.

Let us take a few minutes to talk together about the following:

1. What does 1 Timothy 5:8 teach about serving family?
2. What examples of family service are seen in the Bible?
3. How did Jesus show care for His own family?
4. How can our family serve one another this week?

✒ PRAYER

Caring God, thank You for placing us in families. Thank You for showing us how to love and serve one another. Forgive us when we neglect those closest to us. Teach our family to serve each other with joy and patience. Amen.

♟ FAMILY ACTIVITY

On a scrapbook page, write "Serving Family". Each family member writes one way they will serve someone in the household this week.

August 25
Caring For Our Neighbors

"You shall love your neighbor as yourself." – Mark 12:31

Have you ever considered how showing kindness and love for your community can have an incredible impact on their lives?

Jesus taught that the second greatest commandment is to love our neighbors as ourselves. Families should understand that serving neighbors is a practical way to show God's love in action.

The parable of the Good Samaritan shows what it means to love neighbors. A man was beaten and left on the road. Religious leaders passed by, but the Samaritan stopped, cared for him, and paid for his needs. Jesus said to go and do likewise.

Serving neighbors may mean helping with groceries, offering a listening ear, inviting someone for a meal, or simply greeting them with kindness. Families should look for ways to show love in daily interactions.

Loving neighbors also includes those who may be different from us. Jesus served tax collectors, sinners, and outcasts. Families should remember that everyone is a neighbor in God's eyes.

Living this way means being attentive, generous, and kind. Families who serve neighbors reflect God's love to the world.

Let us take a few minutes to talk together about the following:

1. What does Mark 12:31 teach about serving neighbors?
2. How does the Good Samaritan show love in action?
3. Why does Jesus call us to serve all neighbors, not only those like us?
4. How can our family serve neighbors this week

PRAYER

Loving God, thank You for calling us to love neighbors as ourselves. Thank You for showing us this love in Jesus. Forgive us when we ignore people in need. Teach our family to serve neighbors with compassion and joy. Amen.

FAMILY ACTIVITY

On a scrapbook page, write "Serving Neighbors." Each family member writes one way they will serve a neighbor this week.

August 26
Serving Our Church

"Now you are the body of Christ and individually members of it." –
1 Corinthians 12:27

The church is described as the body of Christ, with each believer being a part of it. First Corinthians 12:27 reminds us that every member matters. Families should understand that serving the church is serving Christ Himself.

The early church shows this clearly. In Acts 2:42-47, believers devoted themselves to teaching, fellowship, prayer, and sharing. They served one another by meeting needs, worshiping together, and encouraging each other. This service strengthened the church and spread the gospel.

Every person has a role in the body. Some teach, some encourage, some give, some lead, and some show mercy. Each part is needed, just as every part of a body is important. Families should see service in church not as optional but as essential.

Jesus Himself served the church by laying down His life. Ephesians 5:25 says Christ loved the church and gave Himself for her. Serving the church means reflecting His sacrifice and care.

Living this way means volunteering, praying for leaders, encouraging fellow believers, and using talents for the church's good. Families should ask, "How can we serve Christ's body together?"

This awareness can guide our family on our spiritual journey and help us as a family to perfectly serve our church and fellow churchgoers.

Let us take a few minutes to talk together about the following:

1. What does 1 Corinthians 12:27 teach about the church?
2. How did the early church serve one another?
3. Why is every member important in the body of Christ?
4. How can our family serve our church this week?

✎ PRAYER

Lord of the Church, thank You for making us part of Your body. Thank You for giving us a place to worship and serve. Forgive us when we neglect the needs of the church. Teach our family to serve faithfully as members of Your body. Amen.

⛪ FAMILY ACTIVITY

On a scrapbook page, write "Serving Our Church". Each family member writes one way they will serve their church this week.

Opening Our Hearts To Our Community

"Let your light shine before others, so that they may see your good works and give glory to your Father who is in heaven." – Matthew 5:16

A simple act of kindness can go a long way. An extra set of hands to help where help is needed can make a world of difference to someone.

Serving God is not limited to home or church. Jesus calls believers to let their light shine in the world. Matthew 5:16 teaches that good works in the community bring glory to God. Families should remember that service is also a mission.

The Bible shows God's people serving their communities. Joseph served Egypt by storing food during famine. Daniel served Babylon with wisdom while remaining faithful to God. Nehemiah served Jerusalem by leading the rebuilding of its walls.

Jesus served communities by healing, teaching, and feeding crowds. He cared for both spiritual and physical needs. Families should follow His example by serving neighbors, schools, workplaces, and towns.

Serving communities may include volunteering, caring for the poor, helping at events, or praying for leaders. It shows the world God's love in action.

Living this way means being salt and light, preserving goodness, bringing flavor, and shining truth. Families who serve their communities point people to Christ.

Let us take a few minutes to talk together about the following:

1. What does Matthew 5:16 teach about good works?
2. How did Joseph, Daniel, and Nehemiah serve their communities?
3. How did Jesus serve people in practical ways?
4. How can our family serve our community this week?

PRAYER

Light of the World, thank You for calling us to shine for You. Thank You for giving us opportunities to serve beyond our home. Forgive us when we keep our light hidden. Teach our family to serve our community with love and boldness. Amen.

FAMILY ACTIVITY

On a scrapbook page, write "Serving Our Community". Each family member writes one way they will serve their community this week.

Serving the Poor

"Whoever is generous to the poor lends to the Lord, and he will repay him for his deed." – Proverbs 19:17

When was the last time you and your family helped someone in need in your community? Perhaps you volunteered at a soup kitchen, or did a blanket drive during winter months to help those that didn't have enough to keep themselves warm during cold weather.

Serving the poor is close to God's heart. Proverbs 19:17 says generosity to the poor is like lending to the Lord. Families should remember that caring for the needy is serving Christ Himself.

The Bible shows God's concern for the poor. He commanded Israel to leave part of their harvest for the needy. The prophets rebuked those who oppressed the poor. Jesus said in Matthew 25 that serving "the least of these" is serving Him.

The early church also cared for the poor. Acts 6 shows them appointing deacons to distribute food fairly. Paul collected offerings for struggling believers.

Serving the poor means sharing food, clothing, resources, and time. It also means treating them with dignity and respect. Families should not see the poor as a burden but as people loved by God.

Living this way shows compassion and obedience. It teaches children to value generosity over selfishness and builds a heart that reflects Christ.

Let us take a few minutes to talk together about the following:

1. What does Proverbs 19:17 teach about serving the poor?
2. How does the Bible show God's care for the poor?
3. How is serving the poor also serving Christ?
4. How can our family help the poor this week?

PRAYER

Compassionate God, thank You for caring for the poor and needy. Thank You for blessing us so we can bless others. Forgive us when we ignore those in need. Teach our family to serve the poor with love and generosity. Amen.

FAMILY ACTIVITY

On a scrapbook page, write "Serving the Poor". Each family member writes one way they can give or share with someone in need this week.

Showing Compassion For Those Who Are Dealing With Heartache

"Religion that is pure and undefiled before God the Father is this: to visit orphans and widows in their affliction." – James 1:27

Not all families are perfectly whole. In some cases, kids might only have a mom or dad, or have lost both parents. For others, a woman or man could have lost their spouses and are mourning.

James 1:27 teaches that true religion includes caring for widows and orphans. Families should understand that serving the most vulnerable is a mark of genuine faith.

The Bible often commands care for widows and orphans. God is described as "Father of the fatherless and protector of widows" (Psalm 68:5). Israel was told not to oppress them but to show justice and mercy.

Jesus showed compassion for the vulnerable. He raised a widow's son, healed children, and welcomed the overlooked. The early church also provided for widows, showing God's love in practical ways.

Serving widows and orphans today means supporting those who have lost family, caring for children in need, visiting the elderly, and helping single parents. Families can be a source of comfort and hope.

Living this way reflects God's heart. Families who serve the vulnerable become His hands and feet in a hurting world.

Let us take a few minutes to talk together about the following:

1. What does James 1:27 teach about true religion?
2. How does the Bible describe God's care for widows and orphans?
3. How can serving the vulnerable show God's love?
4. How can our family care for widows or orphans this week?

PRAYER

Father of the fatherless, thank You for showing compassion to the vulnerable. Thank You for calling us to serve widows and orphans. Forgive us when we forget them. Teach our family to reflect Your heart in serving those in need. Amen.

FAMILY ACTIVITY

On a scrapbook page, write "Serving Widows and Orphans". Each family member writes one way they can help someone who is lonely or without family support.

August 30

Living Faithfully in the Small, Everyday Moments

"The righteous who walks in his integrity—blessed are his children after him." –
Proverbs 20:7

This verse doesn't talk about big achievements or public faith. It talks about walking, day after day, with integrity. Quiet faithfulness. The kind that happens when no one is watching.

Integrity is formed in ordinary moments. How we speak when we're tired. How we respond when things don't go our way. How we treat one another when patience runs thin. These choices shape a home more than we often realize.

This verse reminds families that faith leaves a mark. Not through perfection, but through consistency. Children are shaped by what they see lived out: honesty, humility, repentance, and trust in God during everyday life.

Walking faithfully does not mean never failing. It means returning to what is right. It means owning mistakes and choosing to keep moving forward with God's help. God uses that kind of faithfulness to bring blessing in ways we may not see right away.

As the month comes to an end, this verse invites families to reflect on how faith is lived at home. Not perfectly, but sincerely. A family that chooses integrity in small moments is leaving something lasting behind.

Let us take a few minutes to talk together about the following:

1. What does integrity look like in everyday family life?
2. Why do small choices matter more than big moments?
3. How do our actions affect others in our home?
4. What is one small area where our family can choose faithfulness today?

PRAYER

Faithful God, thank You for caring about how we live each day. Thank You for working through small, faithful choices. Forgive us when we overlook the importance of integrity. Help our family walk honestly before You, trusting You to use our faithfulness to shape what lasts. Amen.

FAMILY ACTIVITY

On a scrapbook page, write the title **"Walking With Integrity"**. Draw simple footsteps or a path. Each family member writes one small habit or choice they want to work on: honesty, patience, kindness, or forgiveness. Leave space to return later and reflect on how choosing integrity shaped your family.

August 31
Serving for God's Glory

"So, whether you eat or drink, or whatever you do, do all to the glory of God." – 1 Corinthians 10:31

The ultimate purpose of serving is not recognition, success, or even the good of others. It is the glory of God. First Corinthians 10:31 teaches that everything we do should honor Him. Families should remember that service is worship.

The Bible shows people serving for God's glory. David defeated Goliath not for his own fame but to show that God saves. Elijah called down fire so the people would know the Lord is God. Jesus glorified the Father in everything He did, especially through the cross.

Serving for God's glory means keeping the right motive. Good works are not for praise but for pointing others to Him. Families should ask, "Does this honor God?" in their service. If the answer is yes, then even small tasks like sweeping floors or sharing a smile become acts of worship.

Living this way means serving cheerfully, humbly, and faithfully. Families who serve for God's glory find joy and peace, knowing they are pleasing Him.

Let us take a few minutes to talk together about the following:

1. What does 1 Corinthians 10:31 teach about purpose in service?
2. What examples in Scripture show serving for God's glory?
3. Why is motive important in service?
4. How can our family serve for God's glory this week?

PRAYER

Glorious God, thank You for giving us life and purpose. Thank You for calling us to honor You in all we do. Forgive us when we serve for our own praise. Teach our family to serve for Your glory alone. Amen.

FAMILY ACTIVITY

On a scrapbook page, write "Serving for God's Glory." Each family member writes one act of service they will do this week with the goal of glorifying God.

SEPTEMBER

September 1
Trusting God's Promises

"For no matter how many promises God has made, they are 'Yes' in Christ." – 2 Corinthians 1:20

The Bible is full of God's promises: promises to never leave us, to forgive us, to give us strength, and to prepare a place for us. Second Corinthians 1:20 reminds us that every promise of God finds its fulfillment in Jesus. Families should hold tightly to these promises, especially when life feels uncertain.

The Bible shows God keeping His promises over and over. He promised Abraham descendants, and it came true. He promised Israel a land, and they entered it. He promised a Savior, and Jesus came. Every fulfilled promise strengthens faith in the promises still ahead.

Trusting God's promises requires faith. Sometimes His promises take time, like Abraham waiting for Isaac. Sometimes they seem impossible, like Israel facing the Red Sea. Yet God never fails. Families must remind themselves that His Word is always true.

Living in trust means memorizing His promises, praying them, and applying them in daily life. When fear or doubt arises, families can answer with God's promises.

Let us take a few minutes to talk together about the following:

1. What does 2 Corinthians 1:20 teach us about God's promises?
2. What examples show God fulfilling promises in Scripture?
3. Why does trusting promises strengthen faith?
4. How can our family live by God's promises this week?

PRAYER

Promise-Keeping God, thank You for never breaking Your Word. Thank You for fulfilling every promise in Christ. Forgive us when we doubt or forget what You have said. Teach our family to trust Your promises in every situation. Amen.

FAMILY ACTIVITY

On a scrapbook page, write "Trusting God's Promises". Each family member writes one promise from Scripture to hold onto this week.

September 2
Learning to Listen Before We Speak

"To make an apt answer is a joy to a man, and a word in season, how good it is!" –
Proverbs 15:23

This verse reminds us that words matter. Not just what we say, but when we say it. A well-timed word can bring clarity, comfort, or peace in a way that rushed words never can.

In family life, it's easy to speak quickly. Emotions run high. Schedules are full. Reactions come before reflection. This verse gently calls families to slow down and pay attention, especially in moments that feel tense or confusing.

Listening first helps words land better. It creates space to understand what someone else is carrying before responding. A word spoken at the right time can soften hearts and calm situations that might otherwise escalate.

This kind of wisdom doesn't come naturally. It grows as families learn to pause, pray, and ask God for guidance before speaking. God cares deeply about how words are used within a home, because words shape trust and relationships.

For families, this verse is an invitation to practice patience with one another. Not every moment requires a response right away. Sometimes the best thing a family can do is listen first and trust God to help shape the words that come next.

Let us take a few minutes to talk together about the following:

1. Why is it hard to slow down before speaking?
2. How can listening change the way conversations go in our family?
3. What does a "word in season" look like?
4. When has a well-timed word helped our family before?

PRAYER

Wise God, thank You for caring about the words we speak. Thank You for offering wisdom when we pause and listen. Forgive us when we speak too quickly or without thought. Help our family listen well and speak words that bring peace, understanding, and care. Amen.

FAMILY ACTIVITY

On a scrapbook page, write the title **"Words Spoken at the Right Time"**. Draw a speech bubble or an ear. Each family member writes one situation where they want to practice listening before speaking. Leave space to return later and reflect on how slowing down changed conversations.

September 3
Trusting God in Trials

"Count it all joy, my brothers, when you meet trials of various kinds, for you know that the testing of your faith produces steadfastness." – James 1:2–3

When was the last time you experienced tough times? Perhaps a challenge of faith, friendship or even work problems?

Trials are part of life. James 1:2-3 teaches that trials test faith and produce steadfastness. Families should remember that trusting God in trials grows stronger faith and deeper dependence on Him.

The Bible shows people trusting God in trials. Job lost everything but declared, "The Lord gave, and the Lord has taken away; blessed be the name of the Lord." Paul and Silas sang hymns in prison. Daniel prayed faithfully even when threatened with lions.

Trusting God in trials does not mean pretending pain is easy. It means holding onto God's promises when life is hard. Trials remind us that this world is temporary and that God is preparing us for eternity.

Families should remember that God uses trials to refine faith, strengthen love, and teach perseverance. Romans 8:28 promises that God works all things for the good of those who love Him.

Living this way means praying during trials, encouraging each other, and remembering that God is always present. Families who trust Him in hard times show His strength to the world.

Let us take a few minutes to talk together about the following:

1. What does James 1:2–3 teach about trials?
2. What examples show people trusting God in trials?
3. How do trials produce steadfast faith?
4. How can our family trust God in trials this week?

PRAYER

Steadfast God, thank You for being with us in trials. Thank You for using hardships to grow our faith. Forgive us when we complain or lose hope. Teach our family to trust You in trials and to find joy in Your presence. Amen.

FAMILY ACTIVITY

On a scrapbook page, write "Trusting God in Trials". Each family member writes one trial they are facing and one promise they will hold onto.

September 4
Building a Home That Feels Safe

"In the fear of the Lord one has strong confidence, and his children will have a refuge." – Proverbs 14:26

This verse speaks quietly about something every family wants: a sense of safety. Not just physical safety, but emotional and spiritual security, a place where people can rest without fear.

Strong confidence does not come from having everything under control. It comes from trusting God. When God is honored in a home, stability grows. Children sense it. They feel it in how problems are handled and how love is shown.

The verse connects a parent's trust in God with a child's sense of refuge. That does not mean families never struggle. It means that even in hard seasons, there is a place to land. A home shaped by trust in God becomes a shelter, not a source of fear.

Families build this kind of home slowly. Through consistency. Through honesty. Through choosing faith over panic when things go wrong. God uses those quiet choices to create confidence that lasts.

This verse reminds families that faith shapes the atmosphere. When God is trusted, peace grows. A home that looks to Him becomes a place where children, and adults, feel safe, known, and cared for.

Let us take a few minutes to talk together about the following:

1. What makes a home feel safe to you?
2. How does trusting God affect the way we handle problems?
3. Why do you think children need a sense of refuge at home?
4. What is one way our family can build confidence and trust today?

PRAYER

Faithful God, thank You for being our refuge and strength. Thank You for offering security that does not depend on circumstances. Forgive us when fear shapes our reactions. Help our family trust You more deeply, so our home becomes a place of confidence, peace, and care. Amen.

FAMILY ACTIVITY

On a scrapbook page, write the title **"A Home of Refuge"**. Draw a house with open doors or sheltering arms. Each family member writes one thing that helps them feel safe and supported at home. Leave space to return later and note how trusting God shaped your family's sense of peace.

Becoming a Place of Encouragement for One Another

"For I have derived much joy and comfort from your love, my brother, because the hearts of the saints have been refreshed through you." – Philemon 1:7

This verse is simple and personal. It speaks about the kind of love that brings relief to others, not through grand gestures, but through steady care. It reminds us that encouragement can quietly strengthen people in ways we may never fully see.

In families, encouragement matters more than we often realize. Words spoken at the right moment, patience shown during stress, or kindness offered when someone is struggling can refresh hearts that feel worn down.

Refreshing others does not require having perfect answers. It comes from being present, listening well, and choosing compassion instead of criticism. God uses these small acts to bring comfort and stability within a home.

Family life includes tired days, misunderstandings, and moments when someone feels overlooked. This verse reminds us that love expressed through encouragement can change the tone of a home. It can restore trust and lift spirits.

When families choose to encourage one another, they reflect God's care. A home shaped by encouragement becomes a place where hearts are strengthened rather than drained, and where love points back to God's grace at work among His people.

Let us take a few minutes to talk together about the following:

1. What does encouragement look like in our family?
2. Why do words of comfort matter during hard days?
3. How can encouragement change the atmosphere in our home?
4. Who in our family might need encouragement right now?

PRAYER

God of comfort, thank You for using love to refresh weary hearts. Thank You for the ways You encourage Your people through one another. Forgive us when we withhold kindness or speak carelessly. Help our family become a place of encouragement, reflecting Your grace and care in how we treat one another. Amen.

FAMILY ACTIVITY

On a scrapbook page, write the title **"Refreshing One Another"**. Draw a heart, a cup of water, or open hands. Each family member writes one encouraging word or action they want to offer someone in the family this week. Leave space to return later and reflect on how encouragement changed your home.

Faith Like Abraham

"And he believed the Lord, and he counted it to him as righteousness." – Genesis 15:6

Abraham is often called the father of faith. Genesis 15:6 tells us that he believed God, and it was counted to him as righteousness. Families should remember that faith is not about perfect actions but about trusting God's promises.

God called Abraham to leave his home and go to a land he had never seen. Abraham obeyed. God promised him descendants as numerous as the stars, even though he and Sarah were old. Abraham believed. God asked him to trust even with Isaac, his promised son. Abraham obeyed, and God provided.

Romans 4:20–21 says Abraham did not waver in unbelief but grew strong in faith, fully convinced that God was able to do what He promised. Faith like Abraham's is not about knowing the whole plan but trusting the One who does.

Families should learn from Abraham that faith requires obedience, patience, and trust. It may involve waiting, sacrifice, or risk. But faith always pleases God, who rewards those who believe.

Let us take a few minutes to talk together about the following:

1. What does Genesis 15:6 teach about Abraham's faith?
2. How did Abraham show faith in action?
3. Why is Abraham called the father of faith?
4. How can our family show faith like Abraham this week?

PRAYER

Faithful God, thank You for Abraham's example of trust. Thank You for showing us that faith pleases You. Forgive us when we doubt or hesitate to obey. Teach our family to walk in faith like Abraham, trusting Your promises. Amen.

FAMILY ACTIVITY

On a scrapbook page, draw stars. Each family member writes one promise of God they want to trust this week. Title the page "Faith Like Abraham".

September 7

Inspired by Moses

"By faith he left Egypt, not being afraid of the anger of the king, for he endured as seeing him who is invisible." – Hebrews 11:27

Moses is another great example of faith. Hebrews 11:27 reminds us that he endured as if seeing the invisible God. Families should learn from Moses that faith keeps eyes fixed on God, not on fear.

Moses faced many challenges. He stood before Pharaoh, led Israel through the Red Sea, guided them in the wilderness, and interceded for them when they sinned. Each step required faith.

Faith like Moses means obedience even when the task feels impossible. Moses trusted God to provide words, miracles, and strength. He saw God part the sea, provide manna, and give the law at Sinai.

Families today can follow Moses' example by trusting God in big challenges. Whether in school, work, or relationships, faith means remembering that God is greater than fear.

Living this way means praying for courage, obeying God's call, and remembering His presence. Families who trust like Moses will see God do mighty things.

Let us take a few minutes to talk together about the following:

1. What does Hebrews 11:27 teach about Moses' faith?
2. How did Moses show faith in Egypt and the wilderness?
3. Why does faith require fixing eyes on God instead of fear?
4. How can our family show faith like Moses this week?

📖 PRAYER

Mighty God, thank You for Moses' example of faith. Thank You for showing that You are greater than fear. Forgive us when we let challenges overwhelm us. Teach our family to trust You as Moses did and to endure by faith. Amen.

⛰ FAMILY ACTIVITY

On a scrapbook page, draw parted waters. Each family member writes one fear they will trust God with this week. Title the page "Faith Like Moses".

September 8
Triumphant Like David

"David said to the Philistine, 'You come to me with a sword and with a spear and with a javelin, but I come to you in the name of the Lord of hosts.'" – 1 Samuel 17:45

David's faith is remembered in his victory over Goliath. First Samuel 17:45 shows that David's confidence was not in himself but in the Lord. Families should remember that true faith faces giants by trusting God's power.

David was young, small, and inexperienced in battle. Goliath was tall, armed, and terrifying. Yet David believed that the battle belonged to the Lord. He took a stone and a sling, and God gave him victory.

Faith like David means trusting God's strength when we feel weak. It means facing problems, temptations, and fears with confidence in God. Families may not face giants like Goliath, but they face challenges in daily life. Faith brings courage to face them.

David's faith also grew through worship. He sang psalms, praised God, and sought His presence. Families should remember that worship strengthens faith.

Living with David-like faith means focusing on God's greatness, not problems. It means serving God boldly, even when others doubt.

Let us take a few minutes to talk together about the following:

1. What does 1 Samuel 17:45 teach about David's faith?
2. How did David show trust in God against Goliath?
3. Why does faith give courage to face challenges?
4. How can our family show faith like David this week?

PRAYER

Victorious God, thank You for David's bold faith. Thank You for showing us that You are stronger than any giant. Forgive us when we focus on problems instead of Your power. Teach our family to walk in faith like David. Amen.

FAMILY ACTIVITY

On a scrapbook page, draw a sling and stone. Each family member writes one "giant" they will face with faith this week. Title the page "Faith Like David".

Trust Like Daniel

"When Daniel knew that the document had been signed, he went to his house where he had windows in his upper chamber open toward Jerusalem. He got down on his knees three times a day and prayed." – Daniel 6:10

Daniel's faith is shown in his commitment to prayer. Daniel 6:10 tells us that even when a law was passed against prayer, Daniel continued faithfully. Families should remember that faith is shown in consistent devotion, even under pressure.

Daniel served God faithfully in Babylon, a foreign land with many idols. He refused to eat forbidden food, interpreted dreams, and stood firm in prayer. His faith led him into the lions' den, but God shut the lions' mouths.

Faith like Daniel means courage to obey God when the world pressures us to compromise. It means staying faithful in prayer, reading Scripture, and trusting God's power.

Families should learn that prayer is a vital act of faith. Daniel's faithfulness in prayer prepared him for trials. Families can strengthen their faith by praying daily together.

Living this way means making prayer a priority, even when busy or pressured. Faith like Daniel inspires boldness and perseverance.

Let us take a few minutes to talk together about the following:

1. What does Daniel 6:10 teach about Daniel's faith?
2. How did Daniel show trust in God in Babylon?
3. Why is consistent prayer a sign of faith?
4. How can our family show faith like Daniel this week?

PRAYER

Faithful God, thank You for Daniel's example of prayer and courage. Thank You for protecting him in the lions' den. Forgive us when we neglect prayer or give in to pressure. Teach our family to walk in faith like Daniel, trusting You fully. Amen.

FAMILY ACTIVITY

On a scrapbook page, draw a lion. Each family member writes one way they will stay faithful to God in prayer this week. Title the page "Faith Like Daniel".

September 10
Mary's Incredible Faith

"And Mary said, 'Behold, I am the servant of the Lord; let it be to me according to your word.'" – Luke 1:38

Mary, the mother of Jesus, showed remarkable faith. Luke 1:38 records her response to the angel's message. She called herself the Lord's servant and accepted His plan. Families should remember that faith is surrender to God's will.

Mary was young and likely afraid, yet she trusted God's word. She accepted a role that would bring questions and challenges, but her faith was steady. She believed that God's promise of a Savior would come through her.

Faith like Mary means saying "yes" to God's plan, even when it is difficult. It means surrendering personal desires and trusting His wisdom. Families can learn from Mary to accept God's will with humility and trust.

Mary's faith was also expressed in worship. In Luke 1:46-55, she sang the Magnificat, praising God for His power and mercy. Faith grows through praise and gratitude.

Living this way means surrendering daily decisions to God, praying "Your will be done," and praising Him in every circumstance. Families who walk in faith like Mary reflect true trust and devotion.

Let us take a few minutes to talk together about the following:

1. What does Luke 1:38 teach about Mary's faith?
2. How did Mary show surrender and trust?
3. Why is saying "yes" to God's plan an act of faith?
4. How can our family show faith like Mary this week?

PRAYER

Sovereign God, thank You for Mary's example of humble faith. Thank You for showing us what it means to surrender to Your will. Forgive us when we resist Your plans. Teach our family to walk in faith like Mary, trusting You completely. Amen.

FAMILY ACTIVITY

On a scrapbook page, draw an open hand. Each family member writes one area where they will surrender to God this week. Title the page "Believe Like Mary".

September 11

Learn From Peter

"So Peter got out of the boat and walked on the water and came to Jesus." –
Matthew 14:29

Peter is remembered for both his bold faith and his moments of fear. In Matthew 14:29, he stepped out of the boat to walk on water toward Jesus. Families should remember that faith sometimes means stepping out of comfort zones to trust God.

When Peter kept his eyes on Jesus, he walked on water. When he looked at the waves, he began to sink. Jesus reached out His hand and saved him, teaching that faith is strengthened when we stay focused on Him.

Faith like Peter means being willing to take risks in obedience. It means trusting Jesus more than fear. Families can learn that faith will sometimes fail, but Jesus is always ready to lift us up.

Later, Peter grew into a leader filled with faith. He preached at Pentecost, healed the sick, and endured persecution with courage. His story shows that God grows faith through experience and forgiveness.

Living this way means stepping out in obedience, even when it feels risky. Families who walk in Peter-like faith will see God work powerfully.

Let us take a few minutes to talk together about the following:

1. What does Matthew 14:29 teach about Peter's faith?
2. What happened when Peter looked at the waves instead of Jesus?
3. How does God grow our faith through both success and failure?
4. How can our family step out in faith this week?

✐ PRAYER

Saving God, thank You for teaching us through Peter's example. Thank You for lifting us when our faith falters. Forgive us when we look at problems instead of You. Teach our family to keep eyes fixed on Jesus and walk in faith. Amen.

♟ FAMILY ACTIVITY

On a scrapbook page, draw waves and a boat. Each family member writes one step of faith they will take this week. Title the page "Step into Obedience".

September 12

Faith Like the Centurion

*"When Jesus heard this, he marveled and said, 'Truly, I tell you, with no one in Israel
have I found such faith.'" – Matthew 8:10*

The Roman centurion showed remarkable faith when he asked Jesus to heal his servant. He believed Jesus could heal with a word. Matthew 8:10 tells us that Jesus marveled at his faith. Families should remember that true faith trusts God's authority completely.

The centurion understood authority. He commanded soldiers and knew they obeyed his word. He believed Jesus' authority was even greater. that sickness and creation obeyed Him.

Faith like the centurion means believing God's Word is enough. Families do not need signs or proof when they trust His promises. They believe because He is faithful.

Jesus praised this Gentile's faith, showing that faith is not limited by background or status. Anyone who trusts Jesus can experience His power.

Living this way means honoring Jesus as Lord, trusting His Word, and resting in His authority. Families who trust like the centurion live with peace, knowing God is in control.

Let us take a few minutes to talk together about the following:

1. What does Matthew 8:10 teach about the centurion's faith?
2. Why did he believe Jesus could heal with a word?
3. What does this story teach about God's authority?
4. How can our family show faith like the centurion this week

✐ PRAYER

Lord of Authority, thank You for showing us the centurion's faith. Thank You for reminding us that Your Word is powerful. Forgive us when we doubt or demand proof. Teach our family to trust Your authority completely. Amen.

⛁ FAMILY ACTIVITY

On a scrapbook page, write "Never Stop Believing." Each family member writes down one promise of Jesus they will trust this week.

September 13

The Woman at the Well

"The woman left her water jar and went away into town and said to the people,
'Come, see a man who told me all that I ever did. Can this be the Christ?'" –
John 4:28–29

The Samaritan woman at the well experienced life-changing faith when she met Jesus. John 4:28–29 tells us she left her water jar and told others about Him. Families should remember that faith responds by sharing the good news.

This woman had a troubled past, but Jesus spoke to her with love and truth. He revealed that He was the Messiah. Her faith grew quickly, and she became one of the first to share His message.

Faith like the woman at the well means leaving behind old ways and boldly telling others about Jesus. Families should learn that faith is not only private; it overflows into testimony.

Her story shows that Jesus welcomes everyone, regardless of background. Faith transforms hearts and inspires others.

Living this way means sharing personal stories of God's work, inviting others to church, and speaking about Jesus naturally in conversation.

Families who live this way shine the gospel in their community. Together, we can inspire others through our experiences of faith and unyielding trust.

Let us take a few minutes to talk together about the following:

1. What does John 4:28-29 teach about the woman's response?
2. How did Jesus show grace and truth in this story?
3. Why does faith lead to sharing the good news?
4. How can our family share about Jesus this week

✐ PRAYER

Living Water, thank You for transforming the woman at the well. Thank You for showing us that faith leads to testimony. Forgive us when we keep silent about You. Teach our family to share boldly about Jesus with others. Amen.

⚖ FAMILY ACTIVITY

On a scrapbook page, write "What we Learned From the Woman at the Well". Each family member writes one way they will share about Jesus this week.

The Blind Man That Showed Courage and Faith

"He answered, 'Whether he is a sinner I do not know. One thing I do know, that though I was blind, now I see.'" – John 9:25

In John 9, Jesus healed a man born blind. When questioned by leaders, the man simply testified, "I was blind, now I see." Families should remember that faith often begins with simple trust in what Jesus has done.

The blind man did not have all the answers. He could not explain every detail. But he knew what Jesus had done for him. His simple testimony was powerful and undeniable.

Faith like the blind man means trusting Jesus even without all the details. It means focusing on His work, not on arguments. Families should be encouraged that faith does not require knowing everything, but believing in what He has done.

His story also shows courage. He testified about Jesus even when pressured by authorities. True faith stands firm even under opposition.

Living this way means remembering personal testimonies and sharing them confidently. Families can strengthen faith by telling stories of God's goodness.

Let us take a few minutes to talk together about the following:

1. What does John 9:25 teach about the blind man's faith?
2. Why is testimony powerful, even without full knowledge?
3. How did the man show courage in his faith?
4. How can our family share what God has done for us this week?

✒ PRAYER

Healing God, thank You for opening the eyes of the blind man. Thank You for reminding us that faith begins with trusting Jesus. Forgive us when we are silent about Your work. Teach our family to testify with courage and gratitude. Amen.

Family Activity

On a scrapbook page, write "Thankful Like the Blind Man." Each family member writes one thing Jesus has done for them to thank Him this week.

September 15
Trusting God When We Don't Know What to Do

"We do not know what to do, but our eyes are on you." – 2 Chronicles 20:12

This sentence is spoken in the middle of fear. God's people were facing a situation they could not solve. There was no clear plan, no easy solution, and no guarantee of safety. Instead of pretending confidence, they admitted the truth: they didn't know what to do.

What stands out is where they turned next. They did not panic or rush ahead. They fixed their attention on God. This verse shows faith not as certainty, but as dependence. It is faith that speaks honestly and still chooses trust.

Families experience moments like this often. Decisions feel heavy. Problems feel bigger than wisdom or experience. This verse gives permission to admit uncertainty without giving in to fear. Faith does not require having answers, it requires knowing where to look.

Jehoshaphat's prayer shows that God honors faith that turns toward Him in weakness. God responded with guidance and deliverance, not because His people were strong, but because they trusted Him when they were unsure.

For families, this verse is deeply reassuring. Faith does not mean always knowing the next step. Sometimes it simply means saying, *"God, we don't know—but we're looking to You."* That kind of faith draws a family closer to God and to one another.

Let us take a few minutes to talk together about the following:

1. Why do you think God's people admitted they didn't know what to do?
2. How is this verse an example of real faith?
3. When has our family felt unsure about the next step?
4. What does it look like for our eyes to be on God?

PRAYER

Faithful God, thank You for welcoming us when we come to You without answers. Thank You for meeting Your people in moments of uncertainty. Forgive us when fear takes over or pride keeps us from asking for help. Help our family keep our eyes on You, trusting You to guide us when we don't know what to do. Amen.

FAMILY ACTIVITY

On a scrapbook page, write the title "Our Eyes Are on You". Draw a simple path or open hands lifted upward. Each family member writes one situation where they need God's guidance. Leave space to come back later and write how trusting God helped your family move forward.

September 16
Stepping Forward While Trusting God

"Nothing can hinder the Lord from saving, whether by many or by few." –
1 Samuel 14:6

Jonathan spoke these words quietly, not to a crowd, but to the armor-bearer standing beside him. There was no guarantee of success. No full plan. Just a deep trust in who God is and what He is able to do.

This verse shows faith that moves forward without demanding certainty. Jonathan did not know how God would act, but he believed God was not limited by numbers or strength. His confidence rested in God, not in circumstances.

Families often face moments like this. Decisions must be made without all the information. Steps are taken without knowing how things will turn out. This verse reminds us that faith does not wait for perfect conditions.

Trusting God sometimes means moving forward carefully but confidently, believing that God is able to work even when resources feel small or options feel limited. God's power is not reduced by what we lack.

For families, this example is encouraging. Faith is not about being fearless. It is about trusting God enough to take the next step. A family that learns to rely on God's strength rather than their own discovers that He is faithful to meet them along the way.

Let us take a few minutes to talk together about the following:

1. What stands out to you about Jonathan's faith?
2. Why is it hard to trust God when outcomes are uncertain?
3. How does this verse change the way we think about limitations?
4. What is one step our family needs to take in faith right now?

PRAYER

Mighty God, thank You for showing us that You are not limited by what we see. Thank You for working through trust and obedience. Forgive us when fear holds us back. Help our family take steps of faith, trusting You to work beyond our strength and understanding. Amen.

FAMILY ACTIVITY

On a scrapbook page, write the title "Taking the Next Step in Faith". Draw a single step or a path moving forward. Each family member writes one situation where they want to trust God and move forward in faith. Leave space to return later and reflect on how God met your family as you trusted Him.

Faith Like the Woman Who Touched Jesus' Cloak

"For she said to herself, 'If I only touch his garment, I will be made well.'" –
Matthew 9:21

Faith is sometimes quiet but powerful. In Matthew 9:21, a woman who had suffered for twelve years believed that touching Jesus' cloak would heal her. Families should remember that even small acts of faith bring great results.

The woman had been sick and excluded from society. She pushed through the crowd, believing in Jesus' power. Jesus honored her faith, saying, "Take heart, daughter; your faith has made you well."

Faith like this woman's is personal and determined. It seeks Jesus in hope and trust, even when others discourage. Families can learn that faith does not need recognition, it simply needs to trust Jesus.

Her story also shows that Jesus notices individuals. In a large crowd, He stopped for her. Families should remember that faith connects us personally to Jesus, who knows each need.

Living this way means coming to Jesus in prayer, believing He hears, and trusting His power. Quiet faith is still mighty in His sight.

Let us take a few minutes to talk together about the following:

1. What does Matthew 9:21 teach about faith?
2. How did the woman show determination and trust?
3. Why does Jesus honor even small acts of faith?
4. How can our family show faith like this woman this week?

PRAYER

Compassionate Lord, thank You for healing the woman who touched Your cloak. Thank You for noticing every act of faith. Forgive us when we doubt or hold back. Teach our family to come to You with simple, trusting faith. Amen.

FAMILY ACTIVITY

On a scrapbook page, write "Faith Like the Woman." Each family member writes one quiet act of faith they will take this week.

September 18
The Centurion at the Cross

"When the centurion and those who were with him, keeping watch over Jesus, saw the earthquake and what took place, they were filled with awe and said, 'Truly this was the Son of God!'" – Matthew 27:54

Faith often grows when we witness God's power. At the cross, a Roman centurion declared Jesus was the Son of God. Families should remember that even in dark moments, God reveals truth that leads to faith.

This centurion had likely seen many crucifixions, but none like this. He saw darkness cover the land, the temple curtain torn, and the earth quake. His heart was moved to confess faith in Jesus.

Faith like this centurion's recognizes who Jesus is, even when others reject Him. Families should learn that faith is strengthened by paying attention to God's works in daily life.

His story shows that no one is too far from faith. Even a Roman soldier became a witness. Families can be encouraged that faith can grow in unexpected places and people.

Living this way means being attentive to God's presence in trials, confessing Jesus boldly, and sharing faith with others.

Let us take a few minutes to talk together about the following:

1. What does Matthew 27:54 teach about the centurion's faith?
2. How did witnessing God's power bring him to faith?
3. Why is it important to confess Jesus as the Son of God?
4. How can our family notice God's works and confess faith this week?

PRAYER

Holy God, thank You for revealing Jesus as Your Son at the cross. Thank You for moving hearts, even in dark times. Forgive us when we miss Your works around us. Teach our family to notice Your power and confess faith boldly. Amen.

FAMILY ACTIVITY

On a scrapbook page, write "Faith at the Cross." Each family member writes one way they saw God at work this week.

September 19
Faith Lived Out at Home

*"And he went down with them and came to Nazareth and was submissive to them.
And his mother treasured up all these things in her heart." – Luke 2:51*

This verse gives us a quiet glimpse into Jesus' family life. After a moment that revealed His divine understanding, Jesus returned home and lived under the authority of His parents. The Son of God chose obedience within a family setting.

Faith here is not shown through miracles or teaching crowds. It is shown through submission, patience, and everyday faithfulness. Jesus honored God not only in public ministry, but also in the ordinary rhythms of home life.

Families can learn from this moment. Faith is not only practiced in church or special moments. It is lived out in how family members relate to one another, through respect, listening, and care. God values obedience and humility within the home.

Mary's response is also telling. She treasured these things in her heart. Some parts of faith are not immediately understood, but they are remembered, reflected on, and trusted to God. Families often walk this same path, holding onto God's work even when it unfolds slowly.

Living faith at home means choosing God's ways in daily interactions. It means honoring one another, practicing patience, and trusting God to work through ordinary family life. A home shaped by faith becomes a place where God's presence is quietly known and deeply felt.

Let us take the next couple of minutes to discuss the following questions as a family:

1. What does this verse show us about Jesus' life at home?
2. Why do you think obedience and humility matter in family life?
3. How can faith be lived out in ordinary, everyday moments?
4. What is one way our family can honor God in our home this week?

📖 PRAYER

Faithful God, thank You for showing us that faith is lived out in everyday life. Thank You for the example of Jesus, who honored You through obedience and humility at home. Forgive us when we separate faith from daily family life. Help our family live in ways that honor You, trusting You to work through even the quiet moments. Amen.

⛪ FAMILY ACTIVITY

On a scrapbook page, write **"Faith at Home"**. Each family member writes one way they can live out faith in the home this week, through respect, kindness, patience, or obedience. Leave space to return later and reflect on how choosing faith shaped your family's time together.

September 20

Living Like Paul

"I have fought the good fight, I have finished the race, I have kept the faith." –
2 Timothy 4:7

When we read the Bible, we come across many figures that shows us what a life of faith looks like. Paul is one such person that we can learn from daily.

Paul's life shows enduring faith. Near the end of his life, he declared in 2 Timothy 4:7 that he had fought the fight, finished the race, and kept the faith. Families should remember that faith is not just for a moment but for a lifetime.

Paul's journey included hardships: shipwrecks, beatings, prison, and rejection. Yet he remained faithful to Christ. He preached the gospel boldly, planted churches, and encouraged believers. His faith endured to the end.

Faith like Paul's means perseverance. It does not quit when life is hard. It keeps trusting Jesus through trials, temptations, and opposition. Families should be encouraged that faith grows stronger when tested.

Paul's life also shows joy in service. Even in prison, he wrote letters full of hope. His faith was rooted in knowing Christ deeply. Families should learn that lasting faith comes from relationship with Jesus, not circumstances.

Living this way means finishing strong, praying daily, staying in Scripture, serving faithfully, and encouraging others. Families who walk with Paul-like faith will leave a legacy of trust.

Let us take the next couple of minutes to discuss the following questions as a family:

1. What does 2 Timothy 4:7 teach about Paul's faith?
2. How did Paul persevere through hardships?
3. Why does enduring faith matter more than short bursts of faith?
4. How can our family keep the faith to the end?

PRAYER

Faithful Lord, thank You for Paul's example of endurance. Thank You for showing us that faith is a lifelong journey. Forgive us when we grow weary or distracted. Teach our family to fight the good fight and finish the race faithfully. Amen.

FAMILY ACTIVITY

On a scrapbook page, draw a race track. Each family member writes one way they will "keep the faith" this week. Title the page "Faith Like Paul."

September 21

Hannah's Story

"I prayed for this child, and the Lord has granted me what I asked of him." –
1 Samuel 1:27

Have you ever prayed so hard for something, wishing God could immediately grant your prayers? Perhaps you were praying that you would be included in a sports team, or that you would get a promotion at work.

If there is one example of patience and faith that we can learn from, it is from Hannah.

Hannah's story is a picture of faith in prayer. For years she longed for a child and cried out to the Lord. In 1 Samuel 1:27, she declared that God had answered her prayer by giving her Samuel. Families should remember that faith waits on God in prayer and trusts His answer.

Hannah's faith was not shallow. She prayed with tears, pouring out her heart before God. She promised that if He gave her a son, she would dedicate him back to the Lord. When Samuel was born, she kept her promise and brought him to serve at the temple.

Faith like Hannah's means praying persistently, even when it takes time. It means trusting that God hears and answers in His way and His time.

Her story also shows faith in surrender. She gave Samuel to God's service, showing that every blessing belongs to Him. Families should learn that faith means dedicating children, resources, and plans to God's glory.

Living with Hannah-like faith means praying faithfully, keeping promises to God, and trusting Him with our hearts' desires.

Let us take the next couple of minutes to discuss the following questions as a family:

1. What does 1 Samuel 1:27 teach about answered prayer?
2. How did Hannah show faith in her persistence and surrender?
3. Why is faith required when we wait in prayer?
4. How can our family pray with Hannah-like faith this week?

✎ PRAYER

Listening God, thank You for hearing Hannah's prayer. Thank You for granting her request and showing Your faithfulness. Forgive us when we stop praying too soon. Teach our family to pray with persistence and to surrender blessings back to You. Amen.

♟ FAMILY ACTIVITY

On a scrapbook page, write "Faith Like Hannah". Each family member writes one prayer request they will keep bringing to God this week.

September 22
Elijah's Example

"Elijah came near to all the people and said, 'How long will you go limping between two different opinions? If the Lord is God, follow him.'" – 1 Kings 18:21

Have you ever had to defend your faith in front of others? Elijah sure did, and he had courage when the situation looked less than favorable for him.

Elijah showed bold faith on Mount Carmel. Surrounded by prophets of Baal, he declared that the Lord is God and called for a test. When fire fell from heaven, the people bowed and confessed, "The Lord, he is God!" Families should remember that faith means standing firm even when outnumbered.

Elijah's faith was not in himself but in God's power. He soaked the altar with water to prove that only God could answer. His prayer was simple, asking God to reveal Himself. God responded with fire that consumed everything.

Faith like Elijah's means refusing to compromise. It means calling people to worship God alone. Families should learn that faith is courageous, even when culture goes the other way.

Elijah's story also reminds us that faith sometimes leads to discouragement. After his bold stand, he grew weary and afraid. God met him gently, showing that faith is also about depending on God's care. Living this way means speaking truth, trusting God's power, and finding strength in His presence.

Families who walk in Elijah-like faith shine light in dark places. So, don't be afraid to set an example of staying strong in faith, even when it might feel challenging at times.

Let us take the next couple of minutes to discuss the following questions as a family:

1. What does 1 Kings 18:21 teach about Elijah's boldness?
2. How did God prove His power on Mount Carmel?
3. Why does faith require courage when we feel outnumbered?
4. How can our family stand firm like Elijah this week?

📖 PRAYER

Almighty God, thank You for showing Your power through Elijah. Thank You for proving that You alone are God. Forgive us when we compromise or stay silent. Teach our family to stand firm in faith and to trust Your strength. Amen.

♟ FAMILY ACTIVITY

On a scrapbook page, draw a flame. Each family member writes one area where they want to stand firm in faith this week. Title the page "Faith Like Elijah".

September 23

Esther's Triumph

"For if you keep silent at this time, relief and deliverance will rise for the Jews from another place... And who knows whether you have not come to the kingdom for such a time as this?" – Esther 4:14

Imagine standing up for what's right when the odds are against you. Perhaps you had to face a bully in your class in the past, or you needed to address unfair behavior in the workplace.

Esther's faith shines in her courage to act. When her people faced destruction, she risked her life by approaching the king. Esther 4:14 reminds us that God places His people in specific times and places for His purpose. Families should remember that faith trusts God's plan and steps forward with courage.

Esther could have remained safe in the palace, but she chose to act. She fasted, prayed, and then risked everything to intercede for her people. Her faith saved lives and revealed God's providence.

Faith like Esther's means believing that God has a purpose for where we are. Families should see daily situations, school, work, neighborhood, as opportunities to serve His plan.

Her story also shows that faith requires action. She said, "If I perish, I perish," showing her trust in God's will. Families should learn that courage flows from faith in God's control.

Living this way means stepping out in courage, interceding for others, and trusting that God has placed us where we are for His purposes.

Let us take the next couple of minutes to discuss the following questions as a family:

1. What does Esther 4:14 teach about God's purpose?
2. How did Esther show faith in her courage?
3. Why does faith sometimes require risk?
4. How can our family act with Esther-like faith this week?

📖 PRAYER

Sovereign Lord, thank You for Esther's example of courage and trust. Thank You for showing that You place us where we are for a reason. Forgive us when we stay silent or avoid hard choices. Teach our family to walk with faith like Esther. Amen.

♟ FAMILY ACTIVITY

On a scrapbook page, write "Courage Like Esther". Each family member writes one situation where they will act with courage this week.

September 24

Choosing God Together as a Family

"So Jacob said to his household and to all who were with him, 'Put away the foreign gods that are among you and purify yourselves and change your garments.'" –
Genesis 35:2

This moment comes during a turning point for Jacob and his family. God was calling them forward, but before they could move on, something had to be addressed inside the household. Faith was not only a personal decision for Jacob, it became a family matter.

Jacob spoke directly to his household. He understood that walking with God required intentional choices, not just belief. Old attachments had to be left behind so the family could move forward in obedience and trust. This was about aligning daily life with God's direction.

Families today face similar moments, even if they look different. Distractions, habits, or priorities can quietly take God's place at the center of home life. This verse reminds us that faith involves ongoing choices about what we allow to shape our hearts and homes.

Choosing God together as a family does not mean perfection. It means willingness. It means pausing, listening, and being honest about what needs to change. God honors families who desire to follow Him, even when the process feels uncomfortable.

This passage shows that faith grows when families move in the same direction. When God is placed first, homes are reshaped—not all at once, but steadily. A family that chooses God together learns to walk forward with clarity, unity, and renewed trust in His guidance.

Let us take the next couple of minutes to discuss the following questions as a family:

1. Why do you think Jacob spoke to his whole household, not just himself?
2. What kinds of things can quietly distract families from following God?
3. Why is it important for families to choose obedience together?
4. What is one small change our family can make to put God first?

✐ PRAYER

Faithful God, thank You for guiding families with patience and grace. Thank You for calling Your people to walk with You together. Forgive us when we allow distractions to take Your place. Help our family choose You daily, trusting You to guide our steps and shape our home according to Your will. Amen.

♟ FAMILY ACTIVITY

On a scrapbook page, write "Choosing God Together". Each family member writes one thing they want to give more attention to God: time, prayer, obedience, or trust. Leave space to return later and reflect on how choosing God shaped your family's days.

September 25
Faith Like Gideon

"The Lord said to him, 'Peace be to you. Do not fear; you shall not die.'" –
Judges 6:23

Gideon's story shows faith that grows through God's patience. When God called him to deliver Israel, Gideon felt weak and afraid. Judges 6:23 records God's reassurance: "Do not fear." Families should remember that faith begins small but grows as we trust God's Word.

Gideon asked for signs to confirm God's call. God answered, showing patience. With only 300 men, Gideon defeated Midian's massive army because God gave the victory. Faith trusts God's strength, not numbers.

Faith like Gideon's means admitting weakness but trusting God's power. Families should learn that God often chooses unlikely people to show His glory.

His story also shows that peace comes from trusting God. Gideon built an altar and called it "The Lord is Peace." Faith replaces fear with God's peace.

Living this way means obeying God's call even when we feel small. Families who walk in Gideon-like faith discover that God's strength is enough.

Let us take the next couple of minutes to discuss the following questions as a family:

1. What does Judges 6:23 teach about Gideon's faith?
2. How did God show patience in growing Gideon's faith?
3. Why does faith mean trusting God's strength over numbers?
4. How can our family serve God with Gideon-like faith this week

PRAYER

Patient God, thank You for choosing Gideon and showing Your strength through weakness. Thank You for giving peace that removes fear. Forgive us when we doubt Your call. Teach our family to trust You and walk in faith like Gideon. Amen.

FAMILY ACTIVITY

On a scrapbook page, draw 300 torches. Each family member writes one way they will trust God's strength instead of their own this week. Title the page "Faith Like Gideon".

September 26
The Faithful Trio
Shadrach, Meshach, and Abednego

"If this be so, our God whom we serve is able to deliver us from the burning fiery furnace, and he will deliver us out of your hand, O king. But if not, be it known to you, O king, that we will not serve your gods." – Daniel 3:17–18

Shadrach, Meshach, and Abednego are remembered for their unwavering faith. When ordered to bow to a golden image, they refused. They trusted that God could save them, but even if He did not, they would still obey Him. Families should remember that faith means trusting God's power while standing firm no matter the outcome.

The king ordered them thrown into the fiery furnace. Yet God was with them in the fire. A fourth figure appeared" one like the Son of God. The flames did not harm them, and they came out without even the smell of smoke. Their faith testified to God's power.

Faith like these three men's is steadfast. It is not based on circumstances but on devotion to God. Families should learn that faith is tested when obedience is costly, yet God's presence sustains.

Their story reminds us that God may deliver miraculously or allow trials, but either way, He is faithful. Families who trust Him will never be alone in the fire.

Let us take the next couple of minutes to discuss the following questions as a family:

1. What does Daniel 3:17–18 teach about faith?
2. How did Shadrach, Meshach, and Abednego show courage?
3. Why is faith more about trusting God than expecting outcomes?
4. How can our family stand firm like these men this week

PRAYER

Delivering God, thank You for being with Shadrach, Meshach, and Abednego in the fire. Thank You for promising never to leave us. Forgive us when we compromise or give in to fear. Teach our family to trust You in every trial. Amen.

FAMILY ACTIVITY

On a scrapbook page, draw flames. Each family member writes one situation where they will stand firm in obedience this week. Title the page "Faith in the Fire".

September 27
Rahab's Resilience

"By faith Rahab the prostitute did not perish with those who were disobedient, because she had given a friendly welcome to the spies." – Hebrews 11:31

Have you ever watched a spy thriller movie where the odds were stacked up against the hero of the film? Today's iconic figure was in such a position.

Rahab's faith is a story of trust and courage. In Hebrews 11:31, she is honored for welcoming Israel's spies. Families should remember that faith is not limited by background, anyone who trusts God is welcomed into His family.

Rahab lived in Jericho, a city marked for destruction. Yet she believed the God of Israel was the true God. She risked her life by hiding the spies and asking for protection. Her faith saved her and her household.

Her story also shows God's grace. Though she had a sinful past, faith transformed her future. She became part of Israel, and even part of the family line of Jesus.

Faith like Rahab's means trusting God's mercy, taking risks for Him, and welcoming His people. Families should learn that faith brings salvation and new beginnings.

Living this way means believing God can redeem any past and using opportunities to stand with His people.

Let us take the next couple of minutes to discuss the following questions as a family:

1. What does Hebrews 11:31 teach about Rahab's faith?
2. How did Rahab show courage and trust in God?
3. What does her story teach about grace and redemption?
4. How can our family act with Rahab-like faith this week?

📖 PRAYER

Redeeming God, thank You for Rahab's faith and courage. Thank You for showing us that anyone who trusts You is welcomed. Forgive us when we judge by appearances or doubt Your grace. Teach our family to walk in faith like Rahab. Amen.

👪 FAMILY ACTIVITY

On a scrapbook page, write "Faith Like Rahab". Each family member writes one way God has redeemed their story, or one way they can welcome others into His family this week.

September 28
Caleb's Story

"But my servant Caleb, because he has a different spirit and has followed me fully, I will bring into the land into which he went." – Numbers 14:24

Caleb showed faith when most doubted. When the spies returned from exploring Canaan, ten gave fearful reports. But Caleb and Joshua declared, "We can take the land because the Lord is with us." Families should remember that faith trusts God even when others doubt.

God honored Caleb's faith. Numbers 14:24 says he had a different spirit and followed God fully. While others perished in the wilderness, Caleb lived to see the Promised Land.

Faith like Caleb's means standing apart from fear and unbelief. Families should learn that faith may put us in the minority, but God rewards those who trust Him.

Caleb's story also shows endurance. He was 85 years old when he claimed his inheritance, still strong in faith. Faith means trusting God's promises for a lifetime.

Living this way means choosing faith over fear, speaking truth boldly, and holding onto God's promises. Families who trust like Caleb will see His faithfulness.

Let us take the next couple of minutes to discuss the following questions as a family:

1. What does Numbers 14:24 teach about Caleb's faith?
2. How did Caleb and Joshua respond differently than the other spies?
3. Why does faith sometimes mean standing apart from the crowd?
4. How can our family show Caleb-like faith this week?

📖 PRAYER

Faithful God, thank You for Caleb's example of courage and endurance. Thank You for rewarding those who follow You fully. Forgive us when we give in to fear. Teach our family to trust You boldly like Caleb. Amen.

⚠ FAMILY ACTIVITY

On a scrapbook page, write "Faith Like Caleb". Each family member writes one promise of God they will hold onto, even when others doubt.

Joseph: More Than Just The Favorite Son

"As for you, you meant evil against me, but God meant it for good." – Genesis 50:20

Imagine being bullied by your own brother because of their jealousy, so much so that you get taken to a faraway land?

Joseph's life shows faith in God's providence. Sold by his brothers, enslaved, and imprisoned, he still trusted God. In Genesis 50:20, he declared that God turned evil into good to save many lives. Families should remember that faith believes God works all things for good.

Joseph remained faithful in every situation. He served well in Potiphar's house, resisted temptation, and trusted God in prison. Eventually, he rose to power in Egypt and saved his family during famine.

Faith like Joseph's means seeing beyond present trials. Families should learn that God's hand works even in hardships. What others intend for harm, God can use for blessing.

Joseph's story also shows forgiveness. Instead of revenge, he forgave his brothers. Faith means trusting God with justice and choosing mercy.

Living this way means trusting God's plan in every season, serving faithfully where we are, and forgiving those who hurt us.

Let us take the next couple of minutes to discuss the following questions as a family:

1. What does Genesis 50:20 teach about God's providence?
2. How did Joseph show faith through trials?
3. Why is forgiveness an act of faith?
4. How can our family show Joseph-like faith this week?

✎ PRAYER

Sovereign God, thank You for Joseph's story of faith and forgiveness. Thank You for working all things for good. Forgive us when we doubt Your plan. Teach our family to trust You in hardships and to forgive like Joseph. Amen.

▲ FAMILY ACTIVITY

On a scrapbook page, write "Faith Like Joseph". Each family member writes one area where they will trust God's plan this week.

<h1 style="text-align:center">September 30</h1>
<h1 style="text-align:center">Faith Like Jesus</h1>

"And being found in human form, he humbled himself by becoming obedient to the point of death, even death on a cross." – Philippians 2:8

Jesus Himself is the perfect example of faith. Philippians 2:8 tells us He humbled Himself and obeyed the Father to the point of death. Families should remember that true faith is obedience to God's will, even when it costs everything.

Jesus trusted the Father completely. He prayed in Gethsemane, "Not my will, but Yours be done." His faith led Him to the cross, where He secured salvation for the world.

Faith like Jesus means full surrender. It means trusting God's plan even in suffering. Families should learn that obedience is the highest expression of faith.

His faith was also filled with love. He laid down His life willingly. Families should remember that faith is not only belief but action rooted in love.

Living this way means daily surrender: trusting God's Word, obeying His commands, and serving with love. Families who walk in Jesus-like faith reflect Him to the world.

Let us take the next couple of minutes to discuss the following questions as a family:

1. What does Philippians 2:8 teach about Jesus' faith?
2. How did Jesus show trust in the Father's will?
3. Why is obedience the highest form of faith?
4. How can our family walk in Jesus-like faith this week

✎ PRAYER

Obedient Savior, thank You for showing perfect faith in the Father. Thank You for laying down Your life in love. Forgive us when we resist surrender. Teach our family to walk in faith like You, obeying with trust and love. Amen.

⚶ FAMILY ACTIVITY

On a scrapbook page, draw a cross. Each family member writes one way they will obey God this week.

OCTOBER

October 1
Called to Holiness

"But as he who called you is holy, you also be holy in all your conduct, since it is written, 'You shall be holy, for I am holy.'" – 1 Peter 1:15–16

Holiness is not optional for God's people. First Peter 1:15-16 commands believers to be holy because God is holy. Families should understand that holiness means being set apart for God, living differently from the world.

The Bible shows that God's holiness is His perfection and purity. He is separate from sin and full of righteousness. When He calls His people to holiness, He invites them to reflect His character in their lives.

Israel was called to be a holy nation. They were given laws, sacrifices, and worship practices to remind them of God's holiness. In the New Testament, believers are called holy because of Christ's sacrifice. Through Jesus, we are forgiven and empowered to live holy lives.

Holiness is not about perfection on our own, it is about obedience through the Spirit. Romans 12:2 tells us not to conform to the world but be transformed by renewing our minds. Families should remember that holiness starts in the heart and flows into words and actions.

Living in holiness means choosing purity over sin, truth over lies, kindness over anger, and worship over selfishness. Families should encourage one another to live as God's holy people daily.

Let us take the next couple of minutes to discuss the following questions as a family:

1. What does 1 Peter 1:15-16 teach about holiness?
2. How is God's holiness shown in the Bible?
3. Why does God call His people to holiness?
4. How can our family live as holy people this week?

PRAYER

Holy God, thank You for calling us to reflect Your holiness. Thank You for making us holy through Jesus' sacrifice. Forgive us when we compromise with sin. Teach our family to live set apart for You in everything we do. Amen.

FAMILY ACTIVITY

On a scrapbook page, write "What It Means To Live A Holy Life". Each family member writes down what it means to live a holy life.

October 2
Holy in Our Thoughts

"Finally, brothers, whatever is true, whatever is honorable, whatever is just, whatever is pure, whatever is lovely, whatever is commendable, if there is any excellence, if there is anything worthy of praise, think about these things." – Philippians 4:8

Holiness begins in the mind. Philippians 4:8 calls believers to focus their thoughts on things that are true, pure, and praiseworthy. Families should understand that holiness is not only about actions but about the thoughts that shape them.

The Bible often links the mind with holiness. Romans 12:2 speaks of renewing the mind to be transformed. Colossians 3:2 says to set our minds on things above, not on earthly things.

Sin often begins with thoughts: envy, anger, pride, or lust. Holiness means guarding the mind and filling it with God's truth. Jesus Himself taught that sin starts in the heart and mind before it shows in actions.

Families should learn to filter what they allow into their minds through books, music, screens, and conversations. Choosing what is pure and true protects holiness.

Living with holy thoughts means memorizing Scripture, praying often, and encouraging positive conversations at home. Families who guard their minds will live lives that honor God.

Let us take the next couple of minutes to discuss the following questions as a family:

1. What does Philippians 4:8 teach about our thoughts?
2. Why is holiness connected to the mind?
3. How can sin begin in thoughts before actions?
4. How can our family keep our thoughts holy this week?

✐ PRAYER

Pure God, thank You for giving us Your Word to guide our thoughts. Thank You for calling us to think about what is true and pure. Forgive us when we let wrong thoughts fill our minds. Teach our family to honor You in our thinking. Amen.

⚑ FAMILY ACTIVITY

On a scrapbook page, write "Holy in Our Thoughts". Each family member writes down one area where they will aim to choose something pure to protect holiness.

October 3
Learning to Trust God One Day at a Time

"This is the day that the Lord has made; let us rejoice and be glad in it." –
Psalm 118:24

Today's Bible study reminds us to pay attention to the day in front of us. God does not promise to give tomorrow's strength today. Instead, He gives what is needed for *this* day. Faith often grows when we learn to trust God in the present, rather than worrying about what comes next.

Families can easily feel pulled in many directions, thinking ahead, managing schedules, and carrying concerns about the future. This verse gently brings hearts back to the moment. Today is a gift from God, even if it feels ordinary or challenging.

Rejoicing does not mean ignoring difficulties. It means choosing to recognize God's presence in the middle of them. Some days are joyful and light; others are heavy and uncertain. God is present in all of them. Gratitude helps families see His faithfulness, even when answers are not clear.

Living one day at a time teaches trust. It helps families slow down and rely on God's provision instead of their own planning. When families learn to receive each day as God's gift, anxiety loosens its grip and faith has room to grow.

This verse invites families to practice faith daily, not by having everything figured out, but by choosing trust, gratitude, and obedience in the moment they are given.

Let us take the next couple of minutes to discuss the following questions as a family:

1. Why do you think God wants us to focus on today instead of worrying about tomorrow?

2. What makes it hard to trust God one day at a time?

3. How can gratitude help our family see God's presence today?

4. What is one way we can rejoice in today, even if it's not perfect?

PRAYER

Faithful God, thank You for giving us this day. Thank You for meeting us in ordinary moments and uncertain times. Forgive us when we worry about what we cannot control. Help our family trust You one day at a time, receiving today as a gift from Your hand. Amen.

FAMILY ACTIVITY

On a scrapbook page, write "Today Is God's Gift". Each family member writes one thing from today they are thankful for, even if it seems small. Leave space to return later and add reminders of how God showed His faithfulness in everyday moments.

October 4
Learning Obedience Through Everyday Choices

"But be doers of the word, and not hearers only, deceiving yourselves." – James 1:22

This verse reminds us that faith is meant to be lived, not just talked about. Hearing God's Word is important, but obedience is where faith takes shape. What we believe becomes visible through what we do.

In family life, this truth shows up every day. It appears in how conflicts are handled, how promises are kept, and how kindness is shown when it would be easier to react in frustration. Obedience is often practiced in small, unseen moments.

God's Word guides families toward actions that reflect His character. When families choose to live out what God teaches, faith becomes part of daily life rather than something reserved for special times or places.

This verse also serves as a gentle warning. It is possible to know God's truth without allowing it to shape behavior. God calls families to move beyond listening and into faithful action, trusting that obedience leads to growth and maturity.

When families practice obedience together, they grow in unity and trust. God uses these shared choices to strengthen hearts and shape homes that reflect His truth and grace.

Let us take the next couple of minutes to discuss the following questions as a family:

1. What does it mean to be a "doer" of God's Word?
2. Why is it sometimes easier to listen than to obey?
3. How can obedience show up in everyday family situations?
4. What is one way our family can put God's Word into action this week?

PRAYER

Faithful God, thank You for giving us Your Word to guide our lives. Forgive us when we hear Your truth but fail to live it out. Teach our family to obey with willing hearts, trusting that Your ways lead to life and peace. Help us honor You through our actions each day. Amen.

FAMILY ACTIVITY

On a scrapbook page, write "Living Out God's Word". Each family member writes one practical way they can put God's teaching into action this week: through kindness, honesty, forgiveness, or service. Leave space to return later and reflect on how obedience shaped your family's days.

October 5
Holy in Our Relationships

"A new commandment I give to you, that you love one another: just as I have loved you, you also are to love one another." – John 13:34

Holiness is not only about personal purity, it is about how we treat others. John 13:34 reminds believers to love one another as Christ has loved us. Families should remember that holy relationships are marked by love, forgiveness, and respect.

The Bible shows that love is the foundation of holiness. First Corinthians 13 describes love as patient, kind, not envious or proud. Families should learn that holiness in relationships reflects God's love.

Jesus loved sacrificially, laying down His life. Families are called to love in the same way: serving, forgiving, and encouraging one another.

Holy relationships require effort. They involve listening, showing patience, and resolving conflict peacefully. Families should remember that forgiveness keeps relationships holy and strong.

Living this way means practicing love at home first, then extending it outward to friends, neighbors, and church. Families who live with holy relationships shine Christ's love to the world.

Let's discuss the following questions for the next couple of minutes:

1. What does John 13:34 teach about relationships?
2. How is love connected to holiness?
3. How did Jesus model holy love?
4. How can our family make relationships more holy this week?

PRAYER

Loving God, thank You for calling us to love one another as Jesus loved us. Thank You for showing us true holiness through His sacrifice. Forgive us when we fail to love or forgive. Teach our family to live with holy relationships. Amen.

FAMILY ACTIVITY

On a scrapbook page, write "Holy in Our Relationships". Each family member writes one way they will show love to another person this week.

October 6

Our Choices Must Be Guided By Faith

"Choose this day whom you will serve... But as for me and my house, we will serve the Lord." – Joshua 24:15

We make decisions every day. Some are basic decisions, such as what to wear, what to eat. Others are more faith driven, such as how we can grow in our service to God and our communities.

What we need to remember, is that holiness involves the choices we make daily. Joshua 24:15 records Joshua's declaration that his household would serve the Lord. Families should remember that holiness is not only about big moments but about daily decisions that honor God.

Israel faced a choice: serve the idols of the nations or serve the Lord. Joshua called them to decide clearly. Holiness always requires a decision to follow God above all else.

The Bible shows the importance of holy choices. Daniel chose not to defile himself with the king's food. Joseph chose to flee from temptation in Potiphar's house. Ruth chose to follow Naomi's God instead of returning to Moab. Each choice revealed a holy heart.

Families should understand that choices shape character. Small decisions, what to watch, how to speak, whether to forgive, add up to a holy or unholy life. Holiness means consistently choosing God's way.

Living with holy choices means asking, "Does this please God?" before deciding. Families who make choices together based on Scripture will honor Him in their homes.

Let's discuss the following questions for the next couple of minutes

1. What does Joshua 24:15 teach about choices?
2. What examples of holy choices are found in Scripture?
3. Why do small decisions matter in holiness?
4. How can our family make choices that honor God this week?

✎ PRAYER

Righteous God, thank You for giving us the freedom to choose. Thank You for showing us the best way in Your Word. Forgive us when we choose sin or selfishness. Teach our family to make holy choices that honor You. Amen.

♟ FAMILY ACTIVITY

On a scrapbook page, write "Holy in Our Choices". Each family member writes one decision they will make this week to serve the Lord.

Holy in Our Attitude

"Do all things without grumbling or disputing, that you may be blameless and innocent, children of God without blemish." – Philippians 2:14–15

Have you ever had to do a household chore that made you feel unhappy? Or have you ever felt like going to church or Bible study is too much effort to begin with?

Holiness is reflected not only in actions but in attitudes. Philippians 2:14-15 teaches that believers should avoid grumbling and disputing. Families should remember that a holy life shines through a spirit of joy, gratitude, and humility.

Israel in the wilderness often grumbled against God. Their complaints showed lack of trust. In contrast, Paul urged believers to shine like lights in the world by their attitudes.

Jesus modeled a holy attitude. Though He suffered, He did not complain. He accepted God's will with humility. Families should learn that holiness means cultivating a heart that reflects Christ's character.

A holy attitude includes gratitude, patience, humility, and joy. It turns daily chores into worship and trials into opportunities for trust. Families should encourage each other to check attitudes, not just behaviors.

Living this way means remembering that God looks at the heart. Families who live with holy attitudes will create homes full of peace and light.

Let's discuss the following questions for the next couple of minutes:

1. What does Philippians 2:14-15 teach about attitudes?
2. How did Israel show unholy attitudes in the wilderness?
3. How did Jesus model a holy attitude?
4. How can our family reflect holiness in our attitudes this week?

PRAYER

Holy God, thank You for calling us to shine as Your children. Thank You for Jesus' example of humility and joy. Forgive us when we complain or argue. Teach our family to live with holy attitudes that glorify You. Amen.

FAMILY ACTIVITY

On a scrapbook page, write "Holy in Our Attitude". Each family member writes one attitude they will change or improve this week.

October 8
Habits Can Shape Our Lives For The Better

"Discipline yourself for the purpose of godliness." – 1 Timothy 4:7

What would you consider to be a good habit? Is it keeping your room or house neat and tidy, going to church every Sunday or checking in with friends who need support during difficult times?

Holiness is shaped by daily habits. First Timothy 4:7 reminds believers to discipline themselves for godliness. Families should remember that holiness is not accidental; it comes from intentional habits of faith.

The Bible shows the importance of godly habits. Daniel prayed three times daily. Jesus often withdrew to pray. The early church devoted themselves to teaching, fellowship, breaking bread, and prayer.

Holy habits include reading Scripture, praying regularly, attending worship, practicing gratitude, and serving others. These habits form character and draw us closer to God.

Families should understand that unholy habits, such as neglecting prayer, wasting time, or feeding sin, pull us away from God. Holiness requires choosing habits that grow faith.

Living with holy habits means setting aside time for God, creating family rhythms of prayer and Scripture, and encouraging one another to stay faithful. Families who form holy habits will remain strong in faith through all seasons.

Let's discuss the following questions for the next couple of minutes:

1. What does 1 Timothy 4:7 teach about habits?
2. What examples of holy habits are found in the Bible?
3. How do daily habits shape holiness?
4. How can our family create holy habits this week?

📖 PRAYER

God of Discipline, thank You for showing us the value of godly habits. Thank You for examples of faithful people who prayed and obeyed daily. Forgive us when we neglect holy habits. Teach our family to practice habits that build holiness. Amen.

♟ FAMILY ACTIVITY

On a scrapbook page, write "Our Habits: How Can We Make Them Better". Each family member writes one habit they will practice daily this week.

October 9
Holy in Our Bodies

"Do you not know that your body is a temple of the Holy Spirit within you, whom you have from God? You are not your own, for you were bought with a price. So glorify God in your body." – 1 Corinthians 6:19–20

Did you know that holiness includes how we treat our bodies?

First Corinthians 6:19-20 teaches that our bodies are temples of the Holy Spirit. Families should remember that holiness involves using our bodies for God's glory.

The Bible warns against sin that dishonors the body. Immorality, gluttony, and laziness dishonor God. Instead, we are called to purity, self-control, and service.

Jesus honored God with His body, using His hands to heal, His feet to serve, and His strength to carry the cross. Families should learn that holiness means offering our bodies for God's purposes.

Holiness in the body also includes caring for health. Eating wisely, resting, and working diligently are ways of honoring God. Families should remember that stewardship of the body is part of holiness.

Living this way means saying no to sin and yes to healthy, pure living. Families who honor God in their bodies show respect for His Spirit dwelling in them.

Let's discuss the following questions for the next couple of minutes:

1. What does 1 Corinthians 6:19–20 teach about our bodies?
2. How did Jesus honor God with His body?
3. Why is caring for health part of holiness?
4. How can our family glorify God in our bodies this week?

PRAYER

Holy Spirit, thank You for dwelling in us as Your temple. Thank You for redeeming us with the blood of Jesus. Forgive us when we dishonor our bodies with sin or neglect. Teach our family to glorify You in our bodies. Amen.

FAMILY ACTIVITY

On a scrapbook page, write "Holy in Our Bodies". Each family member writes one way they will honor God with their body this week.

Trusting God to Restore What Was Lost

"You shall eat in plenty and be satisfied, and praise the name of the Lord your God, who has dealt wondrously with you." – Joel 2:26

This verse was spoken to God's people after a season of loss. They had experienced hardship, uncertainty, and the consequences of difficult times. God did not ignore what they had been through. Instead, He promised restoration and reminded them that He was still at work among them.

Families often walk through seasons that feel draining. Time is lost. Energy is spent. Mistakes are made. This verse reminds us that God sees those seasons clearly and is able to restore in ways we could not imagine on our own.

Restoration does not always mean getting back exactly what was lost. Sometimes it means renewed strength, deeper faith, or a clearer understanding of God's care. God's work of restoration reaches beyond circumstances and into the heart.

For families, this verse brings hope. God is not finished with what feels broken or incomplete. He works patiently, often over time, to bring healing and renewal where it is needed most.

Trusting God to restore means believing that He is faithful even after hard seasons. Families who hold onto this promise learn to praise God not only for what they see now, but for what He is still bringing about.

Let us take the next couple of minutes to discuss the following questions as a family:

1. Why is it sometimes hard to believe God can restore what was lost?
2. What kinds of loss do families experience beyond physical things?
3. How does this verse encourage hope after difficult seasons?
4. Where does our family need to trust God's restoring work right now?

📖 PRAYER

Restoring God, thank You for seeing Your people through every season. Thank You for Your promise to renew and restore. Forgive us when discouragement makes it hard to trust You. Help our family place our hope in You, believing that You are still working for good. Amen.

♟ FAMILY ACTIVITY

On a scrapbook page, write "God Restores". Each family member writes one area where they are trusting God to bring renewal, whether in relationships, faith, or hope. Leave space to return later and reflect on how God's restoring work became clear over time.

October 11

Holy in Our Hearts

"Blessed are the pure in heart, for they shall see God." – Matthew 5:8

Have you ever wondered how holiness takes root in our lives?

Today's Bible lesson reminds us that holiness begins in the heart, or more specifically, a pure heart that lives to serve God.

In Matthew 5:8, Jesus promised that the pure in heart will see God. Families should understand that holiness is not about outward appearances but about inner devotion and sincerity.

The Bible teaches that the heart is the center of life. Proverbs 4:23 says, "Keep your heart with all vigilance, for from it flow the springs of life." If the heart is holy, actions and words will reflect holiness too.

King David prayed, "Create in me a clean heart, O God" (Psalm 51:10), after his sin with Bathsheba. He knew that holiness starts within, not only in behavior. God desires truth in the inner being, not outward show.

Jesus rebuked the Pharisees for looking holy outwardly while their hearts were corrupt. Families should learn that holiness is about loving God sincerely, not pretending.

Living with holy hearts means confessing sin, asking God for cleansing, and filling hearts with love for Him.

Families who pursue purity of heart will draw closer to God daily.

Let us take the next couple of minutes to discuss the following questions as a family:

1. What does Matthew 5:8 teach about the heart?
2. Why does holiness begin within rather than outwardly?
3. What can we learn from David's prayer in Psalm 51?
4. How can our family keep our hearts holy this week?

✒ PRAYER

Lord of Purity, thank You for promising that the pure in heart will see You. Thank You for cleansing us through Jesus. Forgive us when our hearts drift from You. Teach our family to keep our hearts holy and devoted to You. Amen.

▲ FAMILY ACTIVITY

On a scrapbook page, write "Holy in Our Hearts". Each family member writes one way they will keep their heart pure for God this week.

October 12
Friendships Shape Our Lives

"Do not be deceived: 'Bad company ruins good morals.'" – 1 Corinthians 15:33

Think for a moment how you would describe a good friend. Is it someone who inspires you to be the best person you can be, or is it someone you can always rely on, no matter what?

Friendships shape the kind of life we live. First Corinthians 15:33 warns that bad company corrupts good character. Families should remember that holiness includes choosing friends who encourage faith and obedience.

The Bible shows examples of holy friendships. Jonathan and David shared a covenant friendship marked by loyalty and faith in God. Ruth and Naomi's bond reflected faithfulness and devotion. Paul encouraged Timothy as a spiritual son.

Unholy friendships, however, can pull people away from God. Solomon's wives turned his heart to idols. Samson's relationship with Delilah led to his downfall. Families should learn that friendships matter deeply in holiness.

Holy friendships build up, encourage, and point us to Christ. They involve honesty, accountability, and shared devotion. Families should encourage children to seek godly friends and be godly friends to others.

Living this way means showing love to everyone but choosing close companions who strengthen faith. Families who value holy friendships create circles that honor God.

Let us take the next couple of minutes to discuss the following questions as a family:

1. What does 1 Corinthians 15:33 teach about friendships?
2. What examples of holy friendships are found in Scripture?
3. How can friends either strengthen or weaken holiness?
4. How can our family encourage holy friendships this week?

PRAYER

Faithful God, thank You for giving us friends and relationships. Thank You for showing us examples of holy friendships in Your Word. Forgive us when we choose relationships that lead us away from You. Teach our family to pursue holy friendships. Amen.

FAMILY ACTIVITY

On a scrapbook page, write "Our Friendships". Each family member writes one quality of a godly friend and one way to be that kind of friend this week.

October 13
Remembering Who God Is When Life Feels Unsteady

"Trust in the Lord forever, for the Lord God is an everlasting rock." – Isaiah 26:4

This verse points us to something solid when everything else feels uncertain. An everlasting rock does not shift, weaken, or disappear. God remains steady even when life around us feels unpredictable.

Families experience seasons of change: new routines, unexpected challenges, and moments when answers are not clear. During these times, it is easy to feel unsettled. This verse reminds us that God does not change with circumstances. He remains faithful and dependable.

Trusting God as our rock does not mean ignoring difficulties. It means choosing where we place our confidence. Families can learn to turn to God together, relying on His strength instead of being overwhelmed by what they cannot control.

Children especially need this assurance. When families show trust in God during unsteady moments, they model where true security is found. God's faithfulness becomes something that is seen and experienced, not just spoken about.

Today's Bible lesson invites families to pause and remember who God is. When trust is placed in Him, hearts grow steadier. A family that leans on God as their rock learns to stand firm, even when life feels uncertain.

Let us take the next couple of minutes to discuss the following questions as a family:

1. What does it mean to trust God as an "everlasting rock"?
2. When does life feel most unsteady for our family?
3. How can trusting God bring peace during uncertain times?
4. What is one way our family can lean on God more fully right now?

PRAYER

Faithful God, thank You for being steady when life feels uncertain. Thank You for being a rock we can depend on in every season. Forgive us when fear replaces trust. Help our family lean on You together, finding peace and strength in who You are. Amen.

FAMILY ACTIVITY

On a scrapbook page, write "God Is Our Rock". Draw a strong rock or foundation. Each family member writes one situation where they want to trust God's strength instead of worrying. Leave space to return later and reflect on how trusting God brought stability and peace.

October 14

Choosing to Honor One Another in Our Home

"Love one another with brotherly affection. Outdo one another in showing honor." –
Romans 12:10

This verse speaks to how God's people are meant to treat one another. Love here is not distant or abstract. It is close, intentional, and expressed through respect. Honor is not something demanded; it is something freely given.

In family life, honor is often tested. Familiarity can lead to impatience. Stress can make words sharper than intended. This verse gently calls families back to a better way—one shaped by affection, humility, and care.

Showing honor means noticing one another. It means listening without dismissing, speaking without tearing down, and choosing kindness even when emotions run high. These choices shape the atmosphere of a home more than rules or routines ever could.

God calls His people to reflect His love through how they treat those closest to them. When families choose honor, trust grows. Hearts soften. Conflicts are handled with greater grace. God's love becomes visible in everyday interactions.

This verse invites families to be intentional. Honor does not happen accidentally. It grows when family members choose to value one another, recognizing that each person is created and loved by God.

Let us take the next couple of minutes to discuss the following questions as a family:

1. What does it mean to show honor to one another?
2. Why is it sometimes hardest to show honor at home?
3. How can words and actions reflect respect in family life?
4. What is one way our family can practice honoring one another today?

✎ PRAYER

Loving God, thank You for teaching us how to love one another well. Forgive us when impatience or selfishness replaces honor. Help our family treat one another with affection, respect, and humility, reflecting Your love in our home each day. Amen.

♟ FAMILY ACTIVITY

On a scrapbook page, write "Honoring One Another". Each family member writes one way they can show honor to someone else in the family this week, through encouragement, listening, kindness, or forgiveness. Leave space to return later and reflect on how choosing honor affected your home.

October 15
Holy in Our Speech

"Set a guard, O Lord, over my mouth; keep watch over the door of my lips!" –
Psalm 141:3

Holiness is often revealed through words long before it is seen through actions. In Psalm 141:3, David does not trust himself to speak rightly on his own. Instead, he asks God to stand guard over his mouth. This prayer reminds families that holy speech begins with dependence on God, not self-control alone.

Words carry weight in family life. They shape trust, build confidence, and leave lasting impressions. Scripture repeatedly reminds God's people that listening matters as much as speaking. James teaches us to be slow to speak and slow to anger, while Proverbs reminds us that gentle words can calm tense situations. God's wisdom directs speech toward peace rather than harm.

Unholy speech does not always sound extreme. It can appear in careless comments, sharp responses, sarcasm, or words spoken in frustration. These moments can quietly damage relationships. Holy speech, by contrast, reflects patience, restraint, and a desire to honor God and one another.

Jesus' warning that people will give an account for every careless word reminds families that speech is not insignificant. Words flow from the heart, and God cares deeply about what they reveal. This truth encourages families to pause before speaking and to invite God's guidance into everyday conversations.

Living with holy speech means choosing words carefully, especially in difficult moments. Sometimes it means remaining silent rather than responding in anger. Other times it means speaking truth with kindness. Families who seek holiness in their words create homes marked by peace, encouragement, and respect for God.

Let us take the next couple of minutes to discuss the following questions as a family:

1. What does Psalm 141:3 teach us about the need for God's help with our words?
2. Why do words have such a strong impact in family relationships?
3. What kinds of speech can quietly cause harm, even if unintentional?
4. How can our family be more intentional about speaking with holiness this week?

PRAYER

God of wisdom, thank You for giving us the ability to speak and communicate. Forgive us for words spoken carelessly or in frustration. Teach our family to pause, listen, and invite You to guard our mouths. Help us use our words to bring life, peace, and honor to You. Amen.

FAMILY ACTIVITY

On a scrapbook page, write **"Holy in Our Speech."** Each family member writes one phrase or sentence they will intentionally use this week to encourage, show kindness, or speak truth with grace. Leave space to reflect later on how these words affected others.

October 16
Choosing What Is Good Together

"Seek good, and not evil, that you may live; and so the Lord, the God of hosts, will be with you." – Amos 5:14

This verse is a clear invitation, not just a command. God calls His people to actively seek what is good. That kind of seeking requires attention, discernment, and intentional choice, especially in everyday life.

Families make many choices each day. Some feel small and routine, others feel weighty and important. This verse reminds us that the direction of those choices matters. Seeking good is not passive; it is a deliberate turning toward what honors God and reflects His character.

Choosing good together shapes the atmosphere of a home. It influences how conflicts are handled, how time is spent, and how priorities are set. When families seek what is good, they invite God's presence into ordinary moments and shared decisions.

This verse also connects seeking good with life and God's nearness. God promises to be with His people as they choose His ways. Families do not walk alone when they commit to pursuing what pleases Him.

Living this out means pausing before decisions and asking what reflects God's heart. It means choosing kindness over bitterness, truth over convenience, and faith over fear. Families who seek good together grow in unity and experience God's guidance along the way.

Let us take the next couple of minutes to discuss the following questions as a family:

1. What does it mean to "seek good" in everyday family life?
2. Why do small choices matter as much as big ones?
3. How does seeking good invite God's presence into our home?
4. What is one choice our family can make today that reflects what is good?

✎ PRAYER

Faithful God, thank You for guiding Your people toward what is good and life-giving. Forgive us when we choose what is easy instead of what is right. Help our family seek what honors You, trusting that You are with us as we follow Your ways. Amen.

⚘ FAMILY ACTIVITY

On a scrapbook page, write "Seeking Good Together". Each family member writes one choice they want to make this week that reflects God's goodness, through kindness, honesty, patience, or obedience. Leave space to return later and reflect on how those choices shaped your family's days.

October 17
Holy in Our Ears

"So faith comes from hearing, and hearing through the word of Christ." –
Romans 10:17

Holiness is shaped not only by what we say and do, but also by what we allow ourselves to hear. Romans 10:17 reminds us that faith grows through hearing the Word of Christ. What enters our ears has the power to shape our thoughts, attitudes, and trust in God.

Throughout Scripture, God calls His people to listen carefully. When Israel was commanded to "hear" the Lord, it was an invitation to pay attention, remember, and obey. Jesus echoed this call when He urged listeners to truly hear His words. Listening has always been closely tied to faithfulness.

The Bible also warns that not every voice leads toward God. From the beginning, listening to the wrong voice brought confusion and sin. Gossip, lies, and constant negativity can quietly influence hearts and weaken faith. Families need wisdom to recognize which voices build up and which ones pull them away from God.

Holy listening involves choosing what strengthens faith. God uses His Word, worship, and wise counsel to guide and encourage His people. When families fill their homes with truth, faith is nurtured and character grows stronger over time.

Living this way requires intention. Families must decide what they welcome into their ears each day. By choosing to listen to Scripture, prayer, and words that honor God, families create space for faith to deepen and holiness to take root.

Let us take the next couple of minutes to discuss the following questions as a family:

1. What does Romans 10:17 teach us about the connection between hearing and faith?
2. Why is listening an important part of holy living?
3. What kinds of voices can distract us from hearing God clearly?
4. How can our family be more intentional about what we listen to this week?

📖 PRAYER

God of truth, thank You for speaking to us through Your Word. Thank You for shaping our faith as we listen to You. Forgive us when we give attention to voices that lead us away from Your truth. Teach our family to listen carefully to what is holy and pleasing to You. Amen.

🛐 FAMILY ACTIVITY

On a scrapbook page, write "Holy in Our Ears". Each family member writes one thing they will choose to listen to this week, such as Scripture, worship music, or encouraging words, that helps build faith and honor God.

October 18
Hands That Serve God

"Whatever your hand finds to do, do it with your might." – Ecclesiastes 9:10

Holiness involves how we use our hands. Ecclesiastes 9:10 reminds believers to work with diligence. Families should remember that hands can serve God or be used for selfishness.

The Bible speaks of holy hands. Psalm 24:3-4 says only those with clean hands and a pure heart may stand in God's presence. First Timothy 2:8 encourages believers to lift holy hands in prayer.

Hands in Scripture also served others. Jesus used His hands to heal, bless children, and break bread. Dorcas used her hands to sew clothes for the needy. Families should learn that holiness is shown in how hands serve, create, and care.

Unholy hands are associated with violence, greed, and sin. Families must choose to use hands for building up, not tearing down.

Living this way means serving others, helping at home, and offering hands to God in worship. Families who use their hands for holiness honor Him daily.

Let us take the next couple of minutes to discuss the following questions as a family:

1. What does Ecclesiastes 9:10 teach about hands?
2. What examples of holy hands are found in the Bible?
3. How did Jesus use His hands to serve?
4. How can our family use our hands for holiness this week?

📖 PRAYER

Creator God, thank You for giving us hands to work and serve. Thank You for Jesus' example of holy hands. Forgive us when our hands are idle or selfish. Teach our family to use our hands for Your glory. Amen.

👪 FAMILY ACTIVITY

On a scrapbook page, draw an outline of each family member's hand. Inside, write one way they will use their hands to serve this week.

October 19

Holy in Our Feet

"How beautiful are the feet of those who preach the good news!" – Romans 10:15

Holiness is not only about what we believe, but also about where our lives take us. Romans 10:15 reminds us that God notices the paths His people walk. Feet that carry the good news are called beautiful because they are used in service to God's purposes.

Throughout Scripture, feet often represent direction and choice. God's Word is described as a light for the path, showing where to step and where to avoid going. Families are reminded that holiness involves daily decisions about the places they go, the activities they choose, and the influences they allow into their lives.

Jesus showed holiness through where He walked. His feet carried Him to places of need: homes of the hurting, crowds of the searching, and ultimately the cross. He did not avoid difficult paths when obedience required Him to walk them. Even washing His disciples' feet showed that holy steps are often steps of humility and service.

For families, holy feet mean being intentional about direction. It means avoiding paths that lead toward temptation or harm and choosing places where love, truth, and service can be shared. Sometimes this looks like going out to serve; other times it looks like choosing not to go where faith could be compromised.

Walking with holy feet is an ongoing choice. When families ask God to guide their steps, He leads them toward paths that reflect His goodness. A family that walks in God's ways becomes a quiet witness, showing others what it looks like to follow Him faithfully.

Let us take the next couple of minutes to discuss the following questions as a family:

1. What does Romans 10:15 teach us about where God calls His people to go?
2. Why do you think the Bible connects feet with direction and choice?
3. How did Jesus show holiness through the places He went?
4. What is one way our family can choose holy paths this week?

📖 PRAYER

Guiding God, thank You for caring about the paths we walk. Thank You for leading Your people with wisdom and purpose. Forgive us when our choices take us away from Your ways. Teach our family to walk with holy feet, going where You lead and reflecting Your love wherever we go. Amen.

🛐 FAMILY ACTIVITY

On a scrapbook page, draw footprints across the page. Title it "Holy Feet". Each family member writes one place they plan to go this week where they can show kindness, encouragement, or service. Leave space to return later and reflect on how God used those steps.

October 20

Making The Right Choices

"I call heaven and earth to witness against you today, that I have set before you life and death, blessing and curse. Therefore choose life, that you and your offspring may live." – Deuteronomy 30:19

Holiness is often lived out through choices. This verse makes it clear that God places decisions before His people and invites them to choose what leads to life. These choices are not only personal, they affect families and future generations.

Family life is filled with decisions, both big and small. Some choices feel obvious, while others are made in the moment, shaped by habits and values. This verse reminds families that choices matter because they shape direction, character, and spiritual health.

Choosing life does not mean choosing what is easiest or most comfortable. It means choosing obedience, truth, and faithfulness, even when those choices require patience or sacrifice. God's call to holiness is always connected to His desire for His people to live well under His care.

This verse also highlights responsibility. God gives guidance, but He allows His people to choose. Families who talk openly about choices, why they matter and where they lead, help one another grow in wisdom and accountability.

Living with holy choices means asking God for discernment each day. Families who choose life together learn to trust God's guidance and experience the blessing of walking in His ways.

Let us take the next couple of minutes to discuss the following questions as a family:

1. Why do you think God connects our choices with life and blessing?
2. How do small choices affect family life over time?
3. What makes choosing obedience difficult sometimes?
4. What is one choice our family can make this week that reflects holiness?

✍ PRAYER

Faithful God, thank You for guiding Your people with truth and wisdom. Forgive us when we choose what is easy instead of what is right. Help our family choose life each day, trusting that Your ways lead to blessing and peace. Teach us to honor You through the choices we make together. Amen.

⚖ FAMILY ACTIVITY

On a scrapbook page, write "Choosing Life Together". Each family member writes one choice they want to make this week that reflects obedience to God, such as kindness, honesty, patience, or trust. Leave space to return later and reflect on how these choices shaped your family's days.

October 21
Guarding Our Thoughts

"For as he thinks within himself, so he is." – Proverbs 23:7

This verse reminds us that what happens in the mind shapes the direction of a life. Thoughts influence attitudes, choices, and eventually actions. God cares about what fills our minds because He knows the heart follows where thoughts lead.

Family life brings many opportunities for thoughts to drift toward worry, frustration, comparison, or resentment. Left unchecked, these thoughts can quietly affect how family members speak and treat one another. This verse invites families to recognize the connection between inner thoughts and outward behavior.

Being holy in our thoughts does not mean ignoring struggles or pretending everything is fine. It means choosing to bring thoughts before God and allowing His truth to correct what is unhealthy or untrue. God's Word helps families recognize which thoughts need to be replaced with trust, gratitude, or patience.

Parents and children alike are shaped by repeated patterns of thinking. When families talk openly about thoughts, especially fearful or negative ones, they create space for God's truth to take root. Over time, minds become more aligned with God's ways.

Living with holy thoughts requires intention. Families who ask God to shape their thinking grow in discernment and peace. As thoughts are guided by truth, homes become places where faith is strengthened and hearts are guarded.

Let us take the next couple of minutes to discuss the following questions as a family:

1. Why do our thoughts have such a strong influence on our actions?
2. What kinds of thoughts can disrupt peace in a home?
3. How does God's Word help guide our thinking?
4. What is one thought our family needs to place before God this week?

PRAYER

God of truth, thank You for caring about our hearts and minds. Forgive us when unhealthy thoughts shape our attitudes and actions. Teach our family to bring our thoughts to You and allow Your truth to guide us. Help us think in ways that honor You and bring peace to our home. Amen.

FAMILY ACTIVITY

On a scrapbook page, write "Holy in Our Thoughts". Each family member writes one thought they want to replace this week with God's truth. Leave space to return later and reflect on how choosing better thoughts shaped your family's days.

October 22
Holy in Our Attitudes

"Better is a patient spirit than a proud spirit." – Ecclesiastes 7:8

Attitudes often set the tone in a home before any words are spoken. This verse reminds us that patience reflects humility, while pride often fuels frustration. God values a spirit that is willing to wait, listen, and respond with restraint.

Family life naturally tests attitudes. Tiredness, unmet expectations, and daily pressures can surface impatience quickly. This verse gently calls families to notice what is happening inside before reacting outwardly.

A patient spirit does not ignore problems. It chooses to respond with wisdom instead of pride. When families practice patience, conflicts soften and understanding grows.

God shapes holy attitudes over time. Families who ask Him to work in their hearts learn that patience creates space for peace and growth within the home.

Let us take the next couple of minutes to discuss the following questions as a family:

1. Why do attitudes matter so much in family life?
2. What situations test our patience the most?
3. How does pride affect our reactions?
4. What can help our family respond with patience this week?

Prayer God of wisdom, thank You for teaching us the value of patience. Forgive us when pride or frustration controls our attitudes. Help our family grow in humility and respond with grace toward one another. Amen.

Family Activity Scrapbook title: "Choosing Patience". Each family member writes one situation where they want to practice a patient spirit this week.

October 23
Using Our Time Wisely

"O Lord, make me know my end and what is the measure of my days; let me know how fleeting I am!" – Psalm 39:4

This verse is a humble prayer. It asks God for awareness, an understanding that time is limited and meaningful. God's people are reminded that days are not endless, and how they are lived matters.

Families often feel rushed. Days fill quickly with responsibilities, activities, and distractions. This verse invites families to pause and remember that time is a gift from God, not something to be spent carelessly or without thought.

Being holy in our time does not mean filling every moment with activity. It means using time wisely, with awareness of what honors God and strengthens relationships. God values moments of faith, rest, and togetherness as much as productivity.

When families recognize how quickly time passes, priorities become clearer. Time spent listening, praying, learning, and loving carries lasting value. God uses these moments to shape hearts over time.

Living this way means asking God to guide how time is used. Families who invite Him into their schedules learn to slow down, choose wisely, and make room for what truly matters.

Let us take the next couple of minutes to discuss the following questions as a family:

1. Why does God want us to be aware that time is limited?
2. What makes it hard for families to use time wisely?
3. How can our family choose better priorities with our time?
4. What is one way we can honor God with our time this week?

✐ PRAYER

God of wisdom, thank You for the gift of each day. Forgive us when we rush through time without seeking You. Teach our family to value our days and use our time in ways that honor You and strengthen our faith. Amen.

♟ FAMILY ACTIVITY

On a scrapbook page, write "Using Time Wisely". Each family member writes one activity they want to be more intentional about this week, such as prayer, rest, conversation, or service. Leave space to return later and reflect on how choosing wisely affected your family.

October 24
Holy in Our Relationships

"Let your love be genuine. Abhor what is evil; hold fast to what is good." –
Romans 12:9

This verse speaks honestly about love. God does not describe love as a feeling that comes and goes, but as something sincere and intentional. Genuine love requires discernment: choosing what is good and turning away from what harms relationships.

Family relationships are close, which makes them meaningful but also challenging. Words spoken quickly, unresolved hurt, or selfish choices can weaken trust. This verse reminds families that holiness in relationships involves active effort to love well.

Holding fast to what is good means choosing patience instead of resentment and forgiveness instead of holding grudges. It means recognizing when attitudes or behaviors are pulling relationships in the wrong direction and turning back toward God's ways.

God calls families to reflect His love through how they treat one another. When love is genuine, homes become places where people feel safe, valued, and cared for—even when disagreements arise.

Living with holy relationships means returning to God's standard for love again and again. Families who commit to sincere love grow stronger, more united, and better able to reflect God's grace to one another.

Let us take the next couple of minutes to discuss the following questions as a family:

1. What does genuine love look like in family life?
2. Why is it sometimes hard to hold fast to what is good?
3. How can our actions strengthen relationships at home?
4. What is one way our family can practice sincere love this week?

✎ PRAYER

Loving God, thank You for showing us what true love looks like. Forgive us when selfishness or frustration harms our relationships. Help our family love sincerely, choosing what is good and honoring You through how we treat one another. Amen.

⚜ FAMILY ACTIVITY

On a scrapbook page, write "Genuine Love at Home". Each family member writes one action they can take this week to strengthen a relationship, such as listening, forgiving, or showing kindness.

October 25
Holy in Our Trust

"Some trust in chariots and some in horses, but we trust in the name of the Lord our God." – Psalm 20:7

This verse contrasts two kinds of trust. Some people place confidence in strength they can see or control. God's people are called to trust in Him instead—His name, His character, and His faithfulness.

Families often face situations that tempt them to rely only on their own resources or plans. Worry can grow when outcomes feel uncertain. This verse gently redirects trust away from human strength and back to God.

Trusting God does not mean ignoring responsibility. It means recognizing that security ultimately comes from Him. Families who trust God learn to bring decisions, fears, and hopes before Him instead of carrying them alone.

When trust is placed in God, peace follows. Even when circumstances are unclear, families can rest knowing God is faithful and present. Trust becomes an anchor that steadies hearts during uncertainty.

Living with holy trust means choosing confidence in God daily. Families who place their trust in Him grow in faith and learn to rely on His strength rather than their own.

Let's take a couple of minutes to discuss the following questions:

1. Why is it tempting to trust in things we can control?
2. What does it mean to trust in the Lord instead?
3. How does trust affect the way families face challenges?
4. What is one concern our family needs to place in God's hands?

✐ PRAYER

Faithful God, thank You for being worthy of our trust. Forgive us when fear leads us to rely on our own strength instead of You. Help our family place our confidence in You, trusting Your faithfulness in every situation. Amen.

⚜ FAMILY ACTIVITY

On a scrapbook page, write "Trusting God Together". Each family member writes one worry or plan they want to trust God with this week. Leave space to return later and reflect on how God provided peace or direction.

October 26
Not Growing Weary in Doing Good

"As for you, brothers, do not grow weary in doing good." – 2 Thessalonians 3:13

This verse speaks to perseverance. It acknowledges something God already knows—that doing what is right can become tiring over time. Faithful living often requires steady effort, especially when results are not immediate or gratitude is not expressed.

Family life is full of opportunities to do good. Parents teach, correct, and encourage day after day. Children learn to obey, share, and show kindness even when it feels difficult. This verse reminds families that God sees faithfulness that continues quietly and consistently.

Doing good is not about recognition. It is about obedience. God calls His people to remain faithful even when the work feels repetitive or unnoticed. This kind of perseverance shapes character and builds endurance rooted in trust in God.

Families may feel weary during long seasons: busy schedules, ongoing challenges, or unresolved struggles. This verse gently encourages families to keep going, trusting that God uses steady faithfulness for His purposes, even when progress feels slow.

Living this way means choosing patience instead of frustration and kindness instead of giving up. Families who encourage one another to continue doing good grow stronger together, relying on God's strength rather than their own.

Let us take the next couple of minutes to discuss the following questions as a family:

1. Why do you think God acknowledges that doing good can be tiring?
2. What are some ways our family might feel weary right now?
3. How does encouragement help us keep going?
4. What is one way our family can continue doing good this week?

⬙ PRAYER

Faithful God, thank You for seeing the efforts of Your people. Thank You for strengthening us when we feel tired. Forgive us when discouragement causes us to lose focus. Help our family continue doing good, trusting You to provide strength and purpose each day. Amen.

⬙ FAMILY ACTIVITY

On a scrapbook page, write "Do Not Grow Weary". Each family member writes one good habit or faithful action they want to continue, even when it feels difficult. Leave space to return later and reflect on how perseverance brought growth and encouragement.

October 27
Holy in Our Example

"Whoever says he abides in him ought to walk in the same way in which he walked." –
1 John 2:6

This verse connects faith directly to daily life. To belong to Christ is not only to believe in Him, but to follow His ways. Walking as Jesus walked means allowing His character to shape how life is lived, especially in ordinary moments.

Family life is where this kind of faith becomes visible. How patience is practiced, how forgiveness is offered, and how love is shown all reveal what it means to follow Christ. These choices are often quiet, but they leave a lasting impact.

Jesus' life was marked by humility, obedience, and compassion. He served others, spoke truth with grace, and trusted the Father completely. Families are invited to reflect these same qualities in how they relate to one another.

Being holy in our example does not mean being flawless. It means being sincere. When families choose to walk in Christ's ways, even imperfectly, they point one another toward faith that is lived, not just spoken.

God uses faithful examples to teach and strengthen His people. A family that seeks to walk as Christ walked grows in unity, trust, and a deeper understanding of what it means to follow Him together.

Let us take the next couple of minutes to discuss the following questions as a family:

1. What does it mean to "walk" as Jesus walked?
2. Why is example so important in family life?
3. What qualities of Jesus stand out most to us?
4. What is one way our family can reflect Christ's example this week?

✍ PRAYER

Faithful God, thank You for showing us how to live through the example of Jesus. Forgive us when our actions do not reflect His ways. Help our family walk in obedience, humility, and love, trusting You to shape our lives each day. Amen.

⚜ FAMILY ACTIVITY

On a scrapbook page, write "Walking as Jesus Walked". Each family member writes one way they want to follow Jesus' example this week, through kindness, service, patience, or obedience. Leave space to return later and reflect on how living this way shaped your family's time together.

October 28
Holy in Service

"Even as the Son of Man came not to be served but to serve, and to give his life as a ransom for many." – Matthew 20:28

Holiness is lived out in service. Matthew 20:28 teaches that Jesus came to serve, not to be served. Families should remember that holiness is expressed in humility and service to others.

The Bible shows holy service in many lives. Jesus washed His disciples' feet. Tabitha sewed clothing for widows. The Good Samaritan cared for a stranger on the road. Each example shows holiness in action.

Service is not about recognition but love. Families should learn that holiness means serving with joy, whether the task is big or small.

Selfishness resists serving. Pride looks for others to do the work. But holy families look for ways to meet needs, comfort the hurting, and help the weak.

Living this way means asking, "How can I help?" and offering service with glad hearts. Families who serve together reflect Jesus' love.

Let us take the next couple of minutes to discuss the following questions as a family:

1. What does Matthew 20:28 teach about service?
2. What examples of holy service are in Scripture?
3. Why does holiness require serving instead of seeking to be served?
4. How can our family serve others this week?

PRAYER

Heavenly Father, thank You for showing perfect love through service. Thank You for washing feet and giving Your life. Forgive us when we refuse to serve. Teach our family to live with holy service each day. Amen.

FAMILY ACTIVITY

On a scrapbook page, write "Holy in Service". Each family member writes one act of service they will do this week.

Give Thanks, Always

"Give thanks in all circumstances; for this is the will of God in Christ Jesus for you." –
1 Thessalonians 5:18

Holiness is shown in gratitude. First Thessalonians 5:18 commands believers to give thanks in every situation. Families should remember that gratitude is not optional, it is God's will.

The Bible shows gratitude in many lives. Hannah thanked God for Samuel. The healed leper returned to thank Jesus. Paul gave thanks in letters, even while in prison. Gratitude reflects a holy heart.

Complaining dishonors God. Israel grumbled in the wilderness and missed blessings. Holy families choose thanksgiving instead of grumbling.

Gratitude changes perspective. Instead of focusing on what is missing, holy hearts thank God for His daily mercies. Families should practice gratitude as a way of living.

Living this way means thanking God in prayer, keeping gratitude journals, and speaking words of thanks to one another. Families who live in gratitude reflect God's goodness.

Let us take the next couple of minutes to discuss the following questions as a family:

1. What does 1 Thessalonians 5:18 teach about gratitude?
2. What examples of thankfulness are found in the Bible?
3. Why does complaining dishonor God?
4. How can our family practice gratitude this week?

PRAYER

Gracious God, thank You for giving us every good gift. Thank You for Your daily mercies. Forgive us when we complain or take blessings for granted. Teach our family to live with holy gratitude always. Amen.

FAMILY ACTIVITY

On a scrapbook page, write "Holy in Gratitude." Each family member writes three things they are thankful for this week.

Holy in Hope

"Rejoice in hope, be patient in tribulation, be constant in prayer." – Romans 12:12

Holiness is rooted in hope. Romans 12:12 calls believers to rejoice in hope, endure in trials, and stay constant in prayer. Families should remember that holy people live with confidence in God's promises.

The Bible shows hope in many stories. Abraham hoped for a son, even when old. The prophets hoped for the Messiah. The early church hoped for Christ's return. Hope sustained them in trials.

Hopelessness leads to despair and sin. But holy hope keeps eyes fixed on God's promises. Families should learn that hope is not wishful thinking—it is confident trust in God's Word.

Hope also brings joy. It allows believers to rejoice even in hardships, because they know God is working. Families should cultivate hope through Scripture, prayer, and fellowship.

Living this way means reminding one another of God's promises daily. Families who live in holy hope encourage the world with their joy.

Let us take the next couple of minutes to discuss the following questions as a family:

1. What does Romans 12:12 teach about hope?
2. What examples of hope are in the Bible?
3. Why is hope different from wishful thinking?
4. How can our family live with holy hope this week

PRAYER

God of Hope, thank You for filling our hearts with promises. Thank You for teaching us to rejoice in hope. Forgive us when we give in to despair. Teach our family to live with holy hope and joy. Amen.

FAMILY ACTIVITY

On a scrapbook page, write "Holy in Hope." Each family member writes one promise of God they will hold onto this week.

The Reward in Perseverance

"But the one who endures to the end will be saved." – Matthew 24:13

Holiness requires perseverance. Matthew 24:13 reminds believers that salvation belongs to those who endure faithfully. Families should understand that holiness is not a short burst of devotion but a lifelong walk.

The Bible shows perseverance in many lives. Job endured suffering without cursing God. Paul pressed on despite persecution. Jesus endured the cross for the joy set before Him.

Perseverance means not giving up when faith is tested. Families should learn that trials are not signs of God's absence but opportunities to grow stronger.

Holy perseverance is powered by God's Spirit.

Living this way means staying faithful in prayer, worship, and obedience, even in hard seasons. Families who persevere leave a legacy of holiness.

Let us take the next couple of minutes to discuss the following questions as a family:

1. What does Matthew 24:13 teach about perseverance?
2. What examples of perseverance are found in the Bible?
3. Why do trials strengthen holiness?
4. How can our family endure faithfully this week?

📖 PRAYER

Faithful God, thank You for strengthening us to endure. Thank You for Jesus, who persevered to the cross. Forgive us when we grow weary or want to quit. Teach our family to live with holy perseverance to the end. Amen.

⛰ FAMILY ACTIVITY

On a scrapbook page, write "Holy in Perseverance". Each family member writes one way they will endure in faith this week.

NOVEMBER

November 1
When Fear Tries to Take Hold

"The Lord is on my side; I will not fear. What can man do to me?" – Psalm 118:6

Fear often arrives quietly. It shows up in worries about the future, concerns over safety, or uncertainty about what lies ahead. This verse reminds God's people that fear does not get the final word when the Lord is near.

The psalmist does not deny the presence of trouble. Instead, he declares confidence in God's nearness. Knowing that the Lord is on his side changes how fear is faced. God's presence brings courage that circumstances alone cannot provide.

Families encounter fear in many forms. Children may fear the unknown, and adults may carry anxieties they try to hide. This verse invites families to bring those fears into the light of God's truth, remembering that He stands with His people.

Trusting God does not mean pretending fear does not exist. It means choosing to lean on God instead of allowing fear to control decisions or responses. When families turn to God together, fear loses its power to divide and overwhelm.

Beginning the month with this reminder helps families place confidence where it belongs. God is present, faithful, and attentive. A family that remembers this truth can face what comes next with steadier hearts and renewed trust.

Let us take the next couple of minutes to discuss the following questions as a family:

1. What kinds of things cause fear in family life?
2. How does knowing the Lord is with us change how we face fear?
3. Why is it important to talk about fear instead of hiding it?
4. What fear does our family need to bring to God today?

📖 PRAYER

Faithful God, thank You for being near to Your people. Thank You for standing with us when fear arises. Forgive us when worry replaces trust. Help our family lean on Your presence, believing that You are faithful and strong in every situation. Amen.

👪 FAMILY ACTIVITY

On a scrapbook page, write "The Lord Is With Us". Each family member writes one fear they want to place in God's hands. Leave space to return later and note how trusting God brought peace or courage.

Learning to Speak Life to One Another

"Anxiety in a man's heart weighs him down, but a good word makes him glad." –
Proverbs 12:25

This verse speaks to something families see every day. Worry and discouragement can quietly settle into hearts, weighing people down in ways that are not always visible. God reminds His people that words have the power to lift that weight.

Family life brings moments of stress, uncertainty, and emotional fatigue. Children and adults alike can carry worries they do not know how to express. This verse highlights how God uses simple, thoughtful words to bring comfort and relief.

A "good word" does not have to be long or dramatic. It may be reassurance, understanding, or gentle truth spoken at the right moment. God works through these words to remind His people that they are seen, loved, and not alone.

Speaking life requires attention. It means noticing when someone is discouraged and choosing to respond with kindness rather than impatience. Families who practice this learn to create homes where burdens are shared and hearts are strengthened.

Living this way reflects God's care. He speaks words of truth and hope to His people, and He invites families to do the same for one another as part of daily faithfulness.

Let us take the next couple of minutes to discuss the following questions as a family:

1. Why do worries sometimes feel hard to talk about?
2. How can words help lift someone who feels discouraged?
3. What makes a word "good" or helpful?
4. Who in our family might need an encouraging word today?

PRAYER

Caring God, thank You for knowing what weighs on our hearts. Thank You for using words to bring comfort and hope. Forgive us when we overlook the needs of others. Help our family speak words that bring encouragement, peace, and life to one another. Amen.

FAMILY ACTIVITY

On a scrapbook page, write "Words That Lift the Heart". Each family member writes one encouraging sentence they want to speak to someone in the family this week. Leave space to return later and reflect on how those words made a difference.

November 3
God's Promise of Peace

"You keep him in perfect peace whose mind is stayed on you, because he trusts in you."
– Isaiah 26:3

When someone mentions the word peace, what do you think about first? Is it trusting God to answer your prayers, never being afraid, or knowing that all is well in the world?

God promises peace to those who trust Him. Isaiah 26:3 teaches that perfect peace comes from focusing on God.

Families should remember that peace is not the absence of problems but the presence of trust in God, and even when we might feel it is hard to do, we should encourage one another with examples that we find in the Bible.

The Bible shows God's peace in many lives. Jesus calmed the storm and gave His disciples peace. Paul wrote of God's peace that surpasses understanding while in prison.

Peace does not depend on circumstances. Families can have peace in sickness, stress, or conflict when their minds stay on God's promises. Holiness means trusting Him instead of being ruled by fear.

Living in God's peace means praying when anxious, reading His Word when troubled, and speaking words of trust instead of worry. Families who trust His promise of peace will reflect calmness in a restless world.

Let us take the next couple of minutes to discuss the following questions as a family:

1. What does Isaiah 26:3 teach about peace?
2. What examples in Scripture show God's peace?
3. Why is peace rooted in trust, not circumstances?
4. How can our family live in God's peace this week?

PRAYER

God of Peace, thank You for promising perfect peace. Thank You for keeping us steady when we trust You. Forgive us when we let worry control us. Teach our family to live in Your promise of peace. Amen.

FAMILY ACTIVITY

On a scrapbook page, write "God's Promise of Peace". Each family member writes one way they will keep their mind on God this week.

Learning to Carry One Another's Burdens

"Bear one another's burdens, and so fulfill the law of Christ." – Galatians 6:2

God did not design His people to walk through life alone. This verse reminds families that part of following Christ is caring for one another in tangible ways. Bearing burdens is an act of love that reflects Christ's heart.

Family members often carry unseen burdens, such as worries, disappointments, fatigue, or fear. These struggles may not always be spoken aloud, yet they affect attitudes and relationships. God calls families to notice one another and respond with compassion.

Remember: Bearing burdens does not mean fixing every problem. Sometimes it looks like listening without rushing to correct, offering patience when someone is overwhelmed, or praying together during uncertain moments. God uses these quiet acts to bring comfort and strength.

This verse also points families back to Christ. Jesus bore the greatest burden on behalf of His people. When families help carry one another's struggles, they reflect His love and obedience in everyday life.

Living this way shapes homes into places of safety and care. Families who learn to carry burdens together grow in unity, trust, and reliance on God's grace rather than their own strength.

Let us take the next couple of minutes to discuss the following questions as a family:

1. What does it mean to "bear" someone else's burden?
2. Why is it sometimes hard to ask for help?
3. How can families support one another without trying to fix everything?
4. Who in our family might need extra care or prayer right now?

PRAYER

Compassionate God, thank You for carrying us when we are weak. Forgive us when we overlook the needs of others or focus only on ourselves. Teach our family to bear one another's burdens with patience, kindness, and love, reflecting the heart of Christ. Amen.

FAMILY ACTIVITY

On a scrapbook page, write "Carrying Burdens Together". Each family member writes one way they can help support someone else in the family this week—through prayer, listening, encouragement, or practical help. Leave space to return later and reflect on how sharing burdens strengthened your family.

November 5
Living Out Faith Through Service

"And I pray that the sharing of your faith may become effective for the full knowledge of every good thing that is in us for the sake of Christ." – Philemon 1:6

This verse reminds us that faith is not meant to remain hidden or private. It is meant to be lived out and shared in ways that reflect Christ. When faith is active, it shapes how God's people serve, give, and care for others.

Service often begins at home. Families have daily opportunities to serve one another through patience, responsibility, and kindness. These small acts may go unnoticed by the world, but God sees them clearly and uses them to grow faith.

Sharing faith does not always require words. It is often shown through actions: helping without being asked, choosing humility, or giving time and attention when it would be easier not to. God works through these choices to make faith visible and meaningful.

This verse points families toward purpose. Service done for Christ strengthens understanding of God's work in and through His people. As families serve together, they grow in gratitude and awareness of God's grace.

Living this way teaches families that faith is not only believed, but practiced. When service flows from love for Christ, God uses it to bless others and deepen faith within the home.

Let us take the next couple of minutes to discuss the following questions as a family:

1. What does it mean to live out our faith through service?
2. Why do small acts of service matter to God?
3. How can serving others strengthen our faith?
4. What is one way our family can serve together this week?

PRAYER

Gracious God, thank You for calling us to live out our faith through love and service. Forgive us when we overlook opportunities to help others. Teach our family to serve willingly and joyfully, so that our lives reflect Christ in all we do. Amen.

FAMILY ACTIVITY

On a scrapbook page, write "Serving Together". Each family member writes one way they can serve someone else this week: at home, in the community, or through prayer. Leave space to return later and reflect on how serving together strengthened your family's faith.

November 6
Steady Obedience Over Time

"Blessed is the servant whom his master will find so doing when he comes." –
Matthew 24:46

This verse speaks about faithfulness that continues quietly. Jesus describes a servant who is simply doing what he was entrusted to do when the master returns. There is no spotlight, no dramatic moment, just steady obedience.

Family life is often made up of routines and responsibilities that feel ordinary. Meals need preparing, work needs doing, and relationships require attention. This verse reminds families that God values faithfulness in everyday living, not just in moments that feel important.

Obedience over time shapes character. When families choose to follow God consistently, praying, forgiving, serving, and trusting Him day by day, they reflect a faith that is rooted and sincere. God sees these choices even when others do not.

This verse also encourages patience. God's timing is not always visible, but His return is certain. Families who live faithfully without growing distracted or discouraged learn to trust God's promises fully.

Living this way means staying attentive to what God has placed before us today. When families remain faithful in their daily responsibilities, they honor God and find blessing in steady obedience.

Let us take the next couple of minutes to discuss the following questions as a family:

1. Why does God value faithfulness in ordinary moments?
2. What does steady obedience look like in family life?
3. How can routines become acts of faith?
4. What responsibility has God entrusted to our family right now?

PRAYER

Faithful God, thank You for seeing our everyday obedience. Forgive us when we grow tired or distracted. Help our family remain faithful in the tasks You have given us, trusting that You are pleased with steady obedience done in love. Amen.

FAMILY ACTIVITY

On a scrapbook page, write "Faithful in Everyday Living". Each family member writes one routine or responsibility they want to handle with greater faithfulness this week. Leave space to return later and reflect on how obedience brought peace and growth.

November 7

God's Promise of Eternal Life

"And this is the promise that he made to us—eternal life." – 1 John 2:25

God promises eternal life to His children. First John 2:25 calls it His gift to those who believe. Families should remember that holiness is lived with hope in life beyond death.

The Bible assures eternal life through faith in Jesus. John 3:16 says whoever believes in Him will not perish but have eternal life. Jesus told the thief on the cross, "Today you will be with me in paradise." Paul declared, "To live is Christ, and to die is gain."

Eternal life is not only the future: it begins now. Knowing Jesus means enjoying fellowship with Him today and forever. Families should learn that God's promise gives joy, hope, and purpose.

This promise removes fear of death. Believers know their lives are secure in Christ. Families who trust this promise can face trials with hope.

Living in this promise means focusing on eternal values, faith, love, and obedience, rather than temporary things. Families who trust God's promise of eternal life live with peace and hope.

Let's discuss the following questions for a couple of minutes:

1. What does 1 John 2:25 teach about eternal life?
2. How does Jesus assure eternal life in John 3:16?
3. Why does this promise bring peace and hope?
4. How can our family live with eternal perspective this week?

PRAYER

Living God, thank You for promising eternal life. Thank You for securing our future in Jesus. Forgive us when we focus on temporary things. Teach our family to live with hope in Your promise of eternity. Amen.

FAMILY ACTIVITY

On a scrapbook page, write "God's Promise of Eternal Life". Each family member writes one way they will focus on eternal values this week.

November 8

God is Close to the Brokenhearted

"The Lord is close to the brokenhearted and saves those who are crushed in spirit." –
Psalm 34:18

Have you ever felt like you were carrying a weight that was just too heavy to hold? Maybe it was a disappointment at school, a disagreement with a friend, or just one of those days where everything seemed to go wrong. In those moments, it can feel like God is far away, watching from a distance while we struggle to keep our heads up.

But today's verse tells us the exact opposite. When our hearts are heavy or "crushed," God doesn't pull away; He draws closer. Think of it like a parent who sees their child fall and scrape their knee. They don't just stand across the yard shouting directions; they run to them, scoop them up, and stay right there until the crying stops.

God is our Heavenly Father, and His heart is full of compassion for us. He knows our private thoughts and our deepest worries, and He promises to be our safe place when life feels overwhelming. We don't have to pretend to be strong when we aren't. We can simply come to Him in prayer and let Him carry the weight for us.

Let's discuss the following questions for the next couple of minutes:

1. Can you remember a time when you felt "crushed in spirit" or really sad?

2. How does it make you feel to know that God is actually *closer* to you during those tough times?

3. What is one thing our family can do to support someone when they are having a "brokenhearted" day?

PRAYER

Heavenly Father, thank You for being so close to us, especially when we feel low. Forgive us for the times we try to fix everything on our own or forget that You are right beside us. Please wrap Your arms around our family today. If any of us are feeling sad or overwhelmed, give us Your peace and remind us that we are never alone. Amen.

FAMILY ACTIVITY

Find a piece of paper and draw a large heart. Inside the heart, have each family member write one thing that has been worrying them or making them feel a bit "crushed" lately. Then, together as a family, draw a cross over the heart to symbolize God's protection and presence over those worries. Take a photo of your "Heart of Peace" and add it to your family scrapbook.

November 9

Holding Fast to What Is Good

"Test everything; hold fast what is good." – 1 Thessalonians 5:21

God calls His people to live with discernment. This verse reminds families that faith involves careful attention: examining what aligns with God's truth and holding tightly to what is good. Following God requires wisdom, not carelessness.

Families are surrounded by many influences. Ideas, habits, and attitudes constantly compete for attention. God does not ask His people to accept everything they hear or see, but to measure it against His truth. What is good is worth keeping; what is not should be let go.

Holding fast requires intention. Good things can be crowded out when life becomes busy or distracting. Families must choose to protect what strengthens faith: time in God's Word, prayer, honesty, and love for one another.

This verse also encourages responsibility. God entrusts families with the task of discernment, guiding children and one another toward what honors Him. These choices shape hearts and direction over time.

Living this way leads to stability. Families who learn to test and hold fast grow grounded in faith. God uses these steady choices to build wisdom, peace, and confidence in His ways.

Let us take the next couple of minutes to discuss the following questions as a family:

1. Why does God want us to be careful about what we accept?
2. What kinds of influences need to be tested in family life?
3. What does it mean to "hold fast" to what is good?
4. What is one good practice our family wants to protect this week?

✎ PRAYER

God of wisdom, thank You for guiding Your people with truth. Forgive us when we accept things without discernment or let go of what is good. Help our family test everything by Your Word and hold firmly to what honors You. Amen.

♟ FAMILY ACTIVITY

On a scrapbook page, write "Holding Fast to What Is Good". Each family member writes one habit, value, or practice they want to keep strong in the family. Leave space to return later and reflect on how guarding what is good shaped your family's days.

November 10
God's Promise of Comfort

"Blessed are those who mourn, for they shall be comforted." – Matthew 5:4

God promises comfort in sorrow. Matthew 5:4 teaches that those who mourn will be comforted. Families should remember that holiness includes trusting God's comfort in grief and hardship.

The Bible shows God's comfort in many lives. Hagar was comforted in the desert when God heard her cries. Elijah was comforted under a broom tree when God sent an angel. Paul described God as the "Father of mercies and God of all comfort."

Comfort does not mean the removal of pain but God's presence in it. Families should learn that He draws near to the brokenhearted and carries them in times of loss.

This promise also calls families to comfort others. Second Corinthians 1:4 says God comforts us so we can comfort others. Sharing comfort is part of holy living.

Living in this promise means trusting God in grief, praying for His nearness, and offering comfort to others who are hurting. Families who believe this promise find peace in hard seasons.

Let's discuss the following questions for the next couple of minutes:

1. What does Matthew 5:4 teach about comfort?
2. What examples of God's comfort are in the Bible?
3. How does God's presence bring comfort in sorrow?
4. How can our family comfort others this week?

PRAYER

God of Comfort, thank You for promising to be near in sorrow. Thank You for healing broken hearts. Forgive us when we forget Your presence in pain. Teach our family to trust Your comfort and share it with others. Amen.

FAMILY ACTIVITY

On a scrapbook page, write "God's Promise of Comfort." Each family member writes one way they will comfort someone else this week.

November 11
God Heals the Hurting

"He heals the brokenhearted and binds up their wounds." – Psalm 147:3

Have you ever had a physical wound, like a scraped elbow or a cut on your finger? You probably went straight to a parent or reached for a bandage to protect the area while it healed. We can see those kinds of injuries, and we know exactly how to treat them. But what about the wounds we can't see?

Sometimes our hearts get "scraped" by mean words, or we feel a deep "cut" when a friend lets us down. These emotional wounds can hurt just as much as a broken bone, and often, we don't know where to turn for a bandage. Today's verse gives us the most beautiful promise: God is the Great Physician of our hearts. He doesn't just watch us from a distance when we are hurting; He gently "binds up" our internal wounds with His love and grace.

Think of God's comfort like a warm, spiritual bandage. He uses His Word, the kindness of others, and the peace of the Holy Spirit to start the healing process. We don't have to hide our hurts from Him. Just like you would show a cut to someone who can help, we can show our hurts to God in prayer. He is patient, He is kind, and He specializes in making broken things whole again.

Let's discuss the following questions for the next couple of minutes:

1. Can you think of a time when someone's words or actions hurt your heart? How did you handle it?

2. What does it look like for God to "bind up" a wound in our family?

3. How can we be "bandages" for each other when someone in our house is having a hard day?

✎ PRAYER

Heavenly Father, thank You for being so tender with our hearts. You know the hurts we carry that no one else can see. We ask that You would heal the places where we feel broken or sad today. Help us to trust Your timing and Your care. Teach our family to be a place of healing and kindness for one another, reflecting Your great love. Amen.

♟ FAMILY ACTIVITY

On a page in your Bible study scrapbook, draw a large heart and title it "God's Healing Hands". Cut out several strips of paper to look like bandages. On each "bandage," write a name of someone you know who might be going through a tough time: a friend, a neighbor, or even a family member. Tape these "bandages" onto the heart and say a short prayer together, asking God to bind up their wounds this week.

November 12
God's Promise of Joy

"You make known to me the path of life; in your presence there is fullness of joy; at your right hand are pleasures forevermore." – Psalm 16:11

God promises joy in His presence. Psalm 16:11 teaches that true joy comes from walking with Him. Families should remember that holiness means seeking joy in God, not in temporary pleasures.

The Bible shows joy as a gift of God. Nehemiah declared, "The joy of the Lord is your strength." Mary rejoiced in God her Savior when told she would bear Jesus. Paul sang hymns in prison. Their joy was rooted in God's presence, not in easy circumstances.

Joy is deeper than happiness. Happiness changes with situations, but joy endures because it is based on God's unchanging promises. Families should learn that joy flows from worship, gratitude, and trust.

Living in this promise means rejoicing in God daily, even in trials. Families who live in His joy become a witness to His goodness.

Let's discuss the following questions for the next couple of minutes:

1. What does Psalm 16:11 teach about joy?
2. What examples of joy are found in Scripture?
3. How is joy different from happiness?
4. How can our family rejoice in God this week?

✒ PRAYER

God of Joy, thank You for filling us with gladness in Your presence. Thank You for joy that endures beyond circumstances. Forgive us when we look for joy in empty places. Teach our family to rejoice in Your promises. Amen.

⛄ FAMILY ACTIVITY

On a scrapbook page, write "God's Promise of Joy". Each family member writes one thing that brings them joy in God.

November 13
God Provides Deliverance

"Call upon me in the day of trouble; I will deliver you, and you shall glorify me." –
Psalm 50:15

Have you ever been so worried about something that it felt like the world was crashing down on you? Perhaps you were worried about a test, or your family was facing financial troubles?

God promises deliverance in times of trouble. Psalm 50:15 assures that when His people call on Him, He answers.

Families should remember that holiness means trusting God's power to rescue, even in the most difficult of times.

The Bible gives many examples of God's deliverance. He delivered Israel from Egypt, Daniel from the lions, and Peter from prison. Each deliverance revealed His power and care.

Deliverance may not always look like we expect. Sometimes God removes the problem, and sometimes He gives strength to endure through it. Paul was delivered from some dangers but endured others for God's glory.

Living in this promise means calling on God in trouble, trusting His way of rescue, and giving Him praise afterward.

Families who believe His promise of deliverance will live with confidence and gratitude. They will know that even when things look bleak, their Heavenly Father is with them, and He will provide deliverances.

Let's discuss the following questions for the next couple of minutes:

1. What does Psalm 50:15 teach about deliverance?
2. What examples of deliverance are in the Bible?
3. Why is deliverance sometimes different from what we expect?
4. How can our family call on God in trouble this week?

PRAYER

Delivering God, thank You for rescuing Your people in every generation. Thank You for promising to answer when we call. Forgive us when we try to solve everything ourselves. Teach our family to trust Your deliverance. Amen.

FAMILY ACTIVITY

On a scrapbook page, write "God's Promise of Deliverance". Each family member writes one time God delivered them and gives thanks.

November 14
God's Healing

"For I will restore health to you, and your wounds I will heal, declares the Lord." –
Jeremiah 30:17

How often have you prayed for healing, not just from illness but also for fixing a broken heart or shattered self-esteem because of something that happened at work or school?

God promises healing. Jeremiah 30:17 declares His power to restore health and mend wounds. Families should remember that holiness means trusting God as the ultimate healer.

The Bible shows many stories of God's healing. He healed Naaman of leprosy, restored Hezekiah's health, and made the lame walk through Jesus' ministry. The apostles healed in His name as the gospel spread.

God's healing includes physical, emotional, and spiritual restoration. Sometimes He heals immediately, sometimes over time, and sometimes He gives ultimate healing in eternity. Families should learn that every kind of healing is in His hands.

Living in this promise means praying for healing, trusting God's will, and caring for bodies and hearts with wisdom. Families who believe this promise find hope in sickness and strength in trials.

Let's discuss the following questions for the next couple of minutes:

1. What does Jeremiah 30:17 teach about healing?
2. What examples of healing are seen in the Bible?
3. Why is healing sometimes immediate and sometimes delayed?
4. How can our family trust God's healing this week

✎ PRAYER

Healing God, thank You for promising restoration. Thank You for sending Jesus, who healed the sick and forgives sins. Forgive us when we doubt Your power. Teach our family to trust Your promise of healing. Amen.

♟ FAMILY ACTIVITY

On a scrapbook page, write "God's Promise of Healing". Each family member writes one area of life where they pray for healing.

November 15
God's Promise of Salvation

"For everyone who calls on the name of the Lord will be saved." – Romans 10:13

Today's verse declares that all who call on the Lord's name will be saved, an incredible promise that reminds us that God listens to our prayers and loves us without end.

The Bible shows this promise fulfilled. The jailer in Philippi was saved when he believed in Jesus. Zacchaeus received salvation when he welcomed Jesus into his home. The thief on the cross was saved by trusting in Him.

Salvation means forgiveness of sin, adoption into God's family, and eternal life. Families should learn that it is not earned but received by faith.

This promise is for all people. No one is too young, old, rich, or poor. Salvation is available to everyone who believes. Families who trust this promise live with assurance and joy.

Families should remember that salvation is God's gift through faith in Jesus.

Living in this promise means sharing the gospel with others, rejoicing in forgiveness, and living as children of God.

Remember this week when you are facing troubles that salvation is a promise that you can rely on.

Let's take the next couple of minutes to discuss the following questions:

1.   What does Romans 10:13 teach about salvation?
2.   What examples of salvation are in the Bible?
3.   How can our family share this promise with others this week?

PRAYER

Saving God, thank You for promising salvation to all who call on You. Thank You for Jesus, who died and rose again for us. Forgive us when we forget the greatness of this gift. Teach our family to rejoice and share this promise. Amen.

FAMILY ACTIVITY

On a scrapbook page, write "God's Promise of Salvation". Each family member writes one way they can share the gospel this week.

November 16

God's Promise of Patience

"The Lord is not slow in keeping his promise, as some understand slowness. Instead he is patient with you, not wanting anyone to perish, but everyone to come to repentance." – 2 Peter 3:9

God loves every person and wants them to find their way back to Him. This promise reminds us that God's timing is driven by His mercy and His desire for a relationship with us.

The Bible shows this promise fulfilled through His long-suffering nature. God was patient with the people in the days of Noah while the ark was being built. He was patient with the Israelites as they wandered in the desert, providing for them even when they complained. Jesus showed this same patience with His disciples, teaching them the same lessons over and over until they truly understood His mission.

Patience means giving us the space to grow, to learn from our mistakes, and to choose His path. Families should learn that God's patience is not an excuse to delay following Him, but a beautiful gift that shows how much He values our souls.

This promise is for all people. No matter how many times we have stumbled or how far we feel we have wandered, God's arms remain open. Families should remember that God's patience is a reflection of His deep, unwavering love for His children. Remember this week when you feel frustrated by delays or your own mistakes that God's patience is a promise you can rely on.

Let's take the next couple of minutes to discuss the following questions:

1. What does 2 Peter 3:9 teach about God's timing?
2. What are some examples of God's patience in the Bible?
3. Why is God's patience considered a gift to our family?
4. How can our family show this same kind of patience to one another this week?

PRAYER

Patient God, thank You for not giving up on us. Thank You for Your mercy that waits for us to turn toward You every single day. Forgive us when we are impatient with Your timing or with the people around us. Teach our family to reflect Your heart by being slow to anger and quick to show love. Amen.

FAMILY ACTIVITY

On a scrapbook page, write "God's Promise of Patience". Each family member writes one area where they are thankful for God's patience in their life, and one way they will practice being more patient with a sibling or parent this week.

November 17
Faithfulness, Promised

"Your kingdom is an everlasting kingdom, and your dominion endures through all generations. The Lord is trustworthy in all he promises and faithful in all he does." –
Psalm 145:13

Psalm 145:13 declares that the Lord is trustworthy in every word He speaks and faithful in every action He takes. This is an incredible promise that reminds us that while people might let us down or circumstances may change, God remains the same yesterday, today, and forever.

The Bible shows this promise fulfilled throughout history. He was faithful to Noah, keeping him safe through the flood. He was faithful to Ruth, providing for her in a foreign land and making her part of the lineage of Jesus. He was faithful to the disciples, sending the Holy Spirit just as He said He would. Every story in Scripture is a building block in the wall of God's proven reliability.

Faithfulness means that God's character is the anchor of our lives. Families should learn that His promises aren't like the ones we sometimes make and break; they are "everlasting." We can build our lives on what He says because His "dominion" outlasts any problem we will ever face.

Families should remember that God's faithfulness is not based on how perfect we are, but on how perfect He is. Living in this promise means looking back at how He has helped us before, trusting Him with our "right now," and speaking about His goodness to the next generation.

Let's take the next couple of minutes to discuss the following questions:

1. What does Psalm 145:13 teach us about the "staying power" of God's promises?
2. Can you think of a story from the Bible where God did exactly what He said He would do?
3. Why is it comforting to know that God's faithfulness doesn't depend on us being perfect?
4. How can our family remind each other of God's faithfulness when we are going through a difficult week?

PRAYER

Faithful God, thank You for being the one constant in our changing world. Thank You for every promise You have kept and for the way You watch over our family. Forgive us when we let our worries grow bigger than our trust in You. Teach our family to rely on Your Word and to be people who are faithful to You and to each other. Amen.

FAMILY ACTIVITY

On a scrapbook page, write "God's Promise of Everlasting Faithfulness." Draw a large tree with many branches. On the trunk, write "God's Character." On the branches, have each family member write one "fruit" of His faithfulness they have seen in their lives this year (like a prayer answered, a fear overcome, or a need met). Keep this as a "Faithfulness Tree" to look back on whenever you feel discouraged.

God's Promise of Righteous Justice

"The Lord works righteousness and justice for all the oppressed." – Psalm 103:6

Today's lesson shines the spotlight on an incredible promise that reminds us that God is not a distant observer of the world's problems; He is a God who sees every hidden hurt and every unfair moment, and He promises to be the defender of the weak.

The Bible shows this promise fulfilled time and again. He saw the suffering of the Israelites in Egypt and moved with power to deliver them from slavery. He spoke through the prophets to warn those who were being greedy or unkind to the poor, promising that He would stand up for the widow and the orphan. Jesus lived out this promise by spending His time with the outcasts and the mistreated, showing us that God's kingdom belongs to those the world often overlooks.

Justice means that God's standard of "right" will always have the final word. Families should learn that while we might see unfairness at school, at work, or in the news, we can trust that God is the ultimate Judge who loves fairness. We don't have to carry the bitterness of being wronged because we know that God is our Advocate.

Living in this promise means standing up for others who are being treated poorly, refusing to seek revenge when we are hurt, and trusting that God's timing for fixing the world is perfect.

Remember this week when you see something that feels unfair that God's justice is a promise that you can rely on.

Let's take the next couple of minutes to discuss the following questions:

1. What does Psalm 103:6 teach about how God feels toward people who are mistreated?
2. What are some examples of God standing up for the "underdog" in the Bible?
3. Why is it helpful for our family to trust God with justice instead of trying to get "even"?
4. How can our family show God's heart for justice by helping someone who is being left out this week?

PRAYER

Just God, thank You for being the one who defends us when life is unfair. Thank You for Your promise to bring righteousness to every situation. Forgive us when we try to take matters into our own hands or when we ignore the unfairness others are facing. Teach our family to love what is right and to trust Your perfect timing to fix all that is broken. Amen.

FAMILY ACTIVITY

On a scrapbook page, write "God's Promise of Justice." Draw a pair of scales. On one side of the scale, write "Our Worries about Unfairness." On the other side, write "God's Perfect Justice." Discuss one situation in the world or in your community that feels "unbalanced" or unfair right now, and write a short prayer next to the scales asking God to bring His righteousness to that situation.

November 19

A Promise of Reward

"And whatever you do, work heartily, as for the Lord and not for men, knowing that from the Lord you will receive the inheritance as your reward." –
Colossians 3:23–24

God promises reward for faithfulness. Colossians 3:23-24 teaches that every act done for Him will be rewarded. Families should remember that holiness means serving God with the right heart.

The Bible speaks often of reward. Jesus said even a cup of water given in His name will not go unnoticed. Paul wrote of crowns of righteousness, life, and glory for those who remain faithful. Hebrews 11 describes heroes of faith looking forward to a better reward.

Reward is not earned by good works apart from faith, it is God's gracious gift to His children. Families should learn that serving with humility and love leads to eternal blessing.

Living in this promise means working with diligence at school, jobs, and chores, remembering that God sees. Families who serve with joy will find strength in His promise.

Let's discuss the following questions for the next couple of minutes:

1. What does Colossians 3:23-24 teach about reward?
2. What examples of reward are found in Scripture?
3. How is reward connected to serving God with the right heart?
4. How can our family serve with joy this week?

✐ PRAYER

Reward-Giving God, thank You for promising blessings to those who serve You. Thank You for seeing every act done in Your name. Forgive us when we work for human approval. Teach our family to live for Your reward. Amen.

♟ FAMILY ACTIVITY

On a scrapbook page, write "God's Promise of Reward". Each family member writes one way they will serve this week with joy.

November 20
Renewal For The Weary

"They who wait for the Lord shall renew their strength; they shall mount up with wings like eagles; they shall run and not be weary; they shall walk and not faint." –
Isaiah 40:31

God promises renewal for the weary. Isaiah 40:31 assures that those who wait on the Lord will gain new strength. Families should remember that holiness means trusting God to refresh tired hearts and bodies.

The Bible shows renewal in many lives. Elijah was renewed with food and rest by an angel. The disciples, weary from ministry, were renewed by time with Jesus. Paul declared that though outwardly wasting away, inwardly he was renewed daily.

Renewal comes from waiting on God: prayer, worship, and stillness. Families should learn that renewal does not come from endless activity but from resting in Him.

This promise encourages families in busy seasons. God renews strength for daily tasks, endurance for trials, and hope for the future.

Living in this promise means slowing down, praying together, and seeking God's Spirit for refreshment. Families who trust this promise will find new strength to walk in holiness.

Let's discuss the next couple of questions for the next two to three minutes:

1. What does Isaiah 40:31 teach about renewal?
2. What examples of renewal are found in the Bible?
3. Why is waiting on God essential for renewal?
4. How can our family seek renewal this week?

📖 PRAYER

Renewing God, thank You for promising strength for the weary. Thank You for lifting us up when we grow tired. Forgive us when we rely on our own energy. Teach our family to wait on You for renewal. Amen.

👪 FAMILY ACTIVITY

On a scrapbook page, write "God's Promise of Renewal". Each family member writes one way they will wait on God this week for new strength.

November 21
God's Promise of Victory

"But thanks be to God, who gives us the victory through our Lord Jesus Christ." –
1 Corinthians 15:57

God promises victory through Jesus Christ. First Corinthians 15:57 reminds believers that through His resurrection, death and sin have been defeated. Families should remember that holiness includes living with confidence in Christ's triumph.

The Bible gives many examples of God granting victory. David defeated Goliath by trusting God's strength. Israel conquered Jericho through obedience. Jesus overcame temptation in the wilderness by relying on God's Word.

Victory is not about personal power but God's deliverance. Families should learn that true victory comes from obedience and faith in Christ, not self-reliance.

This promise assures that struggles with sin, fear, and death are not the end. In Christ, the final victory is already won. Families who trust this promise can live with courage and hope.

Living in this promise means facing challenges with prayer, trusting God's Word in battles, and rejoicing in Christ's resurrection. Families who believe His promise of victory will not live in fear.

Let's discuss the following questions for the next couple of minutes:

1. What does 1 Corinthians 15:57 teach about victory?
2. What examples of God's victories are in the Bible?
3. How is victory rooted in Christ's resurrection?
4. How can our family live in God's victory this week?

PRAYER

Victorious God, thank You for promising triumph through Jesus. Thank You for conquering sin and death. Forgive us when we live in fear or defeat. Teach our family to live in Your victory daily. Amen.

FAMILY ACTIVITY

On a scrapbook page, write "God's Promise of Victory". Each family member writes one area where they will trust Christ for victory this week.

November 22
My Times Are in Your Hands

"My times are in your hands; deliver me from the hands of my enemies, from those
who pursue me." – Psalm 31:15

Life can often feel like a fast-moving river, and sometimes it feels like we're just trying to keep our heads above water. We have schedules to keep, goals to reach, and sometimes, people or problems that seem to be "pursuing" us or causing us stress. In the middle of the rush, it is easy to feel like we have to control every second of our lives to be safe.

Psalm 31:15 reminds us that our "times" are held securely in God's hands.

The Bible is full of people who had to trust that their lives were in God's hands even when things looked uncertain. Think of David, who wrote this Psalm while he was being chased and felt surrounded by enemies. He didn't have a plan for the next hour, but he knew who held his life. Think of Mary, who trusted God's timing for the birth of Jesus, even when she was far from home.

Trusting that our times are in His hands means we can trade our anxiety for peace. Families should learn that God is never surprised by what happens in our day. He isn't rushing to catch up with our problems. He is already there, holding the beginning, the middle, and the end of our story. When we understand this, we can face "enemies" like fear or busy schedules with a calm heart.

Families should remember that being in God's hands is the safest place any of us can ever be. Living in this truth means starting each morning by "handing over" our to-do lists to Him. It means staying calm when plans change unexpectedly and reminding each other that God's timing is always better than ours.

Remember this week, when you feel pressured by time or worried about what's coming next, that your life is held by the One who loves you most.

Let's take the next couple of minutes to discuss the following questions:

1. What does it mean to you personally that your "times" are in God's hands?
2. How did David's trust in God help him when he was facing his enemies?
3. Why is it hard for us to let go of control and trust God's timing for our family?
4. What is one worry about the future that our family can "place in God's hands" today?

✒ PRAYER

Lord of Time, thank You for holding our lives so securely. We confess that we often try to control everything ourselves and get stressed when things don't go our way. Forgive us for our worry and our impatience. Help our family to rest in the knowledge that You see our past, our present, and our future. Teach us to trust Your hands more than our own plans. Amen.

▲ FAMILY ACTIVITY

On a scrapbook page, write "Our Times Are in His Hands." Have each family member trace the outline of their own hand on the page. Inside the outline of your hand, write one thing you are currently worried about or a "time" you are waiting for (like a holiday, a graduation, or a big decision). Then, draw a larger heart around all the handprints to symbolize God's love holding everyone together. Pray as a family, officially "handing over" those specific dates and worries to Him.

November 23

Our Safe Hiding Place

"You are my hiding place and my shield; I hope in your word." – Psalm 119:114

Have you ever played a game of hide-and-seek and found the "perfect" spot? Maybe it was behind a big armchair or under a pile of blankets where no one could find you. In that moment, you felt safe, quiet, and completely hidden from the rest of the world.

Life can sometimes feel like a very loud game of hide-and-seek, but instead of a game, we are looking for a place to go when we feel overwhelmed, sad, or tired. Today's verse gives us the best news: God Himself is our hiding place.

The Bible shows us that God's people have always found safety in Him. Think of David, who wrote many of the Psalms while hiding in actual caves to stay safe. He learned that while the cave offered physical cover, it was God who was truly protecting his heart.

A "hiding place" in God doesn't mean we run away from our problems, but that we go to Him to get the strength to face them. Families should learn that we don't have to carry our fears all by ourselves. When a day feels too "loud" or a problem feels too big, we can "hide" in prayer and find rest. We place our hope in His Word because His promises are the shield that keeps our hearts from getting hurt by worry.

Families should also remember that God's arms are the strongest hiding place in the universe.

Living in this truth means taking "prayer breaks" when things get stressful and reminding each other of God's promises when we feel vulnerable. It means making our home a place where we talk about God's protection more than we talk about our fears.

Let's take the next couple of minutes to discuss the following questions:

1. What does it feel like to have a "hiding place" with God?
2. Can you think of a time in the Bible when God acted as a shield for someone?
3. Why is it important for our family to "hide" in prayer when we are feeling stressed?
4. How can we help each other remember that God is our shield during a busy week?

✐ PRAYER

Protective Father, thank You for being our safe place. Thank You for being the shield that guards our hearts from fear and worry. Forgive us for the times we try to protect ourselves instead of running to You. Help our family to find rest in Your presence today and to always put our hope in Your Word. Amen.

⚑ FAMILY ACTIVITY

On a scrapbook page, write "God is Our Hiding Place". Draw a large, sturdy shield in the center of the page. Inside the shield, have each family member write one thing they sometimes worry about. Then, write a favorite Bible verse across the top of the shield to show how God's Word protects us. Finish by making a "fort" out of blankets in the living room and reading a Bible story together inside your "hiding place".

November 24
Wisdom and Strength for the Day

"I thank and praise you, God of my ancestors: You have given me wisdom and strength, you have made known to me what we asked of you." – Daniel 2:23

Imagine being asked a question that was impossible to answer, but your life depended on getting it right. That is exactly what happened to Daniel. He was a young man facing a huge problem that he couldn't solve on his own. Instead of panicking, he gathered his friends and asked God for help.

When God gave him the answer, Daniel didn't just move on; he stopped to say "thank You." He recognized that any "wisdom" (knowing what to do) and "strength" (having the power to do it) came directly from God.

The Bible shows us that God loves to give these gifts to His children. When Solomon was a new king, he asked for wisdom, and God gave it to him in abundance. When Gideon felt too weak to lead, God gave him the strength to save his people. These stories remind us that we don't have to be the smartest or the strongest people in the room. We just need to be the people who know where to go when we need a "boost." God is always ready to share His wisdom and His power with those who ask.

Relying on God's wisdom and strength changes how a family handles challenges. Families should learn that we don't have to have all the answers for tomorrow. We can simply ask God for the wisdom to handle the next hour and the strength to handle the next chore. When we stop and thank Him, just like Daniel did, we are acknowledging that He is the true Source of everything good in our home. This habit of "thanking before doing" keeps our hearts humble and peaceful.

Remember this week, when you feel like you don't have what it takes, that Daniel's God is your God, too, and He is ready to give you everything you need.

Let's take the next couple of minutes to discuss the following questions:

1. Why did Daniel thank God for "wisdom and strength" before he even solved the problem?
2. Can you think of a time when you didn't know what to do, but God gave you an idea or a "wise" thought?
3. What is one thing our family needs "wisdom" for right now? Let's ask Him for it together.

PRAYER

God of Wisdom, thank You for being the Source of all our strength. Forgive us for the times we try to be smart enough or strong enough on our own and end up feeling tired and frustrated. Today, we ask for Your wisdom to guide our family's choices and Your strength to help us love one another well. Thank You for hearing us every time we call. Amen.

FAMILY ACTIVITY

On a scrapbook page, write "Our Source of Wisdom and Strength." Draw two large "batteries" on the page. Label one "Wisdom" and the other "Strength." Inside the batteries, have each family member write one way they saw God provide these things this week (for example: "He gave me strength to be kind when I was tired" or "He gave me wisdom to finish my homework"). Decorate the batteries with bright colors to represent God's power at work in your home.

November 25

God's Promise of Protection from Temptation

"No temptation has overtaken you that is not common to man. God is faithful, and he will not let you be tempted beyond your ability, but with the temptation he will also provide the way of escape." – 1 Corinthians 10:13

God promises to help His people in temptation. First Corinthians 10:13 teaches that He provides a way out. Families should remember that holiness means resisting sin with His strength.

The Bible shows God's people facing temptation. Joseph fled from Potiphar's wife. Jesus resisted the devil by quoting Scripture. Each victory came from choosing God's way of escape.

Temptation itself is not sin, but giving in is. Families should learn that God's promise is to strengthen us and provide escape routes, through prayer, Scripture, accountability, or leaving the situation.

This promise brings hope. No one is trapped in sin without a way out. Families who trust His promise can walk in holiness daily.

Living in this promise means being alert to temptation, relying on God's Word, and choosing the path of escape He provides. Families who believe His promise will grow in victory over sin.

Let's discuss the following questions for the next couple of minutes:

Family Questions

1. What does 1 Corinthians 10:13 teach about temptation?
2. What examples of victory over temptation are in the Bible?
3. Why does God's promise give hope in temptation?
4. How can our family resist temptation this week?

📖 PRAYER

Faithful God, thank You for promising help in temptation. Thank You for providing ways of escape. Forgive us when we give in instead of resisting. Teach our family to walk in holiness and rely on Your promise. Amen.

⚐ FAMILY ACTIVITY

On a scrapbook page, write "God's Promise of Protection from Temptation." Each family member writes one temptation they will resist with God's help this week.

God's Promise of Presence in Trials

"When you pass through the waters, I will be with you; and through the rivers, they shall not overwhelm you; when you walk through fire you shall not be burned, and the flame shall not consume you." – Isaiah 43:2

God promises His presence in trials. Isaiah 43:2 assures that when His people face overwhelming waters or fiery tests, He is with them. Families should remember that trials are certain, but so is God's presence.

The Bible shows this promise fulfilled. God was with Shadrach, Meshach, and Abednego in the fiery furnace. He was with Daniel in the lions' den. He was with Paul in prison, giving him courage and peace.

God does not promise a life free from trials, but He promises never to abandon His children in them. Families should learn that His presence gives courage and peace no matter how severe the hardship.

Living in this promise means trusting Him when problems seem too big, reminding one another of His nearness, and worshiping Him even in hard times. Families who believe His promise of presence in trials will not be shaken.

Let's discuss the following questions for the next couple of minutes:

1. What does Isaiah 43:2 teach about trials?
2. What examples of God's presence in trials are in the Bible?
3. Why is His presence better than removal of all problems?
4. How can our family trust God in hard times this week?

PRAYER

Present God, thank You for promising to be with us in every trial. Thank You for never abandoning us. Forgive us when we fear instead of trust. Teach our family to rest in Your promise of presence. Amen.

FAMILY ACTIVITY

On a scrapbook page, write "God's Promise of Presence in Trials." Each family member writes one trial they face and a way they will remember God is with them.

November 27

Where Our Help Comes From

"I lift up my eyes to the mountains—where does my help come from? My help comes from the Lord, the Maker of heaven and earth." – Psalm 121:1–2

Imagine you are out for a walk and you come across a hill or a mountain that looks impossible to climb. It's steep, rocky, and seems to touch the clouds. In life, we often face "mountains" that aren't made of dirt and stone. These might be a hard week at work, a difficult subject at school, or a situation at home that feels too big to handle.

When we look at these mountains, our first thought is often, "How am I going to do this?" Today's verse gives us the answer: we don't look *at* the mountain; we look *above* it to the One who made it.

The Bible shows us that when God's people looked to Him, they found help that was bigger than their problems. Think of Peter walking on the water: as long as he kept his eyes on Jesus, he was fine. The moment he looked at the waves (his "mountain"), he started to sink. Think of Nehemiah, who had to rebuild a giant wall while people were trying to stop him. He kept his eyes on God, and the work was finished because his help came from the Lord.

Looking to the Lord for help means admitting that we can't do everything on our own. Families should learn that "lifting our eyes" is a choice we make every morning.

Families who practice looking to God together find that their home is filled with more peace and less panic. We aren't just "getting by"; we are being helped by the Almighty.

Let's take the next couple of minutes to discuss the following questions:

1. What are some of the "mountains" or big challenges our family is facing right now?
2. Why does the Bible remind us that God is the "Maker of heaven and earth"? How does that help us trust Him?
3. How can we remind each other to "look up" when we see someone in our family getting stressed or worried?
4. What is one specific thing we want to ask the Lord to help us with today?

✐ PRAYER

Almighty God, Maker of heaven and earth, thank You for being our Helper. Forgive us for the times we stare at our problems until we feel overwhelmed, instead of looking up to You. Help our family to remember that no mountain is too big for You. We lift our eyes to You today and ask for Your guidance and strength in everything we do. Amen.

♟ FAMILY ACTIVITY

On a scrapbook page, write "Our Help Comes from the Lord." Draw a large, simple mountain range at the bottom of the page. Above the mountains, draw a bright sun or a cloud with the name "GOD" inside it. Have each family member write one thing they need help with inside the mountain area, and then draw an arrow pointing from that worry up to God's name. This symbolizes "lifting your eyes" from the problem to the Solution.

November 28

A Harvest for the Heart

"Let us not become weary in doing good, for at the proper time we will reap a harvest if we do not give up." – Galatians 6:9

Have you ever planted a seed in a garden and then checked on it every single hour to see if it had grown? It can be frustrating when you look at the dirt and see absolutely nothing happening.

The Bible shows us many people who had to wait for their harvest. Think of Noah, who built a massive boat for years while his neighbors probably laughed at him. He didn't see the reason for his hard work for a very long time, but he didn't give up. Think of the farmers Jesus often spoke about in His parables; they understood that you cannot rush a plant. You have to keep watering, keep weeding, and keep trusting the soil.

In our lives, "doing good" can feel tiring, especially when it feels like no one notices or when people aren't kind in return, but God notices, and He is the one who brings the growth.

Families should learn that the best things in life take time to grow. When we choose to be a family that does good, even when it's hard, we are planting seeds of love and faith that will eventually change our home and our community. We don't do good just to get a reward; we do it because it is the right path, and we trust that God's timing for the "harvest" is always perfect.

Families should remember that God provides the strength to keep going even when our own "batteries" feel low. Living in this truth means looking for small ways to "plant" a good deed today without worrying about the results. It means encouraging one another when someone feels like their efforts aren't making a difference.

Let's take the next couple of minutes to discuss the following questions:

1. Why do you think it is so easy to become "weary" when we are trying to do the right thing?
2. Can you think of a time when you did something kind and didn't see a "result" until much later?
3. How can our family help each other "not give up" when things feel difficult this week?
4. What is one "good seed" (a kind action) we can plant together in our neighborhood or school?

PRAYER

Patient God, thank You for the promise that our work for You is never in vain. Forgive us for the times we get tired of doing the right thing and feel like giving up. Give our family the endurance to keep being kind, keep being patient, and keep loving others. Help us to trust Your timing for the harvest in our lives. Amen.

FAMILY ACTIVITY

On a scrapbook page, write "Our Family Harvest." Draw a large basket at the bottom of the page. On small paper "fruit" shapes (like apples or grapes), have each family member write one "good thing" they are currently working on (like "being a better listener" or "helping with chores"). Tape the fruits so they appear to be falling into the basket. This represents the harvest that comes from not giving up!

God's Promise of Eternal Security

"My sheep hear my voice, and I know them, and they follow me. I give them eternal life, and they will never perish, and no one will snatch them out of my hand." –
John 10:27–28

When we are still babies and children, we often feel safest when we are with our parents. The same can be said about feeling safe with God watching over us.

In the Bible, God promises eternal security for His people. John 10:27-28 teaches that no one can snatch believers from Jesus' hand. Families should remember that salvation is safe in Him.

Several notable figures in the Bible experienced this eternal security. Noah's family was safe in the ark. Israel was marked with blood during Passover and spared. The church is sealed with the Holy Spirit as a guarantee of salvation.

Families should learn that God's promise means assurance. Salvation does not depend on feelings or performance but on Christ's finished work.

This promise gives confidence to live boldly for Him. Families who trust eternal security can walk in joy and obedience without fear of being lost.

Living in this promise means resting in God's love, obeying His Word with gratitude, and encouraging others in assurance.

Let's discuss the following questions for the next couple of minutes:

1. What does John 10:27-28 teach about security?
2. What examples of God's protection are in the Bible?
3. Why is eternal security rooted in Christ's work, not ours?
4. How can our family rest in this promise this week?

📖 PRAYER

Good Shepherd, thank You for holding us securely in Your hand. Thank You for promising eternal life. Forgive us when we doubt Your grip. Teach our family to rest in Your eternal security. Amen.

⛪ FAMILY ACTIVITY

On a scrapbook page, write "God's Promise of Eternal Security." Each family member writes one reason they are thankful to belong to Jesus forever.

November 30
God's Promise of His Return

"For the Lord himself will descend from heaven with a cry of command, with the voice of an archangel, and with the sound of the trumpet of God." –
1 Thessalonians 4:16

God promises that Jesus will return. First Thessalonians 4:16 describes His coming with power and glory.

Families should remember that holiness means living with expectation of His return. As parents, we should encourage our children to not lose sight of this truth, and as families, we should constantly remind one another of this important truth.

The Bible speaks often of this promise. Jesus said He would prepare a place and come again. Angels at His ascension told the disciples He would return the same way. Revelation describes Him coming as King of kings and Lord of lords.

This promise gives comfort. Those who have died in Christ will rise. Believers will be with Him forever. Families should learn that His return is certain, even if the timing is unknown.

Living in this promise means staying ready, living holy lives, and encouraging one another with hope. Families who trust His promise of return will live with urgency and joy.

Let's discuss the following questions for the next couple of minutes:

1. What does 1 Thessalonians 4:16 teach about Christ's return?
2. What other Scriptures promise His coming again?
3. Why does this promise bring hope and comfort?
4. How can our family live ready for His return this week?

📖 PRAYER

Coming King, thank You for promising to return. Thank You for giving us hope of eternity with You. Forgive us when we live as if this world is all there is. Teach our family to live with expectation and holiness. Amen.

👪 FAMILY ACTIVITY

On a scrapbook page, write "God's Promise of His Return." Each family member writes one way they will live ready for Jesus this week.

DECEMBER

December 1
Living in Expectation

"Therefore you also must be ready, for the Son of Man is coming at an hour you do not expect." – Matthew 24:44

Did you ever receive a promise and you couldn't wait for it to be fulfilled? Perhaps it was a special present or a trip that would take you to a place you have always wanted to go to?

Jesus promises to return, but the timing is unknown. Matthew 24:44 calls His followers to live ready, since His coming will be sudden. Families should remember that holiness means daily preparation, not waiting until the last minute.

The Bible gives warnings about being unprepared. In Noah's time, people lived as usual until the flood came. Jesus used the parable of the ten virgins, where five were wise and ready while five were unprepared and shut out.

In the parable of the ten virgins, the difference between the wise and the foolish wasn't their appearance or their intention. Both groups were waiting for the bridegroom and both had lamps. The five were called wise because they looked ahead and realized that the wait might be longer than expected, so they brought extra oil in jars to keep their lamps burning.

The other five were unprepared because they only brought enough for the moment, showing they hadn't truly considered the possibility of a delay; when the bridegroom arrived late at night, their lamps had gone out and they were left in the dark.

Living in expectation means walking in obedience every day, not only in moments of excitement. Families should learn that holiness is not about predicting dates but living faithfully until He comes.

This promise brings hope and urgency. Every choice matters. Every act of faith shows readiness. Families who live with expectation shine as lights in the world.

Let's discuss the following questions for the next couple of minutes:

1. What does Matthew 24:44 teach about Christ's return?
2. What examples warn about being unprepared in the Bible?
3. Why is daily readiness more important than predictions?
4. How can our family live ready for Jesus this week?

PRAYER

Lord of Glory, thank You for promising to return. Thank You for reminding us to stay ready. Forgive us when we grow careless or distracted. Teach our family to live every day in expectation of You. Amen.

FAMILY ACTIVITY

On a scrapbook page, write "Living in Expectation." Each family member writes one way they will prepare their heart for Jesus' return this week.

December 2
The Blessed Hope

"Waiting for our blessed hope, the appearing of the glory of our great God and Savior Jesus Christ." – Titus 2:13

The Bible calls Christ's return the blessed hope. Titus 2:13 describes it as the appearing of Jesus in glory. Families should remember that hope in His coming brings joy, strength, and perseverance.

The early church lived in eager anticipation of this hope. They encouraged one another with the words, "The Lord is coming soon." This hope sustained them through persecution and hardship.

Hope in Christ's return is not wishful thinking but certain assurance. His resurrection guarantees He will return in glory. Families should learn that this hope shapes how they live, turning hearts toward eternity.

Living with blessed hope means waiting actively, serving, praying, and sharing the gospel while looking forward to His coming. Families who hold onto this hope will endure trials with faith and joy. So, let's support one another

Let's discuss the following questions for the next couple of minutes:

1. What does Titus 2:13 teach about our hope?
2. How did the early church live with this hope?
3. Why is this hope certain, not uncertain?
4. How can our family live with blessed hope this week?

PRAYER

God of Hope, thank You for promising the glorious return of Jesus. Thank You for giving us certainty in this hope. Forgive us when we lose sight of eternity. Teach our family to wait eagerly and faithfully for Christ's return. Amen.

FAMILY ACTIVITY

On a scrapbook page, write "The Blessed Hope." Each family member writes one reason they look forward to Jesus' return.

December 3
Watching and Waiting

"Therefore, stay awake, for you do not know on what day your Lord is coming." –
Matthew 24:42

Do you ever get impatient when you need to wait for something? Perhaps it is standing at a queue in line for a movie, or sitting in traffic on the way to the beach?

These things pale in comparison when we consider the amazing future we can look forward to.

Jesus commands His people to watch and wait. Matthew 24:42 reminds believers that His coming will be unexpected. Families should remember that holiness means staying alert, not spiritually asleep.

The Bible often speaks of watchfulness. Nehemiah set guards on the wall. The disciples in Gethsemane were told to watch and pray but fell asleep. Jesus urged His followers to keep their lamps burning like servants awaiting their master's return.

Watching and waiting means living with awareness of eternity, guarding against sin, and keeping faith strong. Families should learn that being spiritually awake requires prayer, Scripture, and obedience.

Living this way means not letting distractions or comfort dull readiness. Families who watch and wait will not be surprised when He comes but will rejoice with Him.

Let's discuss the following questions for the next couple of minutes:

1. What does Matthew 24:42 teach about watchfulness?
2. What biblical examples warn about falling asleep spiritually?
3. How can families stay spiritually awake?
4. How can our family stay watchful this week?

✒ PRAYER

Alert God, thank You for teaching us to stay awake in faith. Thank You for promising that Jesus will return. Forgive us when we grow distracted or careless. Teach our family to live watchful and ready. Amen.

⚸ FAMILY ACTIVITY

On a scrapbook page, write "Watching and Waiting." Each family member writes one distraction they will guard against to stay spiritually awake this week.

December 4
Encouraging One Another

"Therefore encourage one another with these words." – 1 Thessalonians 4:18

Hope in Christ's return is meant to bring encouragement. First Thessalonians 4:18 urges believers to comfort one another with this promise. Families should remember that speaking of His coming builds faith and hope.

The context of this verse is Paul's teaching about the resurrection. He assured the church that those who died in Christ would rise when He returns. This was a message of comfort, not fear.

This encouragement is powerful because it changes how we view our temporary struggles. When we remind each other that Jesus is coming back, we are reminding each other that the story doesn't end with pain, sickness, or sadness. Encouragement isn't just about saying "be happy"; it is about pointing one another to the truth that a day is coming when God will make all things new. By sharing this hope, we help our family members lift their eyes above their current problems to see the glorious future God has planned.

Families should learn that encouraging one another with Christ's return strengthens endurance in trials. Talking about His promises turns attention from despair to hope.

Living in this promise means reminding one another of eternity during challenges, sharing Scripture of hope, and rejoicing in the certainty of His return. Families who encourage one another will grow stronger in faith together.

Let's discuss the following questions for the next couple of minutes:

1. What does 1 Thessalonians 4:18 teach about encouragement?
2. How does Christ's return comfort believers who grieve?
3. Why should families speak often about His promises?
4. How can our family encourage one another this week?

PRAYER

Comforting God, thank You for promising Christ's return. Thank You for words that bring hope and strength. Forgive us when we fail to encourage each other. Teach our family to speak Your promises and build one another up. Amen.

FAMILY ACTIVITY

On a scrapbook page, write "Encouraging One Another." Each family member writes one Scripture of hope to share with the family this week.

December 5
Be Found Faithful

"Who then is the faithful and wise servant, whom his master has set over his household... Blessed is that servant whom his master will find so doing when he comes." – Matthew 24:45–46

Jesus calls His followers to be faithful until His return. Matthew 24:45-46 praises the servant found doing his duty when the master returns. Families should remember that hope in Christ's coming should lead to faithfulness in daily life.

The Bible honors faithful people. Noah built the ark in obedience. Joseph served faithfully in prison. The apostles spread the gospel despite persecution. Their faithfulness prepared them for God's blessing.

Faithfulness means doing what God asks every day: loving, serving, forgiving, and living holy lives. Families should learn that waiting for Christ's return is not passive but active obedience.

Living this way means being trustworthy in small things, diligent in responsibilities, and steadfast in worship. Families who live faithful lives will hear the words, "Well done, good and faithful servant."

Let's discuss the following questions for the next couple of minutes:

1. What does Matthew 24:45-46 teach about faithfulness?
2. What examples of faithful people are in Scripture?
3. How does waiting for Christ's return call us to active obedience?
4. How can our family be found faithful this week?

PRAYER

Faithful Lord, thank You for calling us to live wisely and faithfully. Thank You for promising blessing to those who obey. Forgive us when we grow lazy or distracted. Teach our family to be faithful until You return. Amen.

FAMILY ACTIVITY

On a scrapbook page, write "Be Found Faithful." Each family member writes one way they will live faithfully this week.

December 6

The Patience of the Farmer

"Be patient, then, brothers and sisters, until the Lord's coming. See how the farmer waits for the land to yield its valuable crop, patiently waiting for the autumn and spring rains. You too, be patient and stand firm, because the Lord's coming is near." –
James 5:7–8

Imagine a farmer who has just finished planting seeds in a large field. After all that hard work, he doesn't sit by the dirt and yell at the seeds to grow faster. He doesn't dig them up every hour to see if anything is happening. Instead, he waits.

He knows that there are things he can control, like weeding and watering, and things he cannot, like the rain and the sun. Today's verse compares our wait for Jesus to a farmer waiting for a "valuable crop." It reminds us that waiting isn't just "doing nothing"; it is a time of quiet trust and preparation.

The Bible is full of people who had to learn the art of "farmer-like" patience. Think of Abraham and Sarah, who waited decades for the child God had talked about. Think of the Israelites, who waited generations for the Messiah to arrive in Bethlehem. These stories teach us that God's timing is rarely our timing. Just because we don't see the "sprout" yet doesn't mean God isn't working under the surface. Patience means trusting that the One who started the work in our lives is faithful to finish it.

When we realize that the "Lord's coming is near," it gives us a reason to keep doing the right thing, even when we are tired. Families who practice patience together find that they don't get as frustrated by delays because they are looking forward to the ultimate "harvest"—being with Jesus forever.

Families should remember that patience is not just about waiting, but about *how* we act while we wait.

Let's discuss the following questions for the next couple of minutes:

1. Why do you think James used a farmer as an example of patience?

2. What is something you find very hard to wait for? How can trusting God make that wait easier?

3. What does it mean to "stand firm" in our hearts when things are changing around us?

4. How can our family help each other stay patient and kind during a busy or stressful week?

✑ PRAYER

Patient Father, thank You for the reminder that Your timing is perfect. Forgive us for the times we get frustrated and try to rush Your plans. Give our family the patience of the farmer, and help us to stand firm in our faith while we wait for Jesus to return. Strengthen our hearts to keep doing good and trusting You every single day. Amen.

♟ FAMILY ACTIVITY

On a scrapbook page, write "Patiently Waiting for the Harvest." Draw a picture of a small sprout coming out of the ground. Have each family member write one thing they are "waiting on the Lord for" next to the sprout. Decorate the page with drawings of rain clouds and sun to represent God's provision. This page will serve as a reminder that while we wait, God is the one bringing the growth.

December 7
Hope in the Resurrection

"For the trumpet will sound, and the dead will be raised imperishable, and we shall be changed." – 1 Corinthians 15:52

Christ's return brings hope in the resurrection. First Corinthians 15:52 assures that when the trumpet sounds, the dead in Christ will rise, and the living will be transformed. Families should remember that hope in His coming is also hope for eternal life.

The Bible consistently promises resurrection. Job declared, "After my skin has been destroyed, yet in my flesh I will see God." Jesus said, "I am the resurrection and the life." Paul encouraged believers that Christ's resurrection guarantees our own.

This "change" Paul describes is a glorious transition from the brokenness of this world to the perfection of the next. To be "imperishable" means that our new bodies will never grow tired, never get sick, and never feel the weight of sadness or age. Just as a seed must be buried in the ground to become a beautiful flower, our earthly lives are just the beginning of a much grander story. This transformation is the ultimate victory of God over sin, showing us that His love is powerful enough to rebuild and renew everything that was lost.

This promise comforts families who grieve. Death is not the end, but the doorway to eternal life. Families should learn that every believer will be raised in glory, with bodies free from sickness and death.

Living in this promise means grieving with hope, encouraging one another with eternity, and remembering that life on earth is temporary but secure in Christ. Families who hold to this hope find peace even in sorrow.

Let's discuss the following questions for the next couple of minutes:

1. What does 1 Corinthians 15:52 teach about the resurrection?
2. What examples of resurrection hope are in Scripture?
3. How does Christ's resurrection guarantee ours?
4. How can our family live with resurrection hope this week?

✎ PRAYER

God of Life, thank You for promising resurrection. Thank You for giving us hope beyond death. Forgive us when we fear what lies ahead. Teach our family to live in confidence of Your promise. Amen.

♟ FAMILY ACTIVITY

On a scrapbook page, write "Hope in the Resurrection." Each family member writes one reason they are thankful for eternal life in Christ.

December 8

Be Holy Until He Comes

"Since all these things are thus to be dissolved, what sort of people ought you to be in lives of holiness and godliness." – 2 Peter 3:1

Peter reminds believers that the hope of Christ's return should lead to holiness. Second Peter 3:11 asks what kind of people we should be in light of the end of all things. Families should remember that holiness is not optional but essential as we wait for Him.

The Bible shows the call to holiness as preparation for meeting God. Noah lived blamelessly in a corrupt world. Daniel stayed faithful in exile. The early Christians lived set apart lives as they waited for Christ.

Holiness is practical; it means rejecting sin, pursuing righteousness, and living for God's glory. Families should learn that hope in His return motivates holy living today.

Living this way means asking daily, "Would this please God if He came today?" Families who pursue holiness while waiting for Jesus shine His light in the world.

Let's discuss the following questions for the next couple of minutes:

1. What does 2 Peter 3:11 teach about holiness?
2. How does the hope of Christ's return call us to godly living?
3. What examples of holiness do we see in Scripture?
4. How can our family live holy this week while waiting for Him?

PRAYER

Holy God, thank You for calling us to lives of holiness. Thank You for reminding us that Jesus will return. Forgive us when we live carelessly. Teach our family to live holy until He comes. Amen.

FAMILY ACTIVITY

On a scrapbook page, write "Be Holy Until He Comes." Each family member writes one way they will live holy this week in preparation for Jesus' return.

December 9
The Crown of Righteousness

"Henceforth there is laid up for me the crown of righteousness, which the Lord, the righteous judge, will award to me on that day, and not only to me but also to all who have loved his appearing." – 2 Timothy 4:8

Paul speaks of a reward for those who long for Christ's return: the crown of righteousness. Second Timothy 4:8 assures that all who love His appearing will receive it. Families should remember that waiting with love and eagerness brings eternal blessing.

Paul wrote this while near the end of his life. He looked forward with joy, not fear, because he had fought the good fight and trusted God's promise.

The Bible speaks of crowns as rewards for faithfulness. There is a crown of life for those who endure, a crown of glory for shepherds, and here, a crown of righteousness for those who long for Jesus. Families should learn that rewards are not about competition but God's gracious blessing.

To "love His appearing" means more than just knowing Jesus will return; it means our hearts actually ache for that day because we love Him so much. It is like the feeling a child has waiting for a parent to come home from a long trip—you keep looking out the window because you miss them. When we love His appearing, we stop worrying so much about the "stuff" of this world and start focusing on the beauty of His character. This crown isn't a prize for being perfect, but a gift for those whose greatest desire is to finally see the face of their Savior.

Living in this promise means longing for Christ's coming, not clinging to this world. Families who love His appearing live with joyful hope and steady faith.

Let's discuss the following questions for the next couple of minutes:

1. What does 2 Timothy 4:8 teach about reward?
2. Why was Paul joyful as he awaited Christ's return?
3. How does loving His appearing shape our lives?
4. How can our family show love for Christ's return this week?

PRAYER

Righteous Judge, thank You for promising crowns to Your people. Thank You for blessing those who long for Jesus. Forgive us when we cling to this world. Teach our family to love His appearing and live for eternity. Amen.

FAMILY ACTIVITY

On a scrapbook page, write "The Crown of Righteousness." Each family member writes one reason they look forward to Christ's appearing.

December 10
Waiting for the Blessed Hope

"For the grace of God has appeared that offers salvation to all people. It teaches us to say 'No' to ungodliness and worldly passions, and to live self-controlled, upright and godly lives in this present age, while we wait for the blessed hope—the appearing of the glory of our great God and Savior, Jesus Christ." – Titus 2:11–13

Imagine you are waiting for a very special guest to arrive at your home. You wouldn't just sit on the couch and stare at the door in a messy house; you would be busy getting ready. You would clean up, set the table, and make sure everything is in order.

Today's verse tells us that waiting for Jesus to return is very similar. It isn't just about looking at the clock; it is about how we live right now, in "this present age," while we wait for what the Bible calls our "blessed hope."

The Bible often uses the word "hope" differently than we do. In our daily lives, we might say, "I hope it doesn't rain," which means we aren't sure. In the Bible, hope is a "blessed" certainty. Think of Simeon in the temple, who spent his whole life waiting for the first coming of the Savior. He didn't just wait; he lived a life that was "righteous and devout." When he finally held the baby Jesus, his hope became a reality. We are in a similar position today: we know the "guest" is coming, so we live in a way that shows we are expecting Him.

This "blessed hope" is a gift for every person in the family. It gives a teenager the strength to stand up for what is right, and it gives a parent the patience to lead with love. When we talk about Jesus' appearing as our "blessed hope," it takes the fear out of the future. We aren't waiting for a scary event; we are waiting for our Savior, who loves us more than anyone else. Families who wait with this perspective find that their daily lives are filled with a sense of purpose and joy.

Families should remember that our lives today are the best way to show the world that we believe in the promise of tomorrow. Living in this truth means asking ourselves, "Does my behavior today show that I am expecting a King?"

It means choosing to live with a "heaven-first" mindset in everything we do.

Let's take the next couple of minutes to discuss the following questions:

1. Why does the Bible call the return of Jesus a "blessed hope"?

2. What does it mean for "grace" to teach us how to live? Can you think of an example?

3. How does expecting a special guest change the way you act at home? How is that like waiting for Jesus?

4. What is one "worldly passion" (like selfishness or grumbling) our family can work on saying "no" to this week?

Prayer

Glorious Savior, thank You for the blessed hope we have in Your return. Thank You for Your grace that teaches us how to live right now. Forgive us when we get so distracted by this world that we forget You are coming back. Help our family to live self-controlled and godly lives, and fill us with joy as we look forward to the day we see Your glory. Amen.

⚶ FAMILY ACTIVITY

On a scrapbook page, write "Our Blessed Hope." Draw a picture of a large, beautiful doorway. Around the door, have each family member write one "godly action" they want to practice this week (like "helping without being asked" or "using kind words"). This reminds us that we are preparing our hearts and our home for the arrival of our King.

December 11
Comfort to Share

"Praise be to the God and Father of our Lord Jesus Christ, the Father of compassion and the God of all comfort, who comforts us in all our troubles, so that we can comfort those in any trouble with the comfort we ourselves receive from God." –
2 Corinthians 1:3–4

Have you ever felt sad and had a family member give you a big hug or say just the right words to make you feel better? That feeling of being understood and cared for is called comfort. Today's verse tells us that God is the "God of all comfort." This means He has an endless supply of peace and kindness for us whenever we are going through "all our troubles", no matter how big or small those troubles might be.

The Bible shows us that God doesn't just watch our struggles from far away; He steps into them with us. Think of Hagar in the desert, who felt completely alone until God spoke to her and provided for her. Think of the disciples on a stormy sea, terrified until Jesus spoke peace to the waves and to their hearts. God's comfort is like a warm blanket on a cold night; it doesn't always make the winter go away immediately, but it gives us the warmth we need to get through it.

There is a very special reason why God comforts us: "so that we can comfort those in any trouble." God pours His love into our hearts so that our hearts can overflow onto others. Families should learn that when we go through a hard time and experience God's help, we are actually gaining "tools" to help someone else later. Your experience with a difficult test, a mean comment at school, or a stressful day at work becomes a gift you can use to help a sibling or friend who is going through the same thing.

Families should remember that being a follower of Jesus means we are never meant to carry our burdens alone. Remember this week, as you receive comfort from the Father, keep your eyes open for someone who needs you to share it with them.

Let's discuss the following questions for the next couple of minutes:

1. What is the difference between a "hug" and the "comfort of God"?
2. Can you think of a time when God comforted you during a "trouble"? How did He do it?
3. Why does God want us to share the comfort we receive with other people?
4. Who is someone outside our family who might be in "any trouble" right now? How can we comfort them this week?

PRAYER

Father of Compassion, thank You for being the God of all comfort. Thank You that You don't leave us alone in our troubles but stay right beside us. Forgive us for the times we forget to share Your kindness with others. Help our family to be a place of comfort, and give us the words to say to those who are hurting this week. Amen.

FAMILY ACTIVITY

On a scrapbook page, write "Comfort to Share." Draw a large heart in the middle. Inside the heart, write "God's Comfort." Around the outside of the heart, write the names of people your family wants to pray for or encourage this week. On a small sticky note, write one kind thing you can do for one of those people (like sending a text or drawing a picture) and place it on the page.

December 12
Hope That Does Not Disappoint

"And hope does not put us to shame, because God's love has been poured into our hearts through the Holy Spirit." – Romans 5:5

The hope of Christ's return will never disappoint. Romans 5:5 teaches that hope is certain because God's love fills us through the Spirit. Families should remember that biblical hope is secure, not uncertain.

The Bible shows how hope sustained God's people. Joseph held onto hope through years in prison. The prophets proclaimed hope even in exile. The early church hoped for Christ despite persecution.

This hope is different from worldly hope. Worldly hope is uncertain, like hoping for good weather. God's hope is certain because His promises never fail. Families should learn that holiness means living with this confident expectation.

Living in this promise means facing trials without despair, encouraging one another, and holding onto joy. Families who trust this hope will not be ashamed when Christ appears.

Let's discuss the following questions for the next couple of minutes:

1. What does Romans 5:5 teach about hope?
2. How does biblical hope differ from worldly hope?
3. What examples of hope are seen in the Bible?
4. How can our family live with hope that does not disappoint this week?

🕮 PRAYER

God of Hope, thank You for pouring Your love into our hearts. Thank You that our hope in Christ will never disappoint. Forgive us when we lose sight of eternity. Teach our family to live with confident hope each day. Amen.

⛄ FAMILY ACTIVITY

On a scrapbook page, write "Hope That Does Not Disappoint." Each family member writes one reason their hope in Christ is secure.

December 13
Living as Children of Light

"For you are all children of light, children of the day. We are not of the night or of the darkness." – 1 Thessalonians 5:5

Hope in Christ's return calls believers to live as children of light. First Thessalonians 5:5 reminds us that holiness means walking in the light of Christ, not in darkness.

The Bible contrasts light and darkness often. God's first act in creation was to speak light into darkness. Jesus said, "I am the light of the world." John declared that if we walk in the light, we have fellowship with one another and cleansing through Jesus' blood.

Being a "child of the day" means that our lives should be transparent and consistent, regardless of who is watching. Just as the sun reveals everything clearly, living in the light means we don't have to hide our actions or words in the shadows of secrecy. When we walk in the light, we are living in a way that is "ready for inspection" by the Lord at any moment. This doesn't mean we are perfect, but it means that when we do make a mistake, we quickly bring it into the light through confession rather than letting it grow in the dark. It is a life of freedom because there is nothing to hide and everything to celebrate.

Families should learn that living as children of light means honesty, purity, and obedience. It means rejecting hidden sin and living openly before God. Living this way means shining God's light to others through kindness, truth, and love. Families who live as children of light will be ready for Christ's return.

Let's discuss the following questions for the next couple of minutes:

1. What does 1 Thessalonians 5:5 teach about being children of light?
2. How does Scripture contrast light and darkness?
3. Why does hope in Christ call us to walk in light?
4. How can our family live as children of light this week?

PRAYER

God of Light, thank You for calling us into Your truth. Thank You for making us children of the day. Forgive us when we hide in darkness. Teach our family to walk as children of light until Christ returns. Amen.

FAMILY ACTIVITY

On a scrapbook page, write "Living as Children of Light." Each family member writes one way they will shine God's light this week.

December 14
Our Citizenship in Heaven

"But our citizenship is in heaven, and from it we await a Savior, the Lord Jesus Christ." – Philippians 3:20

Hope in Christ's return reminds us where we belong. Philippians 3:20 teaches that our true citizenship is in heaven. Families should remember that they are pilgrims on earth, awaiting their Savior.

The Bible shows many who lived as strangers in this world. Abraham left his homeland, looking forward to God's promises. Moses led Israel to a land not their own. Hebrews 11 calls believers "strangers and exiles on the earth."

Families should learn that holiness means living for heaven's values, not earthly ones. Our words, choices, and priorities should reflect our true home.

This promise encourages families not to grow too attached to the world. Trials, possessions, and successes are temporary. Eternity with Christ is forever.

Living in this promise means longing for heaven, staying faithful, and waiting eagerly for Jesus. Families who live as citizens of heaven keep their eyes fixed on their eternal home.

Let's discuss the following questions for the next couple of minutes:

1. What does Philippians 3:20 teach about citizenship?
2. What examples of "pilgrims" are in the Bible?
3. Why does hope in heaven shape how we live now?
4. How can our family live with heaven's values this week?

✎ PRAYER

Heavenly Father, thank You for making us citizens of heaven. Thank You for promising eternity with Jesus. Forgive us when we cling to the world. Teach our family to live for our true home. Amen.

⚑ FAMILY ACTIVITY

On a scrapbook page, write "Our Citizenship in Heaven." Each family member writes one way they will live for heaven's values this week.

December 15
Growing While We Wait

"But grow in the grace and knowledge of our Lord and Savior Jesus Christ. To him be glory both now and forever! Amen." – 2 Peter 3:18

Hope in Christ's return is not a reason to sit still; it is a call to keep growing. 2 Peter 3:18 reminds us that until the day we see Jesus face-to-face, our mission is to deepen our relationship with Him. Holiness is a journey of becoming more like our Savior every single day.

The Bible often compares our spiritual lives to things that grow, like trees or vines. Jesus said, "I am the vine; you are the branches." If a branch stays connected to the vine, it naturally grows and produces fruit. Paul also prayed that believers would be "rooted and established in love," showing that growth happens when we dig deep into God's Word and spend time in His presence.

True growth is a two-part process: growing in "grace" and in "knowledge." Growing in grace means we become more like Jesus in our character, more forgiving, more patient, and more humble. Growing in knowledge means we aren't just learning facts about the Bible, but we are truly getting to know the heart of the Person who wrote it. Just as a garden needs both rain and sun to thrive, we need both God's unmerited favor and the truth of His Word to mature. This growth ensures that when Christ returns, He finds us not just waiting, but flourishing in our faith.

Families should learn that growth is a daily choice. It means making time to talk about God, to pray together, and to ask for His help in changing our "rough edges." It means being a family that values progress over perfection.

Living this way means checking our "spiritual height" by looking at our actions. Are we more kind than we were last year? Do we trust God more than we did yesterday? Families who grow together in grace will be ready for the day Christ appears in glory.

Let's discuss the following questions for the next couple of minutes:

1. What does 2 Peter 3:18 tell us to do while we wait for Jesus?

2. How is a Christian's life like a growing tree or a garden?

3. What is the difference between knowing *about* Jesus and really *knowing* Him?

4. What is one area where you want to "grow in grace" this week?

PRAYER

Lord Jesus, thank You for being our Savior and our Friend. Thank You for giving us the time and the grace to grow. Forgive us when we become lazy in our faith or stop trying to learn more about You. Help our family to grow stronger in our love for You and for one another every day until You return. Amen.

FAMILY ACTIVITY

On a scrapbook page, write "Growing in Grace." Draw a tall tree with many branches. On the leaves of the tree, have each family member write one thing they have learned about Jesus recently or one way they have seen His grace work in their lives this month.

December 16
Setting Your Sights Higher

"Since, then, you have been raised with Christ, set your hearts on things above, where Christ is, seated at the right hand of God. Set your minds on things above, not on earthly things." – Colossians 3:1–2

Waiting for Christ's return is all about where we choose to focus our attention. Colossians 3:1-2 encourages us to live with a "heavenward" focus. When we realize that our true home is with Jesus, it changes how we view our lives here on earth. Holiness starts in the mind and the heart before it ever shows up in our actions.

The Bible often reminds us that our perspective determines our peace. When the prophet Elisha was surrounded by an enemy army, his servant was terrified. But Elisha prayed for the servant's eyes to be opened, and he saw a heavenly army of fire protecting them. Elisha had his "mind on things above," while the servant was only looking at the "earthly things" (the problem in front of him). When we look at life from God's point of view, our fears get smaller and our hope gets bigger.

Setting our minds on "things above" doesn't mean we ignore our responsibilities on earth, but it means we don't let those responsibilities rule our hearts. It is like looking at a map from a high mountain peak instead of being lost in the thick trees of the valley. From "above," we can see that our current troubles are temporary and that God's plan is moving toward a beautiful conclusion. This perspective helps us value people over possessions and kindness over being right. It allows us to live with a sense of calm because we know that the King who is seated at the right hand of God is in total control.

Families should learn that what we talk about and think about most will eventually shape our character. If we only focus on earthly things, like getting more toys, winning every argument, or being the best at everything, we become stressed and selfish. But when we set our hearts on Jesus, we start to care about the things He cares about.

Let's discuss the following questions for the next couple of minutes:

1. What does it mean to "set your heart" on something?
2. Why is it hard to keep our minds on "things above" when we have a busy day at school or work?
3. How does thinking about Jesus in heaven change how we feel about a problem we have today?
4. What is one "earthly thing" (like a worry or a distraction) you want to replace with a "heavenly thing" today?

✎ PRAYER

Lord Jesus, thank You for being our King and for preparing a place for us with You. Forgive us for the times we get so caught up in the "stuff" of this world that we forget to look up to You. Help our family to set our hearts and minds on Your truth today. Fill our thoughts with Your peace and Your love so that we can reflect You to everyone we meet. Amen.

⛪ FAMILY ACTIVITY

On a scrapbook page, write "Set Your Minds on Things Above." Draw a large upward-pointing arrow in the middle of the page. Inside the arrow, have each family member write one "heavenly thing" (like "Jesus' love," "kindness," or "peace"). Around the outside of the arrow, write some "earthly things" that sometimes distract you, then draw a small "X" over them to show that they aren't your main focus.

<h1 align="center">December 17</h1>

<h1 align="center">Love in Action</h1>

"Dear children, let us not love with words or speech but with actions and in truth." – 1 John 3:18

As we prepare our hearts for Christ's return, God reminds us that true faith is something people can actually see. 1 John 3:18 tells us that love is more than just a nice feeling or a kind thing we say; it is something we *do*. Being a "child of God" means that our love has hands and feet.

The Bible is full of examples of love that moved into action. Think of the Good Samaritan. He didn't just look at the hurt man and say, "I hope you feel better soon." He stopped, used his own supplies to help him, and paid for his stay at an inn. He loved "in truth" by meeting a real need. Jesus did the same for us: He didn't just say He loved us from heaven; He came down to earth and gave His life for us. His love was the ultimate action.

To love "in truth" means our actions match our words. It is easy to say "I love you" to our family members, but it is much harder to show that love when we are asked to help with a chore we don't like or when we have to share something we want for ourselves. Action-oriented love means we look for the "unseen" needs in our home. It means noticing when a parent is tired and helping without being asked, or noticing when a sibling is sad and spending time with them. These small, quiet actions are the loudest way we can tell someone, and God, that we truly love them.

Families should learn that a "lifestyle of action" protects us from becoming selfish. When we are busy looking for ways to serve one another, we don't have as much time to grumble or complain. This kind of love creates a home where everyone feels valued and cared for, not because of what they say, but because of how they treat one another.

Living this way means asking ourselves throughout the day: "How can I turn my love into an action right now?" Families who love this way are shining a bright light in a world that often only looks out for itself. We are showing that we belong to Jesus because we act like Him.

Let's discuss the following questions for the next couple of minutes:

1. What is the difference between "loving with words" and "loving with actions"?
2. Why do you think God cares so much about our actions and not just our thoughts?
3. Can you think of a time someone in our family showed you love through an action this week?
4. What is one "secret" act of service you can do for someone in this house today?

PRAYER

Dear Father, thank You for loving us with the greatest action of all, sending Jesus. Forgive us for the times we say kind words but don't follow them up with kind actions. Teach our family how to see the needs of others and to be quick to help. Help us to love one another in truth and in deed every single day. Amen.

FAMILY ACTIVITY

On a scrapbook page, write "Love in Action." Draw a picture of a pair of hands. Inside the hands, have each family member write one "action" they will do for someone else this week. These should be specific things, like "making my bed," "giving a hug," or "sharing a snack."

December 18
Clothed in Readiness

"Let us then cast off the works of darkness and put on the armor of light." –
Romans 13:12

Hope in Christ's return calls believers to live clothed in holiness. Romans 13:12 describes putting on the armor of light as preparation for His coming. Families should remember that readiness is about how we live, not just what we believe.

The Bible speaks often of clothing as a picture of holiness. Adam and Eve were clothed with garments of grace after sin. Priests wore holy garments to serve in the temple. Revelation describes believers clothed in white robes, symbolizing purity in Christ.

This imagery of "armor" is significant because it reminds us that holiness is a form of protection. When we choose to live in the light—being honest, kind, and pure—we are shielded from the "works of darkness" that lead to regret, broken relationships, and fear. Putting on this armor is like waking up and dressing for a important mission; it requires an intentional choice to leave behind the "pajamas" of spiritual laziness and instead put on the strength of Christ. This light doesn't just show us where to walk; it actually guards our hearts from the shadows of the world, keeping us secure until the Day dawns.

Families should learn that putting on the armor of light means living openly, rejecting sin, and reflecting Christ's righteousness. Darkness hides, but light shines clearly.

Living in this promise means confessing sin, choosing honesty, and walking in obedience. Families who stay clothed in readiness will live with confidence when Christ appears.

Let's discuss the following questions for the next two to three minutes:

1. What does Romans 13:12 teach about readiness?
2. How does Scripture use clothing as a picture of holiness?
3. Why is light contrasted with darkness in this verse?
4. How can our family "put on the armor of light" together this week?

PRAYER

Holy God, thank You for calling us to cast off darkness. Thank You for clothing us with Your light. Forgive us when we hide in sin or try to walk through life unprotected. Teach our family to put on the armor of light and live with the joy and confidence of those who are ready for Christ. Amen.

FAMILY ACTIVITY

On a scrapbook page, write "Clothed in Readiness." Draw the outline of a simple shield or a breastplate. Inside the shape, have each family member write one "work of darkness" to cast off (like "grumbling" or "secrets") and one "light-filled" action to put on this week (like "gratitude" or "honesty").

December 19
The Crown of Glory

"And when the Chief Shepherd appears, you will receive the crown of glory that will never fade away." – 1 Peter 5:4

As we look toward the return of Jesus, the Bible gives us a beautiful title for Him: the "Chief Shepherd." This reminds us that we are His flock, and He is the one who guides us, protects us, and knows each of us by name. 1 Peter 5:4 promises that when He appears, there is a special reward waiting for those who have been faithful to Him—a "crown of glory" that is unlike anything on this earth.

The Bible often uses the imagery of shepherds and sheep to show how much God cares for us. King David famously wrote, "The Lord is my shepherd; I shall not want." Jesus called Himself the "Good Shepherd" who lays down His life for His sheep. A shepherd's job is never finished; he stays with the flock through the dark night and the scary storms. Knowing that our "Chief Shepherd" is coming back means we don't have to worry about being lost or forgotten. He is coming to gather His family together.

Families should learn that following the Shepherd means listening for His voice in the Bible and through prayer. Sometimes the world is very loud and tries to lead us in different directions, but the Chief Shepherd always leads us toward peace and righteousness. When we make decisions as a family, we can ask, "Is this where our Shepherd is leading us?"

Living in this truth means finding security in His leadership. We don't have to be afraid of the future because we know who is leading us there. Families who trust the Chief Shepherd find that they can walk through difficult times with their heads held high, looking forward to the day they receive His glorious "well done".

Let's discuss the following questions for the next couple of minutes:

1. Why do you think Jesus is called the "Chief Shepherd" and not just a "King"?
2. What does a shepherd do for his sheep that Jesus does for us?
3. What do you think a "crown that never fades" looks like?
4. How can our family practice "following the Shepherd's voice" this week?

📖 PRAYER

Chief Shepherd, thank You for watching over our family. Thank You that You know our names and that You never leave us. Forgive us for the times we wander off on our own and stop listening to Your voice. Help us to stay close to You today and to live with the joy of knowing that Your glorious reward is waiting for us. We look forward to seeing Your face! Amen.

👪 FAMILY ACTIVITY

On a scrapbook page, write "The Chief Shepherd and His Flock." Draw a simple shepherd's staff in the middle. Around the staff, have each family member write their name inside a small sheep shape. At the top of the page, draw a crown and write "The Crown of Glory" to remind everyone of the promise waiting for us when He returns.

December 20
The Joy of His Return

"Rejoice in the Lord always; again I will say, rejoice." – Philippians 4:4

Christ's return is a source of joy. Paul's command in Philippians 4:4 to rejoice always is grounded in the Lord's presence and promise to come again. Families should remember that hope in Christ's return fills life with unshakable joy.

The Bible shows joy connected to God's promises. Mary rejoiced at the news of Jesus' birth. The disciples rejoiced when the risen Lord appeared to them. Early Christians rejoiced even in persecution, knowing their hope was secure.

This type of joy is much deeper than just being "happy" when things go well; it is a spiritual anchor that holds us steady even when life is hard. Paul wrote these famous words about rejoicing while he was actually in prison, proving that joy is a decision to trust in God's character rather than our current situation. When we rejoice in the Lord's return, we are celebrating the fact that the "final chapter" of our lives has already been written, and it ends in victory. This joy acts like a light in the window of our hearts, reminding us that no matter how dark the night may feel, the Morning Star is coming, and He is bringing a joy that no one can take away.

Families should learn that joy is not dependent on circumstances but on God's faithfulness. His return guarantees that sorrow and pain will not last forever.

Living in this promise means practicing gratitude, singing praises, and choosing joy even in trials. Families who rejoice in Christ's return shine as witnesses to His goodness.

Let's discuss the following questions for the next couple of minutes:

1. What does Philippians 4:4 teach about joy?
2. What examples of joy are in the Bible?
3. Why is joy unshakable when rooted in Christ's return?
4. How can our family choose joy this week?

✎ PRAYER

Joyful God, thank You for filling our hearts with gladness. Thank You for promising Christ's return. Forgive us when we let sorrow steal our joy. Teach our family to rejoice always in Your promises. Amen.

⛪ FAMILY ACTIVITY

On a scrapbook page, write "The Joy of His Return." Each family member writes one way they will rejoice in the Lord this week.

December 21

The Final Rescue

"So Christ was sacrificed once to take away the sins of many; and he will appear a second time, not to bear sin, but to bring salvation to those who are waiting for him."
– Hebrews 9:28

As we get closer to celebrating Jesus' birth, it is helpful to look at the "big picture" of His mission. Hebrews 9:28 explains that Jesus has two great appearances. The first time He came, He arrived as a baby in a manger to grow up and give His life as a sacrifice for our sins. But the second time He appears, He won't be coming to deal with sin—that work is already finished! Instead, He is coming as a King to complete our final rescue and bring full salvation to everyone who is eagerly waiting for Him.

The Bible is a story of God's rescue plans. Think of Noah's ark, which saved his family from the flood, or the parting of the Red Sea, which saved the Israelites from slavery. Each of these stories was a small "preview" of the ultimate rescue Jesus provides. The first time He came, He rescued our hearts from the power of sin. The second time He comes, He will rescue our whole world from the presence of sin. He is the Hero who finishes what He started.

This "final rescue" is what the Bible calls our "blessed hope." It means that everything that is currently broken—sickness, sadness, and even death—will be completely removed when He appears. We are like people standing on a dock, watching the horizon for a ship that is coming to take us to a beautiful new land. We aren't waiting in fear, because we know the Captain of the ship is our Savior who already gave His life for us. This waiting is filled with confidence because we know that the same Jesus who was faithful to die for us will be faithful to return for us.

Families should learn that being "ready" for Jesus simply means trusting in what He did the first time so we can be excited for what He does the second time. We don't have to be perfect to be rescued; we just have to be "waiting for Him." This means our hearts are pointed toward Him and our trust is placed in His finished work on the cross.

Living in this truth means we can face today's problems with courage. If Jesus has already taken away our sins, we know He loves us enough to bring us safely home. Families who live with this "rescue mindset" find that they are less afraid of the future because they know their Savior is coming to make all things new.

Let's discuss the following questions for the next couple of minutes:

1. What was the difference between why Jesus came the first time and why He is coming the second time?

2. Why is it good news that He isn't coming back to "bear sin" again?

3. How does it feel to know that a "final rescue" is coming for the whole world?

4. How can our family show that we are "waiting for Him" this week?

📖 PRAYER

Our Great Savior, thank You for Your perfect plan. Thank You for coming the first time to take away our sins and for promising to come a second time to bring us home. Forgive us when we forget that You are our Rescuer. Help our family to live with our eyes on the horizon, waiting for the day You appear in glory to make all things right. Amen.

👪 FAMILY ACTIVITY

On a scrapbook page, write "The Final Rescue." Draw a large anchor at the bottom of the page to represent our secure hope. Have each family member write one thing they are glad Jesus will "rescue" us from when He returns (like "sickness," "sadness," or "mean words").

December 22
Safe to the Heavenly Kingdom

"The Lord will rescue me from every evil attack and will bring me safely to his heavenly kingdom. To him be glory for ever and ever. Amen." – 2 Timothy 4:18

As we wait for Jesus to return, we sometimes face "attacks", not just from people, but from things like fear, doubt, or temptation. Today's verse gives us a powerful promise of protection. Paul, who wrote this while he was in prison and near the end of his life, was not afraid. He knew that even if things looked difficult on the outside, the Lord was his Rescuer. He was confident that Jesus would bring him "safely" to his true home: the Heavenly Kingdom.

The Bible is full of stories where God brought His people safely through a crisis. Think of Daniel in the lions' den or Peter being released from prison by an angel. These stories show us that "safety" in God's eyes is more than just staying out of trouble; it is about our souls being guarded so that nothing can pull us away from Him. When we live with our hearts set on Christ's return, we realize that our life is like a journey. There might be some bumps in the road, but the Captain of our soul is making sure we reach the finish line.

The word "safely" in this verse is like a guarantee from God. It means that no matter what we face today, a hard day at school, a worry about the future, or a mistake we've made, God is working behind the scenes to preserve our faith. His rescue isn't just a temporary fix; it is a permanent plan to keep us in His hands until the day the Heavenly Kingdom is fully revealed. This gives us a deep sense of courage because we realize that the most important parts of who we are, our soul and our future with Him, are completely untouchable by the "evil attacks" of this world.

Families should learn that we can face scary things with a "Kingdom perspective." When we pray together, we can remind each other that the Lord is our Shield. We don't have to be strong enough to save ourselves; we just have to be willing to hold onto the hand of the One who is bringing us home. This turns our house into a place of peace instead of a place of worry.

Let's discuss the following questions for the next couple of minutes:

1. What does it feel like to know the Lord is your personal Rescuer?

2. What are some "evil attacks" (like unkind thoughts or fear) that God can help us overcome?

3. How does the promise of a "Heavenly Kingdom" change the way we think about the "hard stuff" on earth?

4. What is one thing our family can do to help each other feel "safe" in God's love this week?

✍ PRAYER

Strong Deliverer, thank You for Your promise to rescue us. Thank You that our future is secure in Your Heavenly Kingdom. Forgive us for the times we let fear make us forget Your power. Protect our hearts and minds today, and bring our family safely through every challenge until we see You face-to-face. To You be glory forever and ever! Amen.

⚶ FAMILY ACTIVITY

On a scrapbook page, write "Safe to the Kingdom." Draw a picture of a strong castle or a fortress. Inside the fortress, have each family member write their name. Around the outside, write things that God protects you from (like "worry," "loneliness," or "danger"). This serves as a visual reminder that you are tucked safely inside God's protection.

December 23

Peace on Earth

"Glory to God in the highest, and on earth peace among those with whom he is pleased!" – Luke 2:14

The angels announced peace at Christ's birth, and true peace will be complete at His return. Luke 2:14 shows that God's glory and peace are united in Christ. Families should remember that holiness means living in the peace He brings now while waiting for perfect peace to come.

Jesus brought peace through forgiveness and reconciliation with God. He also brings peace into hearts, families, and communities. Yet the Bible promises that at His return, wars will cease, and He will reign as the Prince of Peace forever.

This peace is much more than just the "quiet" we feel when the house is still; it is a profound wholeness that comes from being right with God. The angels' song reminds us that peace on earth starts with glory in the highest. When we put God in His proper place, honoring Him as King—peace naturally begins to flow into our lives. This "present peace" acts as a preview of the world to come. Every time we choose to settle a disagreement with kindness or sit quietly in prayer despite a busy schedule, we are experiencing a small piece of the total, worldwide harmony that Jesus will establish across the entire earth when He returns.

Families should learn that Christmas peace is both present and future. We taste it now through faith in Jesus, and we will experience it fully in His kingdom.

Living in this promise means making peace in relationships, forgiving others, and trusting God's peace when anxious. Families who live in His peace today prepare for the eternal peace of His reign.

Let's take a couple of minutes to discuss the following questions:

1. What does Luke 2:14 teach about peace?
2. How did Jesus bring peace in His first coming?
3. How will His return bring perfect peace?
4. How can our family practice peace this week?

PRAYER

Prince of Peace, thank You for bringing reconciliation with God. Thank You for promising a kingdom of peace. Forgive us when we stir conflict. Teach our family to live in peace as we wait for Your return. Amen.

FAMILY ACTIVITY

This peace is much more than just the "quiet" we feel when the house is still; it is a profound wholeness that comes from being right with God. The angels' song reminds us that peace on earth starts with glory in the highest. When we put God in His proper place, honoring Him as King, peace naturally begins to flow into our lives. This "present peace" acts as a preview of the world to come. Every time we choose to settle a disagreement with kindness or sit quietly in prayer despite a busy schedule, we are experiencing a small piece of the total, worldwide harmony that Jesus will establish across the entire earth when He returns.

December 24
Joy to the World

"And the angel said to them, 'Fear not, for behold, I bring you good news of great joy that will be for all the people.'" – Luke 2:1

The birth of Christ is good news of great joy. Luke 2:10 reminds us that His coming brings joy to all people. Families should remember that this joy points to even greater joy when Christ returns.

At His first coming, shepherds rejoiced, wise men rejoiced, and Mary treasured every word with joy in her heart. At His return, all nations will rejoice as He establishes His kingdom forever.

The "great joy" the angel described is special because it is meant "for all the people." It wasn't just a private gift for a few; it was an invitation for the whole world to be reconciled to God. This joy is powerful because it begins by removing fear, the very first thing the angel said was "Fear not." When we realize that Jesus came to be with us, our fears about being alone or being unloved start to melt away. This Christmas joy is like a pilot light in a furnace; it stays lit even in the cold seasons of life, reminding us that the light of the world has arrived and that His warmth will eventually fill every corner of the earth.

Joy is rooted in God's promises, not in circumstances. Families should learn that joy endures through trials because it is anchored in Christ's victory.

Living in this promise means practicing gratitude, celebrating His faithfulness, and looking forward to the eternal joy of His return. Families who live in joy are a witness to His goodness.

Let's discuss the following questions for the next couple of minutes:

1. What does Luke 2:10 teach about joy?
2. How did people respond with joy at Christ's birth?
3. How does His return promise even greater joy?
4. How can our family share joy this Christmas?

✒ PRAYER

God of Joy, thank You for bringing good news of great joy. Thank You for promising eternal joy at Christ's return. Forgive us when we let sorrow or stress steal our joy. Teach our family to rejoice always in You. Amen.

♣ FAMILY ACTIVITY

On a scrapbook page, write "Joy to the World." Each family member writes one way they will share joy with someone else this Christmas.

The King Has Come and Will Come Again

"For to us a child is born, to us a son is given; and the government shall be upon his shoulder." – Isaiah 9:6

Christmas is the celebration of the King who has come. Isaiah 9:6 foretold the birth of a child who would reign with authority. Families should remember that the child born in Bethlehem is also the King who will return in glory.

At His first coming, He came in humility, born in a stable, laid in a manger. At His second coming, He will come in power, riding on the clouds, with the nations before Him. Both comings reveal His love and authority.

The phrase "the government shall be upon his shoulder" is a powerful promise of rest for us. In our world, leaders and governments often struggle or fail, but the Bible tells us that the ultimate weight of the world's future doesn't rest on our shoulders or on any earthly ruler, it rests on His. Because He was born as a child, we know He understands our human struggles; because He is the King who will return, we know He has the power to fix everything that is broken. When we look at the baby in the manger today, we see a King who is so strong that He could afford to be small, and so loving that He chose to be near us.

Families should learn that Christmas is a reminder of both past and future hope. The King came to save us, and the King is coming again to reign forever.

Living in this promise means celebrating Christmas with worship, not only for His birth but also for His return. Families who keep both truths together will experience deeper faith and joy.

Let's discuss the following questions for the next couple of minutes:

1. What does Isaiah 9:6 teach about Christ as King?
2. How do His first and second comings show different aspects of His reign?
3. Why should Christmas remind us of both past and future hope?
4. How can our family worship Christ as King this Christmas?

PRAYER

King of Kings, thank You for coming as a child to save us. Thank You for promising to return in glory. Forgive us when we forget Your reign. Teach our family to celebrate Christmas with hearts full of hope in Your return. Amen.

FAMILY ACTIVITY

On a scrapbook page, write "The King Has Come and Will Come Again." Each family member writes one way they will honor Christ as King today.

December 26
Peaceful Preparation

"So then, dear friends, since you are looking forward to this, make every effort to be found spotless, blameless and at peace with him." – 2 Peter 3:14

The day after Christmas can sometimes feel a little quiet or even a bit sad as the decorations start to come down and the excitement fades. However, for a believer, the "looking forward" never stops. 2 Peter 3:14 reminds us that because we know Jesus is coming back, our lives should be marked by a special kind of effort. We aren't working to earn His love—He already gave that to us at the manger and the cross—but we are working to live in a way that shows we are ready to see Him.

The Bible often uses the idea of "cleansing" to describe our spiritual lives. Just as we might clean the house before guests arrive for Christmas dinner, Peter tells us to keep our hearts "spotless and blameless." Think of the story of the ten bridesmaids waiting for the bridegroom; the ones who were ready had their lamps trimmed and full of oil. They didn't let the waiting make them lazy. Being "at peace with him" means that when Jesus returns, we won't have to hide in shame because we have been living in open, honest fellowship with Him every day.

Living "at peace with him" is the most important part of our preparation. It means that we don't carry around the heavy weight of unconfessed sin or the bitterness of a grudge against someone else. If the "prince of peace" was born in a manger to reconcile us to God, then the best way we can honor Him today is by staying in that peace. This isn't a stressful kind of "effort" where we worry if we are good enough; it is the joyful effort of a friend who wants to be ready when their best friend knocks on the door. It's about keeping short accounts with God and with each other.

Families should learn that holiness is a daily habit. Now that the Christmas presents are opened, we can focus on the "everlasting gifts" of character. We can ask ourselves: "If Jesus came back today, would He find our home filled with peace? Would He find us treating each other with the same love He showed us?"

Living in this truth means not letting our spiritual fire go out just because the holiday is over. Families who live in "peaceful preparation" find that the joy of Christmas lasts all year long. We are a people who live with a "ready" heart, keeping our lives clean and our spirits calm as we wait for the Great Day.

Let's discuss the following questions for the next couple of minutes:

1. Why do we sometimes feel a "let down" after Christmas is over? How does this verse help?
2. What does it mean to be "found at peace" with Jesus?
3. How can we keep our hearts "clean" like a house ready for a special guest?
4. What is one way we can keep the "Christmas spirit" of holiness alive in our home this week?

PRAYER

Lord Jesus, thank You for the joy we had celebrating Your birth. Now, as we look forward to Your return, help us to stay alert and ready. Forgive us for the spots of sin or the lack of peace in our hearts. Teach our family to make every effort to live holy, blameless lives that bring glory to You. May we be found at peace with You whenever You choose to return. Amen.

FAMILY ACTIVITY

On a scrapbook page, write "Peaceful Preparation." Draw a picture of a heart and a cleaning cloth. Each family member writes one "clutter" they want to remove from their heart this week (like "complaining" or "selfishness") and one way they will stay "at peace" with God (like "praying every morning").

December 27
Hidden in Christ

"When Christ, who is your life, appears, then you also will appear with him in glory."
– Colossians 3:4

As the year begins to wind down, it is easy to focus on our own accomplishments or failures. But Colossians 3:4 tells us that for a believer, our "real life" is actually found in Jesus. Right now, the world might not see how special it is to follow Christ; sometimes it feels like our faith is quiet or "hidden."

The Bible promises that when Jesus returns and is revealed to the whole world, the truth about who we are will also be revealed. We won't just be watching His glory, we will be sharing in it!

The phrase "Christ, who is your life" is a powerful reminder of where our energy and identity come from. It means that Jesus isn't just a part of our week or a person we talk about at Christmas; He is the very air we breathe. If Christ is our life, then His return isn't a scary event, it is the moment we finally become who we were always meant to be. This "shared glory" means that all the ways we tried to be like Him on earth, the times we were kind when it was hard, or honest when it was costly, will finally be made clear. We will step out of the shadows of this world and into the perfect light of His presence.

Families should learn that we don't need to look for the world's "glory" or praise. We don't need to be the most popular or the most successful to be important. Our value is "hidden" in Christ, and He is the greatest treasure in the universe. When we realize this, we can live with a quiet confidence, knowing that a glorious day is coming that will make all our earthly efforts worth it.

Let's discuss the following questions for the next couple of minutes:

1. What does it mean for Christ to be your "life"?
2. Why do you think our faith sometimes feels "hidden" from the world?
3. How does it feel to know that you will "appear with Him in glory" one day?
4. How can we treat each other today as people who are "hidden in Christ"?

PRAYER

Lord Jesus, thank You for being our life. Thank You that our true identity and our future are safe with You. Forgive us for the times we try to find our value in what other people think instead of what You say about us. Help our family to live for Your glory today, knowing that one day we will see You and be changed into Your likeness. Amen.

FAMILY ACTIVITY

On a scrapbook page, write "Hidden in Christ." Draw a picture of a treasure chest. Inside the chest, write the names of each family member. Decorate the outside with gold or bright colors to represent the "glory" that will be revealed when Christ returns.

December 28
Standing Firm in Hope

"Therefore, my beloved brothers, be steadfast, immovable, always abounding in the work of the Lord." – 1 Corinthians 15:58

Paul calls believers to stand firm in hope. First Corinthians 15:58 follows his teaching about the resurrection, reminding us that nothing done for the Lord is in vain. Families should remember that Christ's return assures our labor has meaning.

The Bible shows steadfast faith in action. Daniel stood firm in prayer even when threatened. Esther stood firm in courage to save her people. The early church stood firm in witness despite persecution.

This call to be "immovable" is especially important as we look toward the return of Christ. When we realize that Jesus is coming back to make all things new and to reward His faithful servants, it changes how we view our daily "labor." Sometimes, doing the right thing feels exhausting or like it doesn't matter, but Paul tells us that because of the resurrection, every act of kindness, every prayer, and every moment of obedience is being recorded by God. Our work for the Lord is never "in vain" because it is an investment in an eternal kingdom. Like a builder who knows the architect is coming to inspect the foundation, we can work with joy and persistence, knowing that our efforts have lasting, heavenly value.

Families should learn that standing firm means not being moved by fear, temptation, or doubt. The hope of Christ's return anchors us when the world shakes.

Living in this promise means serving with diligence, staying faithful in worship, and encouraging one another to remain immovable in Christ. Families who stand firm will be unshaken in trials.

Let's discuss the following questions for the next couple of minutes:

1. What does 1 Corinthians 15:58 teach about standing firm?
2. What examples of steadfast faith are in Scripture?
3. Why does Christ's return give purpose to our work?
4. How can our family stand firm in hope this week?

PRAYER

Steadfast God, thank You for promising that our labor is not in vain. Thank You for giving us hope in the resurrection. Forgive us when we waver. Teach our family to stand firm and abound in Your work. Amen.

FAMILY ACTIVITY

On a scrapbook page, write "Standing Firm in Hope." Each family member writes one way they will stay steadfast this week.

December 29

The New Heaven and New Earth

*"Then I saw a new heaven and a new earth, for the first heaven and the first earth
had passed away." – Revelation 21:1*

The Bible promises not only Christ's return but also the renewal of creation. Revelation 21:1 describes a new heaven and new earth where sin and suffering are gone forever. Families should remember that hope in Christ includes longing for His perfect kingdom.

The Bible describes this renewal vividly. God will wipe away every tear. Death, mourning, crying, and pain will be no more. The dwelling place of God will be with His people.

This "renewal" doesn't mean God is throwing away His creation; it means He is fixing it, cleaning it, and making it even more beautiful than it was in the beginning. Imagine a precious family heirloom that has become rusty and broken over many years. A master craftsman wouldn't throw it in the trash; he would carefully restore it until it shines like new. That is what God is going to do with the world.

He will remove the "rust" of sin and the "breaks" of sickness, leaving a world where everything, nature, animals, and people, works together in perfect harmony. This is our ultimate "homecoming," where we will finally live in the world exactly as God always intended for us to enjoy it.

Families should learn that this promise assures them of eternal joy and restoration. The brokenness of the world is temporary. God is preparing something better.

Living in this promise means not clinging too tightly to this world but living with hope in eternity. Families who look forward to the new creation will endure trials with peace and anticipation.

Let's discuss the following questions for the next couple of minutes:

1. What does Revelation 21:1 teach about the future?
2. What will be different in the new heaven and new earth?
3. How does this promise give hope in suffering?
4. How can our family live with eternity in mind this week?

✐ PRAYER

Renewing God, thank You for promising a new heaven and new earth. Thank You for assuring us of eternal joy. Forgive us when we cling too tightly to this world. Teach our family to live with hope in Your coming kingdom. Amen.

♟ FAMILY ACTIVITY

On a scrapbook page, write "The New Heaven and New Earth." Each family member draws or writes what they most look forward to in God's renewed creation.

December 30
Come, Lord Jesus

"He who testifies to these things says, 'Surely I am coming soon.' Amen. Come, Lord Jesus!" – Revelation 22:20

The final prayer of the Bible is a longing cry: "Come, Lord Jesus." Revelation 22:20 shows the heart of believers waiting with eager hope. Families should remember that holiness includes praying for Christ's return with joy.

The early church often prayed this word: Maranatha, which means "Come, Lord." They lived daily with the expectation that Jesus could return at any moment.

Families should learn that praying for Christ's return means loving His appearing, longing for His kingdom, and desiring His presence more than worldly comfort.

Living in this promise means aligning priorities with eternity, using time wisely, and keeping hearts ready. Families who pray "Come, Lord Jesus" live with anticipation and joy.

Let's discuss the following questions for the next couple of minutes:

1. What does Revelation 22:20 teach about Christ's return?
2. How did the early church express longing for Jesus?
3. Why should families pray for His coming with joy?
4. How can our family live with this prayer on our lips this week?

PRAYER

Lord Jesus, thank You for promising to come soon. Thank You for preparing a place for us. Forgive us when we grow too attached to this world. Teach our family to pray, "Come, Lord Jesus," with eager hope. Amen.

FAMILY ACTIVITY

On a scrapbook page, write "Come, Lord Jesus." Each family member writes one reason they long for Christ's return.

December 31

The Bright Morning Star

"I, Jesus, have sent my angel to give you this testimony for the churches. I am the Root and the Offspring of David, and the bright Morning Star." – Revelation 22:16

On the final day of the year, the Bible leaves us with a beautiful and hopeful title for Jesus: "The Bright Morning Star." In the natural world, the morning star is the brightest light in the sky just before the sun rises. When you see it, you know that the darkness of the night is almost over and a brand-new day is about to begin. By calling Himself this, Jesus is promising us that no matter how dark the world may seem, His return is the "sunrise" that will change everything.

Throughout the Bible, Jesus is shown as the fulfillment of every promise. As the "Root and Offspring of David," He is the King we have been waiting for. As the "Morning Star," He is our signal of hope. Just as the Israelites looked for the pillar of fire in the wilderness, and the Wise Men looked for the star in the East, we look to Jesus to guide us through the "night" of this life until we reach the eternal day of His kingdom.

The imagery of the Morning Star is especially meaningful because it appears when the night is at its deepest and people are most tired of waiting. It is a light that doesn't just sit in the sky; it announces that the shadows are retreating. When we look at Jesus as our Morning Star, we realize that His return isn't just an end to our current year, but the beginning of an eternal morning where "time" as we know it will be transformed into everlasting joy. This means that as we stand at the edge of a new calendar year, we aren't just moving toward more days and months, but we are moving closer to the Day that will never end—the day when the Sun of Righteousness rises with healing in His wings.

Families should learn that ending a year with Jesus means ending with hope. We can look back at the past 365 days and see God's faithfulness, but we look forward to the future with even more excitement because our Morning Star is shining brightly. We don't have to fear the "unknowns" of next year because we know who holds the future.

Living in this promise means keeping our eyes fixed on Jesus. As we head into a new year, we can commit to being "people of the morning"—living with the joy, energy, and hope of those who know the light has already won. Families who follow the Morning Star will never be lost in the dark.

Let's discuss the following questions for the next couple of moments:

1. Why is a "Morning Star" a good symbol for Jesus' return?
2. How has Jesus been a "light" for our family during this past year?
3. What are you most excited about as we look forward to the "New Day" Christ will bring?
4. How can we help each other keep our eyes on Jesus (our Morning Star) in the coming year?

✎ PRAYER

Lord Jesus, our Bright Morning Star, thank You for bringing us safely to the end of this year. Thank You for being the light that the darkness cannot overcome. Forgive us for the times we lived in fear of the dark instead of trusting in Your light. As we begin a new year, help our family to live with our eyes fixed on You, waiting with joy for the Great Day of Your return. Amen.

♟ FAMILY ACTIVITY

On the final scrapbook page of the year, write "Jesus: Our Bright Morning Star." Draw a large, bright star in the center. Inside the star, have each family member write one thing they learned about Jesus this year. Around the star, write: "Even so, come Lord Jesus!"

Check out another book in the series

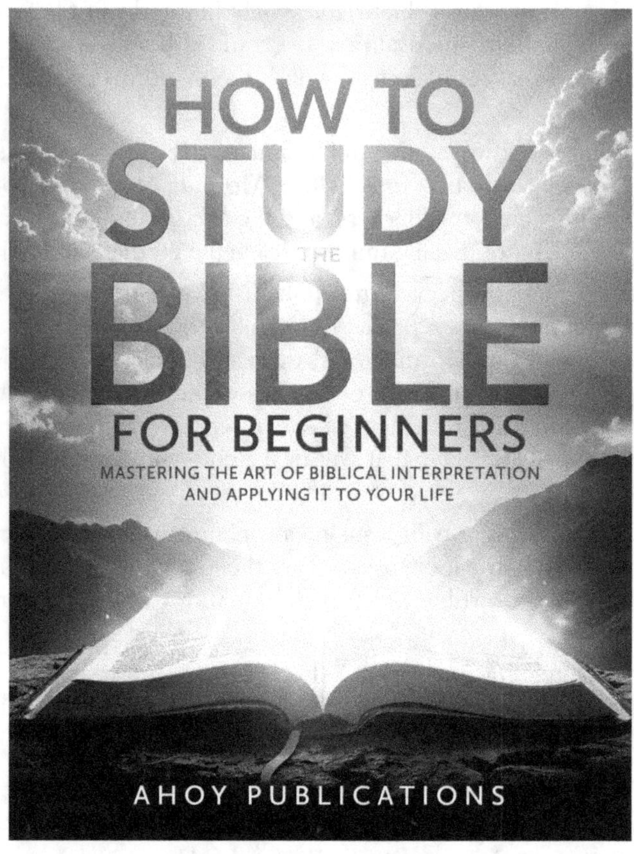

Welcome Aboard, Check Out This Limited-Time Free Bonus!

Ahoy, reader! Welcome to the Ahoy Publications family, and thanks for snagging a copy of this book! Since you've chosen to join us on this journey, we'd like to offer you something special.

Check out the link below for a FREE e-book filled with delightful facts about American History.

But that's not all - you'll also have access to our exclusive email list with even more free e-books and insider knowledge. Well, what are ye waiting for? Click the link below to join and set sail toward exciting adventures in American History.

Access your bonus here
https://ahoypublications.com/
Or, Scan the QR code!